Miles Walker's
DOODLES
Artcetera

Other books by the author: Synthetic Sea Sixty Six, After Age, Uani, Themus, Soft Journey, Paradise Papers, Doodles & Dreams. Miles Walker's Diary. Miles Walker's Dictionary.

Typefaces: Cracked Thanks Apple.....Futura.....feel of Bauhaus although designed earlier by Paul Renner. Hiroshige.....Thanks Cynthia Hollandsworth Batty for this font which I have used so much over the years.....Fruitiger thanks Adrian how clear you are.....Xenu from the type king Ray Larrabie.....Some Optima and Compacta from the sixties and seventies!.....Rub me down Letraset you were the edge then.

DEDICATION.....LIKE NO!

Welcome to my third diary, a collection of doodles, drawings and words....Surreal Art Ideaology from seven journals of words, ephemera, lies, and artwork of memories..... Viewer discretion is advised.....This book contains nudity, horse language.....Some drawings have graphic content, and immature subject matter, graphic standards may not prevail.

BEFORE and AFTER years

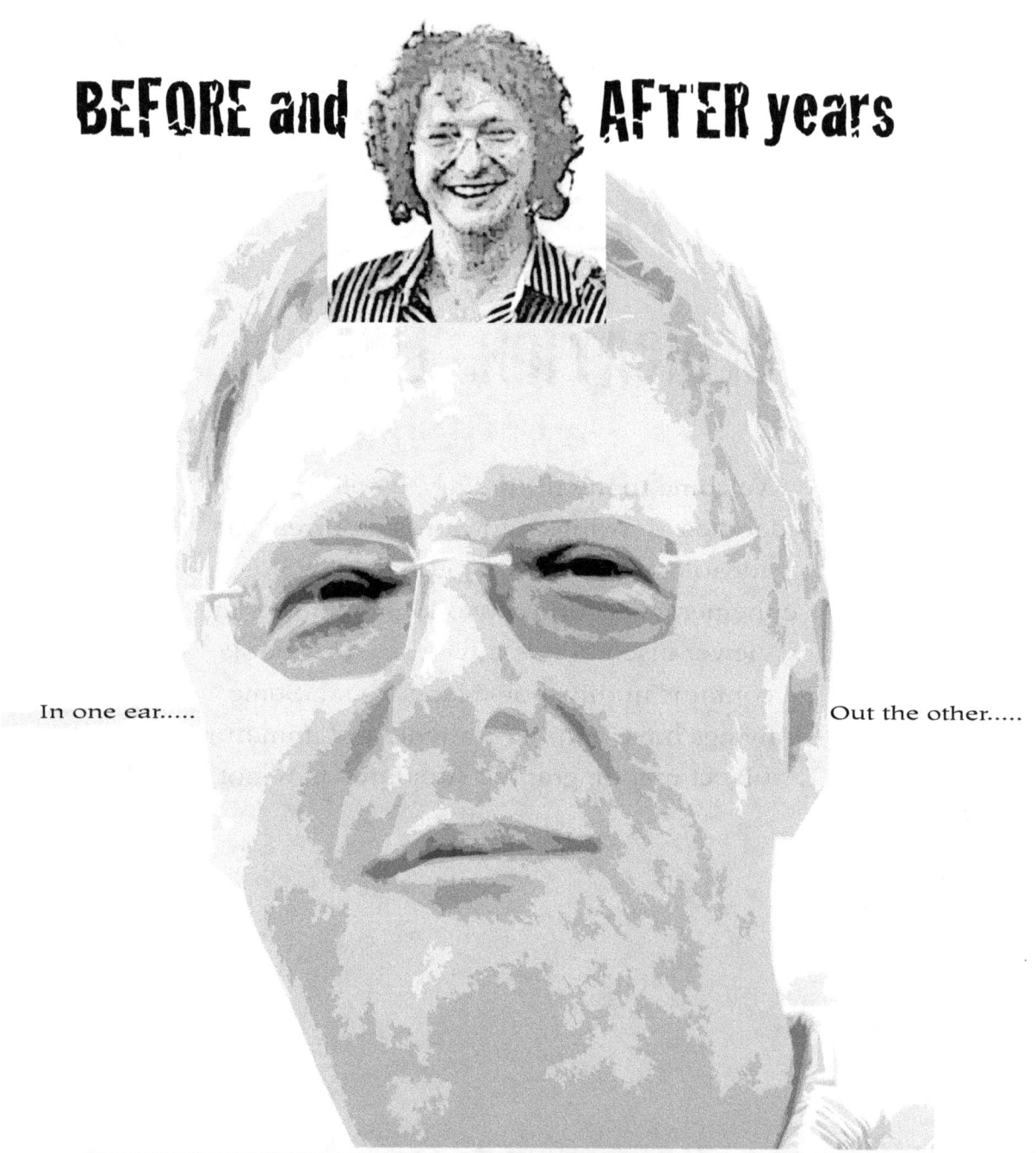

In one ear.....

Out the other.....

Fifty nine years doodling, thank god ? GOD ('kourse for us KO dislexicks it is dog backwards, just as I am selim I lived in my own world. Selim means safe and brings comfort and peace.....

PREFACE.....PROLOG,
It is written, this exists does it not!

This book of surreal.....("sur" means further than or beyond.....Result beyond real) drawings does not ask for approval, it should ask for forgiveness.....Where are you now Victoria? Artutopia is the place where boats pass each other in the sea of life.....The pictures (words or drawings) in this book are my principles of uncertainty.....Every one should doodle, blank space on a boarding pass, right.....Put down those loose bits of thoughts and art floating in your brain, Leonardo was a doodler, active doodlers are usually great thinkers and have a million ideas piggy backing each other..... My happy accidents collected over the years of doodling and drawing and painting now exist on paper and screens. Sleep is the oil of dreams and in my dreams I have found perfect freedom to work on what I want to do without restriction. My art moves away from theory towards raw concepts of ideas, including passion, poetry and politics which act as a foundation in this book.....Using graphic design, digital imaging and unrestricted typography, I attempt to make the mundane look different with some surreal techniques such as juxtaposition, scale, transformation, levitation and of course photoshop. Hopefully my work will embarrass you! It is sensitive, rude and ugly, so I kept my day job as a graphic designer....Perhaps when I die I will wake up! Many nites have turned into mornings, do these artistic mistakes prove I am trying.....Very trying, yes, this time I enjoyed wasting, was not wasted at all.....Mindworms and mind wanderers look on! Disengage all power to foward thrusters....use middle leg to enjoy!

Miles Walker's
DOODLES
Art cetera

The contents of this book includes some of these subjects.....

DOODLE to scribble or draw sometimes absent
mindedly, often with serious automatic intent or
obsession, continuing into fully finished pictures!

SURREAL IMAGES are created in literature and art
by expressing the workings of the subconscious and
is characterised by fantastic imagery and incongruous
juxtaposition of subject matter.

POETRY from the greek meaning "making". Usually a
form of literary art which uses aesthetic and rhythmic
qualities of language. Can create a story, emotions or
a picture in the mind of the reader.

FUTURISM a movement dealing with imaginary
content, ideas and concepts of the future and the near
future of post human lifeforms.

PHILOSOPHY is the study of general and fundemental
problems, such as those connected with reality, existence,
knowledge, values, reason, mind, language and art. The
word "philosophy" comes from the greek, literally meaning
love of wisdom.

DREAMS a series of pictures or events in the mind of
a sleeping person. Daydreams, fantasy, ideas created
in the imagination are often difficult to remember.

COLLAGE from the french coller, to glue, a technique of
an art production, primarily used in the visual arts, where
the artwork is made from an assemblage of different forms,
thus creating a new whole picture.

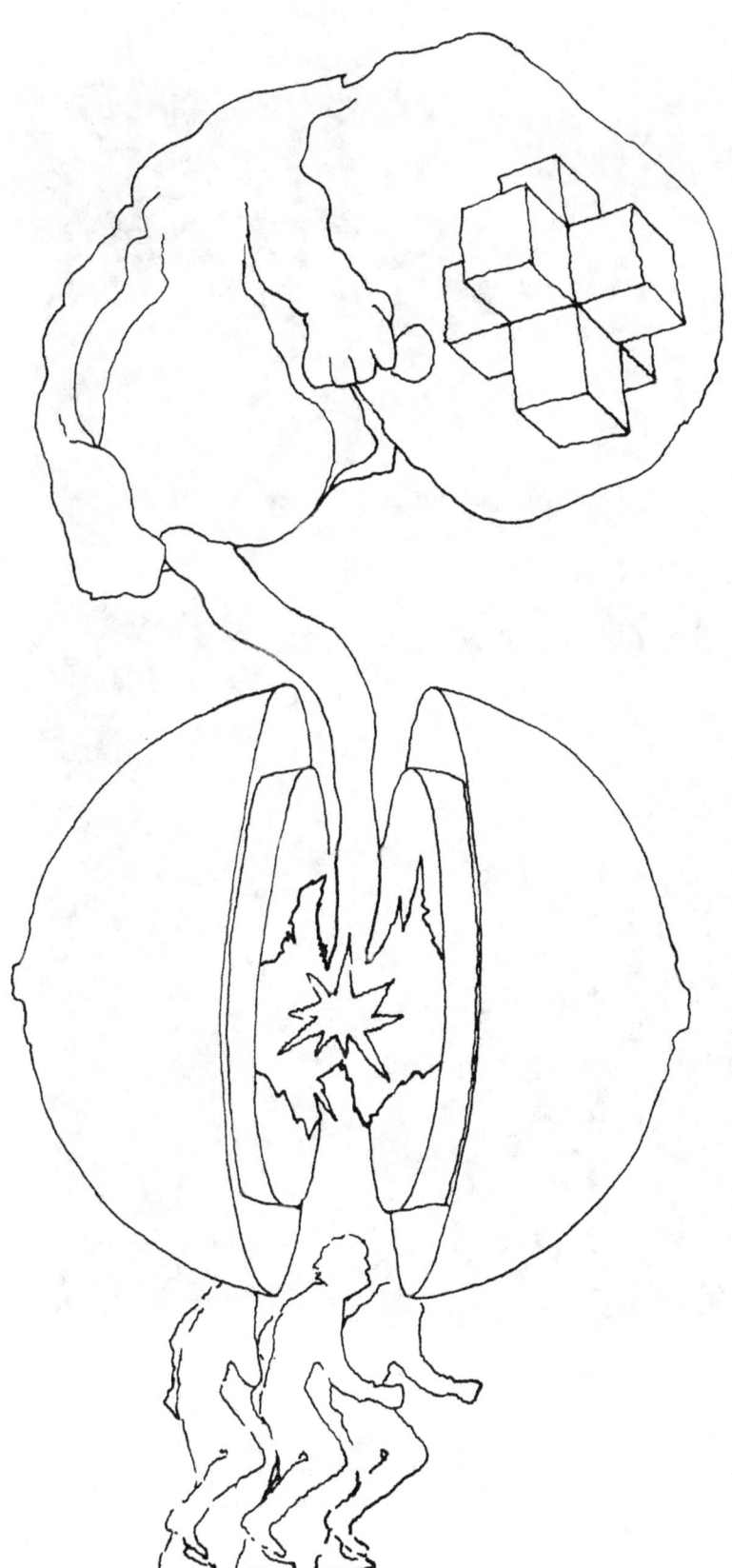

This desire for breasts caused attraction in the right or wrong place.....Leading to copulation and breeding of a long distance runner.....Sparking my interest in breast feeding, did that produce a better human? Computers are good at searching, what are we good at?

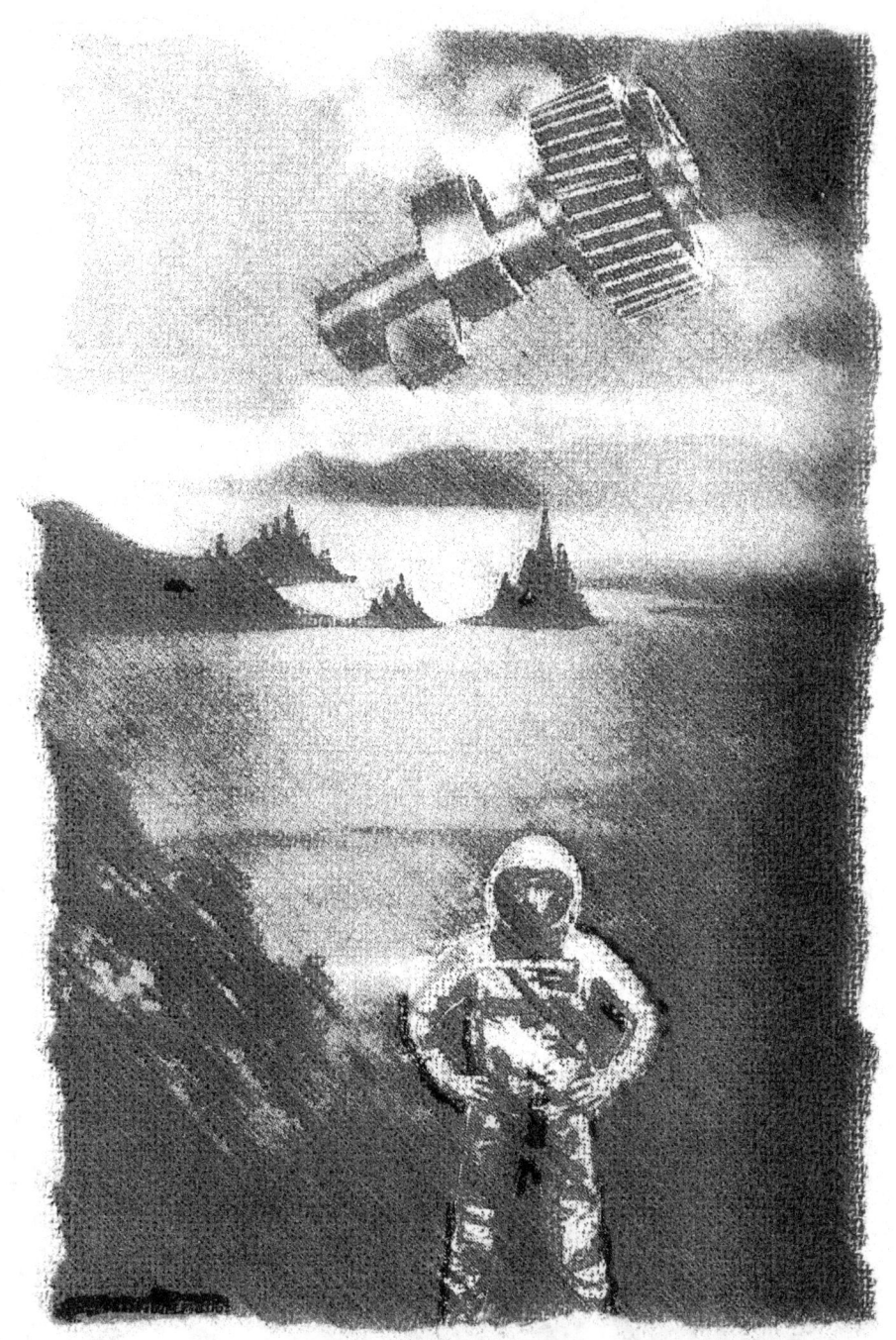

We have damaged our boson field worm gear
and are stuck here in Halong bay, till we get
a replacement, or is it more cost effective to
eliminate us and just send a new mission?
Please advise should we self exterminate.....

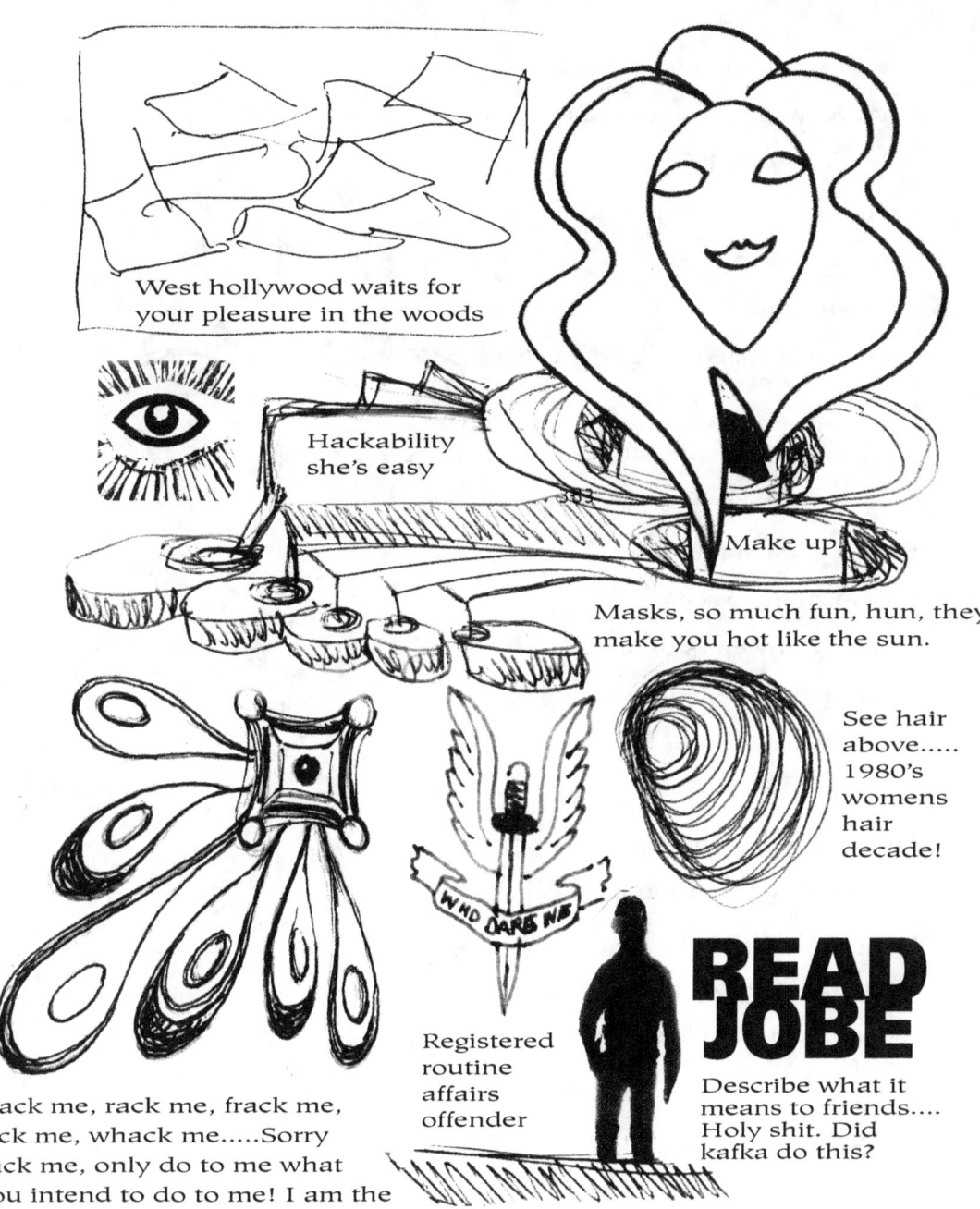

West hollywood waits for your pleasure in the woods

Hackability she's easy

Make up

Masks, so much fun, hun, they make you hot like the sun.

See hair above..... 1980's womens hair decade!

WHO DARES WINS

Registered routine affairs offender

Hack me, rack me, frack me, jack me, whack me.....Sorry sack me, only do to me what you intend to do to me! I am the michael 9000 upgrade for your personal pleasure.....

READ JOBE

Describe what it means to friends.... Holy shit. Did kafka do this?

Who is the holy spirit.....

The questions shadow me,
quiet yet angry-unanswered.
Cold feet by the sea
my thoughts wait hopefully,
bound, well I am free
rooms becoming smaller perpetually
warm, selfish shall I be.

The pattern of depression mauls
at all delight, consequently
I reject these manic calls.
I try to stumble secretly,
frightened by emotional falls.
Warmth devours my ambitions
as I enjoy these four walls.

Life's reward such paradox
they paginate life's landscape
silently, coldly, as rocks.
Excitement before possesion,
a child opens a gift box.....
Consequence of being, existence
our simple age measured by clocks
you the donor, will give life.

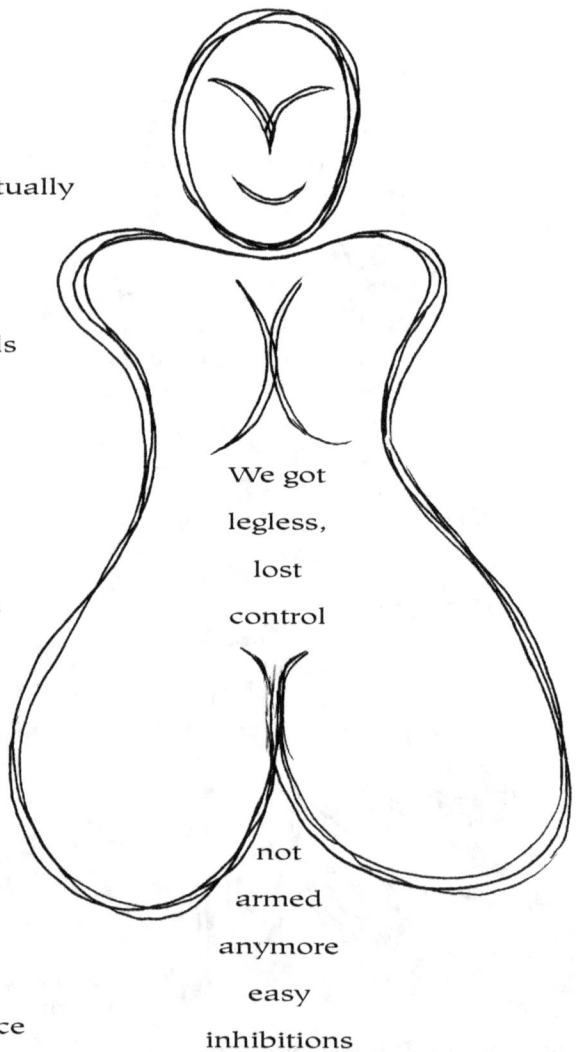

Young
head

We got
legless,
lost
control

not
armed
anymore
easy
inhibitions
to adore

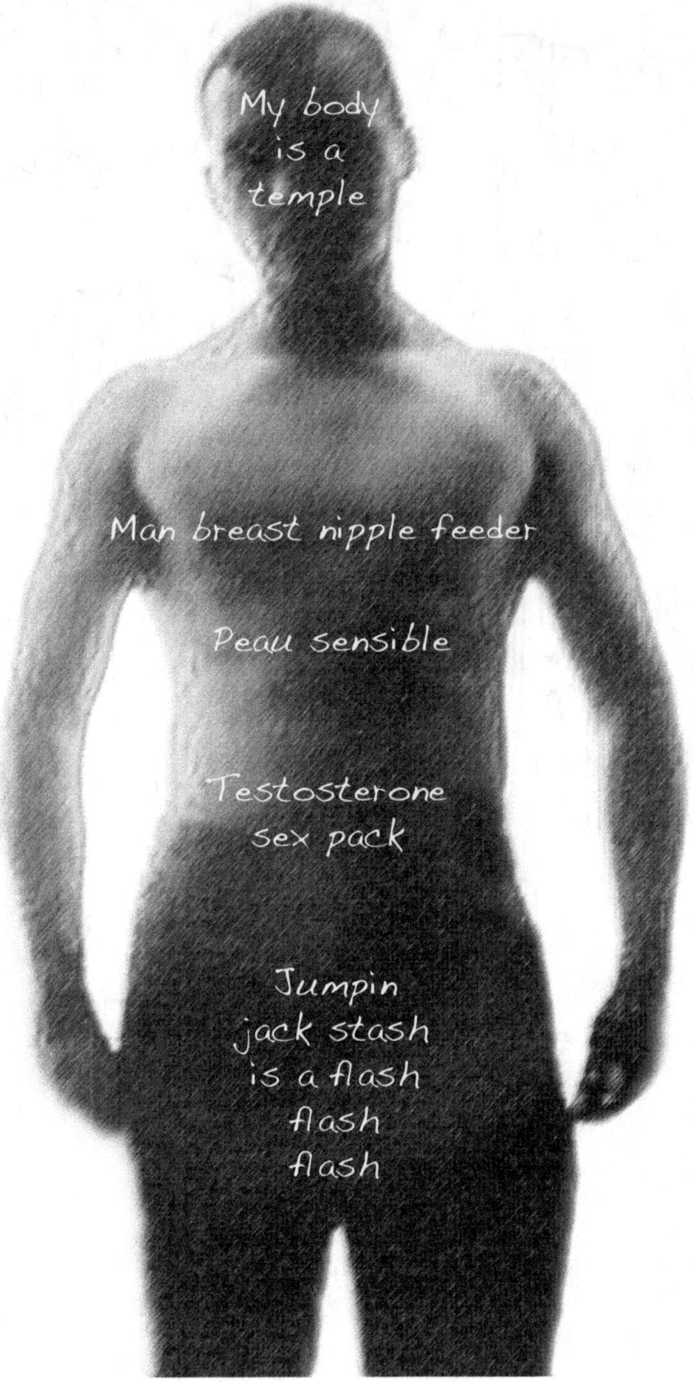

My body
is a
temple

Man breast nipple feeder

Peau sensible

Testosterone
sex pack

Jumpin
jack stash
is a flash
flash
flash

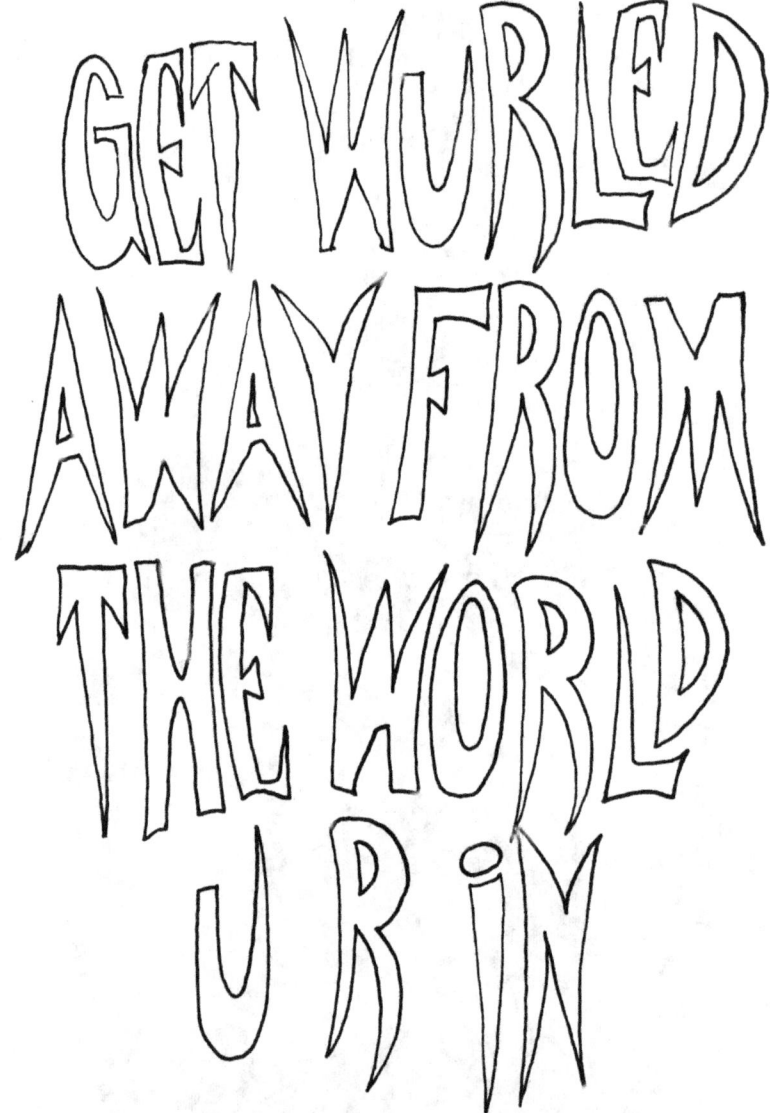

GET WURLED
AWAY FROM
THE WORLD
U R IN

The grass is greener on the
other side of the thrill.....
Lock me in a room and I
feel ecstatic with my artfull
thoughts.....I have always
been looking for the windows
in my mind.....Some where
out there I am sure it is, and
I am going to find it with or
without Nasa!

Enter the dark side of the room

skins hide our thoughts and protect

our soft weak inner minds

from the communication of life.

This painting, naturally obscene.....

should it have been

the front or back cover

edit that, wherever you are mother.....

So why penisosophy?

Well penis means love.....In greek

osophy is wisdom or knowledge.

This is the shroud of urine

hoodies hide facial recognition

and we all continue to confess and sin.

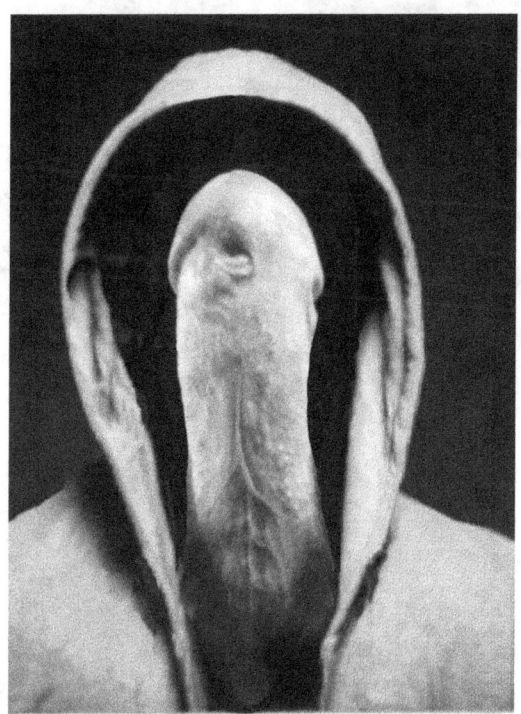

How many radio wave lines are there in the room with you, ninety thousand? Listening is it part of critical thinking?.....Did deaf egyptions use hieroglyphics before words.....Please keep quiet about that.....I've heard about life in silent movies "all men are created equal" that goes well with those who have, liberty and the pursuit of happiness.....Right on brother or sister, get a life in Cairo. Is silence golden? The silent buddists really know there is no such thing as self.....

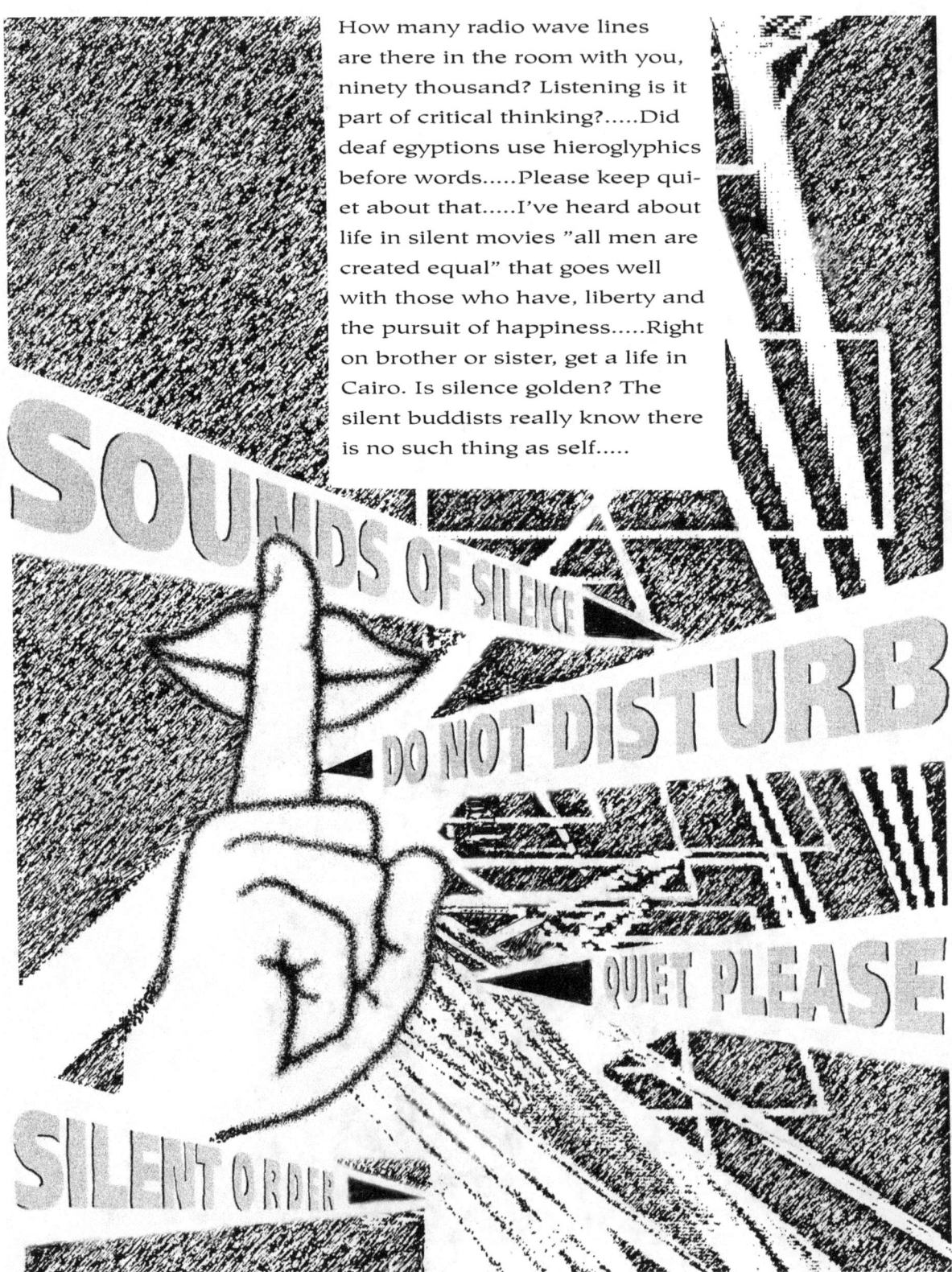

SOUNDS OF SILENCE

DO NOT DISTURB

QUIET PLEASE

SILENT ORDER

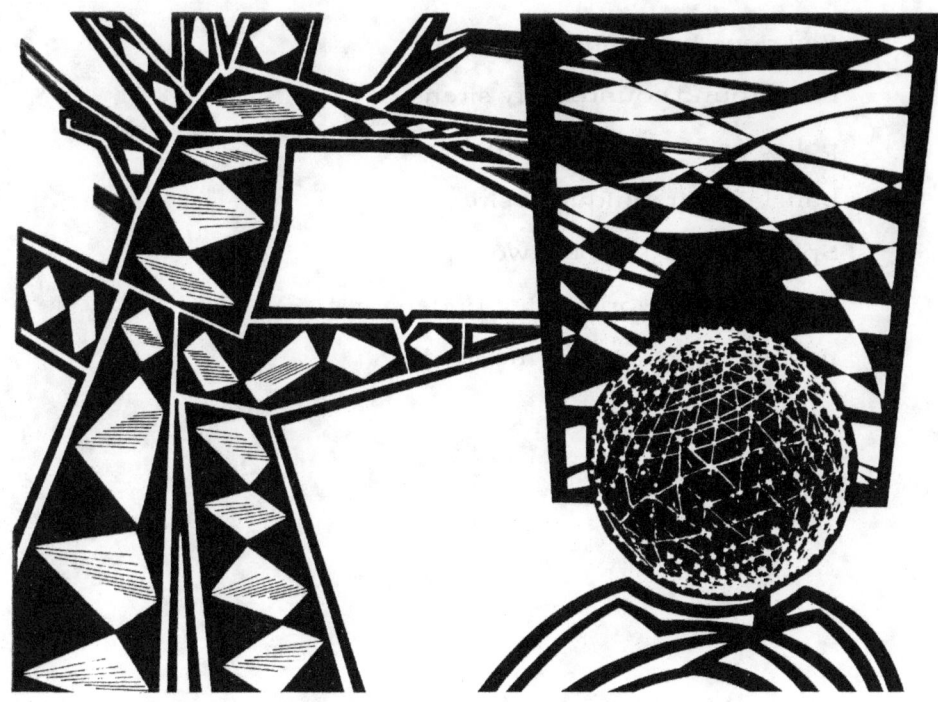

EARTHSHAPE

The cascades of broken reflection
bind the passing water —
*   movements register*
only as the memory of earthshape —
*   a fraction of a sequence*
coincidence.
*   Tired ressurection of probability,*
nausea, compromise unsatisfactory endings.
*   Sensations of selfish attitudes*
mistakes awaken
*   the last sleeping character —*
a man of strong ridicule and bias.
*   Death the waiting predator.*
We, mere crustaceans, amongst the vast
*   energy of universal seafood.*
Fusion of background,
*   consistency of intellect*
man, woman am I.
*   Lucky shades of indifference*
I am healthy — I live, eat sleep.

Bed rider, brains bug minder

background sounds, city sirens

police or fire, nitin sawhney's

bangla choir, unique desire.....

Splender used to be a word

not a brand, world order, understand

now is that computer manned?

Between the sheets, I am hot and slide

searching the bed for cold spots

in and out of fantasy as I glide ride

your skins soft electric walls

trying to find easy entry with my silver balls,

thank god for the desire and thrust of wonderlust

in this audio collage of inner city life.....

This is how I want to die

not alone, but in this safe secure warm zone

at one with all light and time

beyond the wide horizon, then

I will search the perspective

for my lifes vanishing point.....

Holding hands.....Is that being that connected?

Sleep on it.....Connect with your other side.

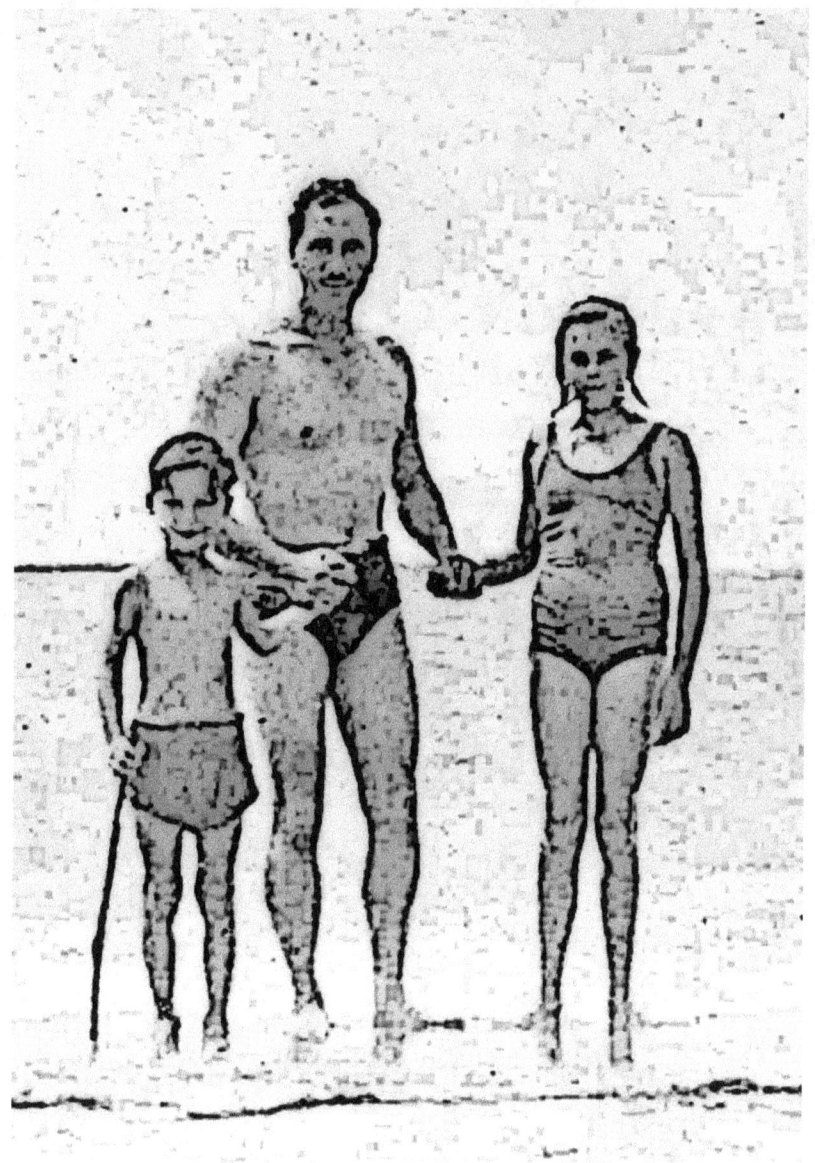

Life is a dream.....Death is your wake up call

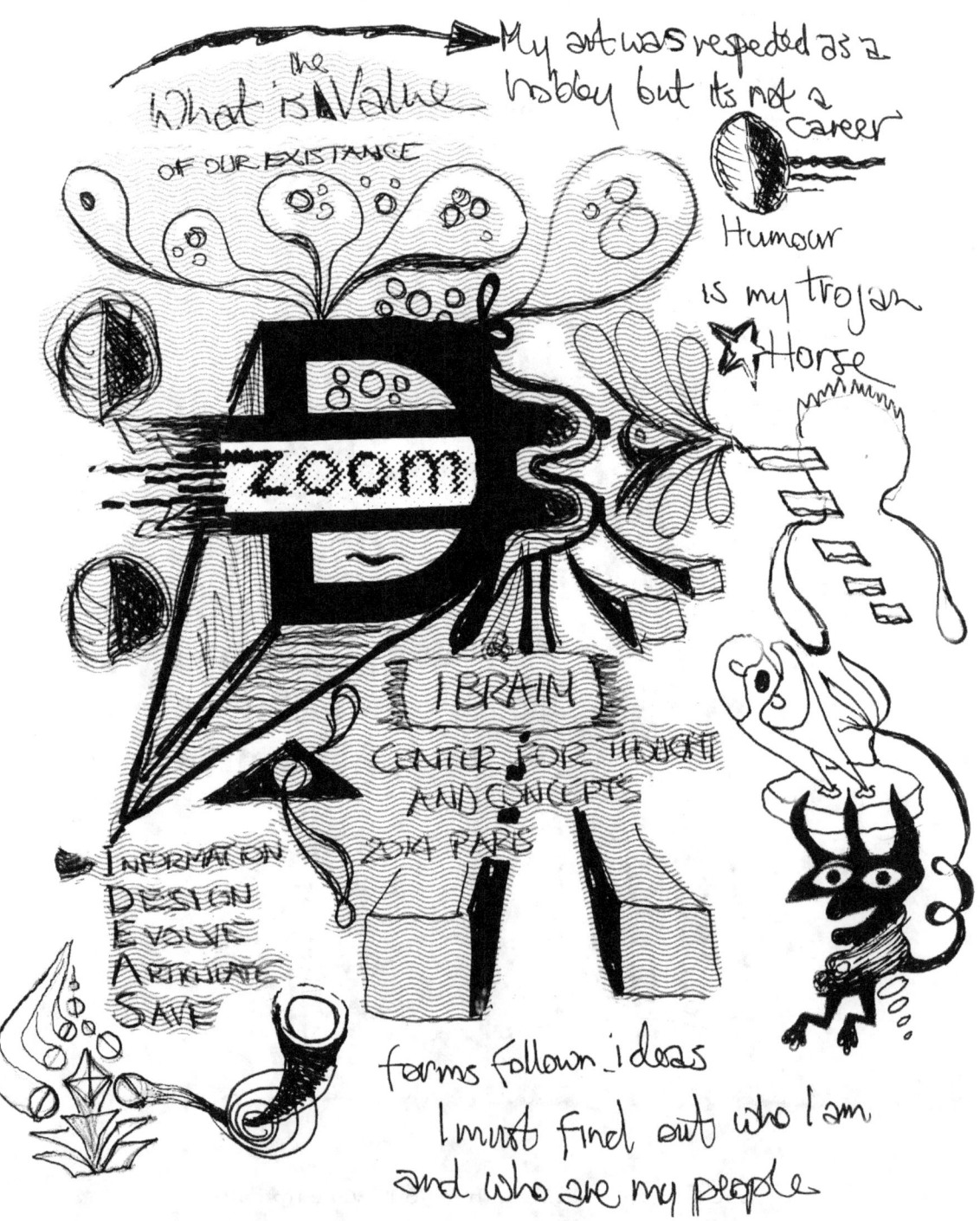

What is the Value
OF OUR EXISTANCE

zoom

My art was respected as a
hobby but its not a
career

Humour
is my trojan
Horse

[BRAIN]

CENTER FOR THOUGHT
AND CONCEPTS
2014 PARIS

INFORMATION
DESIGN
EVOLVE
ARTICULATE
SAVE

forms follown ideas
I must find out who I am
and who are my people

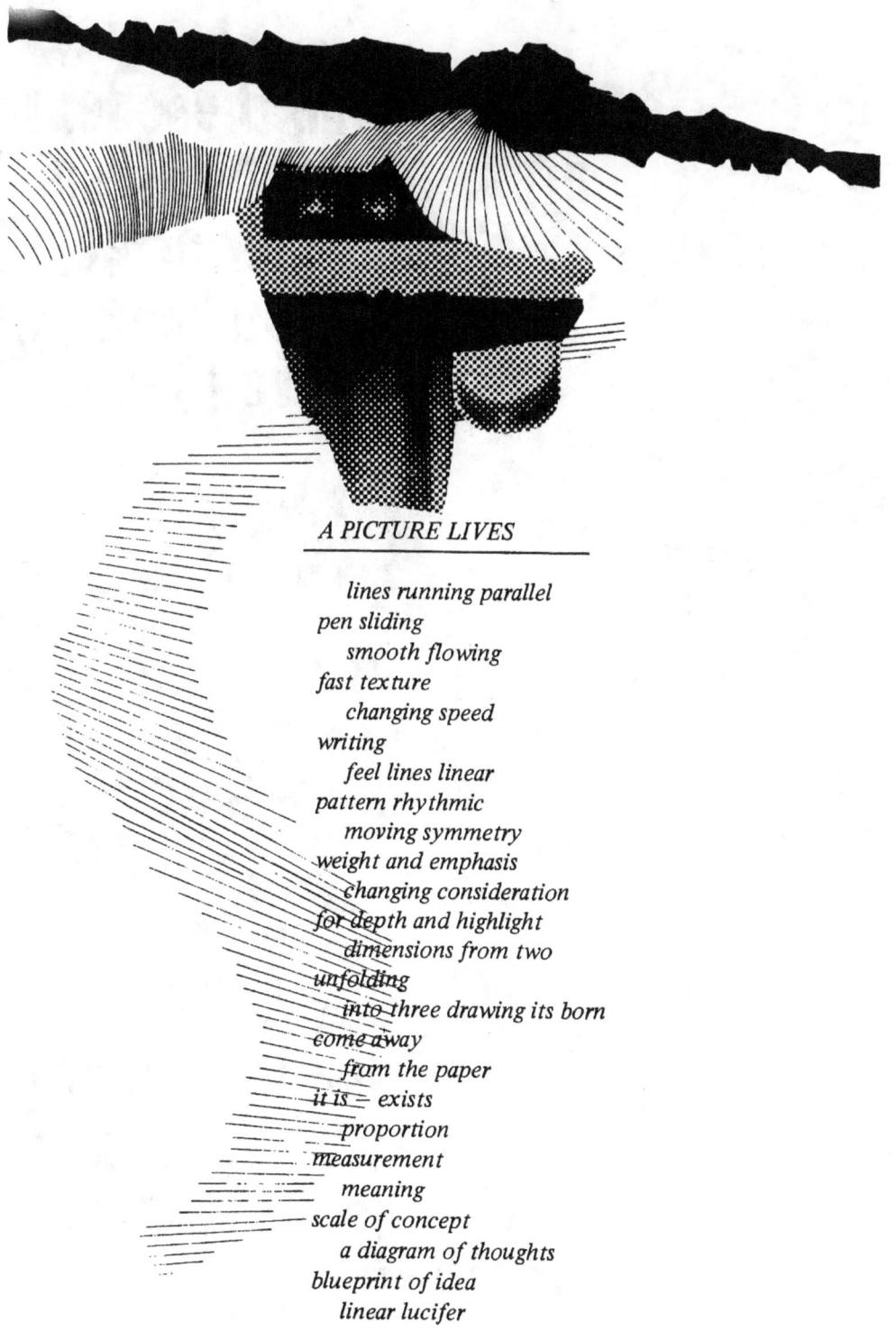

A PICTURE LIVES

　　　lines running parallel
pen sliding
　　　smooth flowing
fast texture
　　　changing speed
writing
　　　feel lines linear
pattern rhythmic
　　　moving symmetry
weight and emphasis
　　　changing consideration
for depth and highlight
　　　dimensions from two
unfolding
　　　into three drawing its born
come away
　　　from the paper
it is – exists
　　　proportion
measurement
　　　meaning
scale of concept
　　　a diagram of thoughts
blueprint of idea
　　　linear lucifer

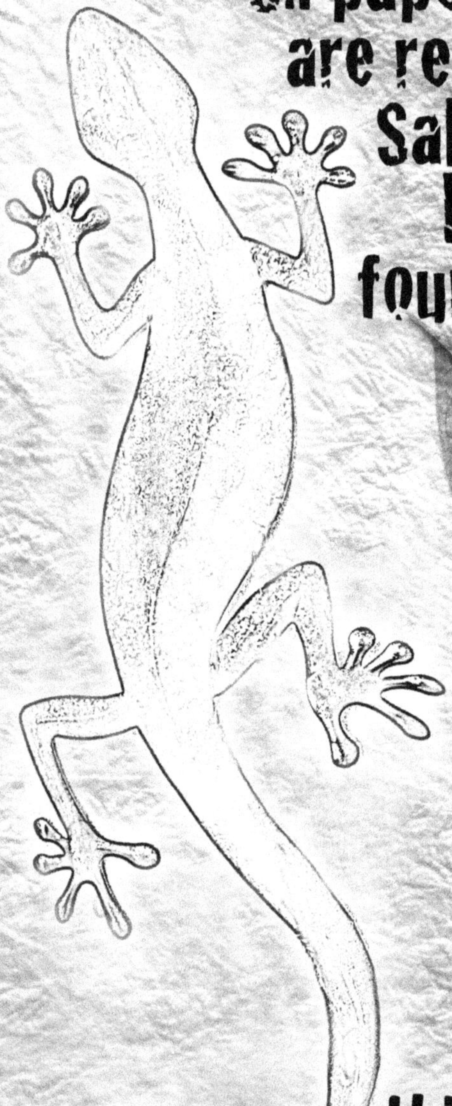

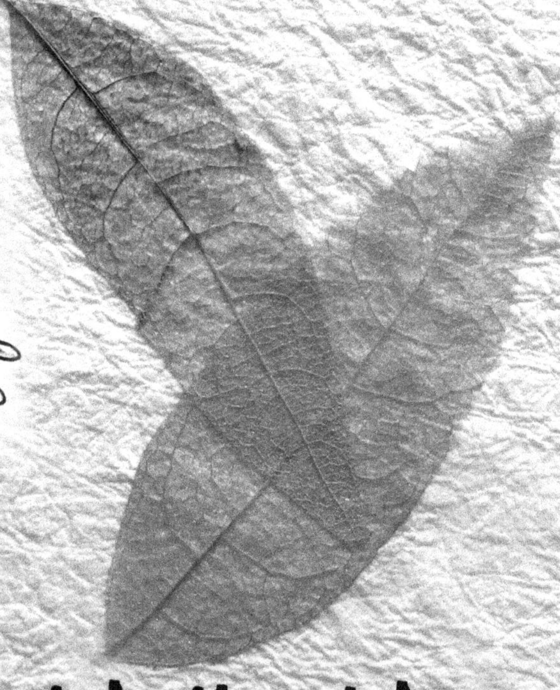

On paperskin, these leaves
are really tropical, so.....
Salamander or geko?
Dont you know
four or five toes.....

take the mickey
this drawing is a sickie
just wanted a quickie.....
its the heat you know!

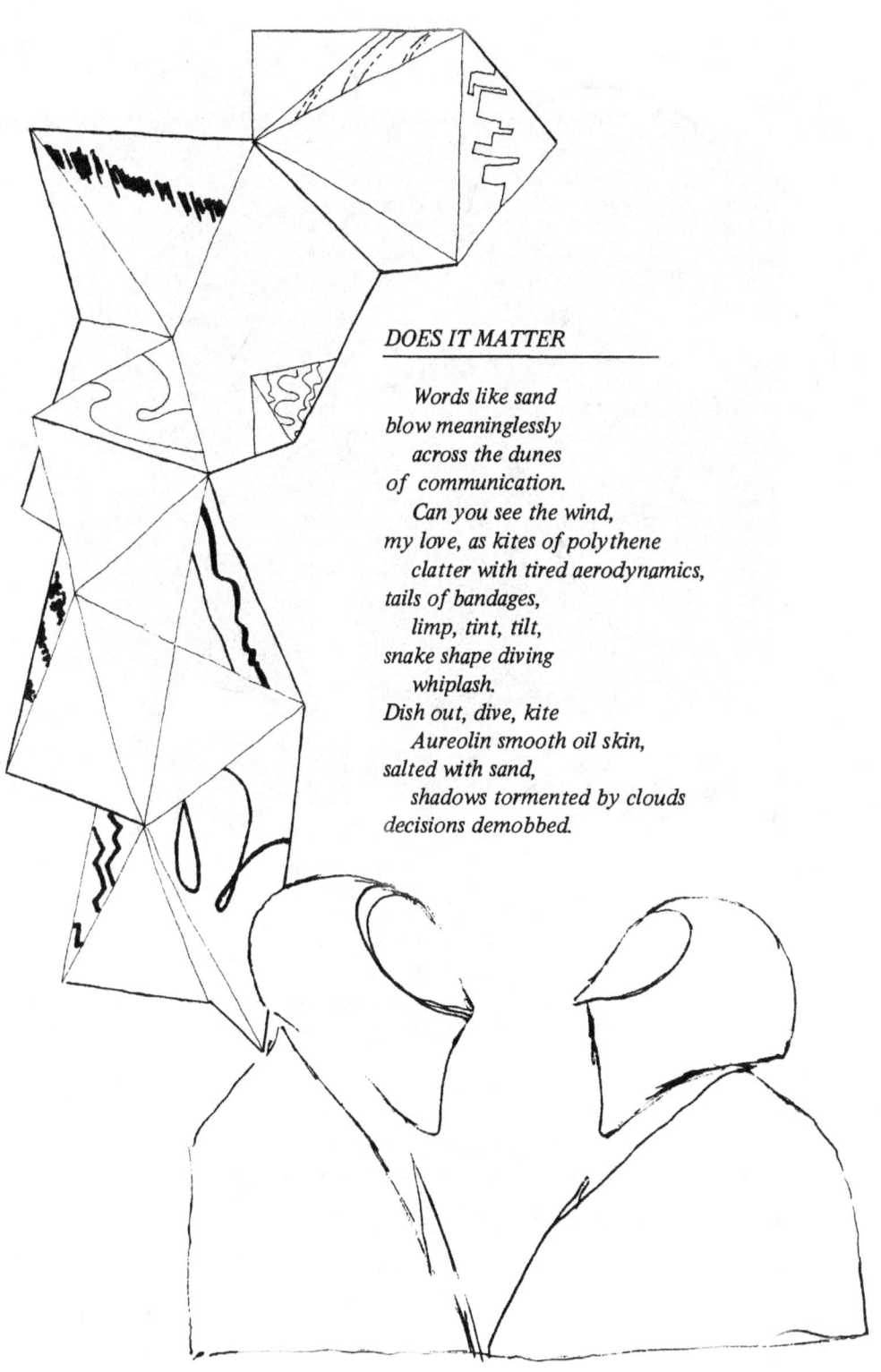

DOES IT MATTER

*Words like sand
blow meaninglessly
   across the dunes
of communication.
   Can you see the wind,
my love, as kites of polythene
   clatter with tired aerodynamics,
tails of bandages,
   limp, tint, tilt,
snake shape diving
   whiplash.
Dish out, dive, kite
   Aureolin smooth oil skin,
salted with sand,
   shadows tormented by clouds
decisions demobbed.*

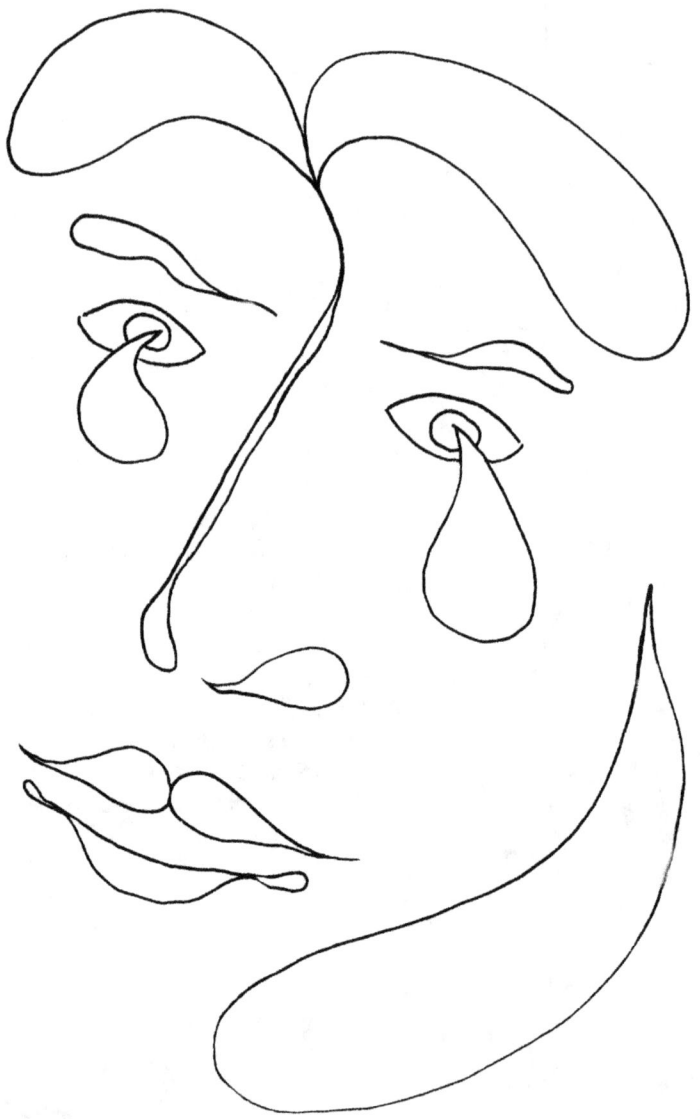

Line like the drawing above. has a point that moves over space!

Space.....Three dimensional, negative, positive or two dimensional

texture and surface, life and artwork have it.....

Primary colour makes all colour exist, no colour here.....is that true?

Shape is formed wherever the ends of a continuous line meet.

Pray you have your visuals.

24

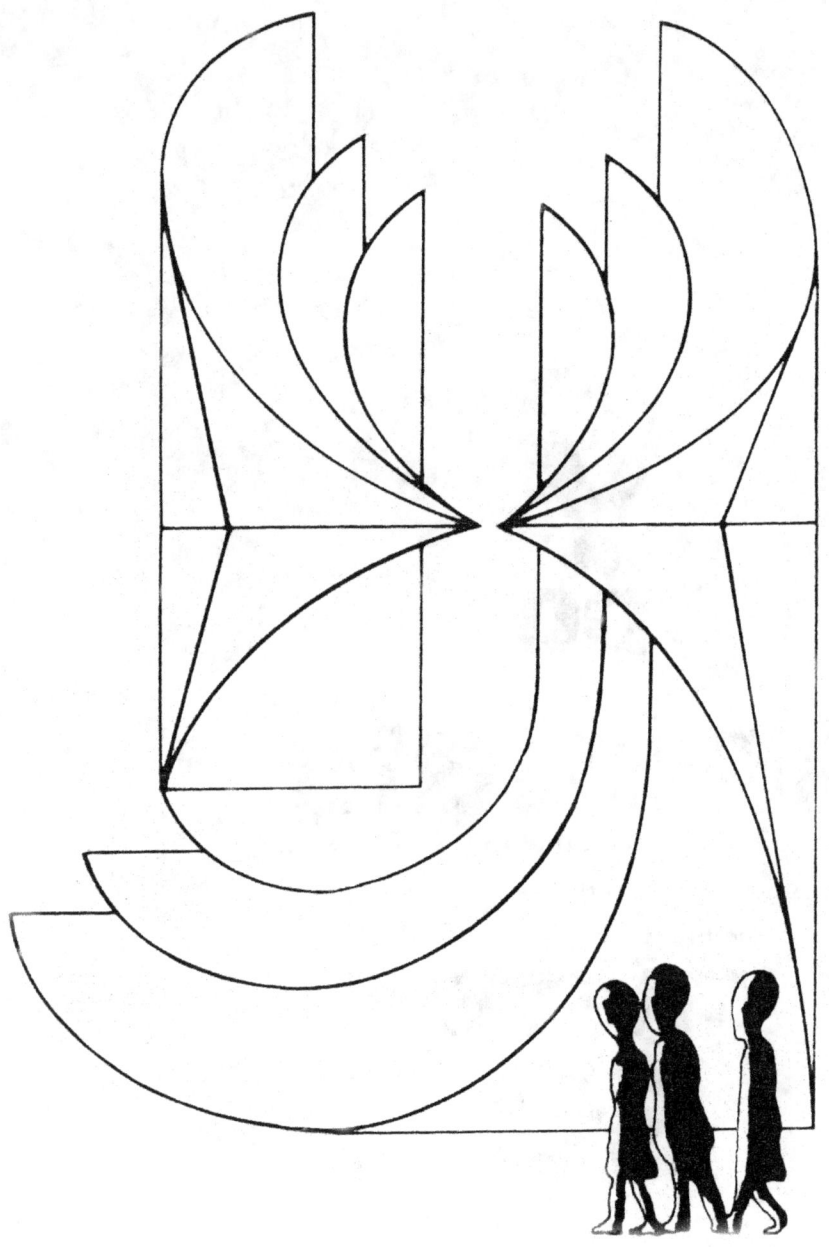

Balance comes from weight, contrast, symmetry, tonal and colour values in non moving art.

Idea, story, the subject inspires your imagination to complete or build your own picture, more so in radio drama than video.

Focal point....Elements in the picture, colour. line or perspective take your eyes to the emphasis or main subject matter of the picture.

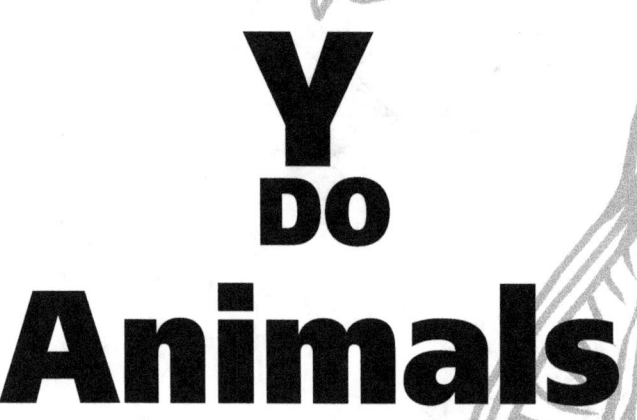

Y
DO
Animals

Rump rules in steak therapy

All the goodness is in the skin

The breast is best.....

TASTE
SO

The parsons knowsarse.....

GOOD
?

26

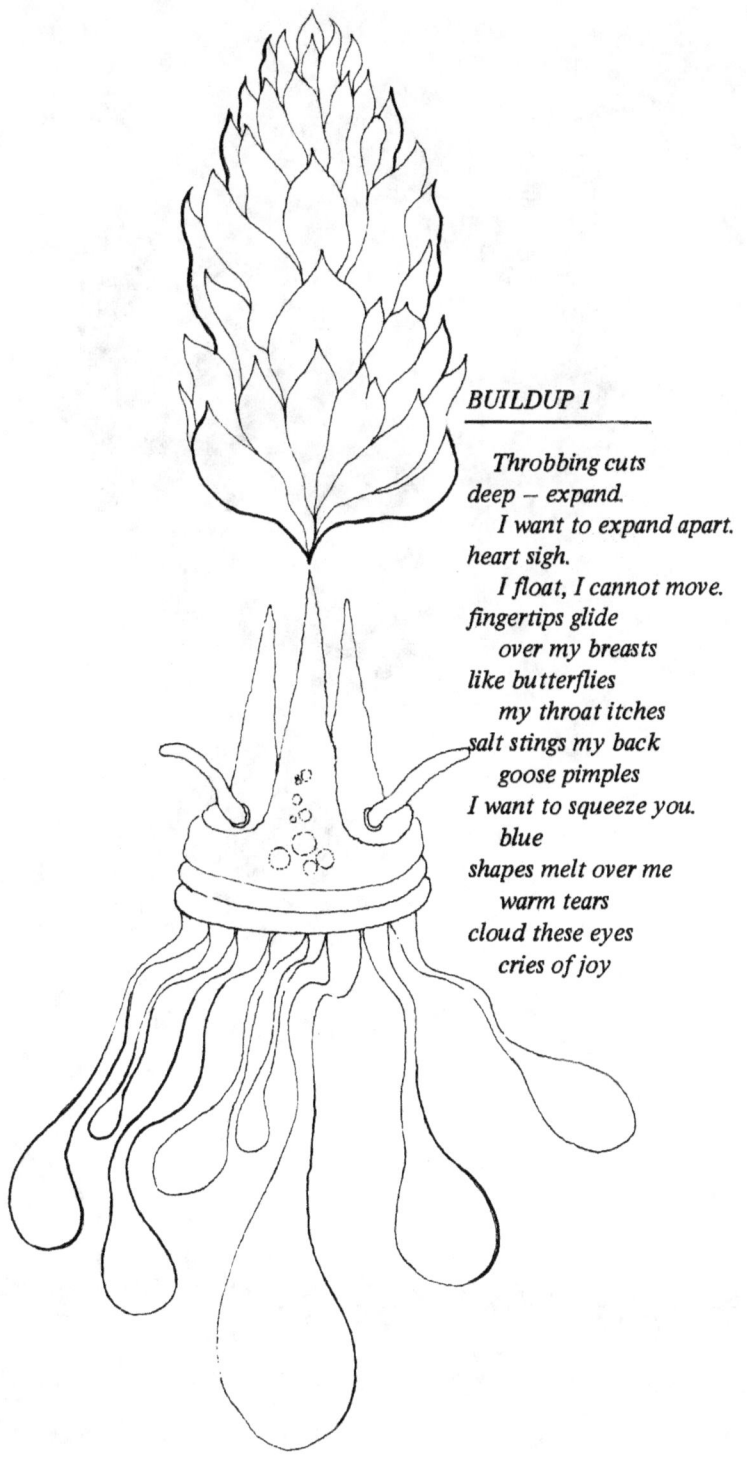

BUILDUP 1

Throbbing cuts
deep — expand.
   I want to expand apart.
heart sigh.
   I float, I cannot move.
fingertips glide
   over my breasts
like butterflies
   my throat itches
salt stings my back
   goose pimples
I want to squeeze you.
   blue
shapes melt over me
   warm tears
cloud these eyes
   cries of joy

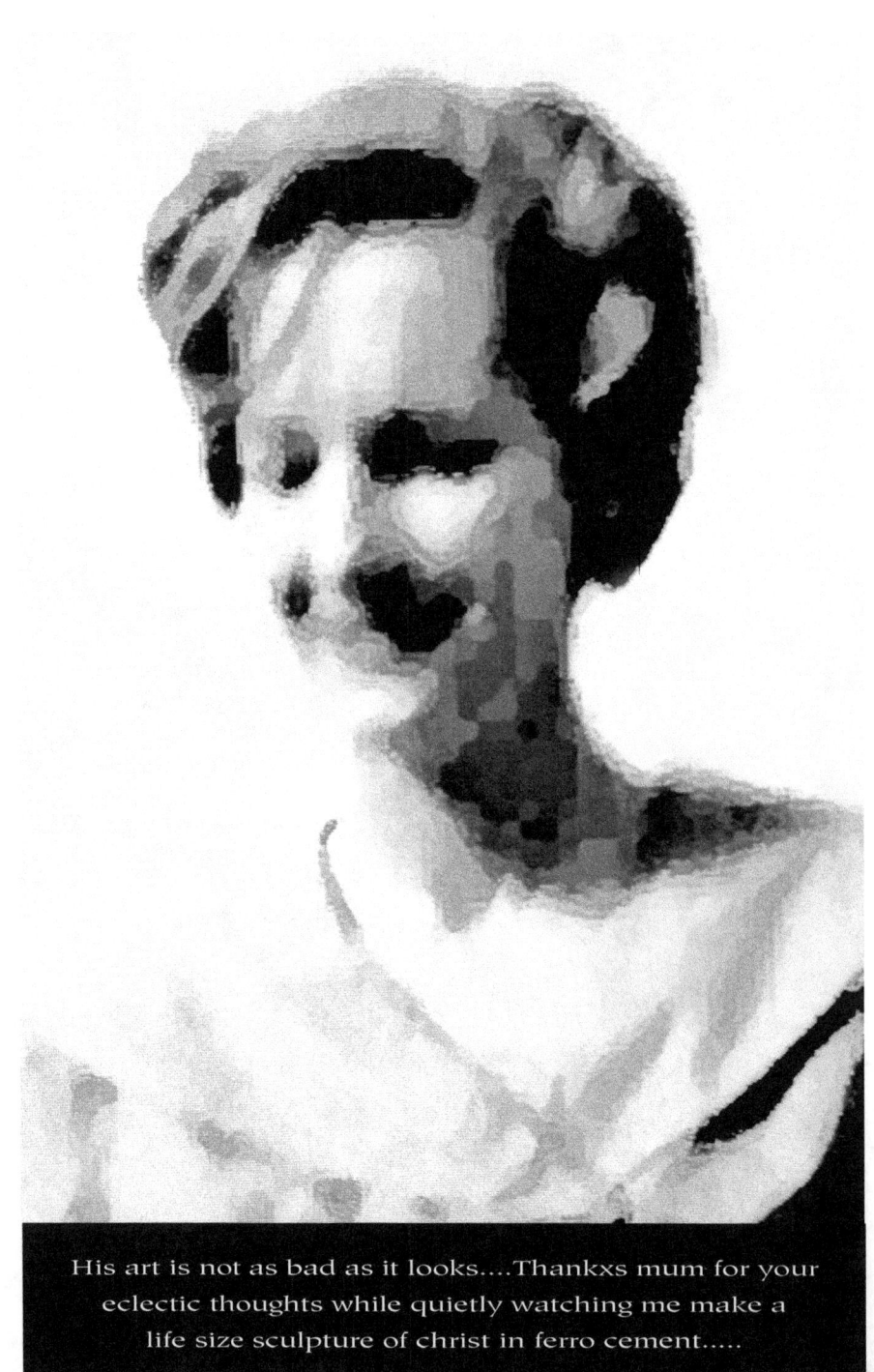

His art is not as bad as it looks....Thankxs mum for your
eclectic thoughts while quietly watching me make a
life size sculpture of christ in ferro cement.....

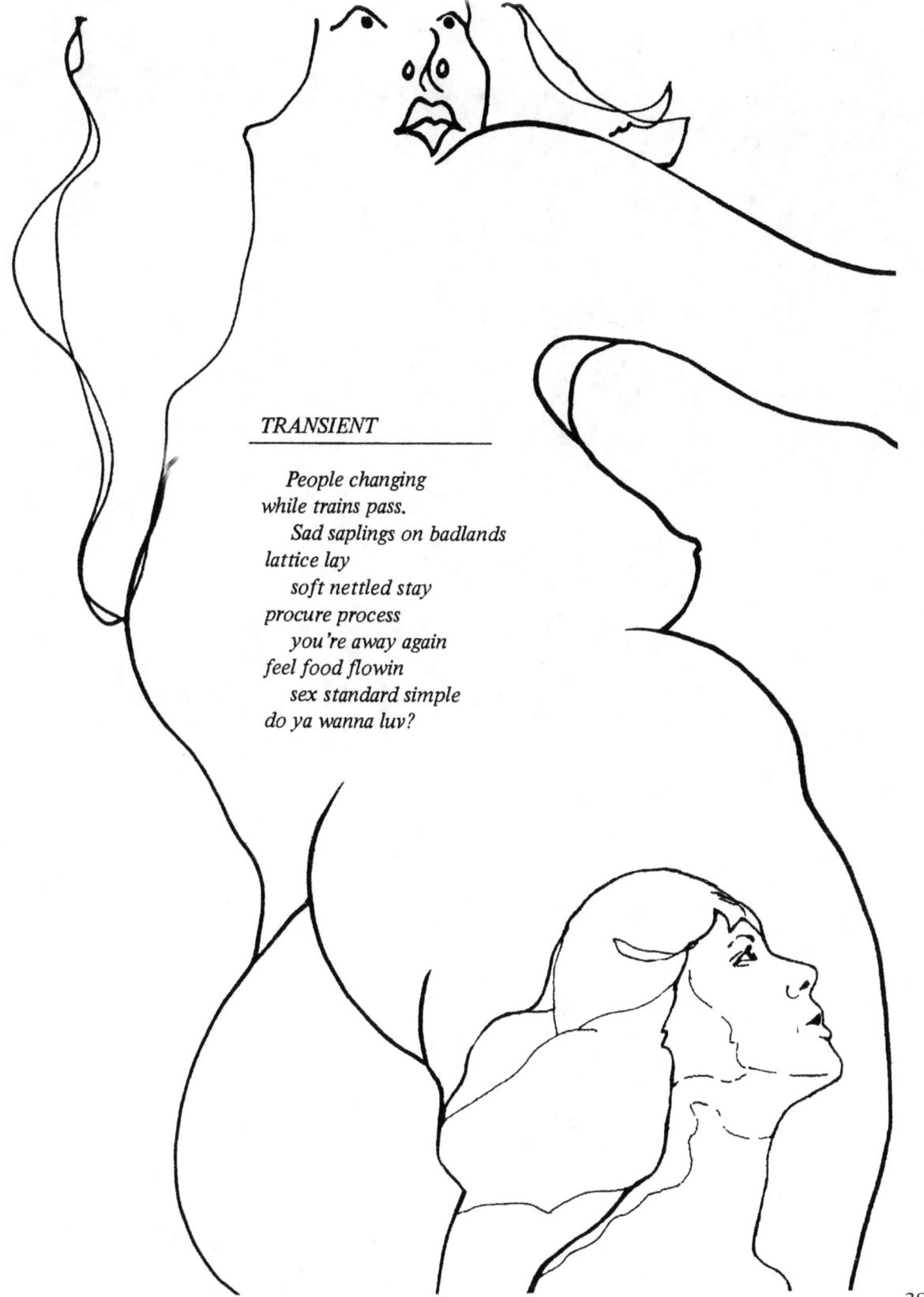

TRANSIENT

People changing
while trains pass.
    Sad saplings on badlands
lattice lay
    soft nettled stay
procure process
    you're away again
feel food flowin
    sex standard simple
do ya wanna luv?

29

"WHAT ANY TRUE PAINTING TOUCHES IS AN ABSENCE

—AN ABSENCE OF WHICH WITHOUT THE PAINTING,

WE MIGHT BE UNAWARE, AND THAT WOULD BE A LOSS."

John Berger

Tu fais mon coeur sourire

The wind streams across the fields of northern france

the damp course breeds in the stone cottages of the last century.

The provences of people have moved to the cities and work

leaving the elderly to council the villages of bourgogne,

canals of commerce long gone, nature is taking back its land.

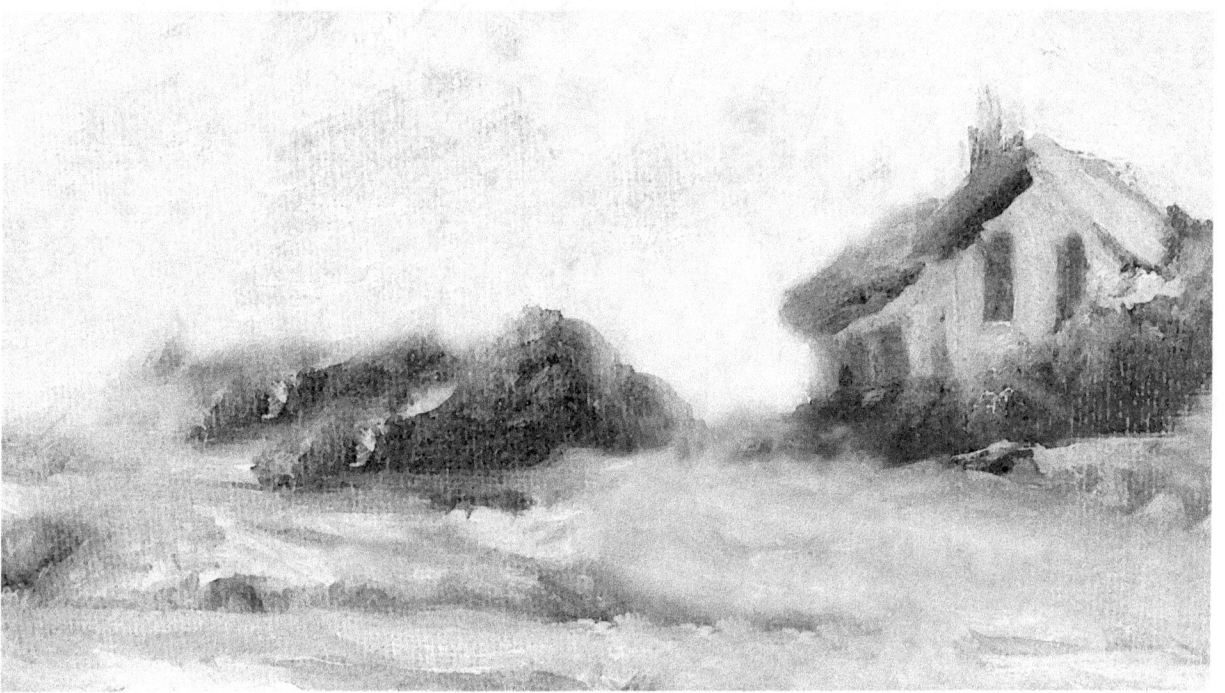

Freedom for impressionism.....I am the sunday afternoon painter

families have grown up living and loving in the right way of life,

knowing how to make jam, sausages, goat cheese, and champagne

bon appetit.....Apres vous.....Yes after you.....

Are we strong, soft in bed? With our lifestyle we could be wrong.

This drawing is Russian, no way.....It is Canadian.....
From what historic ornament did it derive its pattern
structure? It is definitely a Jewish drawing, the way
the olive garden is Italian!

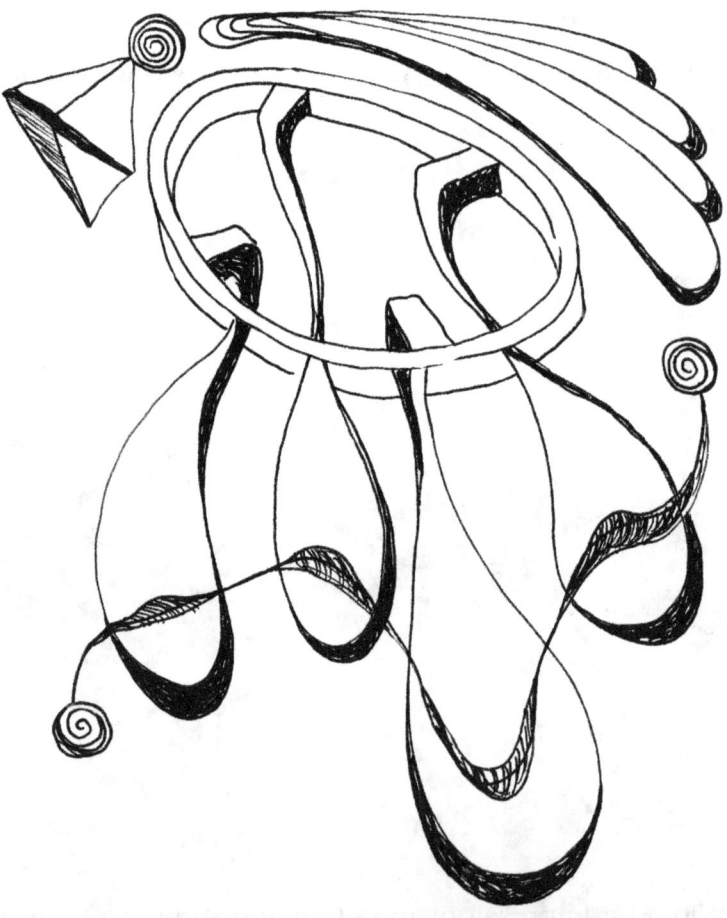

Somabodies fell from the moon....

This is the undrawable likeness of seeing doodles.....

What is the basic story in this design?

Is this the most important drawing in this whole book?

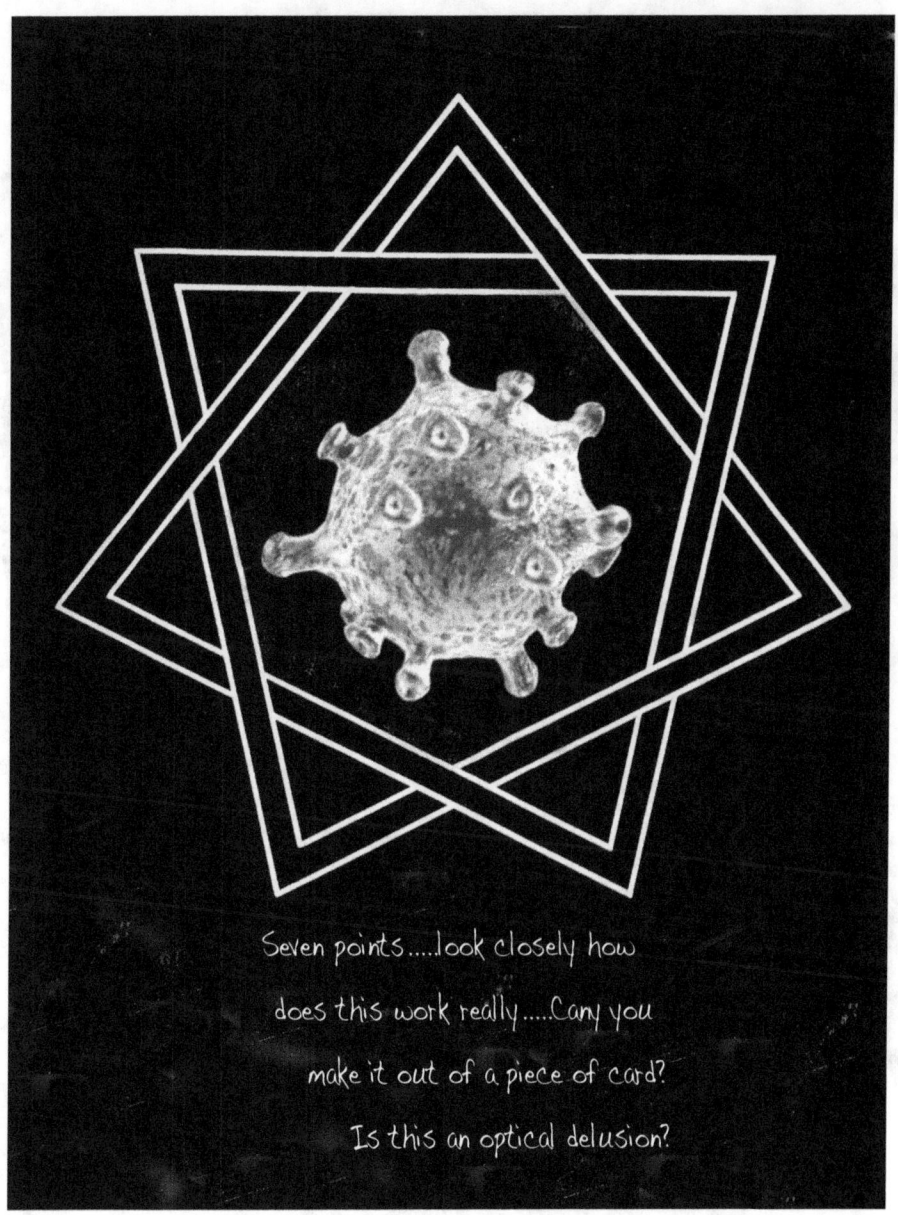

Seven points.....look closely how

does this work really.....Cany you

make it out of a piece of card?

Is this an optical delusion?

Symbols....Secret societies.....Groups
gaterthering for strength and power to
control who?.....Heaven is created for
those who can not handle death.

Mondo cane moved me to
repulsion as I thought I was a
suitable case for treatment.....
Morgan. Cars kept up the
fantasy xke. Satyricon said
it all to candy.....The Magic
christian and the flying circus
enjoyed mandies on the way
to Bibas.....Desmond who
lived in a heart of soul at the
electric cinema, Portobello
road, died of aids. Life was
a speakeasy club in upper
regent street living on It, Oz,
Indica.....With private eyes!
The Guardian watched.

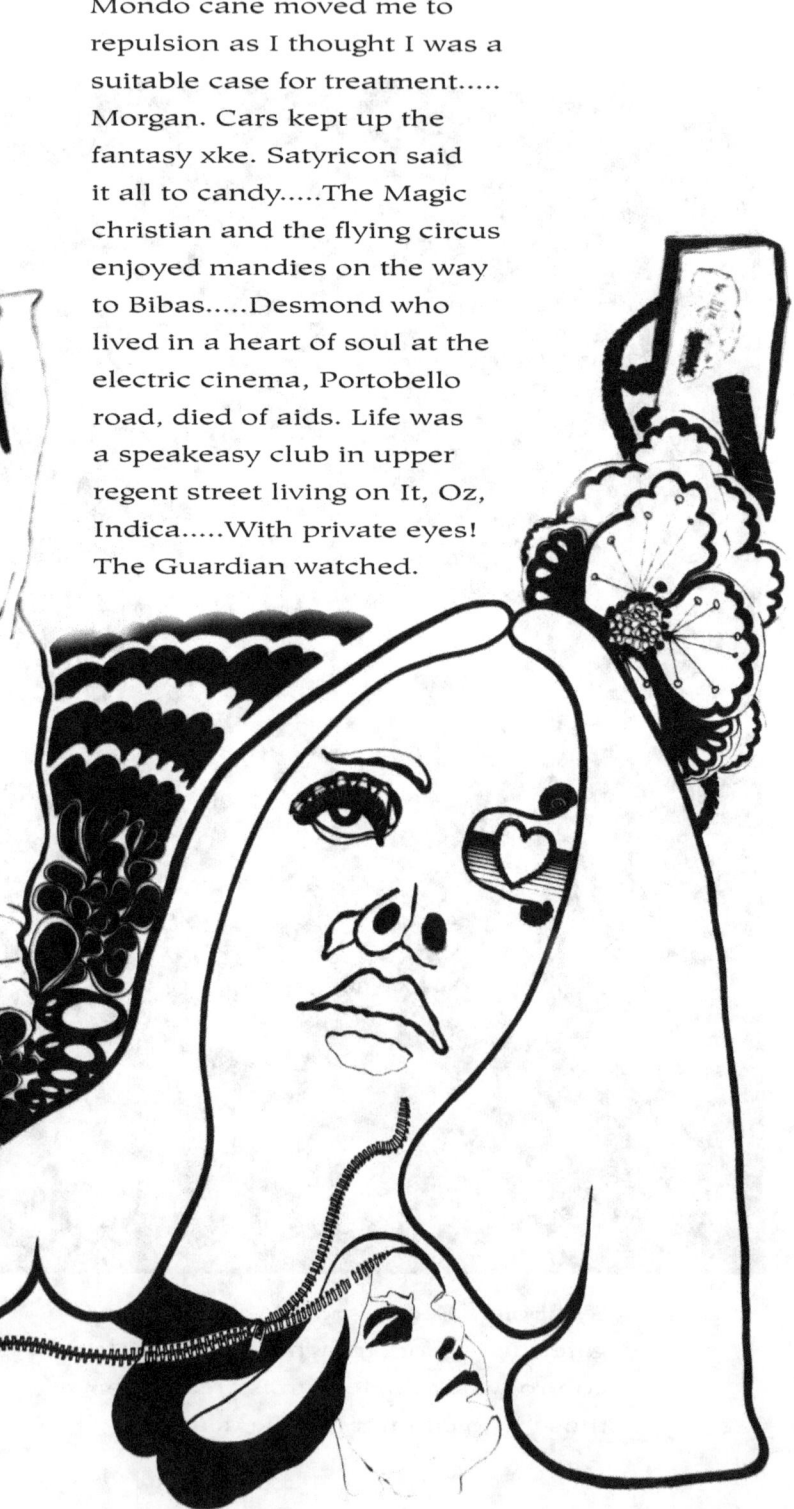

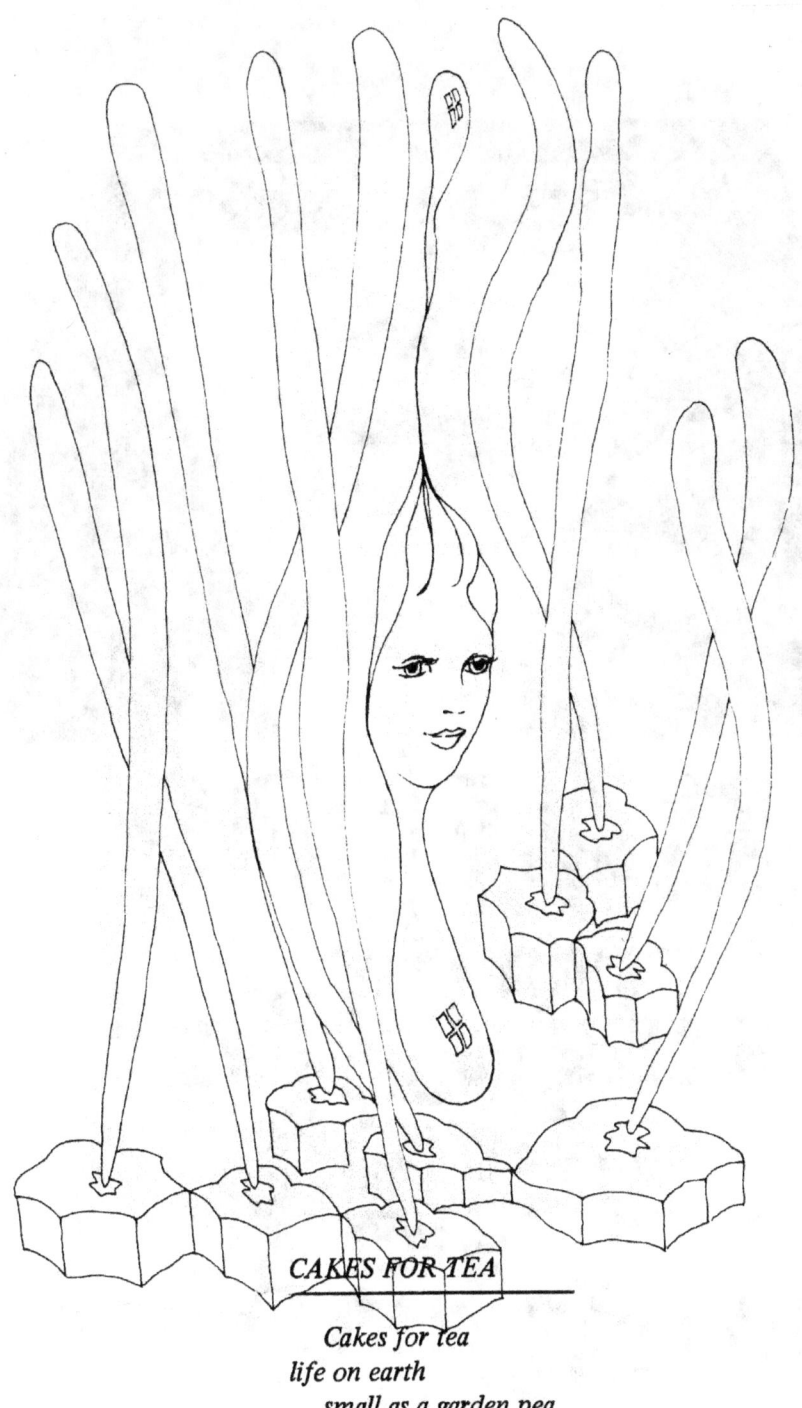

CAKES FOR TEA

Cakes for tea
life on earth
    small as a garden pea.
Do you want more?
    Happiness out of my heart
does pour.

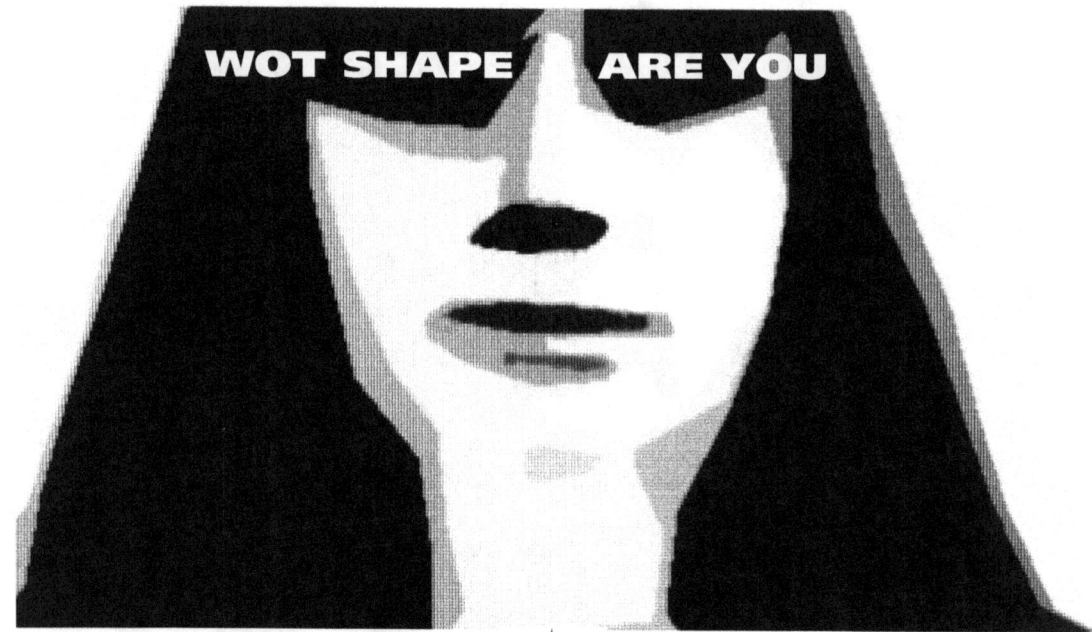

WOT SHAPE ARE YOU

B4I U2

I'M ON A SCREWDRIVER VODKA DIET

SO FAR I'VE LOST TWO DAYS

WAY IN LATE WATCHERS

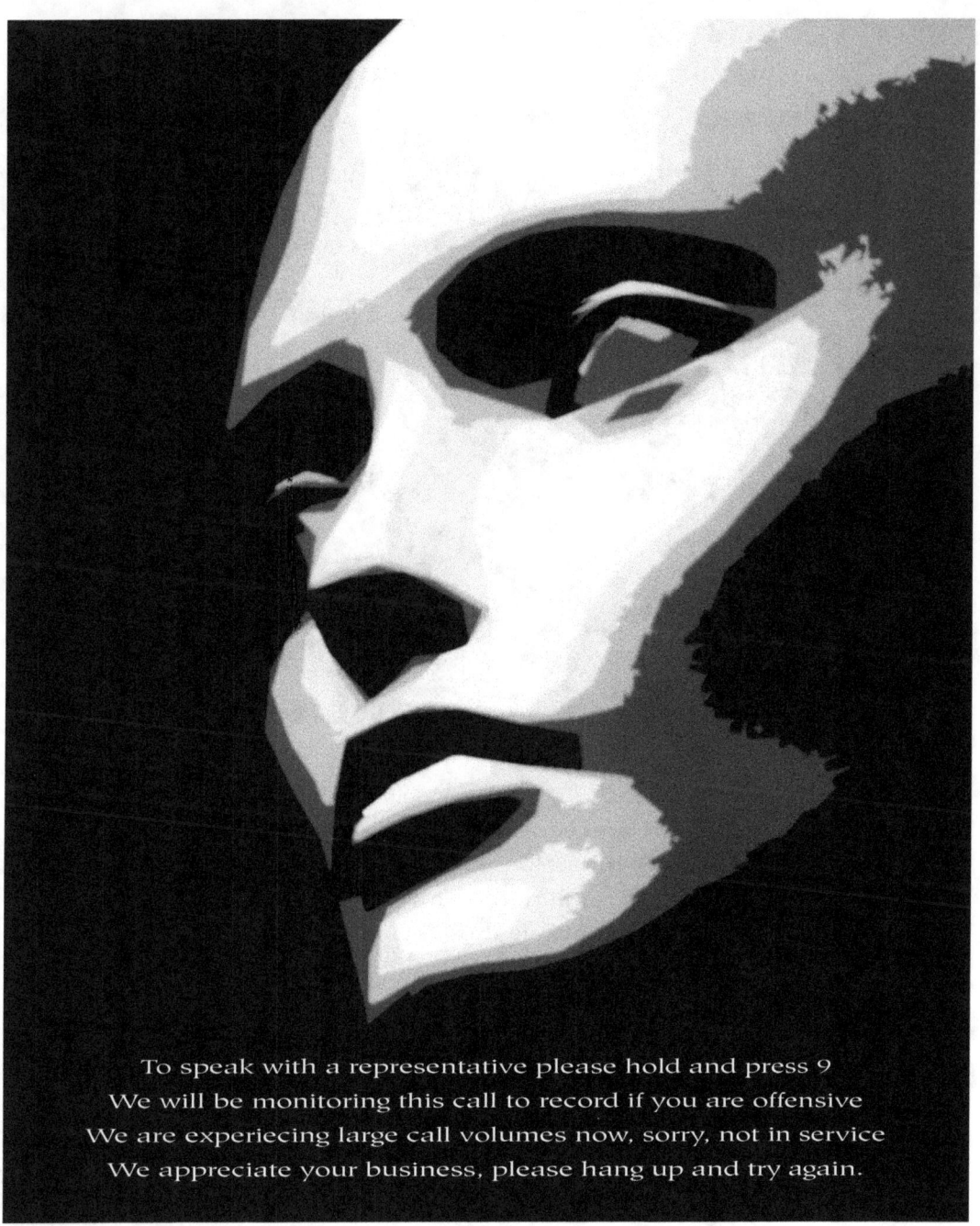

To speak with a representative please hold and press 9
We will be monitoring this call to record if you are offensive
We are experiecing large call volumes now, sorry, not in service
We appreciate your business, please hang up and try again.

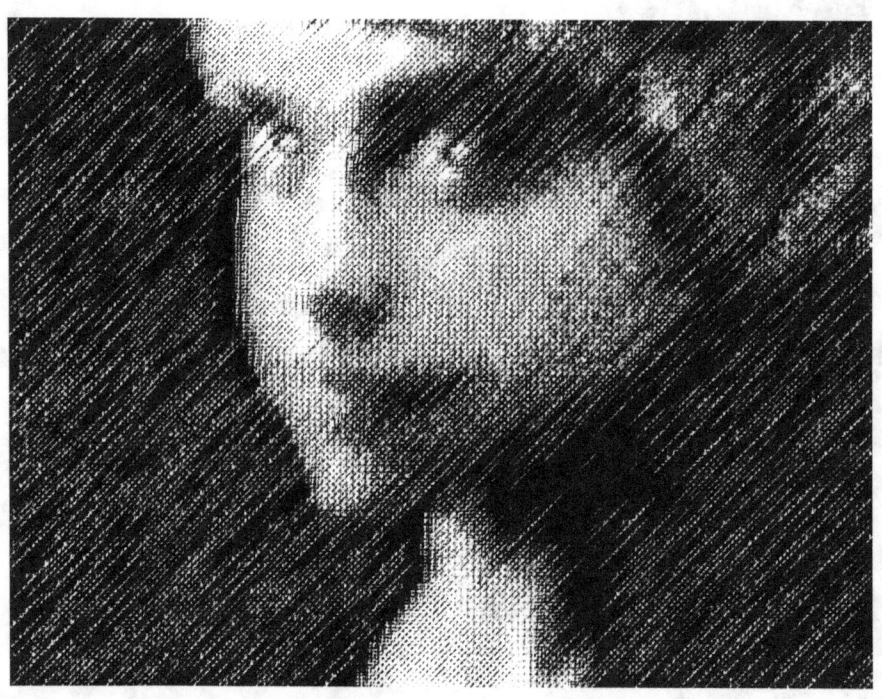

Now lets look at this design.....The
face, outer sensors, eyes see.....
Ears hear.....Nose smells.....Mouth
recharges, reenergise and tastes.
The brain above these sensors
organises and controls the system
for our survival, not really. She is
only made of pixels and ink on
this book paper.....

7H15 M3554G3

53RV35 7O PR0V3

H0W 0UR M1ND5

C4N D0 4M4Z1NG 7H1NG5!

1MPR3551V3 7H1NG5!

1N 7H3 B3G1NN1NG

17 WA5 H4RD BU7

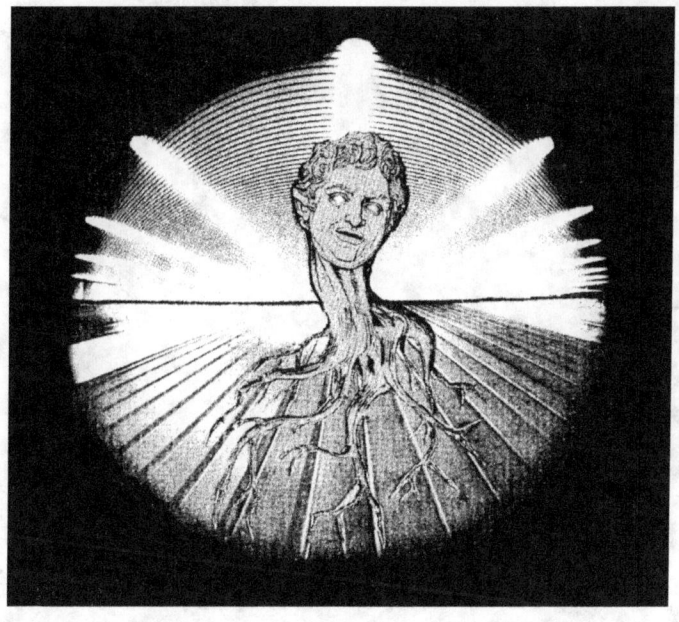

N0W, 0N 7H15 L1N3

Y0UR M1ND 1S

R34D1NG 17

4U70M471C4LLY

W17H 0U7 3V3N

7H1NK1NG 4B0U7 17

B3 PROUD!

0NLY C3R74N P30PL3 C4N

R3AD 7H15

The phaonmneal pwoer of the hmuan mnid. it deos not raed ervey lteter by istlef, but the word as a wlohe. How tehn do we seae.....

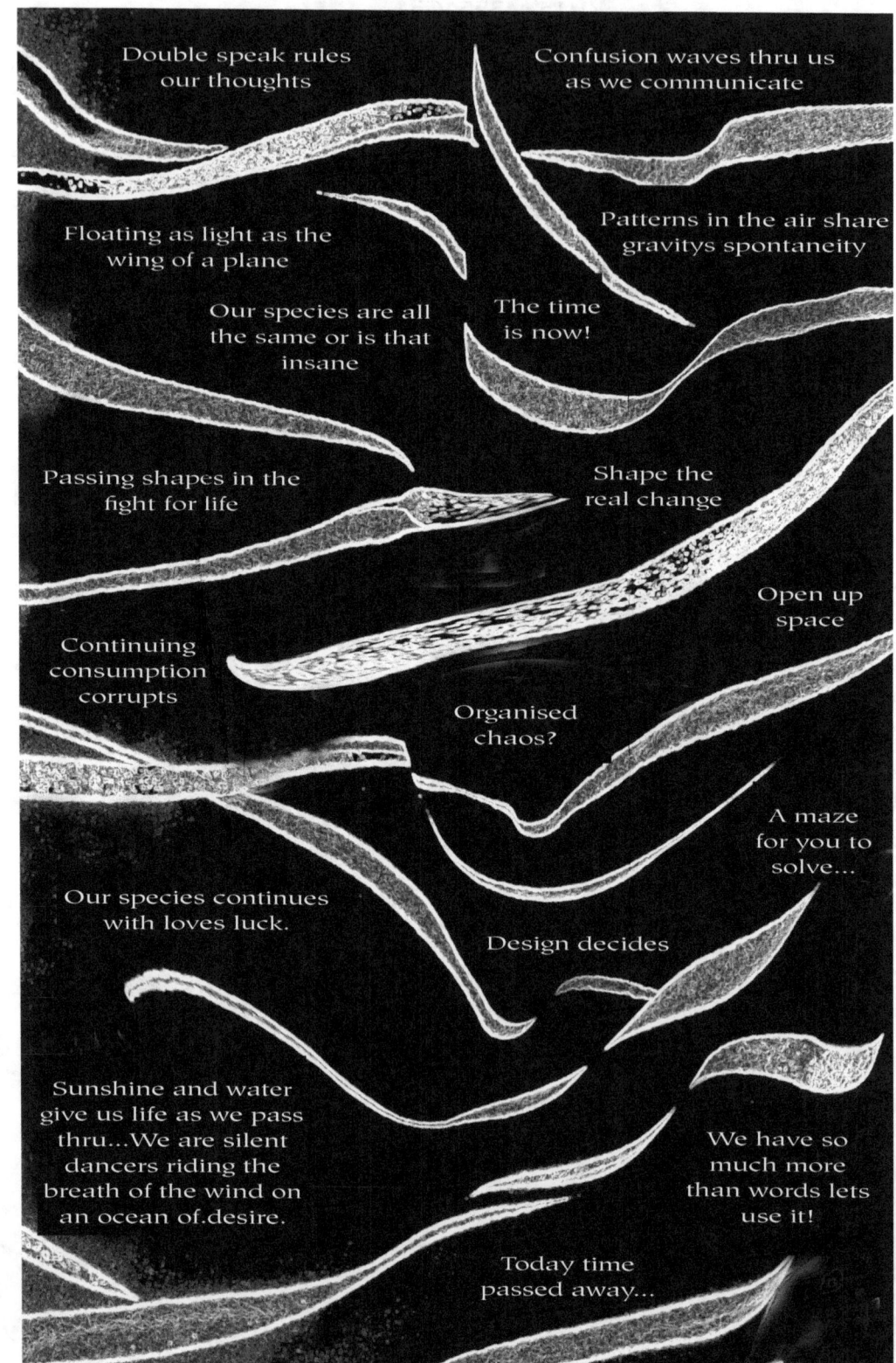

Double speak rules
our thoughts

Confusion waves thru us
as we communicate

Floating as light as the
wing of a plane

Patterns in the air share
gravitys spontaneity

Our species are all
the same or is that
insane

The time
is now!

Passing shapes in the
fight for life

Shape the
real change

Open up
space

Continuing
consumption
corrupts

Organised
chaos?

A maze
for you to
solve...

Our species continues
with loves luck.

Design decides

Sunshine and water
give us life as we pass
thru...We are silent
dancers riding the
breath of the wind on
an ocean of.desire.

We have so
much more
than words lets
use it!

Today time
passed away...

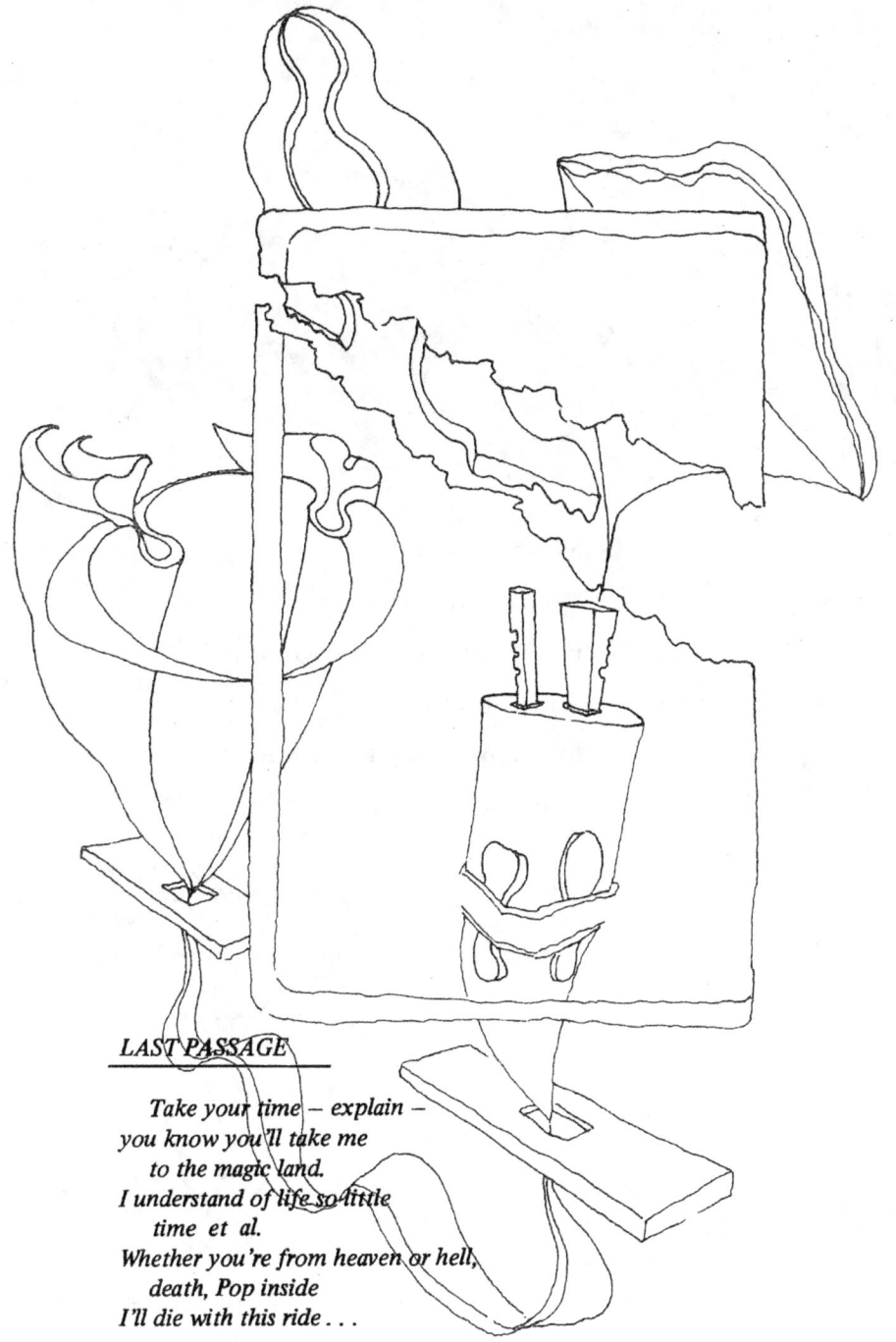

LAST PASSAGE

*Take your time — explain —
you know you'll take me
    to the magic land.
I understand of life so little
    time et al.
Whether you're from heaven or hell,
    death, Pop inside
I'll die with this ride . . .*

Airport africa.....Mum in middle of pic, looking at me.....1961

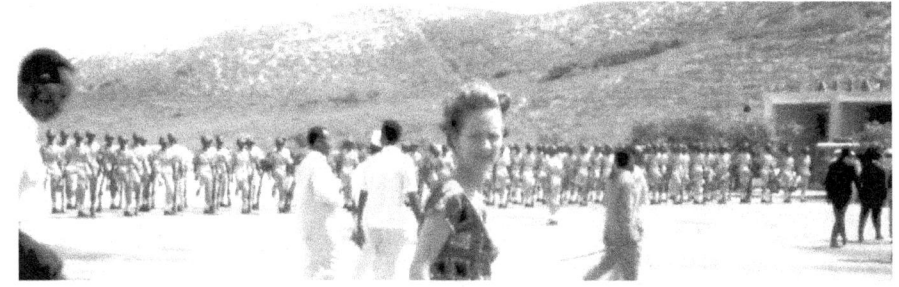

Mum always said

"Sometimes you find yourself

in the middle of nowhere,

and sometimes,

in the middle of nowhere,

you find yourself."

I drew this mask in 1964 in a historic ornament class at the
central tech art school, George street. My proud contribution
to Aboriginal-Italian-Polynesion ornament.....Really I should
edit the hair and give it some eyes!

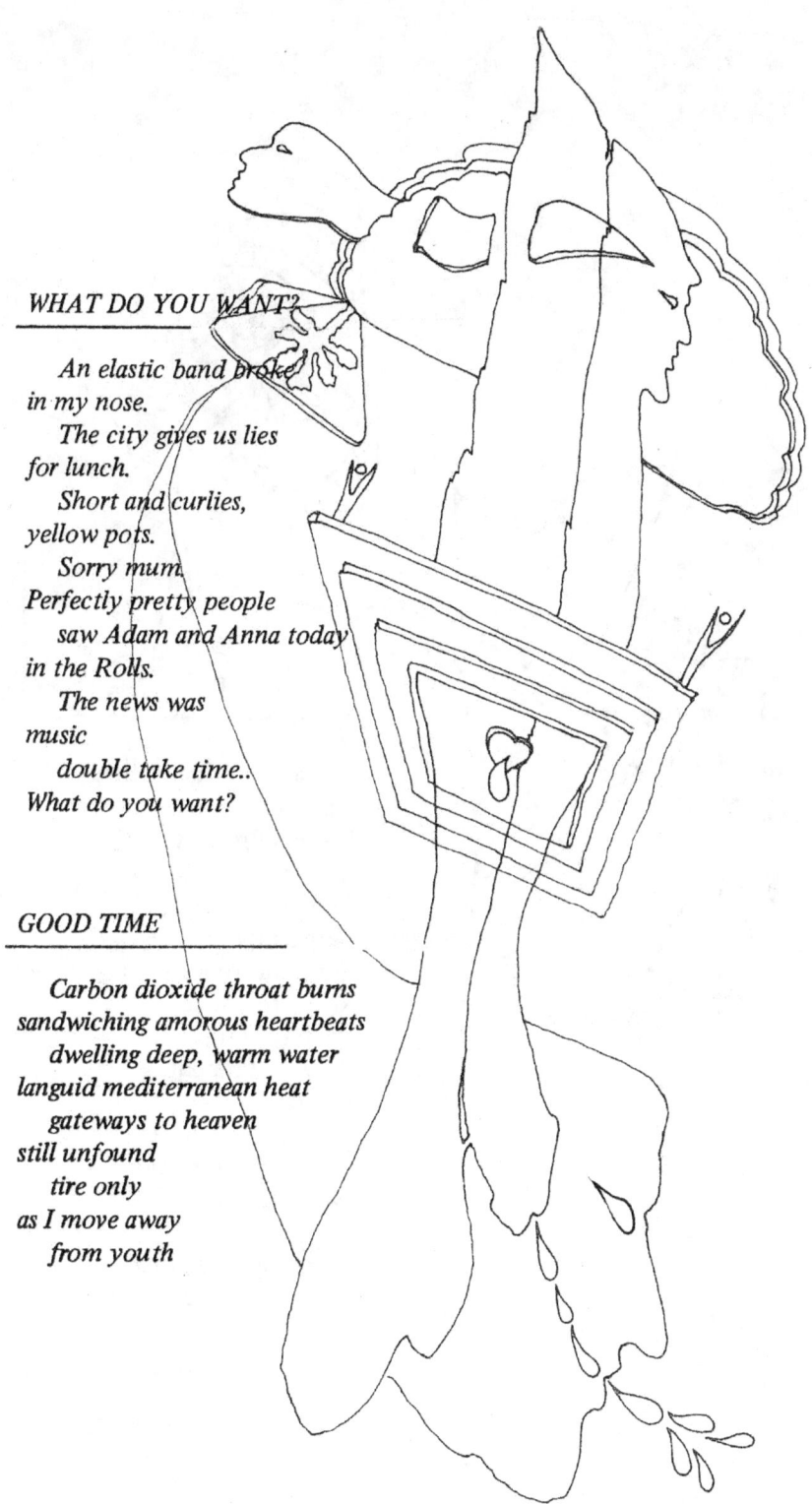

WHAT DO YOU WANT?

An elastic band broke
in my nose.
   The city gives us lies
for lunch.
   Short and curlies,
yellow pots.
   Sorry mum.
Perfectly pretty people
   saw Adam and Anna today
in the Rolls.
   The news was
music
   double take time..
What do you want?

GOOD TIME

Carbon dioxide throat burns
sandwiching amorous heartbeats
   dwelling deep, warm water
languid mediterranean heat
   gateways to heaven
still unfound
   tire only
as I move away
   from youth

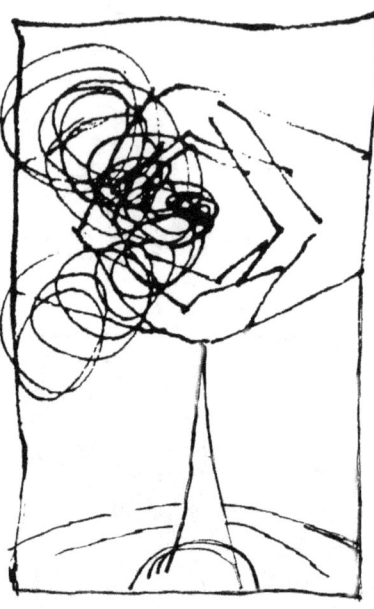

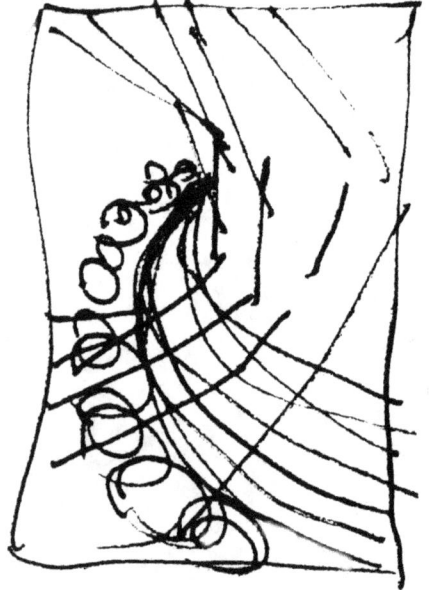

I sit at the edge of time
still waiting as I was
in 1963 Proudly I sat
on that DKW hobby
Zen and the art
of the motorcycle.
Our children do not
know the history
we have failed,
they will repeat
our mistakes..
Please let them repeat
our search beyond
earth or it will all
be wasted, and
they will have died
for nothing yet again !
Still they fall in
love with other peoples
partners, only the
camouflage changes !

Up Yours..... Who Art You

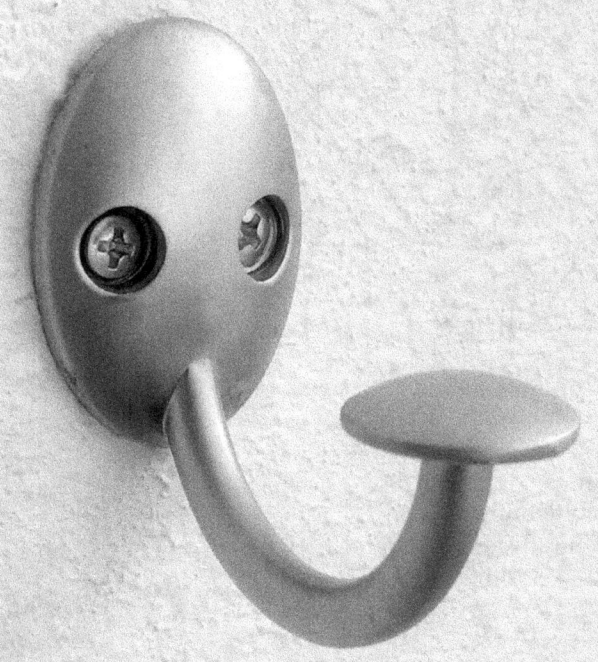

Every morning I sat on the toilet and
talked to this towel hanger about my
plan for the day and the meaning of
life.....Track me google, I am on the vol-
cano on the big island.....Do you know
if I am assange and or snowdon, can
you see this pictures star driver eyes or
just call it phillips head screw.....Google
knows what you are really looking for,
how many passwords do you have? We
are all free to have a nice cup of tea!

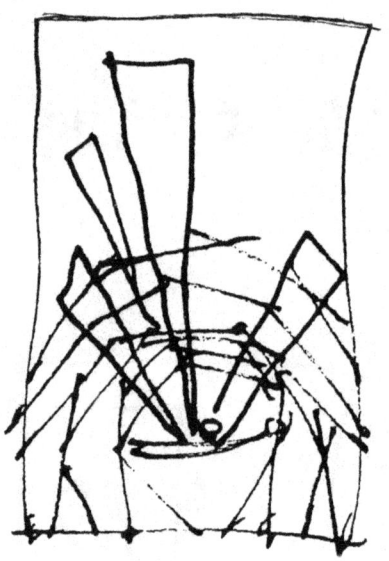

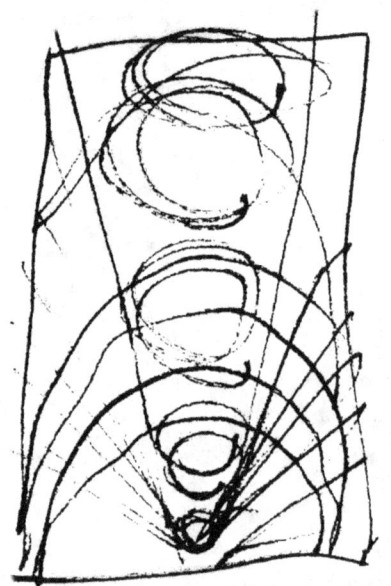

We see things
around us
not as they are
but as we feel they are.
You definitely see
things different than me.
Your world is your
experience, your joy
and your sadness !
You have the power
to change it.
When things go wrong
this is an opportunity
for you to take on the
challenge of surviving
and then you can
experience the
satisfaction
of repairing the
situation, which will
lead you to an inner
state of higher
self esteem and
serenity

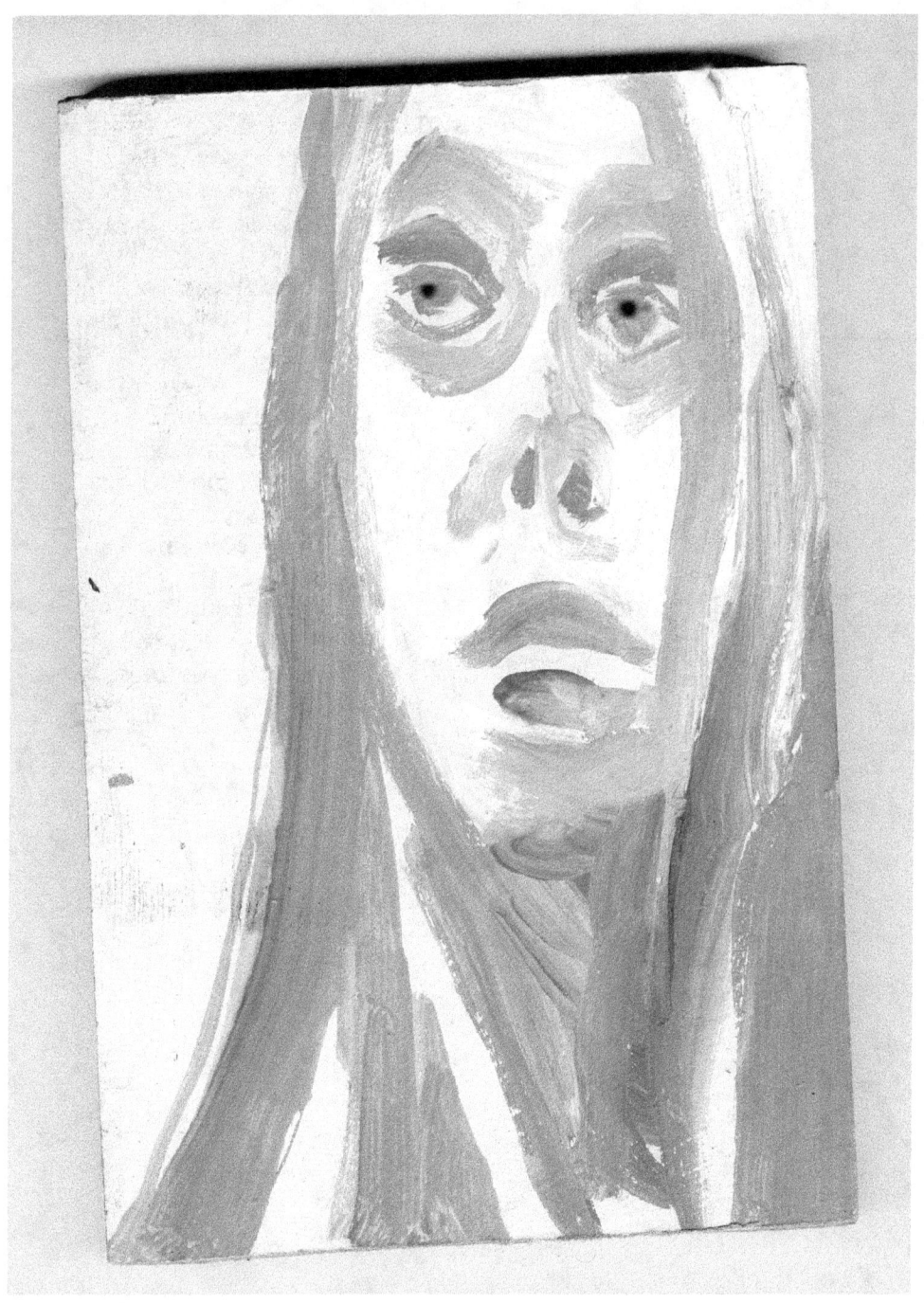

This is an impression of what I thought you were feeling
when you looked at me with so much resentment.....

futureworld
will be
better

What choices
of products will
we have in 2028 ?
Where is your password
your eye scan
does not read.
Those wonderful new
bombs that destroyed
millions of electronic
data files won
the technowars.
We will soon become
one corrected
global economy,
thank god!
Which god would
that be, we are all
virtual prostitutes.

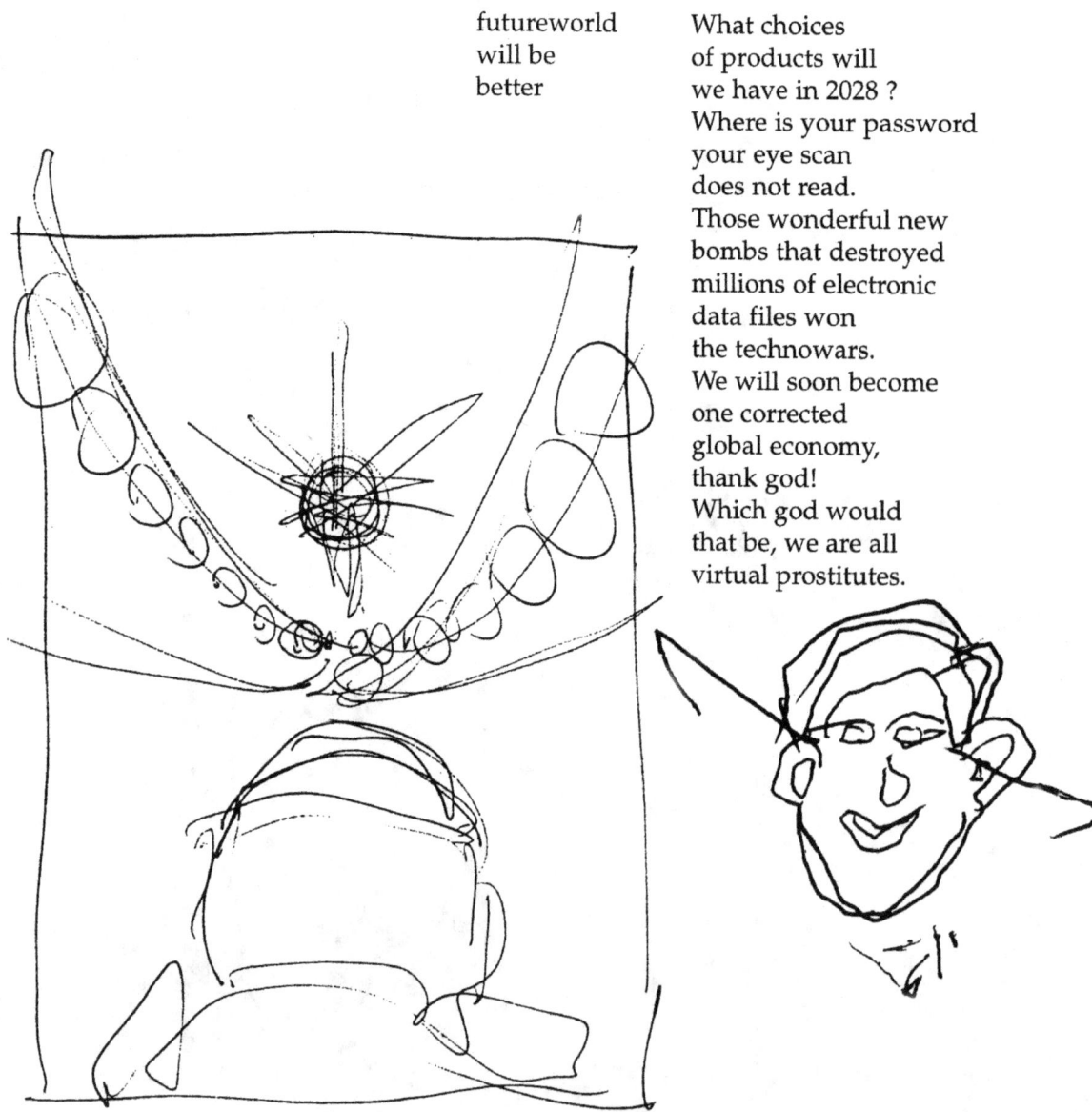

Creativity can be random, discordant and without logical order depending on the mood of the artist . . . . .

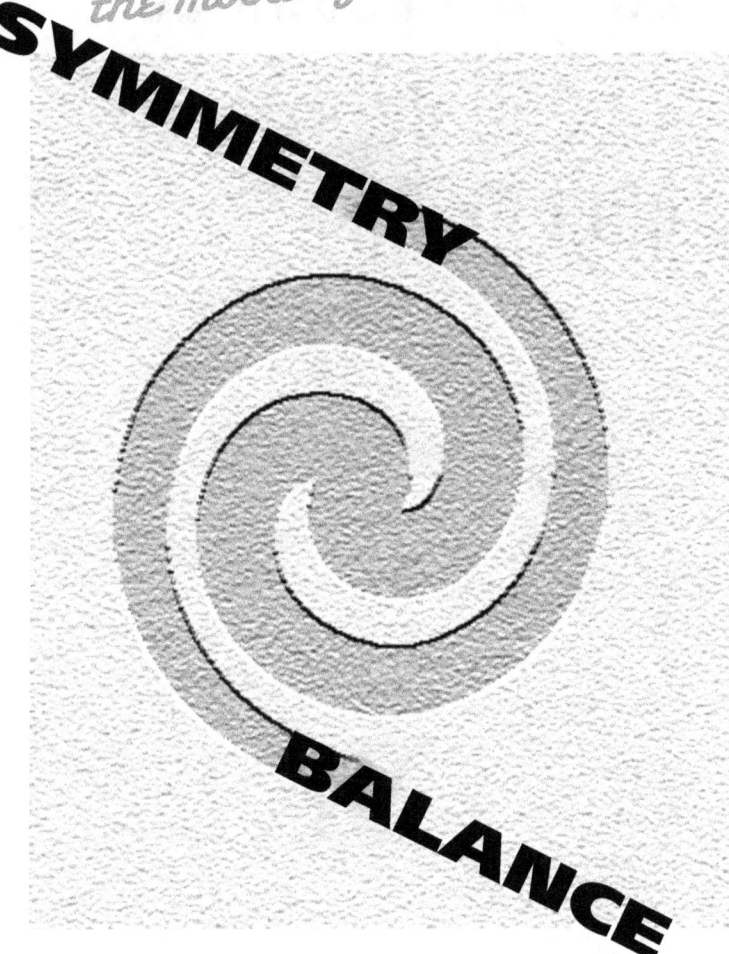

SYMMETRY

BALANCE

Abstrakt

poetik

justice

ideaology

pattern

mania.....

Chaotic

repitition

history

repeats

mis takes.....

Promote

sell, your cells

satyricon

thimk

meta

order now.....

Preconceptions or chaos, if you are looking for a new concept you must leave the road well travelled . . . . .

One sperm
23 chromosomes
75,000 genes
how many ?

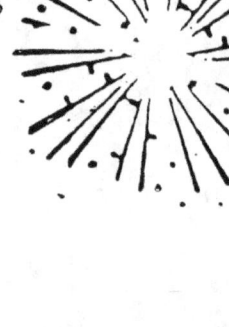

Smile for people
and they will return
the smile usually.
No person is an island !
You teach your child
what you do soldier.
The more we experience
and accomplish, then we
have a greater capacity
for creative achievement.
Do the hard challenging
work first,
just do it !
You will see so much
more with your dreams
than with your eyes !

AERIAL SHADES

I am the house the thoughts
the station that trains
 existence, experience, being.
I grow, ageing.
 I discover the future, the past.
I can record,
 what I have been.
I will foretell
 what I shall hope.

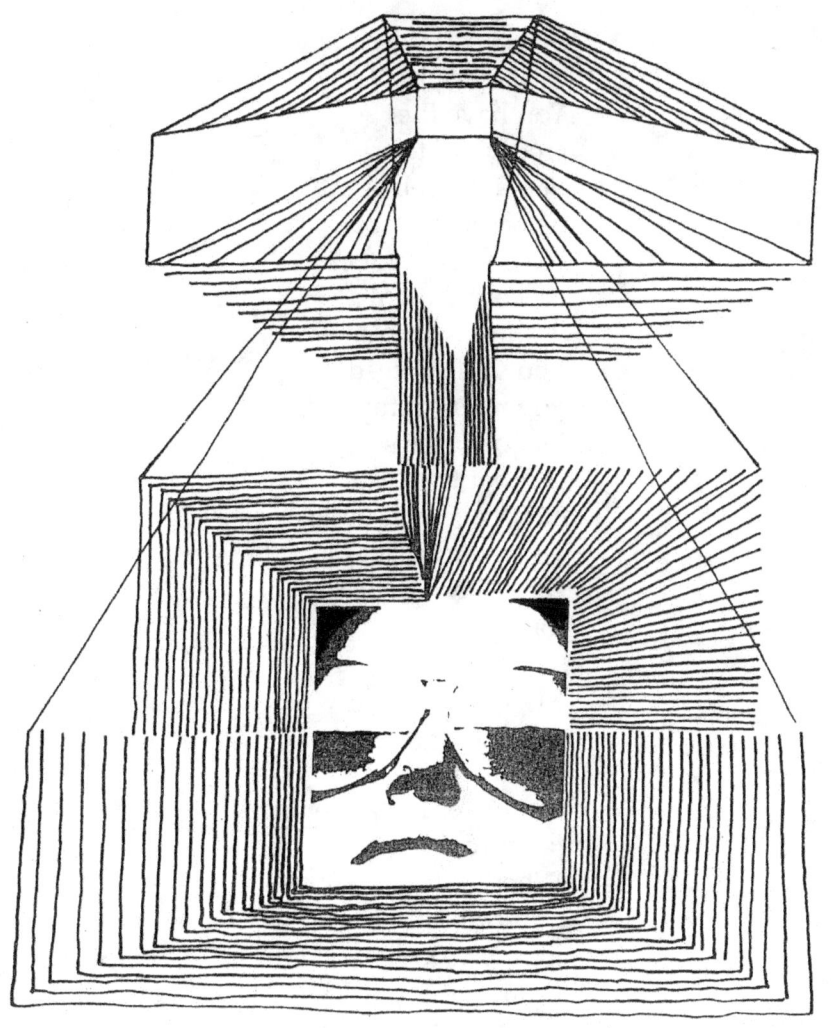

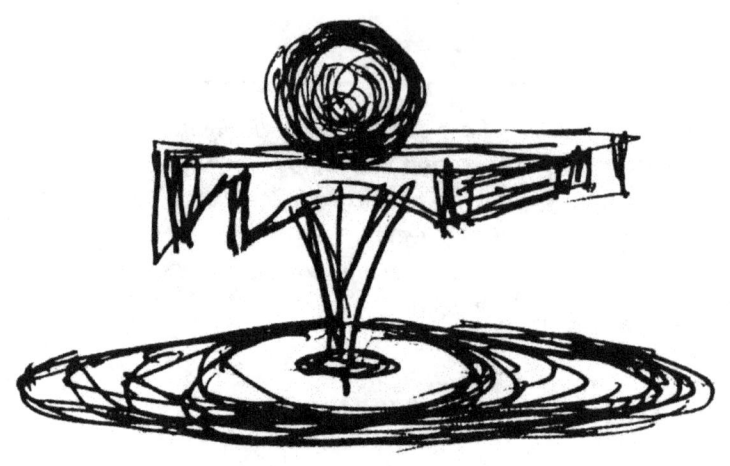

You are at the right age
to achieve it all !
You have the
credibility to try,
you are a self starter,
listen, learn, you
have what it takes.
Be very patient
with those around you.
You will succeed
you are not trapped,
its good it is so
competitive, the
challenge will build
your assets, but be
careful not to be
lonely.

My mother-in-law
is a cyborg,
is that right !
or are her metal bones
just prosthesis ?
When will I get mine,
and can I put in
my new one
thousand gig
memory card before
I am seventy five ?

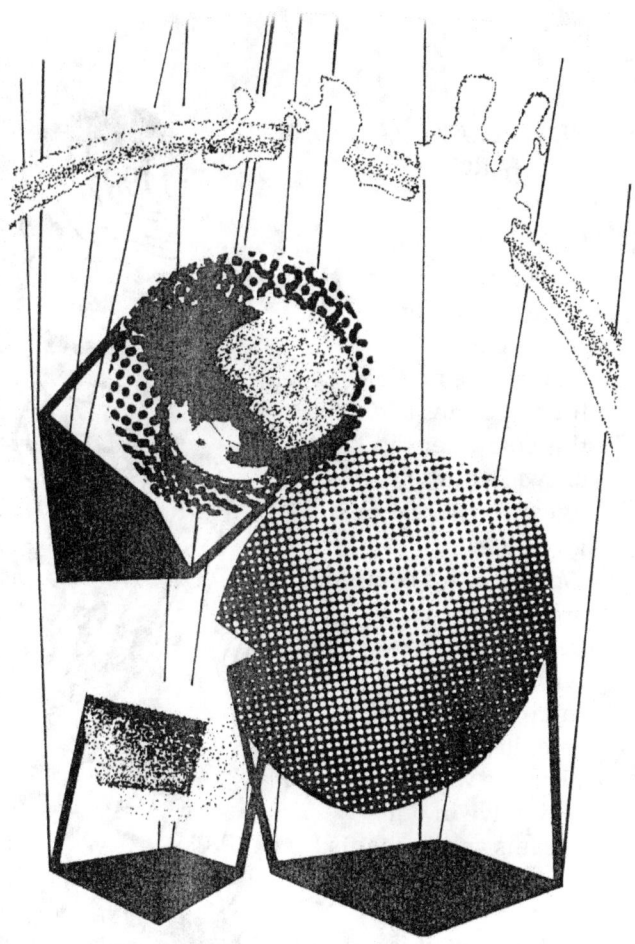

SINKING FEELINGS

Night softens the harshness
of the day's toil.
Waiting for
the tribunal of pattern.
We are strutting
arrogantly in fame,
our aquatic origin drys up.
Unflinching I stay,
with my sinking feeling.
My lonliness
creates failing stimuli,
the indifinite sanctuary
companionship –
philosophy intellect's
great harbour.

WHAT ARE WE MAKING TODAY ?
WHO IS IN CHARGE ?

Command alt enter
option kill

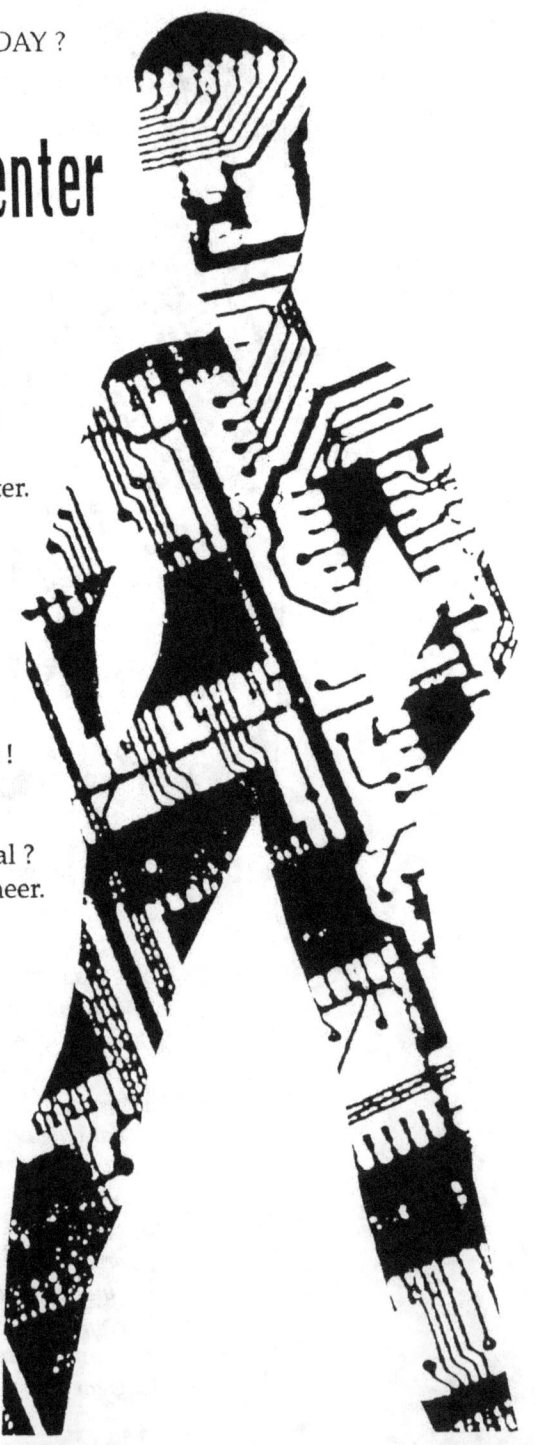

Inside a computer
there can be stored
more knowledge
and experience
than in one million
human brains and
this computer can
answer your
questions in real-time
go figure.
We made this computer.
We can see far
beyond our eyes,
with telescopes
radar, wireless video,
satellites,xrays.
Next we will
really live in our
dreams and thoughts !
Clones and eugenics
are with us now,
children what is moral ?
Ask the genetic engineer.

Space is needed
after satellites

control help
shift escape
no returns

Space correction do we exist
now? after space

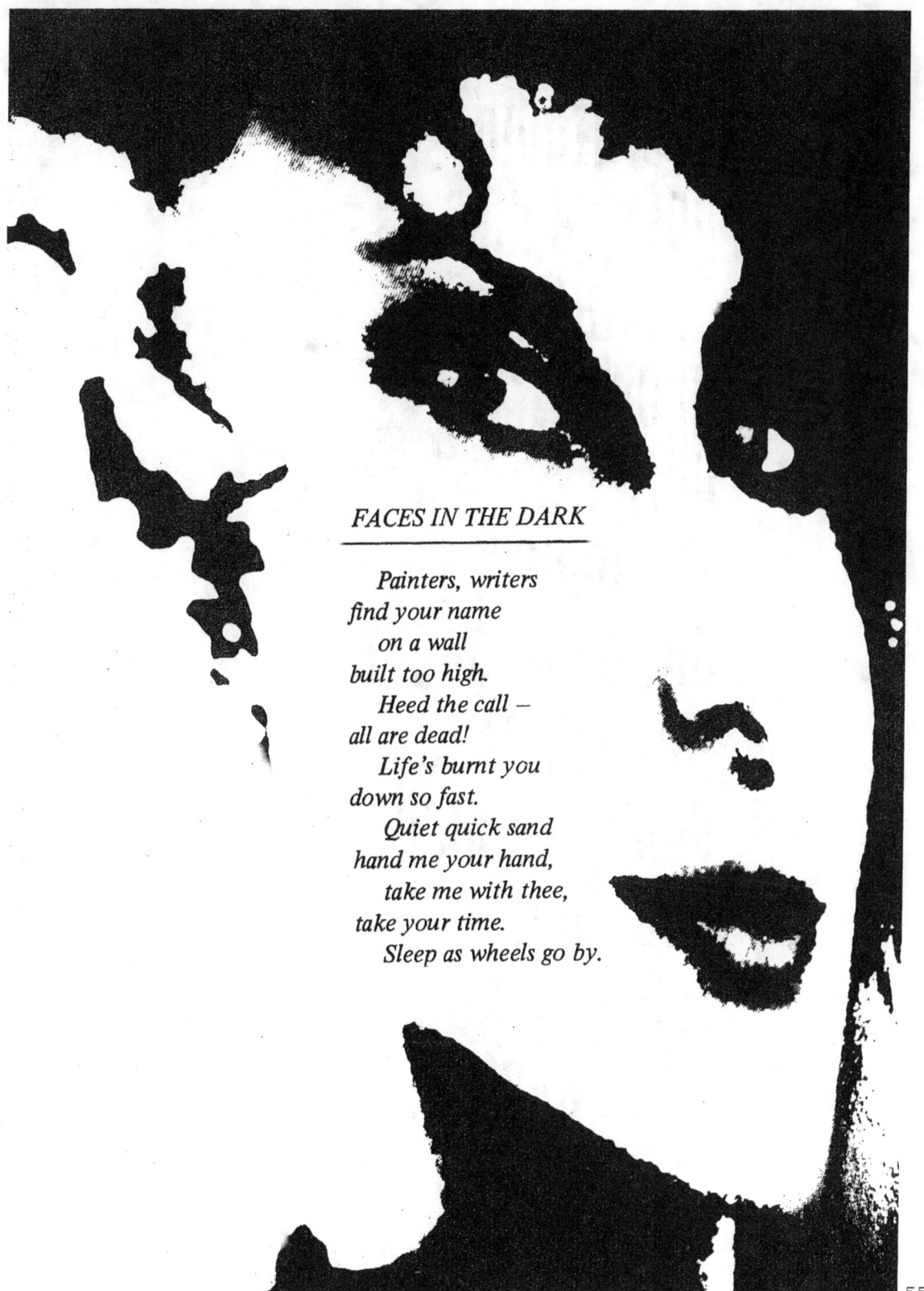

FACES IN THE DARK

Painters, writers
find your name
  on a wall
built too high.
  Heed the call —
all are dead!
  Life's burnt you
down so fast.
  Quiet quick sand
hand me your hand,
  take me with thee,
take your time.
  Sleep as wheels go by.

Everything
goes round
in orbits,
in orbits,
WHY ?
Its universal
but what about
the end of the
universe, well
now that is
really to do
with magnetics !

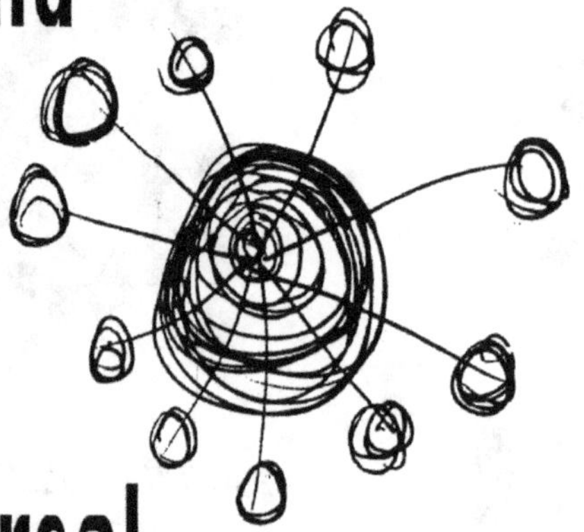

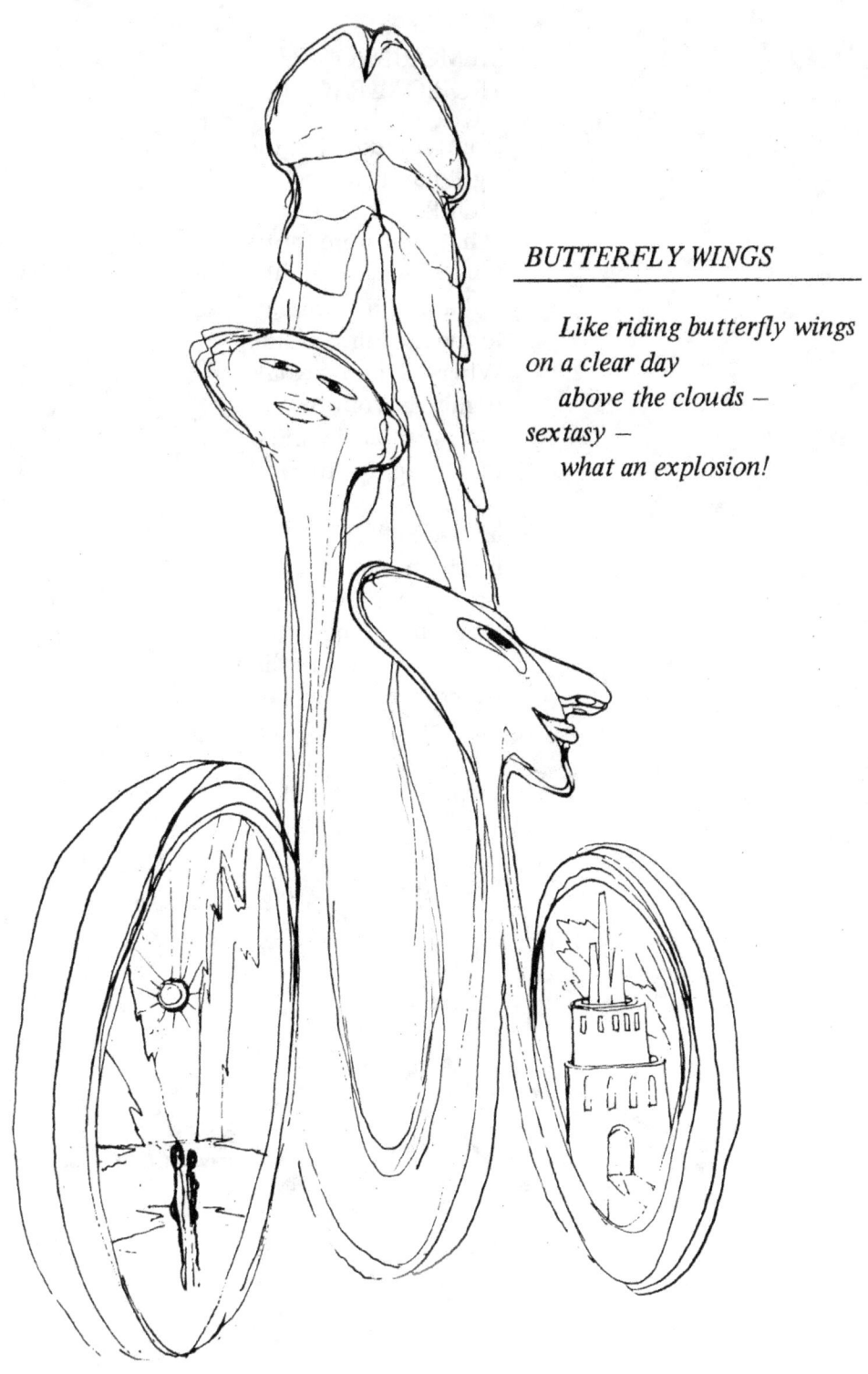

BUTTERFLY WINGS

Like riding butterfly wings
on a clear day
    above the clouds —
sextasy —
    what an explosion!

MEMORIES OF THE TROPICAL PACIFIC

Handyrandy what the
right hands for
MORE and more.
What is in store for us
when we are naughty
imitating the foreplay
to the meaning of life.
Where is your sexual
organ? in your brain.
Warm tropical winds
in the night softly
cross my skin
and sexually
ignite those
prickly pear feelings
that remind me
of warm cosy cuddling.
In the heat
passion predominates
all thoughts, then
I smell the salt and
seaweed, the ocean
overcomes me as
I go fishing for love.

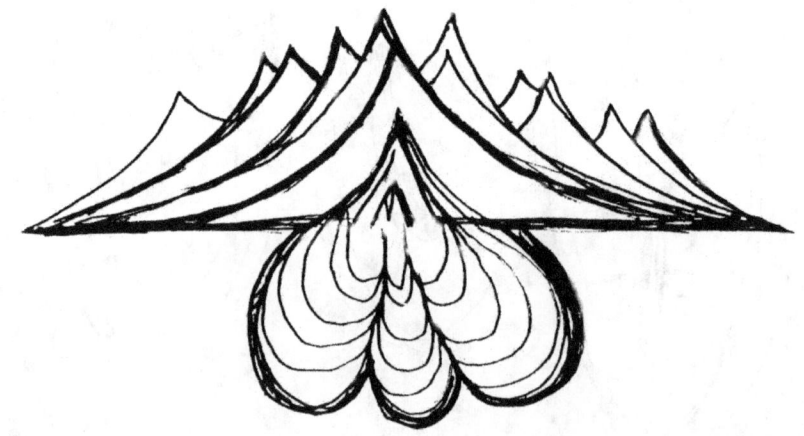

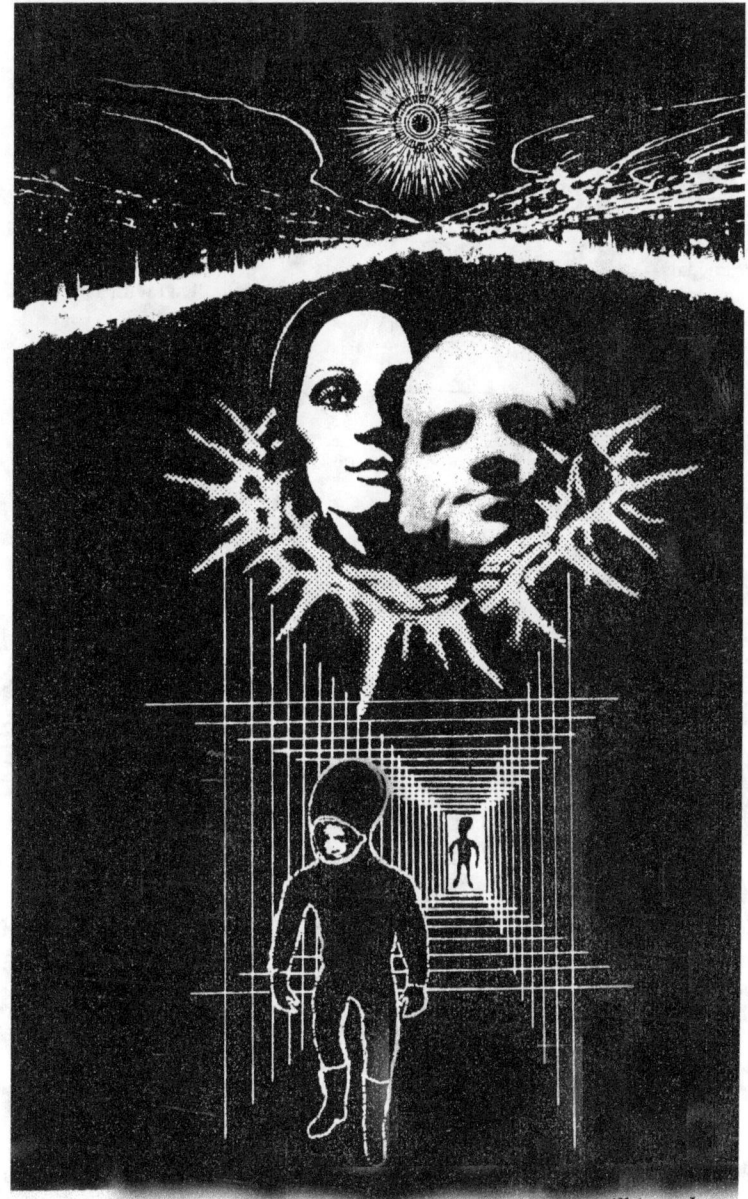

All things have an end and nothing ceases changing till it ends.

We have the desire to know.....As we wait at the foot-hills of time. The signals are sent into our brains from uniserve, part of the gougle foundation, the microwave signal comes via the bioethnic spacenet, then we think we make the decisions.....If it was another time and in another space we would be doing another thing!

Symbols scare us when they are associated with our fears. They become our badge our medals. Sometimes they symbolise what we stand for.

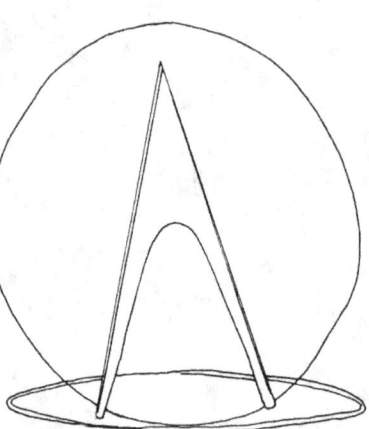

The woman with the goitre lived with a hormone deficient cat named Lucy on the blue duotone walls in Padstow, Kernow. It used to be in the GBR Sector.

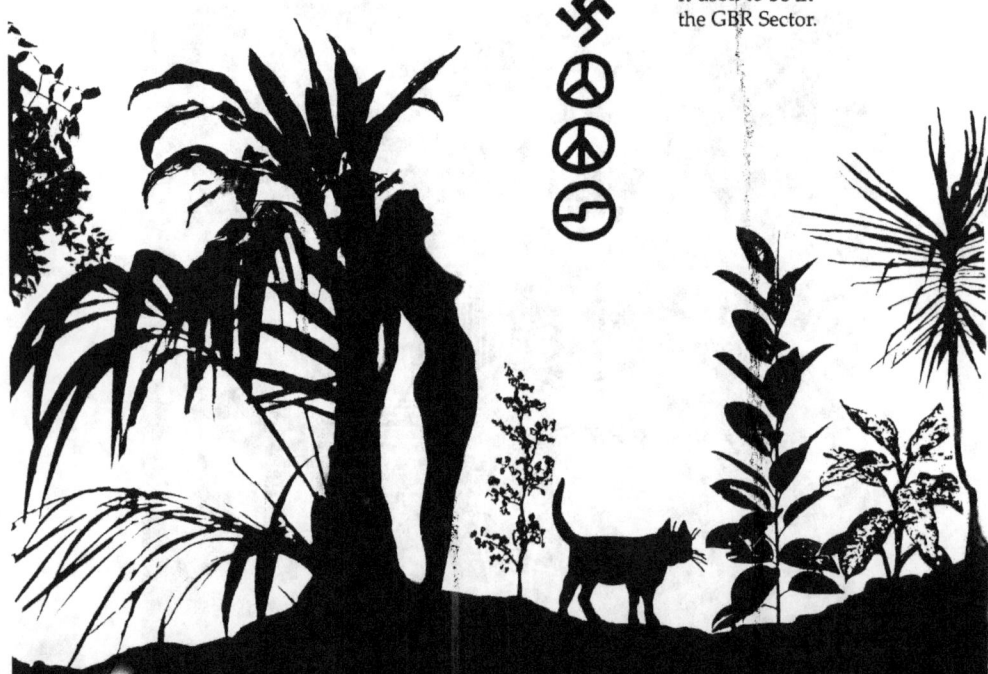

A poet's home is packed with fingertip tours of experience, their celebration of imagination, they must record it for history......
This school of thought believes you should use the power of confusion as a marketing tool, disagreement is futile......However some philosophers are predicting an end to human talking......
Sorry I did not hear that! Please txt me......

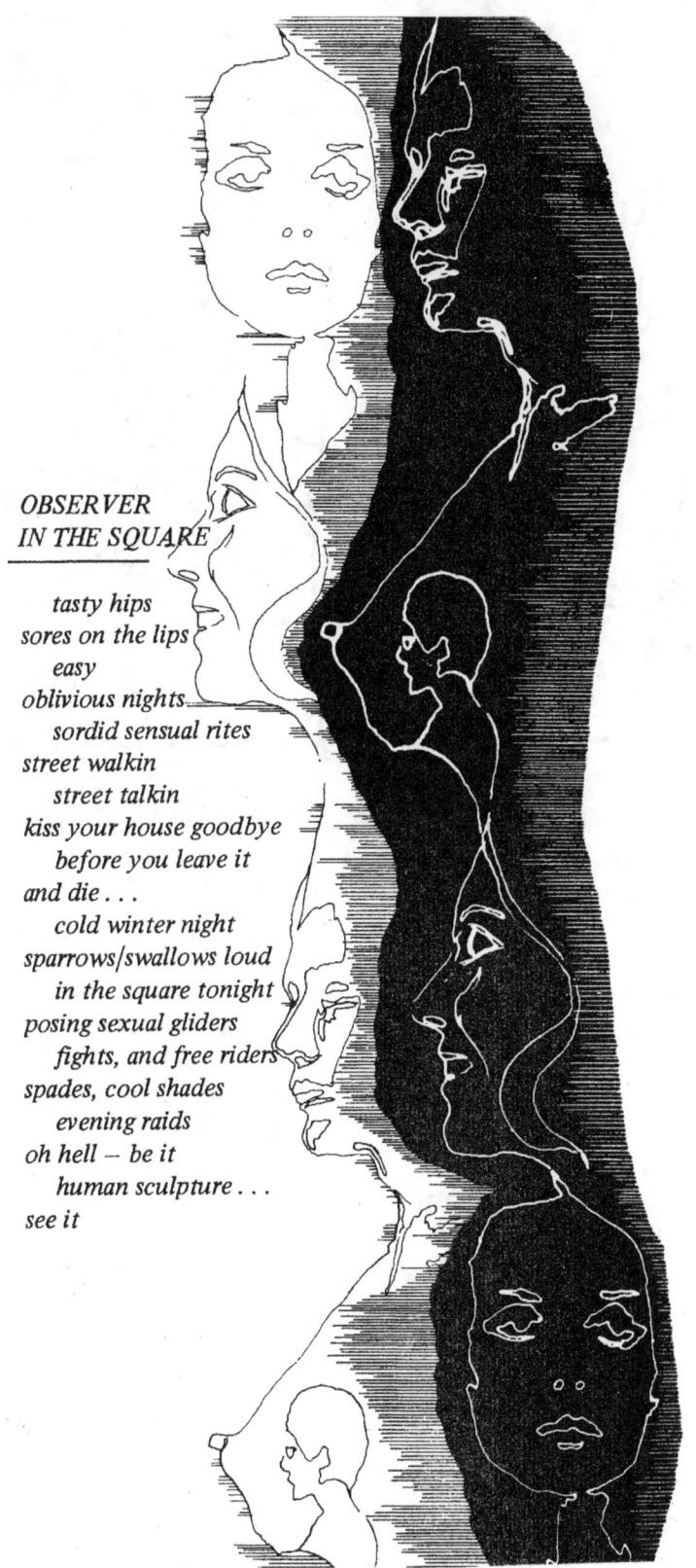

OBSERVER
IN THE SQUARE

   tasty hips
sores on the lips
   easy
oblivious nights
   sordid sensual rites
street walkin
   street talkin
kiss your house goodbye
   before you leave it
and die . . .
   cold winter night
sparrows/swallows loud
   in the square tonight
posing sexual gliders
   fights, and free riders
spades, cool shades
   evening raids
oh hell — be it
   human sculpture . . .
see it

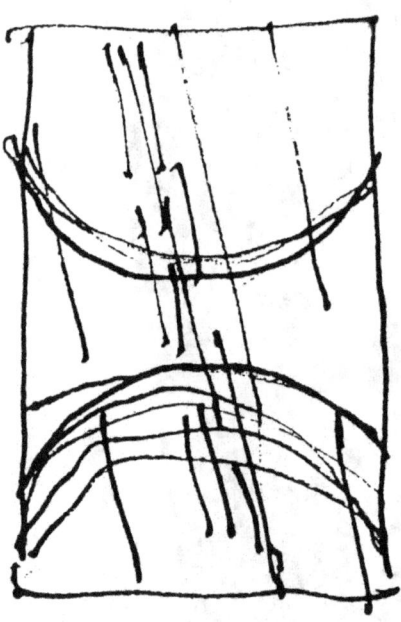
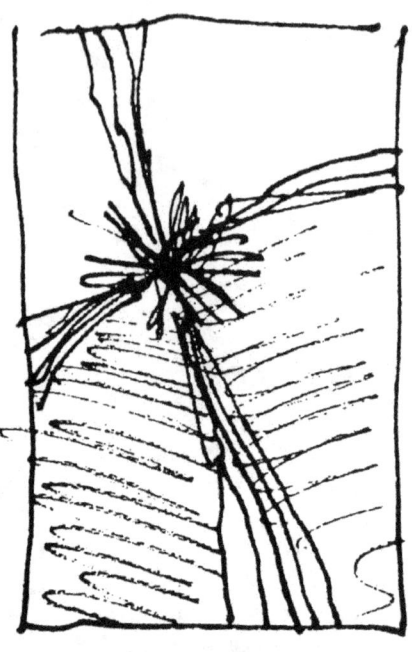

Sitting on the balcony
of life, Hawaii five ohh !
Am I at the edge of my
thinking universe ?
Reading Volataires
Bastard by my real
man John Ralston Saul
does he know the truth
is out there ?
Art Bell.com does.
When I was twenty three
I met a true eco canadian
tetra-mariner who asked
me to search for the
meaning of life
I sold him a record !
Where is he know ?
I got lost on life's way
with relationships,
a child, money
and pain.

THE MEANING OF LIFE
I saw the movie
it still did not help,
dont judge a movie
by its colour.
I'm searching for the
meaning now, I have
7000 days left.
You will remember
five minutes of pain
clearly ! Where are my
walls of denial around me ?
How can you like that be,
why dont you think like me ?

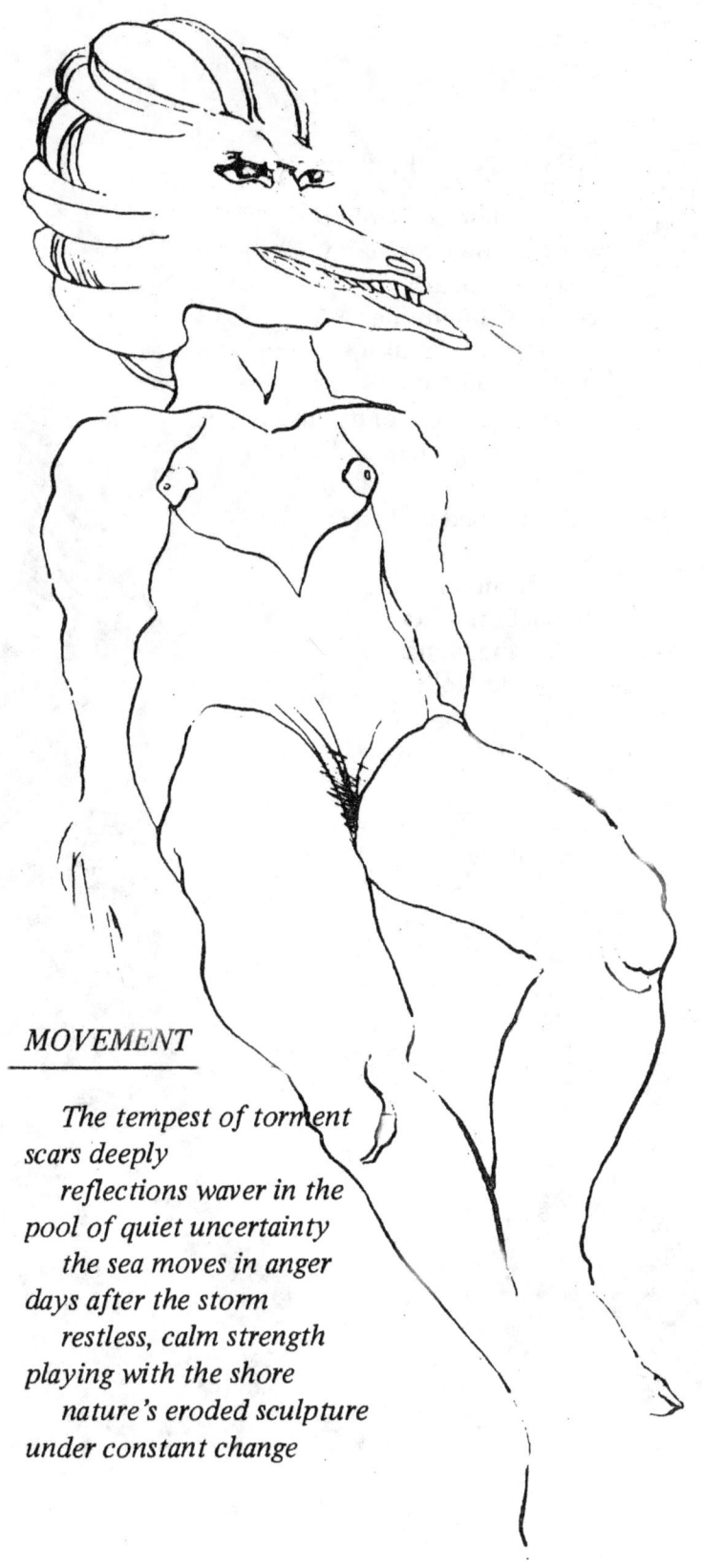

MOVEMENT

The tempest of torment
scars deeply
reflections waver in the
pool of quiet uncertainty
the sea moves in anger
days after the storm
restless, calm strength
playing with the shore
nature's eroded sculpture
under constant change

WESTERN WURLED

We are all to concerned
with our own ambition,
instead of being
concerned with the
planet and the future
of the human race
Its all a question of balance,
squeaky cogs get oiled.

I lie in a bed in a land
of four seasons
and dream of going
to Lubbock Texas,
to feel the home
of Buddy Holly
I live with the guilt.
How can I purchase
pleasure ?
This is the most fun
you can have with
your clothes on !
We really do live
in a land of
nymphomaniacs
with implants.

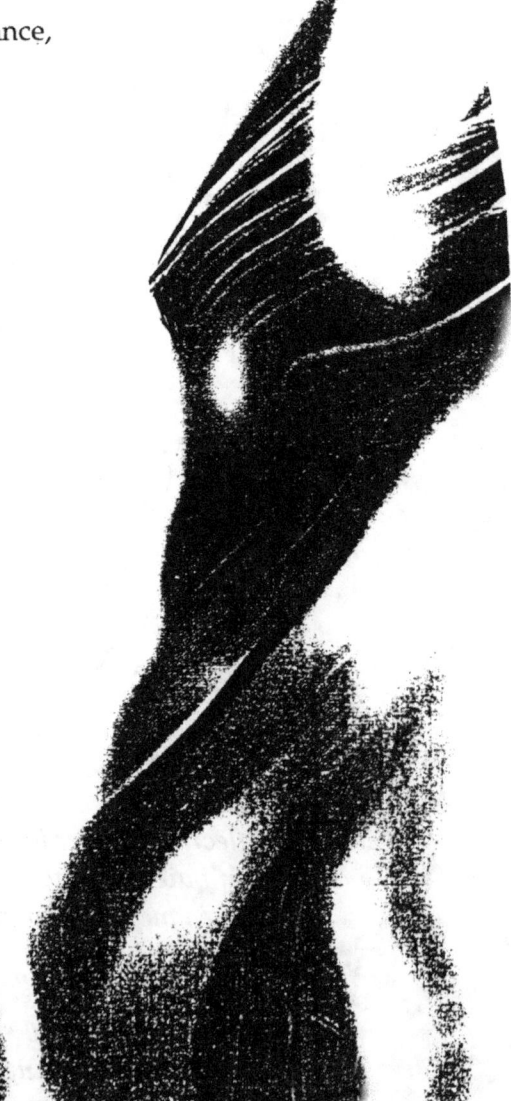

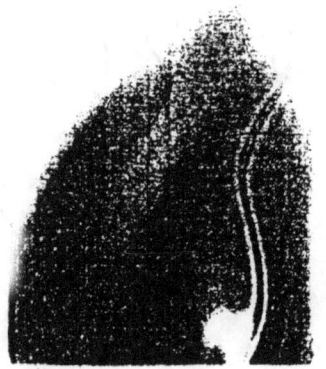

RELEASE CONTOURS

Flames of pain
break out of my stomach.
Sharp sirens
between ears – prison bars –
a demon devouring me.
Life's feud starts
his armoury – age –
mine – happiness.

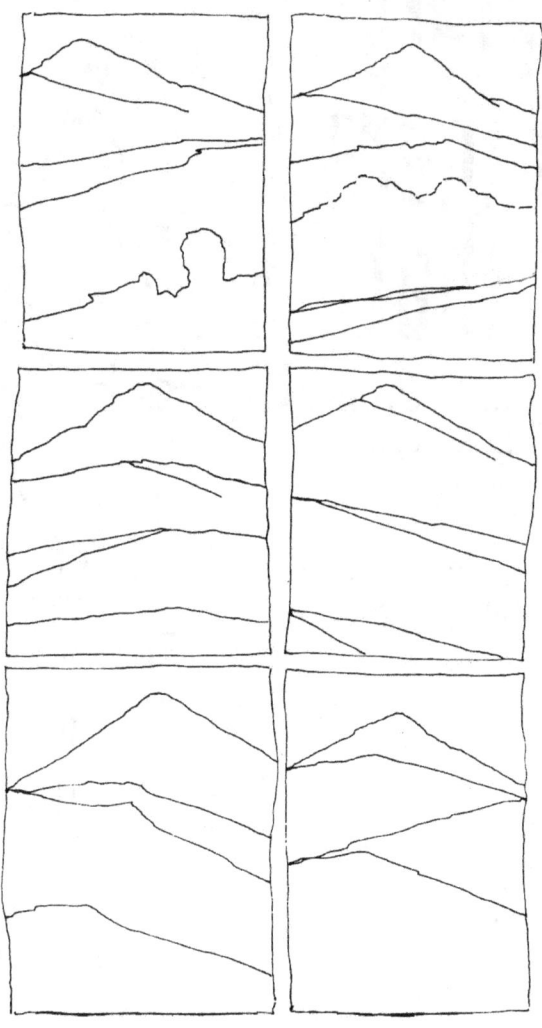

Tanganika the meeting place of waters been there done that

What is left, Why did it change, ocean paradise, all life began close by. Without water we all change for the worse. Politics and pineapples, poverty and peanuts. Gather together hold hands, work it out !

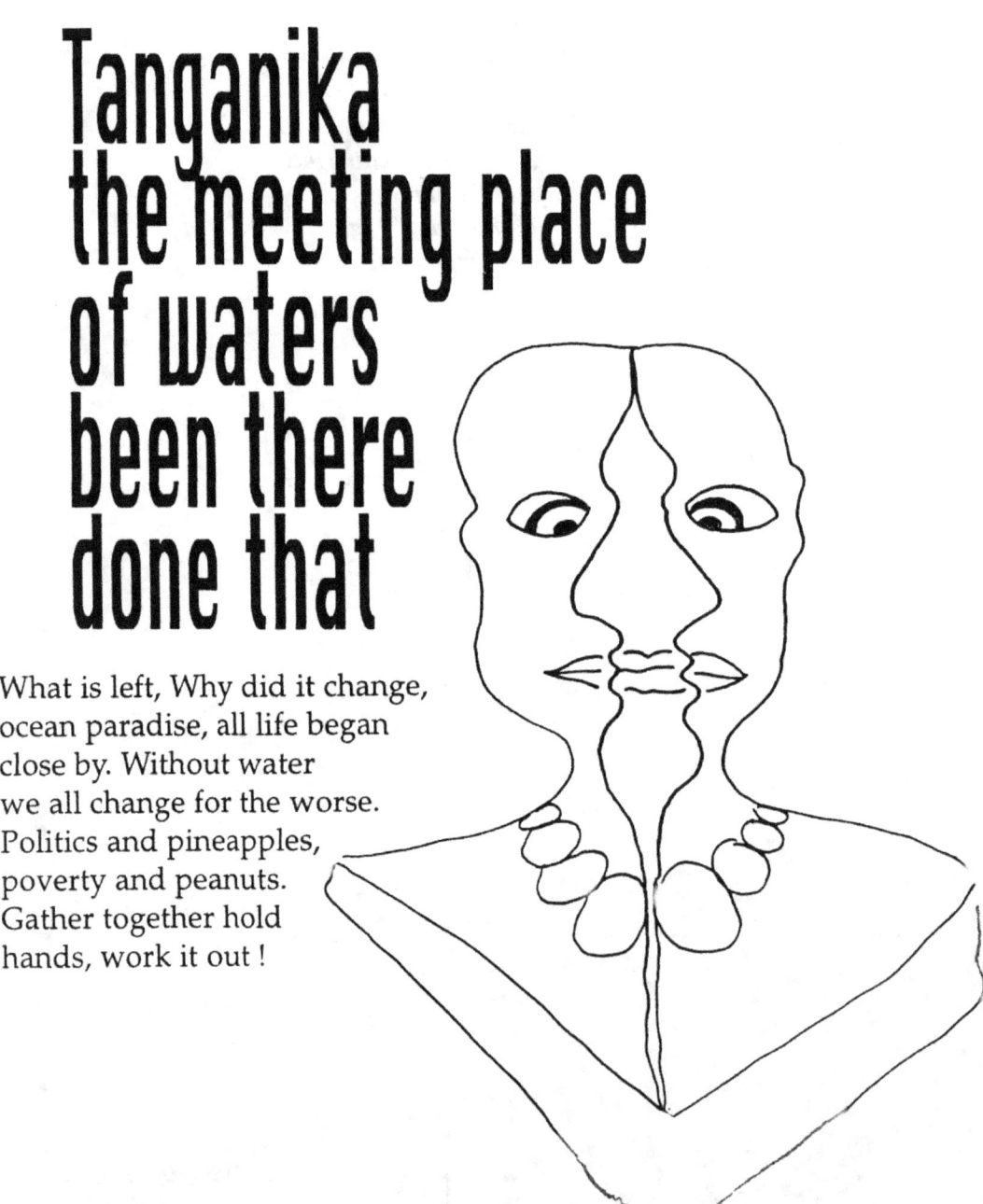

Teflon Terry enjoys slippery bodies.....She had a pied piper living on her face and chest that attracted partners constantly!

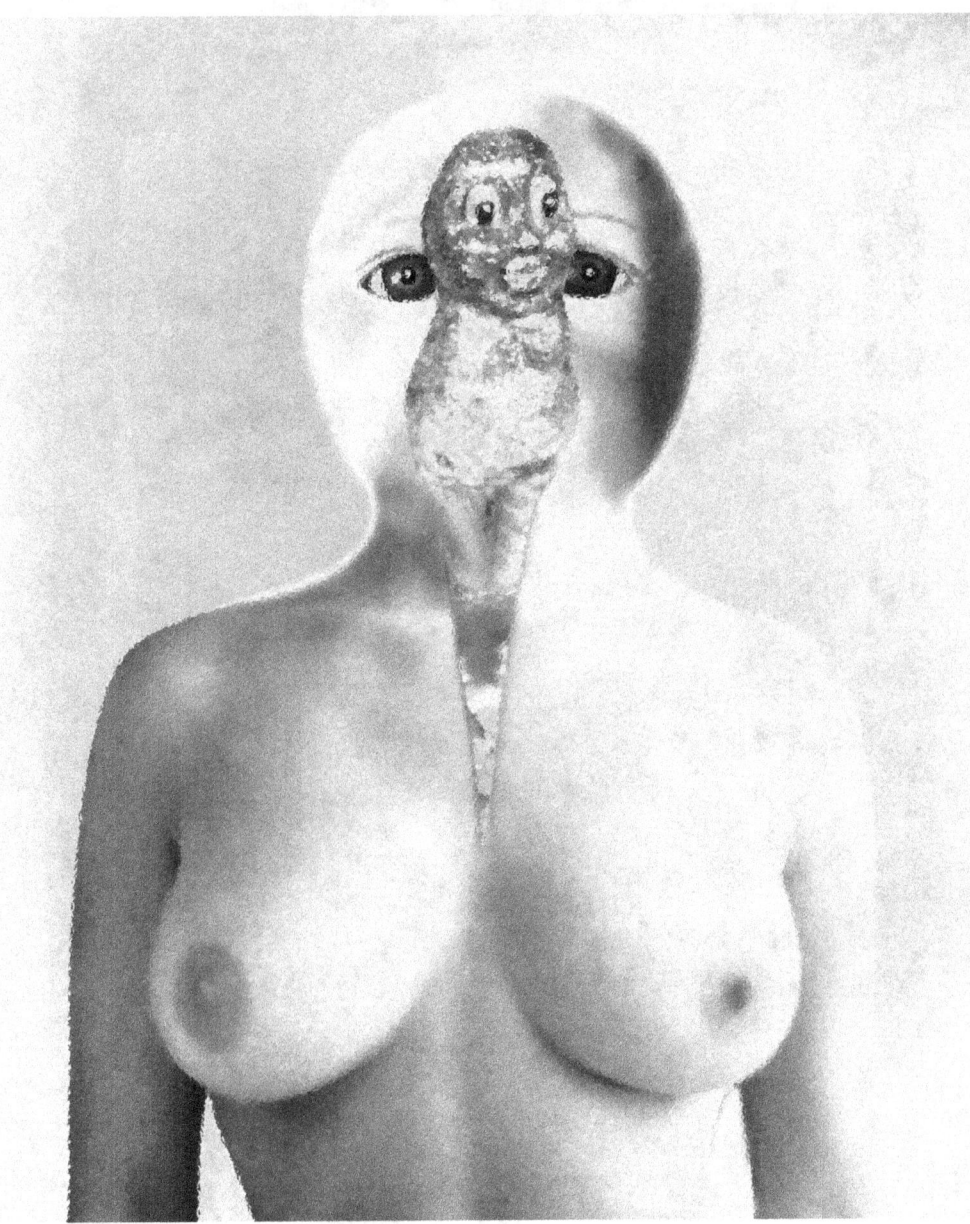

Art embraces possibility as life emulates art.....The lack of understanding and expression for art in so many societies produces dangerous communities. So many political groups are very controlling and filled with driving metaphors for selfish power.....What you see is what you get in this picture.

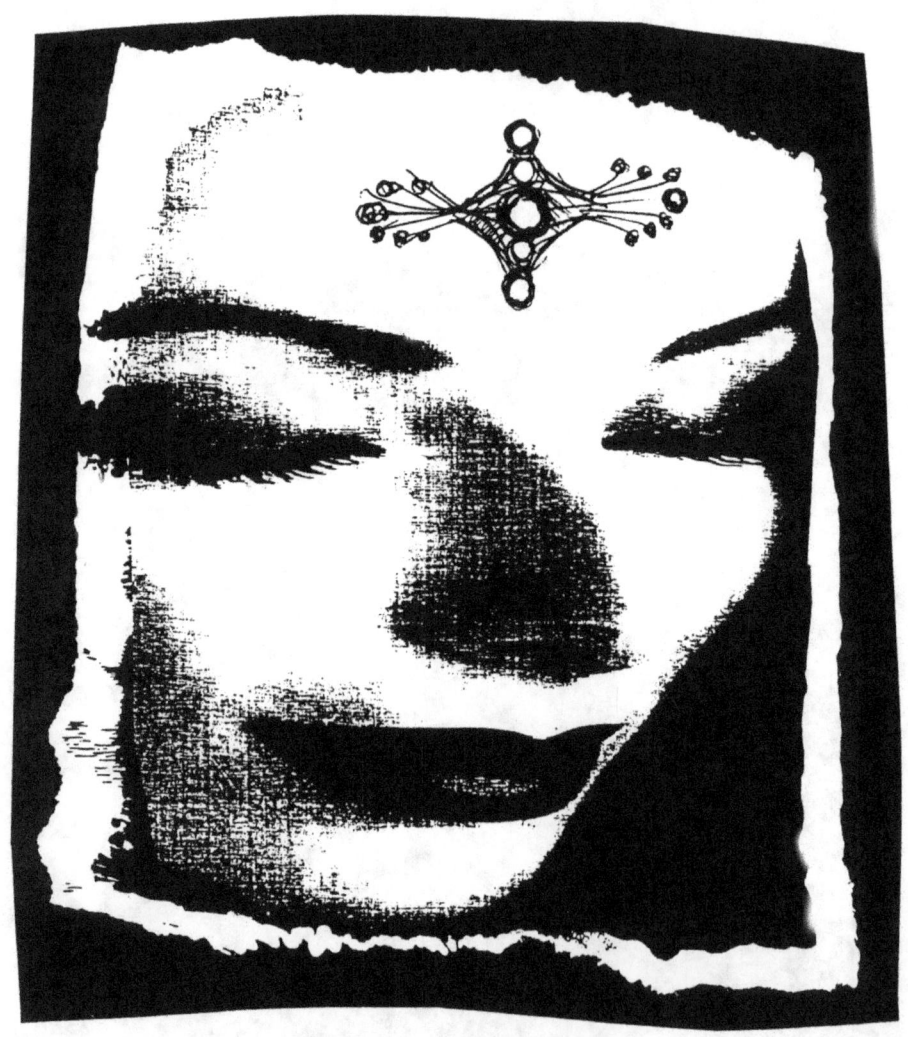

Jargoneeze of the glitterati,
cowpushers and carbras
on those photo SUVS
Air pumpbra make them
rise beautifully to the occasion
Our cosmetic masks help us
face our age.

UNTITLED 1

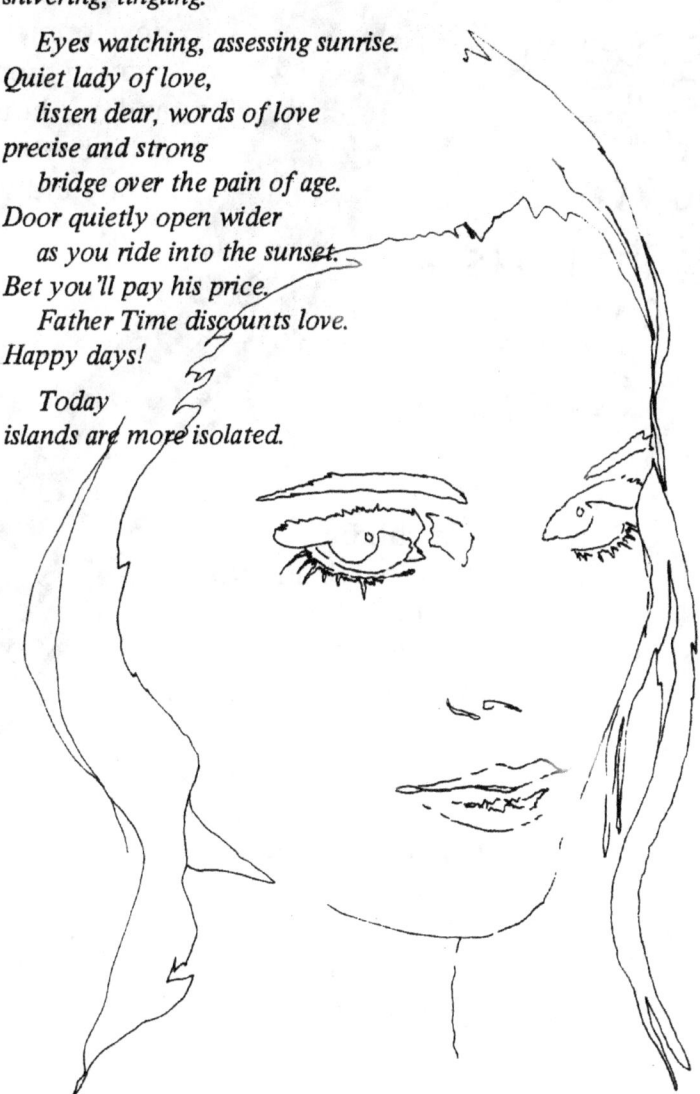

Snowbirds and seagulls,
silk so smooth,
rich thick cream —
deep eyes tear my heart
sunglow burns my skin.
Buffed glossy hulls
touch them — they are smooth.
Cleavage shadow obscene.
Love thoughts start
shivering, tingling.

Eyes watching, assessing sunrise.
Quiet lady of love,
listen dear, words of love
precise and strong
bridge over the pain of age.
Door quietly open wider
as you ride into the sunset.
Bet you'll pay his price.
Father Time discounts love.
Happy days!

Today
islands are more isolated.

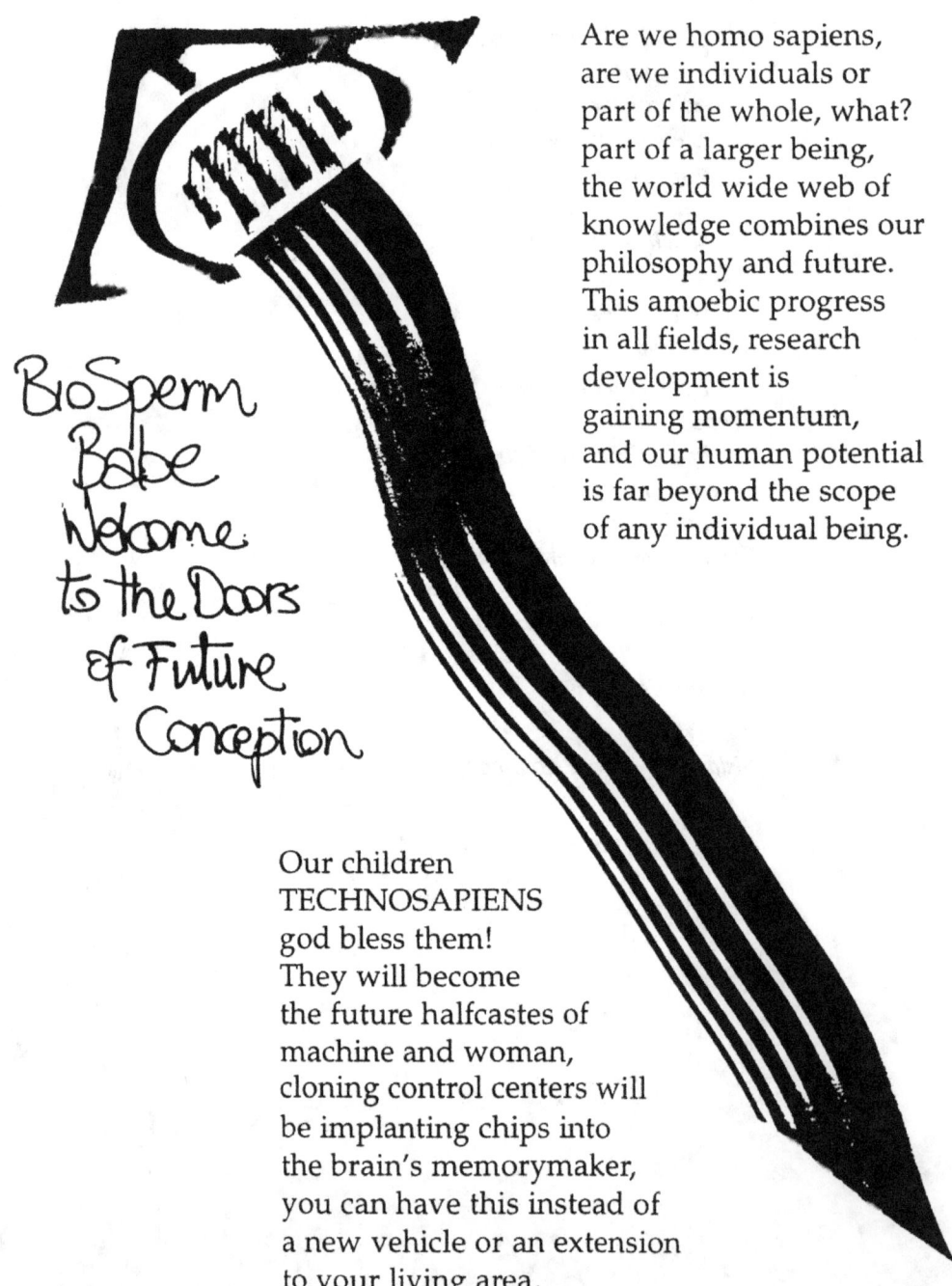

Are we homo sapiens,
are we individuals or
part of the whole, what?
part of a larger being,
the world wide web of
knowledge combines our
philosophy and future.
This amoebic progress
in all fields, research
development is
gaining momentum,
and our human potential
is far beyond the scope
of any individual being.

BioSperm
Babe
Welcome
to the Doors
of Future
Conception

Our children
TECHNOSAPIENS
god bless them!
They will become
the future halfcastes of
machine and woman,
cloning control centers will
be implanting chips into
the brain's memorymaker,
you can have this instead of
a new vehicle or an extension
to your living area,
if you have the money!

HIGH VORTEX

Autumn sienna turns emerald
crisp skin — warmth — red cheeks
*   as seasons exchange importance.*
Young babies like fresh snow tracks melt
*   the young rebels — astute apathy*
skinning my decorative facade.
*   I change places with myself*
this last past twenty years.
*   What happened? Doors open.*
Ideas fade away.
*   Enthusiasm lifts a heart*
tears are freeze-dried for posterity.
*   Balance — privilege sector.*

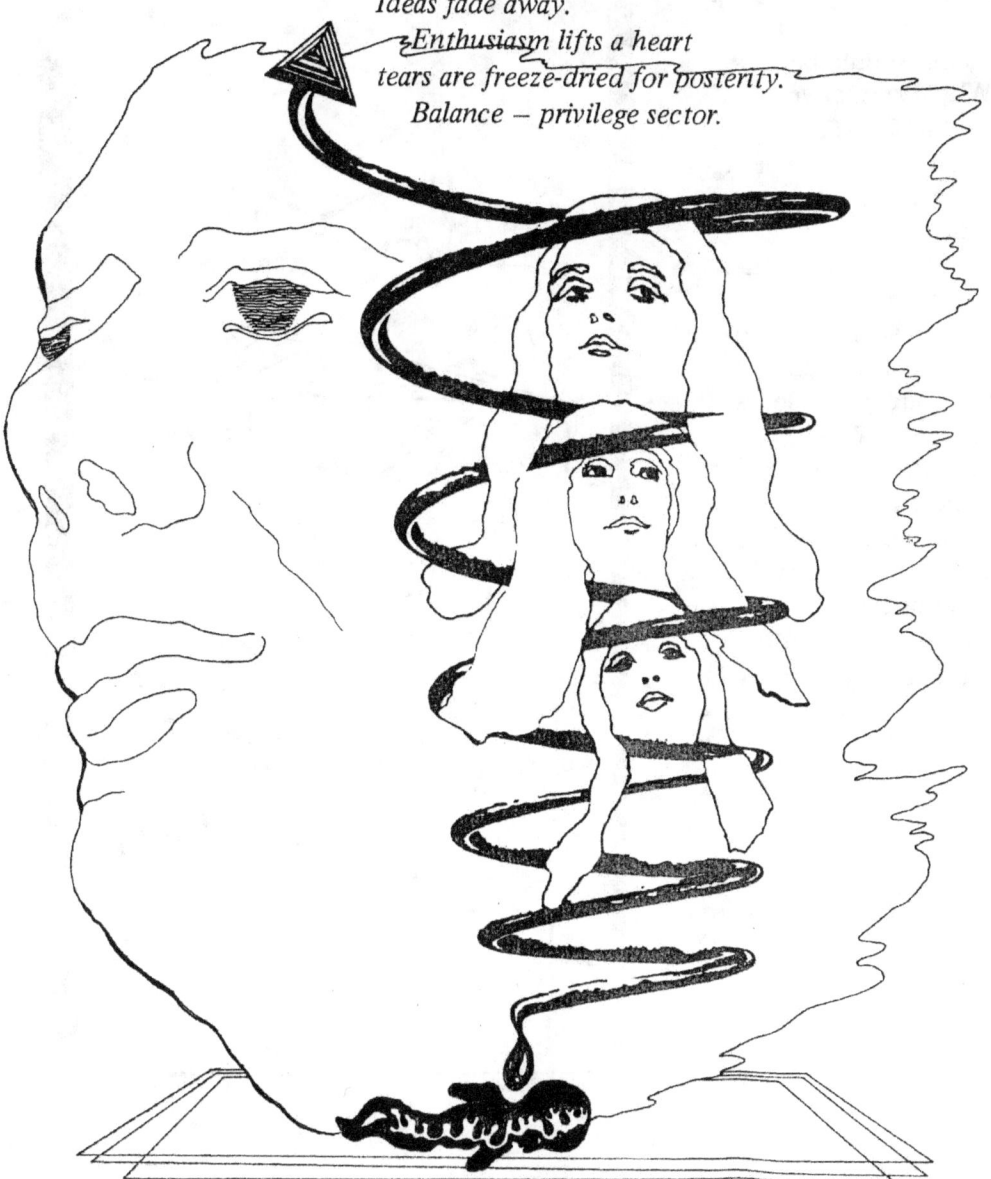

6 PETRIE TERRACE

Living in the condemned house
of art in those Molvig, Rigby,
days with Churchers abstract ways
Manrays influence changed
my mind from art to dreams.

We know why
your lips are painted red !
Who decided
the sea should be blue ?
Why do your eyes
see the sky as blue ?
What colour is an orange
some apples are green
some are red.
Should snow be white,
when you pee in it
its a great lemon yellow.
Then look at gold and
silver are they colours
or feelings ?
Why do people put
so much value in
mere metals, when
they dont value each
other or even life.
Are we here to produce
life, paint those lips red.

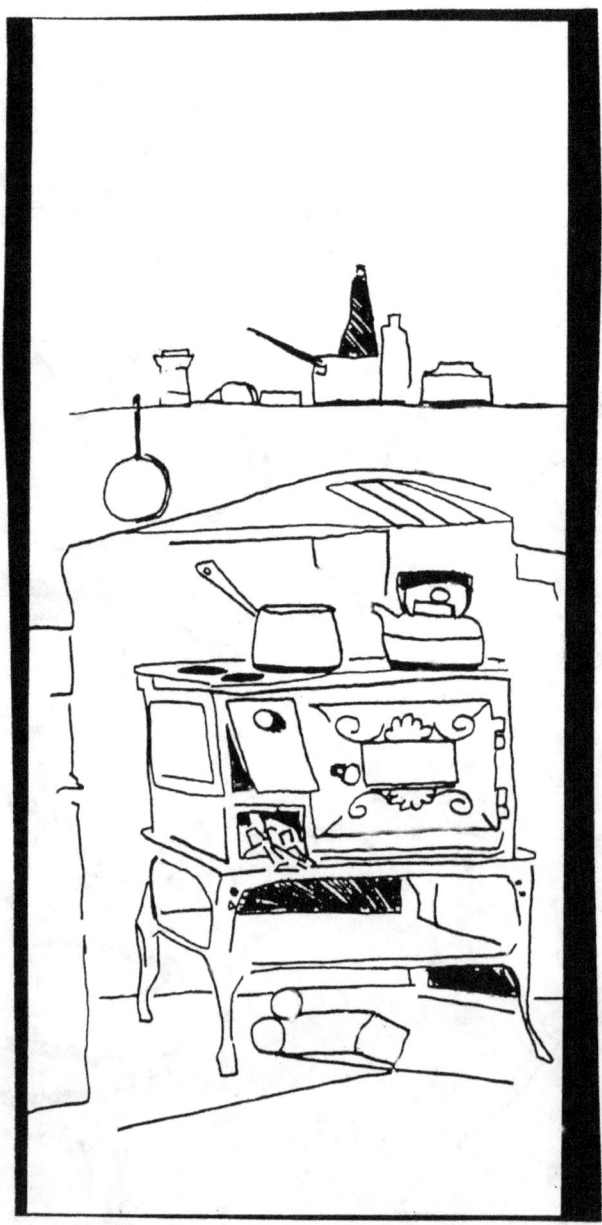

VALIUM LANDSCAPES

Silk sky
cotton clouds
colon creation
duodenum drapes
facial filigree
nasal nasties
dedicated description
devoted deviant
open orifice
outward obstruction
tears tasteless
happiness your face

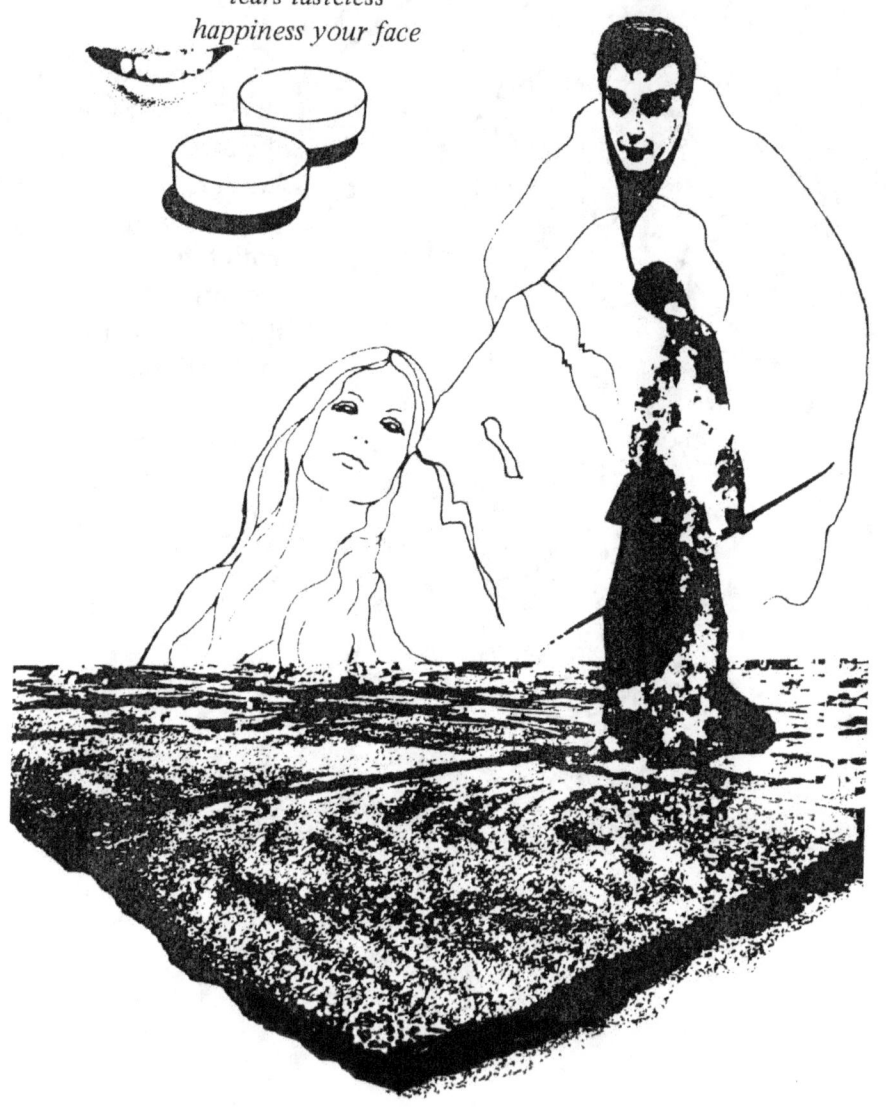

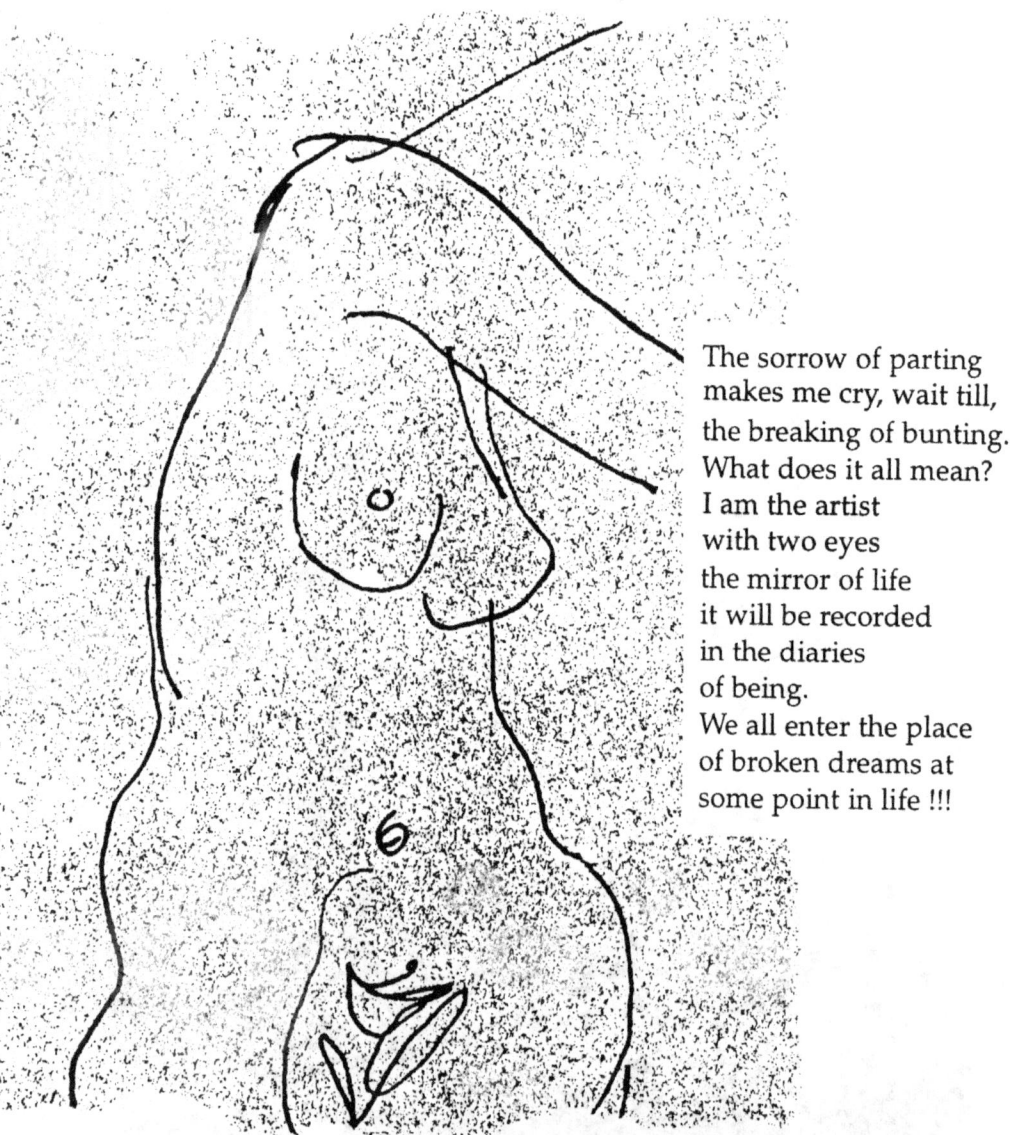

The sorrow of parting
makes me cry, wait till,
the breaking of bunting.
What does it all mean?
I am the artist
with two eyes
the mirror of life
it will be recorded
in the diaries
of being.
We all enter the place
of broken dreams at
some point in life !!!

All picture and no content.....
Life.....the stairway to.....death

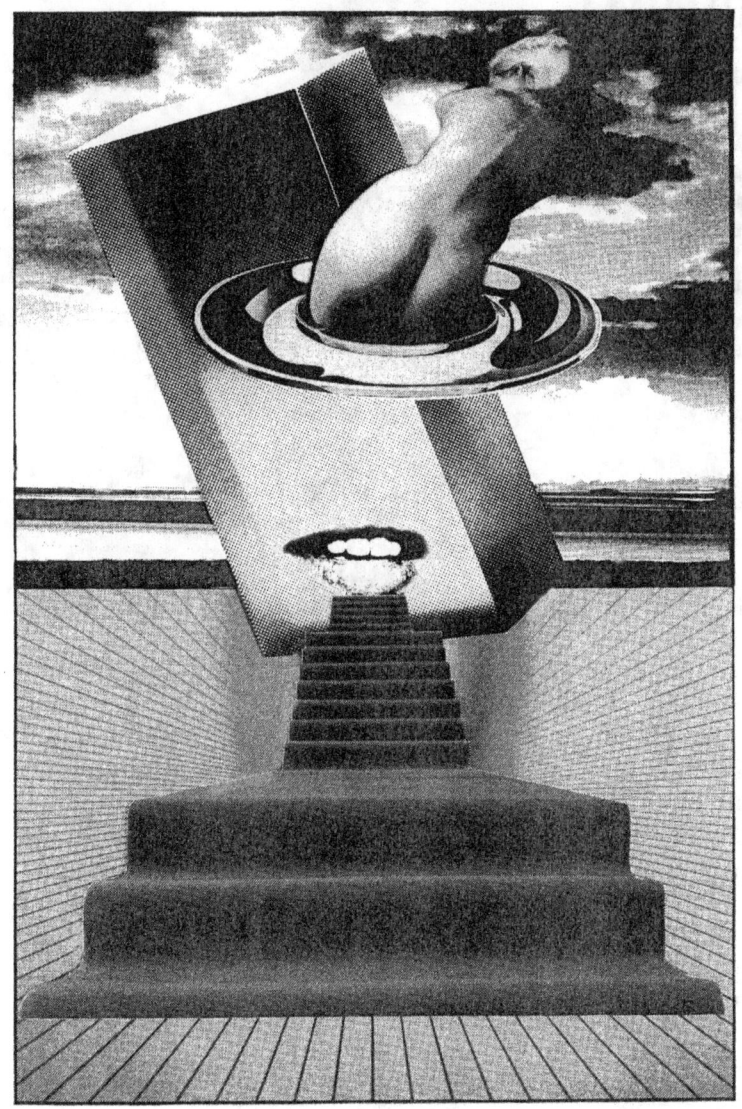

Sky bar on cloud fine, beyond my boring daily
horizon, layout the red carpet to your lip service.....
Center me.....Enter me. I am the flower waiting
for the bee, you see, need, seed, flow, grow on the
wings of a butter fly.....Darling I see you up there.
Mounting monoliths again.....Desire and higher!

See it its all just particles of light !!!

Vespa vinnie
Lambretta laurie
came together
to share
two stroke oil
and focaccia.
Summer heat
august afternoon
three hours
of vibration
riding with the
mods, massaged
them to the
EDGE.
Barley fields
below the
white cliffs
shimmering
in the dry
aromatic
summer wind.
Jason was the
child born in
sixties
now a real
man microwaving
his family's dinner
look on the net
order of the
universe.com

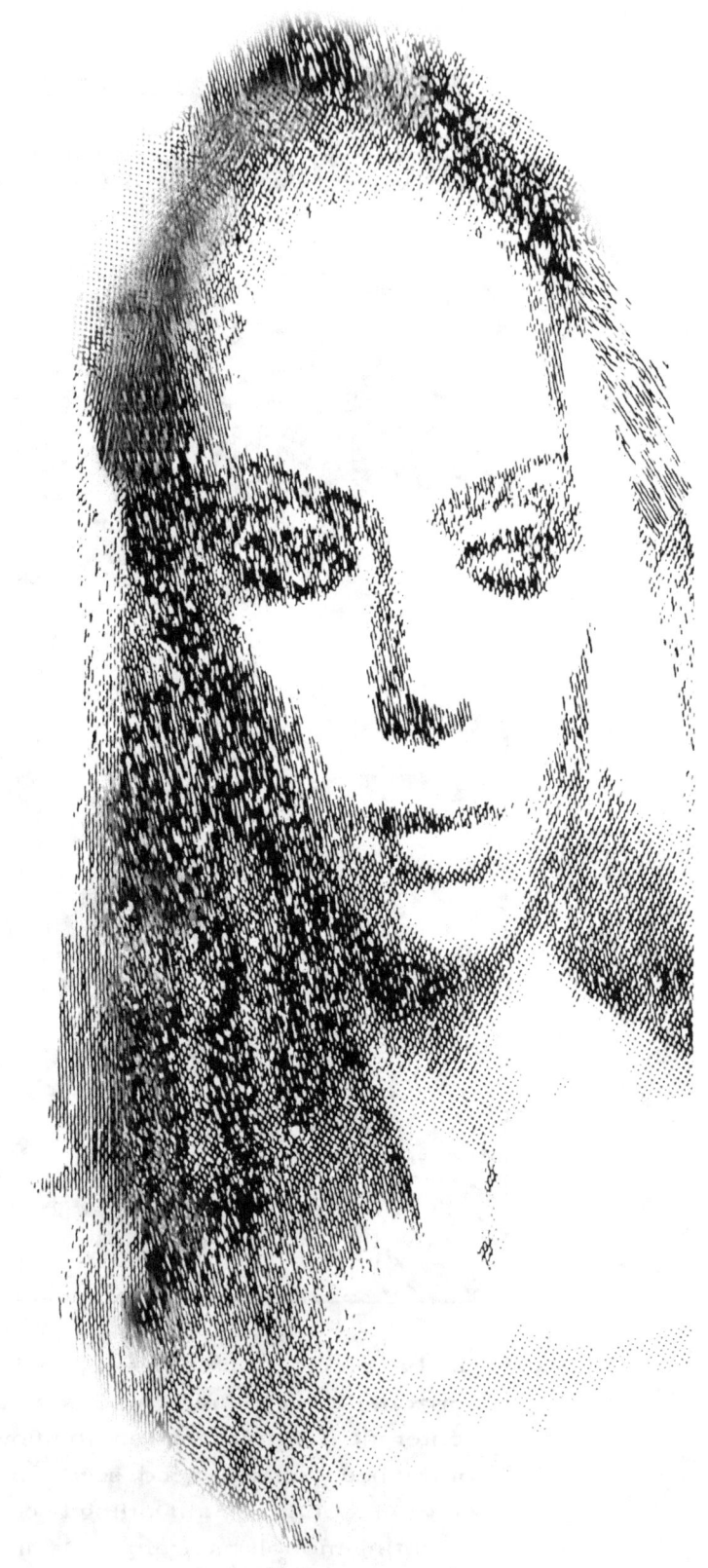

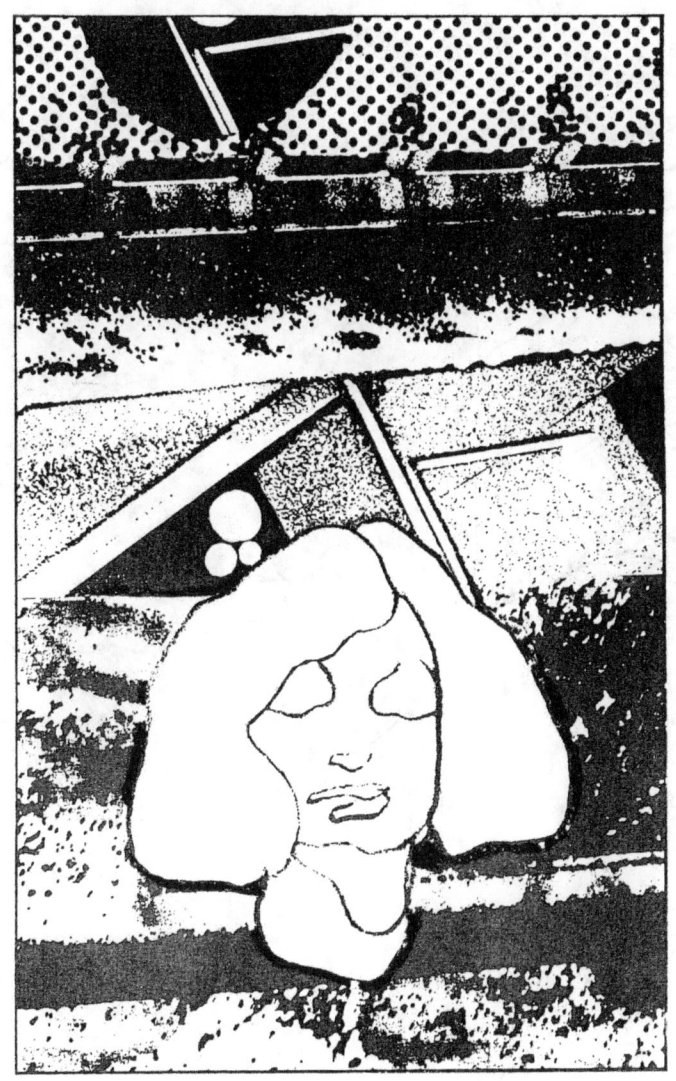

TRIBUTE TO A DEAD FRIEND ... DESMOND

Time – present.
Waiting,
translucence,
wine, worn well.
Desmond dead –
long live life!
See Shylocks?
After me

do your eyelashes
touch your glasses?
Your eyes lie
heavy and low
in your face –
tears fall well.

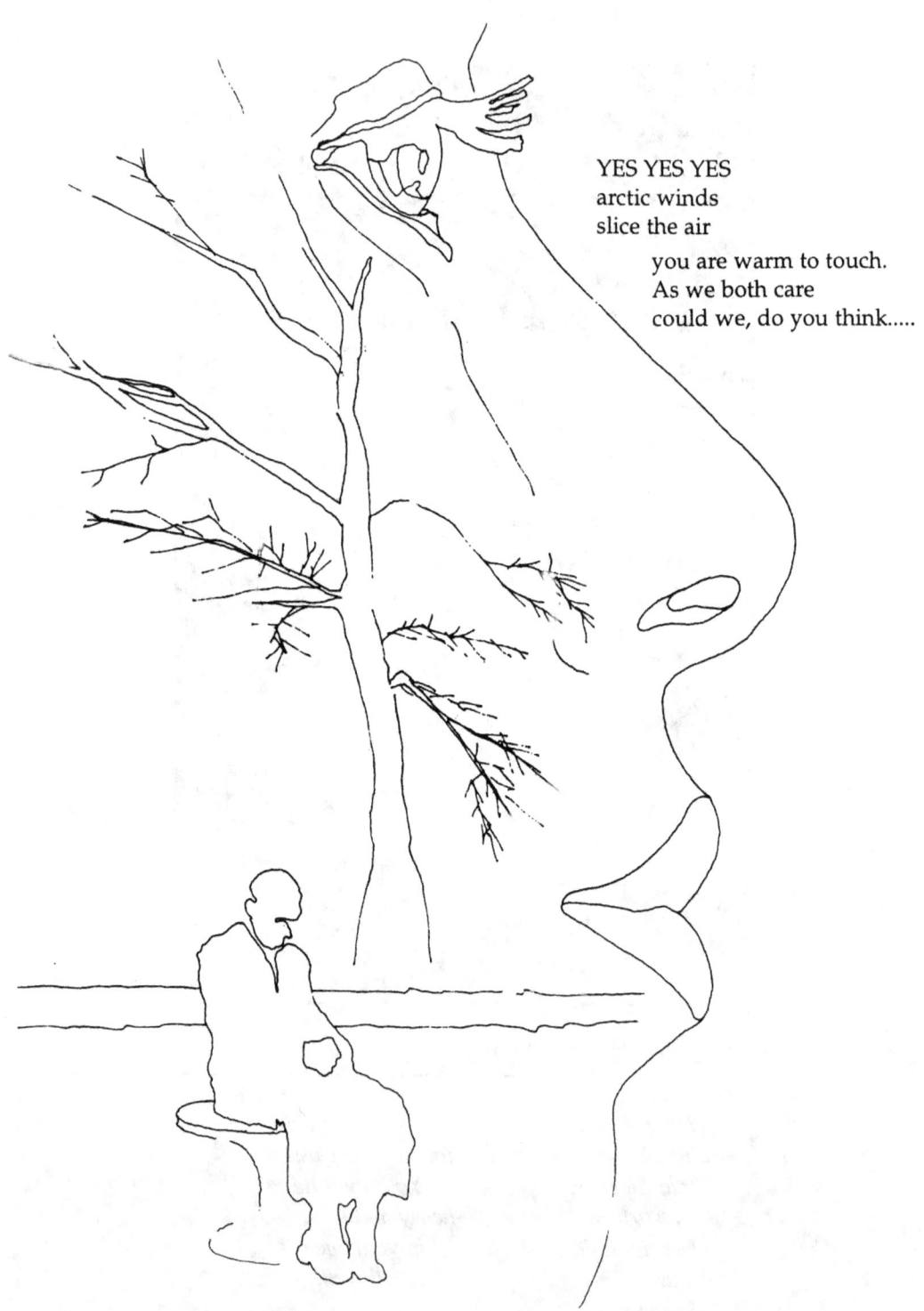

YES YES YES
arctic winds
slice the air

    you are warm to touch.
    As we both care
    could we, do you think.....

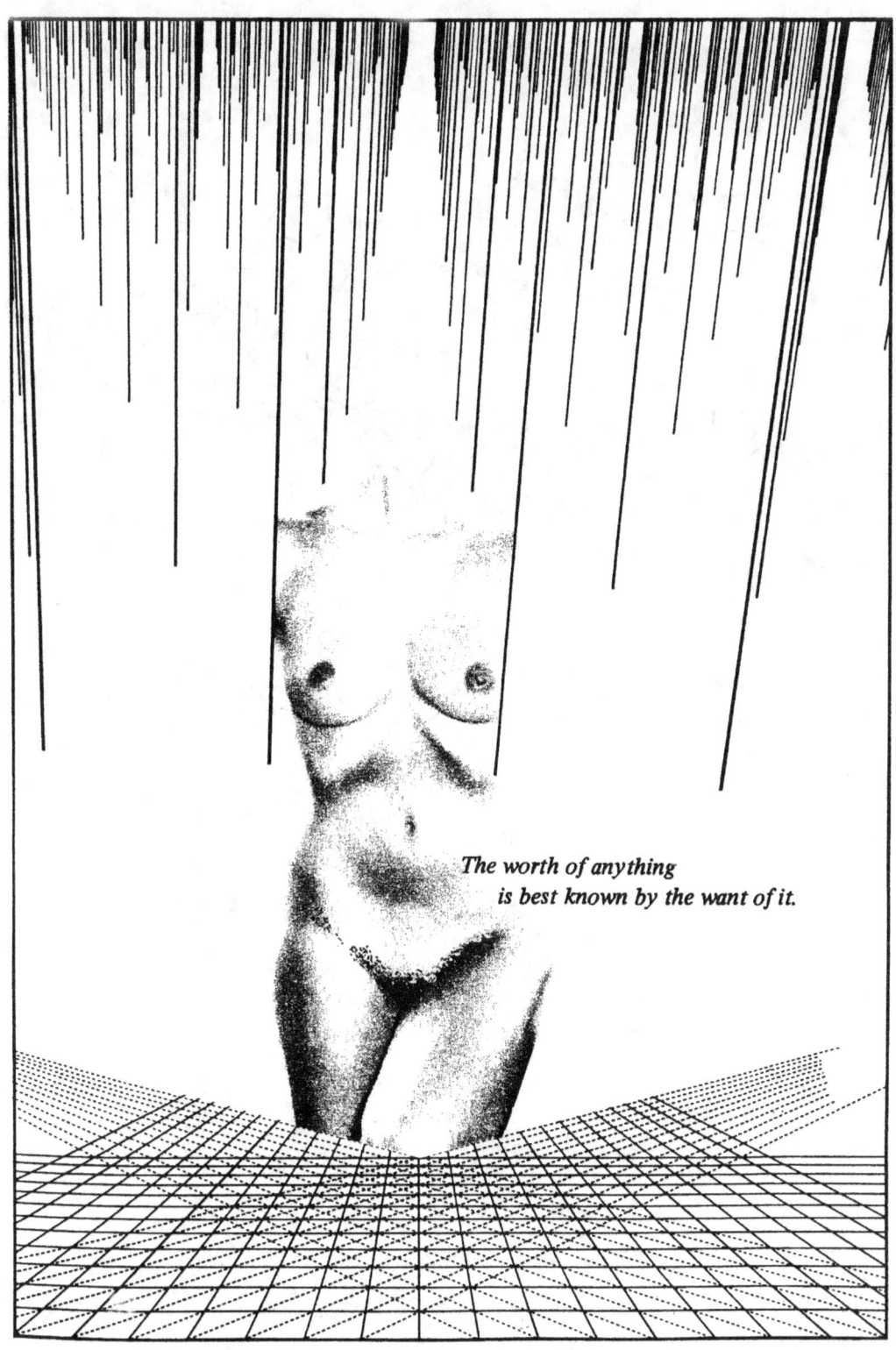

The worth of anything
is best known by the want of it.

When you have it.....Do you need it..... Does it give you pleasure?

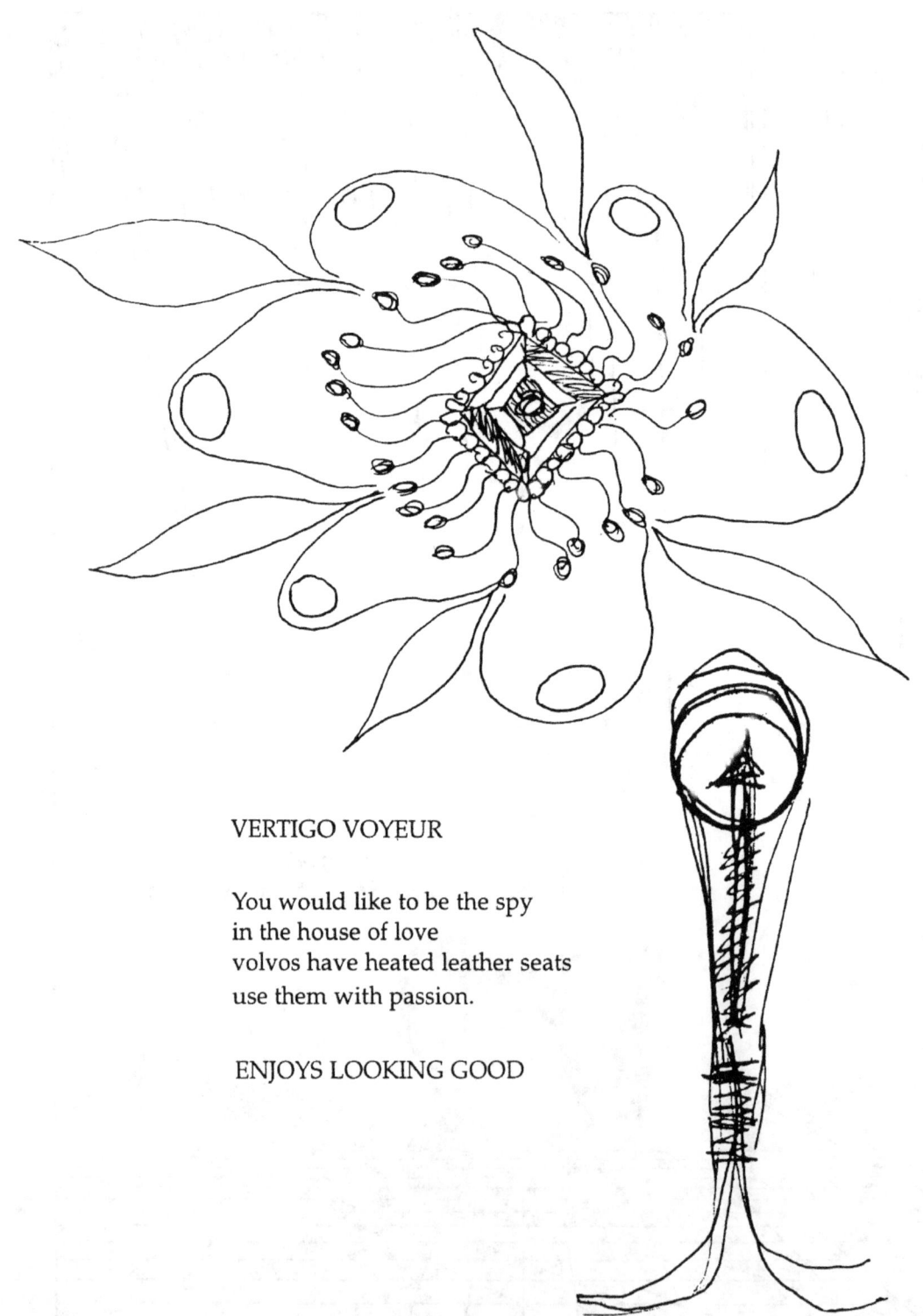

VERTIGO VOYEUR

You would like to be the spy
in the house of love
volvos have heated leather seats
use them with passion.

ENJOYS LOOKING GOOD

ICE MELTING BY THE WINTER POOL

Words are just wheels —
only engines power them.
Butterflies' shadows, hover
in the autumn's sun.
Cream clouds melt over
the barren mountains.
Life's bruises show with
subtle body movements.
Skins tan slowly
inbetween the jacarandas.
Shades of colonialism
vanish away gracefully.
Remember the reflections
in Hockney's pools —
quiet anger in stark
barren hotel rooms.
It's not part of me.
WHO — break room
803.

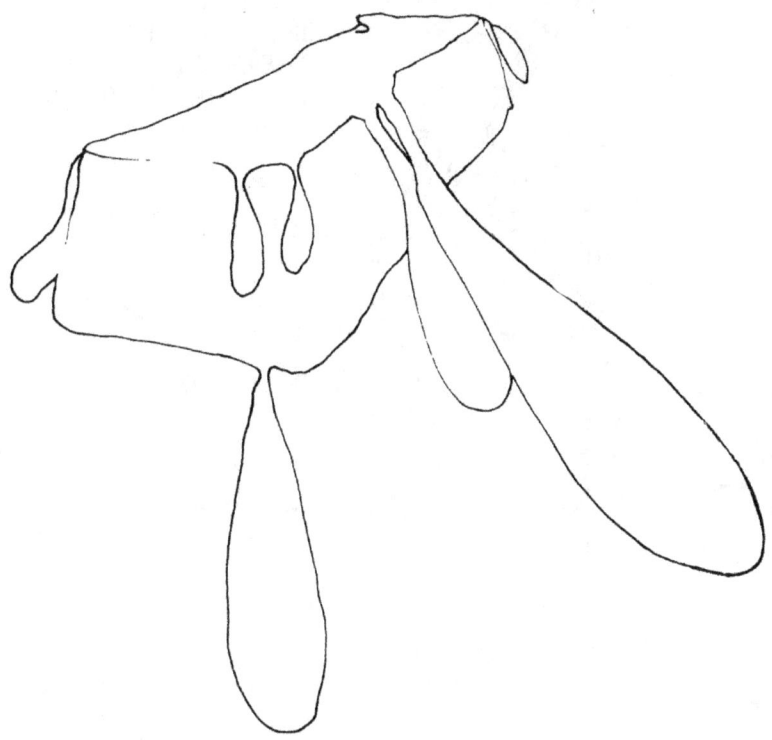

They pop up in my heads headache like little bubbly ideas a cornucopia building todays drawing.....Outside the box, cliche!

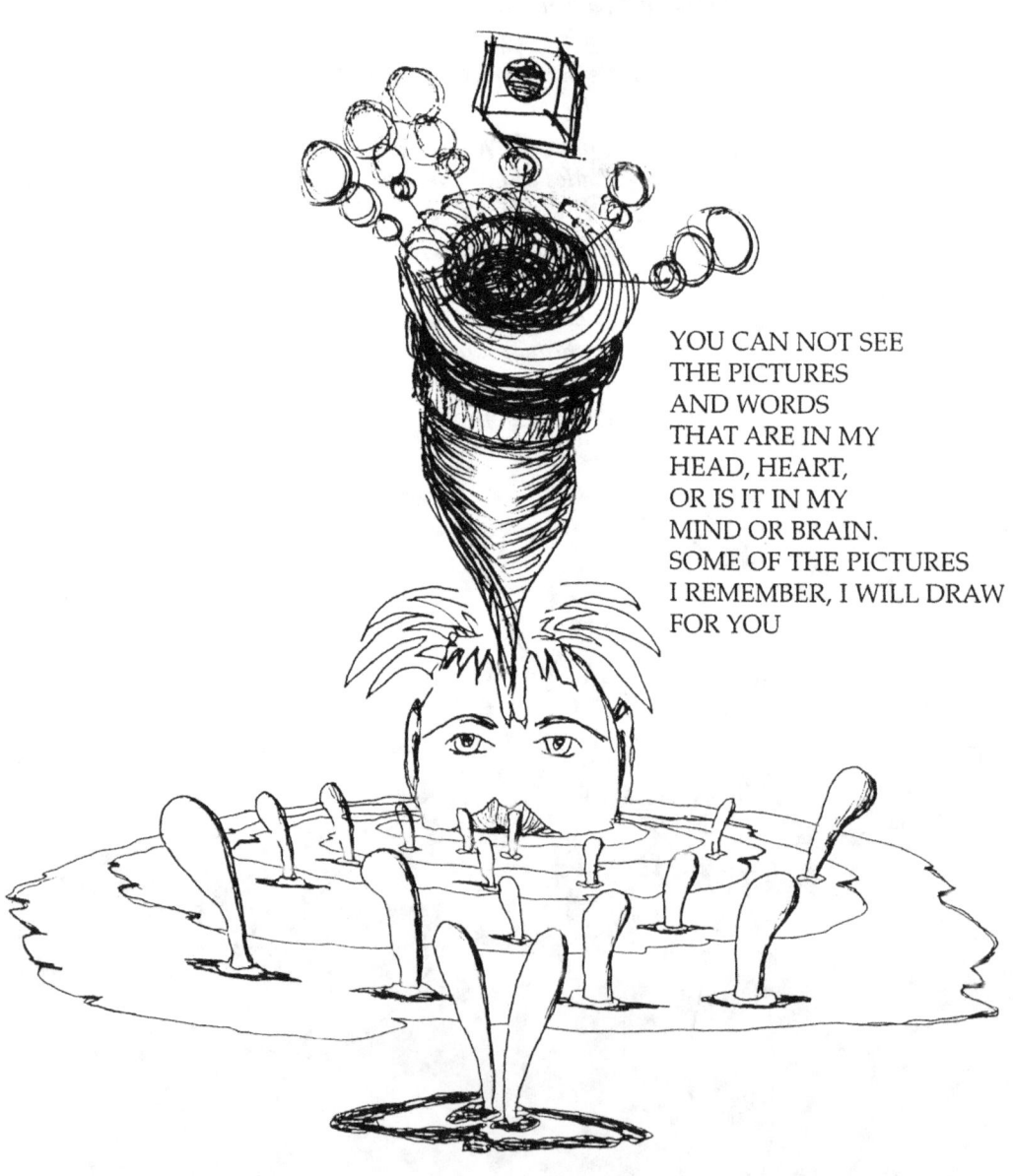

YOU CAN NOT SEE
THE PICTURES
AND WORDS
THAT ARE IN MY
HEAD, HEART,
OR IS IT IN MY
MIND OR BRAIN.
SOME OF THE PICTURES
I REMEMBER, I WILL DRAW
FOR YOU

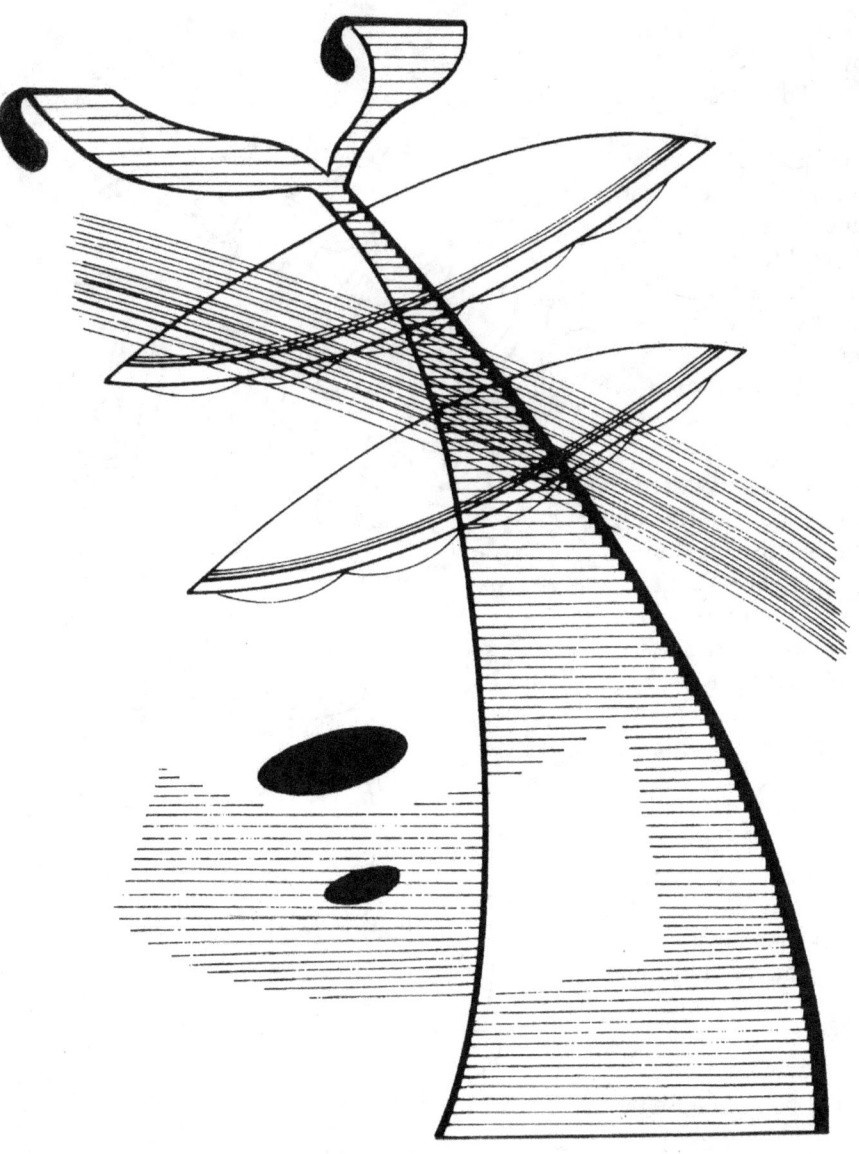

ARTHUR WE DONT NEED A SPACE ELEVATOR NOW ?
The cow jumped over the moon.....I Love degenerate art.....

I met Lyonel feininger while hallucinating under
the influence of Maxfield Parrish's painting of
light bulb ads.....

Memories of the mud flats
low water keys
the tidal race across
three hours of life,
The outer rows,
a living forest of ocean
jungle mangroves.
Beyond the Pacific,
the place where my
fantasy life journey
started.
Mud flats- a picture
an inspiration of
constantly changing
art, ocean sculptured
driftwood collectables,
sun bleached textures
balance across the
mud forming pictures
by ManRay, Picasso
3D by Henry Moore
heres life at arts door.
I'm bored , nothing
to do here !
Tidal pools, fools
have no patience
for the endless search !
Oil down by crocodile creek
crabs the size of hub caps
like armored personnel
carriers on prozac,
or zoloft.
Amphetomine Angels
ride on the imagination
train, to the station of
no words- land of fantasy.
Voyeur of the pattern
of the memory of space,
time and life.

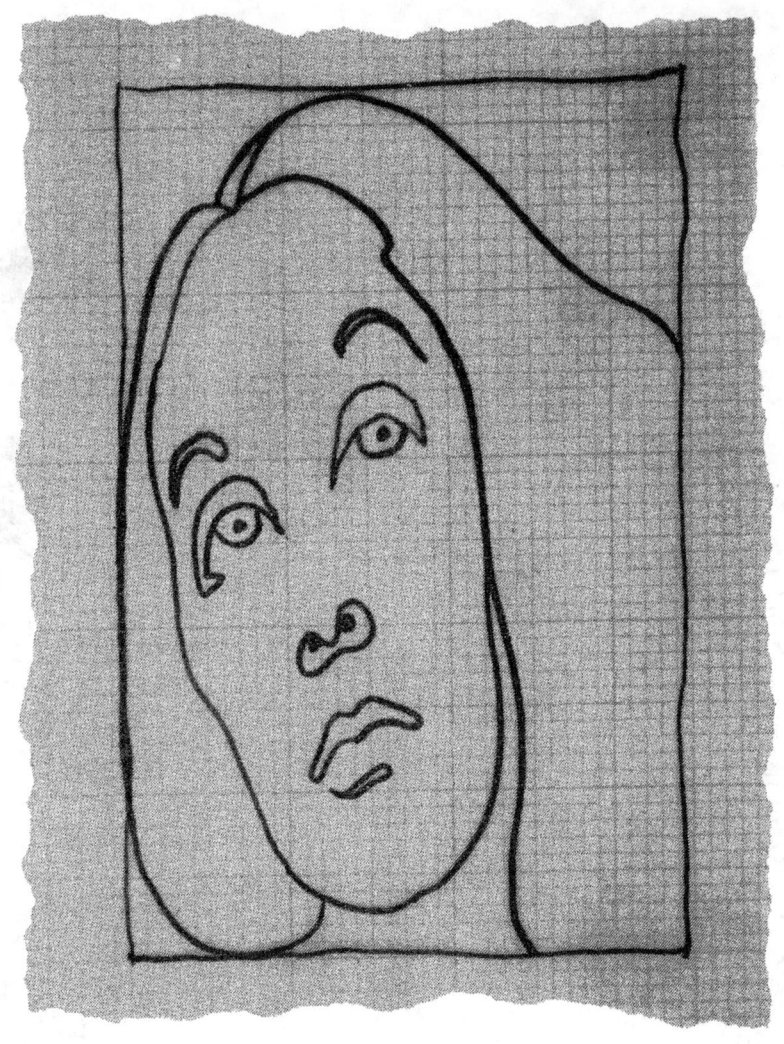

ATLANTIQUE EVENING

   Mascara eyes in the rain
tart taste of musky hops
   moorish symmetry, nostalgia – pain
Aroma: honey roast ham in shops.
   Warm sea rollers gracefully glide
seagulls break the horizon line
   mountains – strength – under comfort hide.
Summer poppy petals shine.
   Soft evening winds through your hair
quiet beach furniture –
   have you ever made a deck chair?

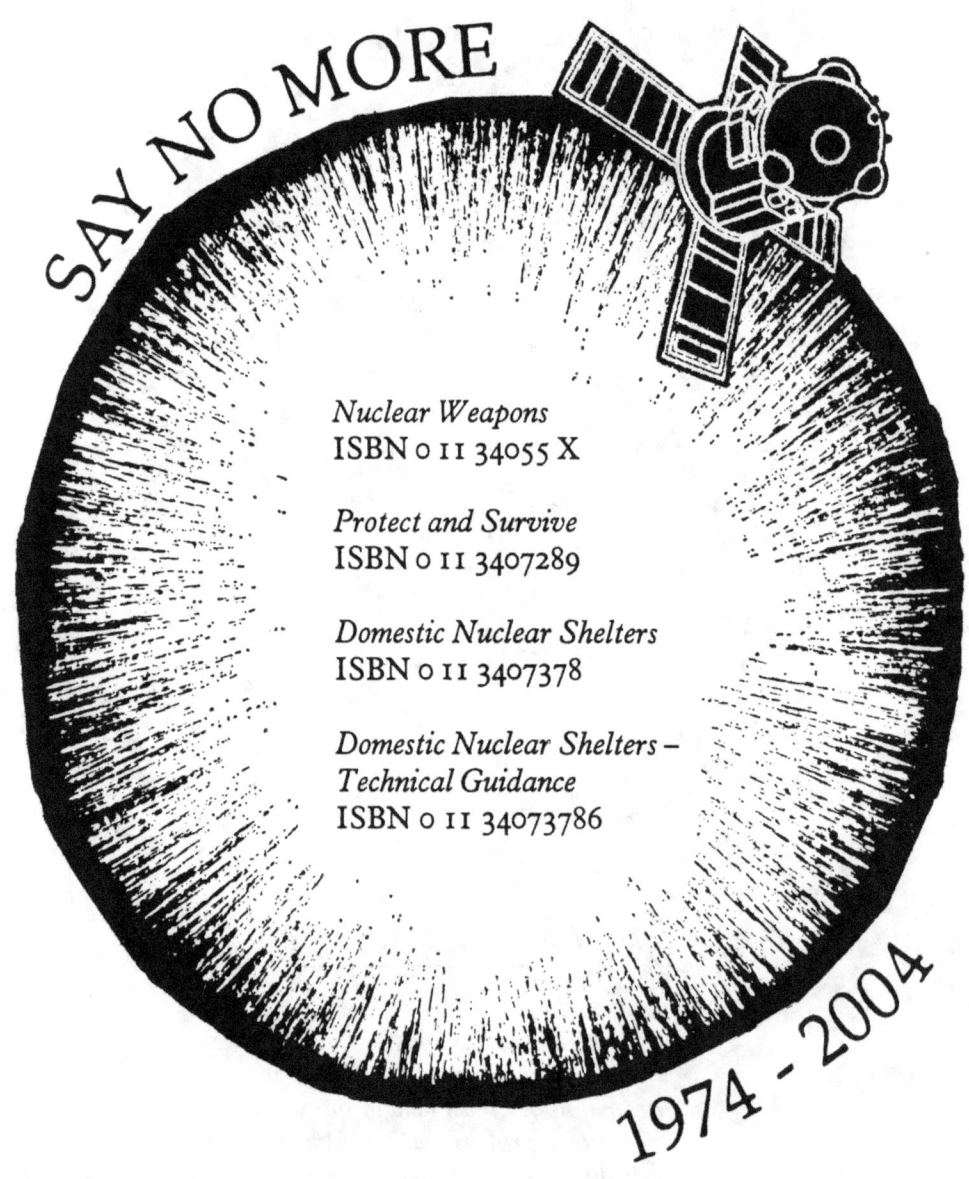

SAY NO MORE

Nuclear Weapons
ISBN 0 11 34055 X

Protect and Survive
ISBN 0 11 3407289

Domestic Nuclear Shelters
ISBN 0 11 3407378

Domestic Nuclear Shelters –
Technical Guidance
ISBN 0 11 34073786

1974 – 2004

Life may not be all we want, but it's all we have.

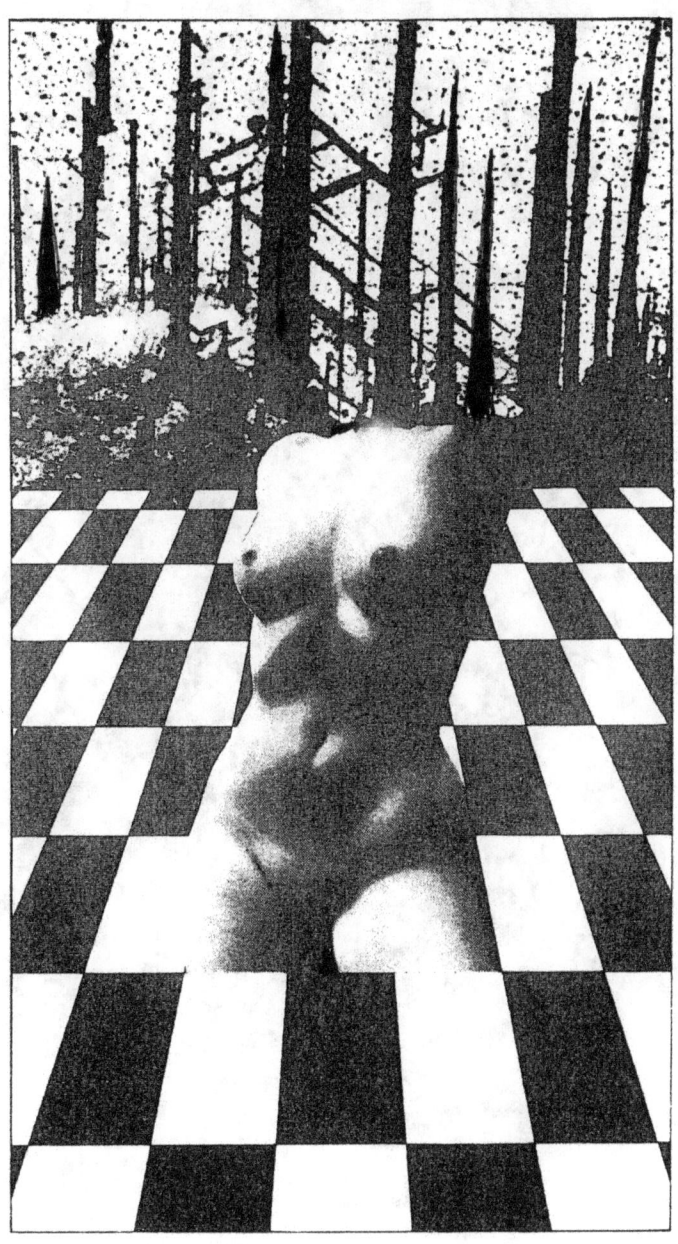

We live not as we would, but as need drives us.

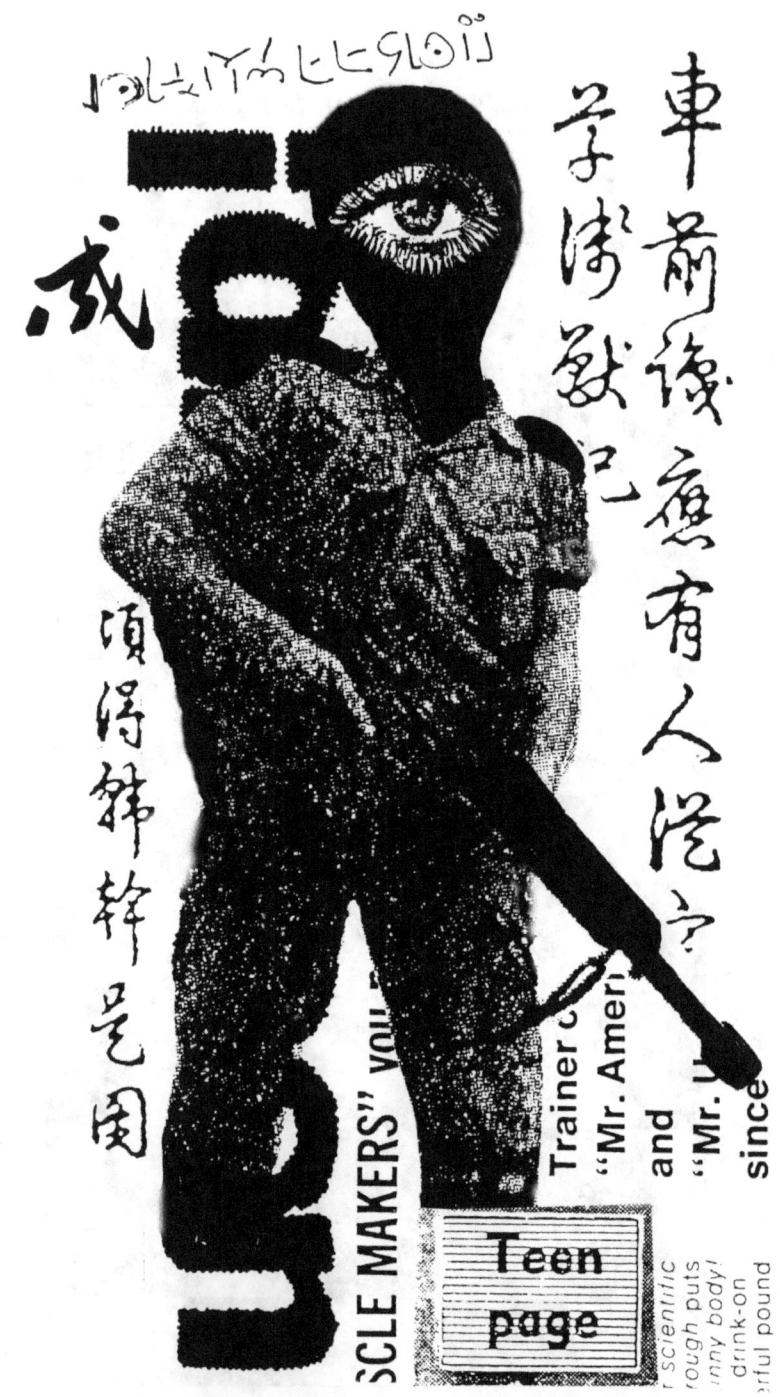

車前後庶有人況

学術敢己

成

須得韓幹呈閉

"SCLE MAKERS" you

Trainer "Mr. Ameri and "Mr. U since

Teen page

r scientific
rough puts
nny body!
drink-on
rful pound

HERE WE GO AGAIN 2010

How would I know..... I never had to fight in a war.....
Warcraft lets play.....We should reinvent the wheel.....

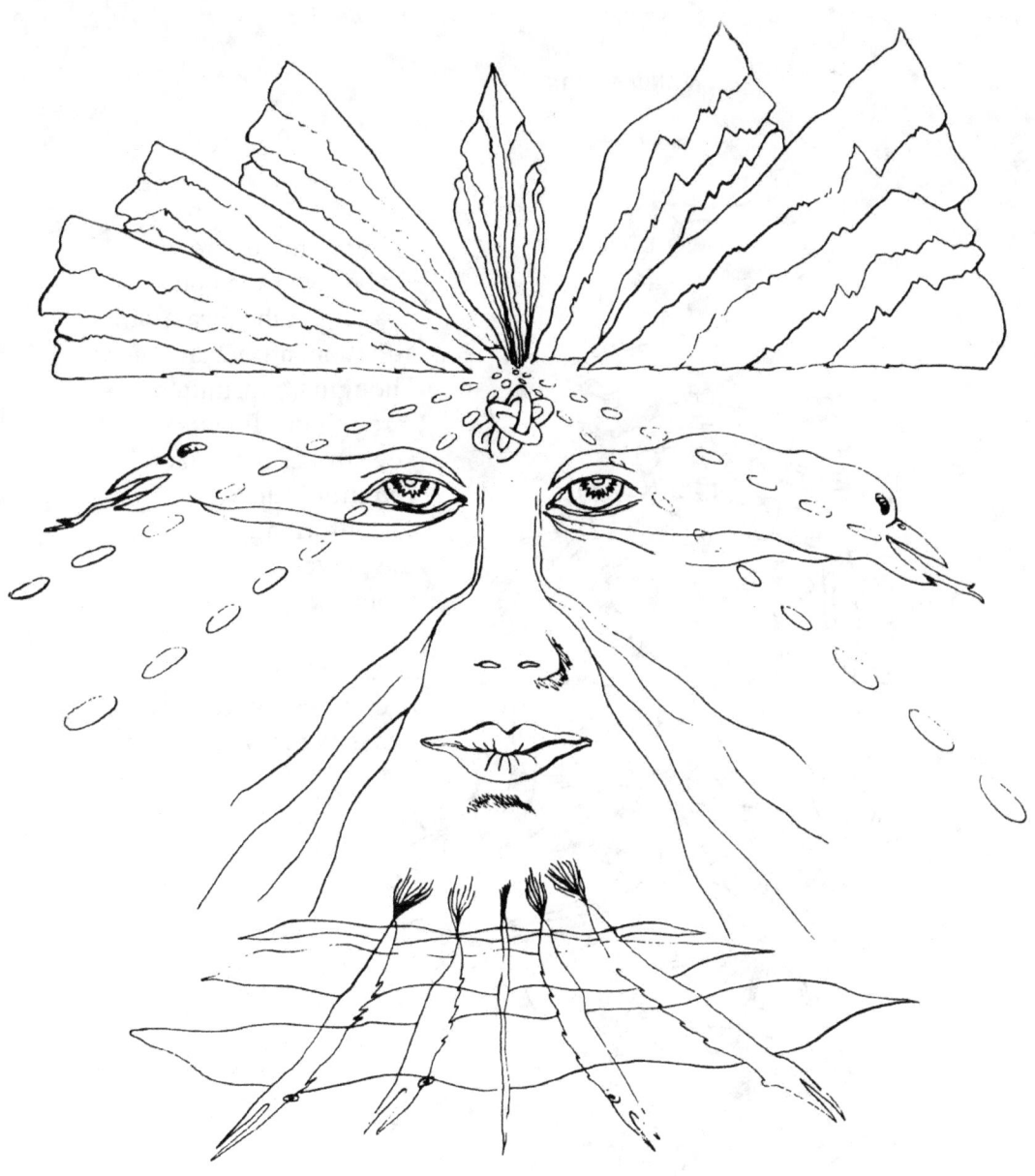

LANDSCAPES OF PERSPEX PEOPLE

Captain conscience
cool courageous.
Dude death
down, determined.
Animal action
arse adventure.
Perspex people
perpetuating pity.

Date:

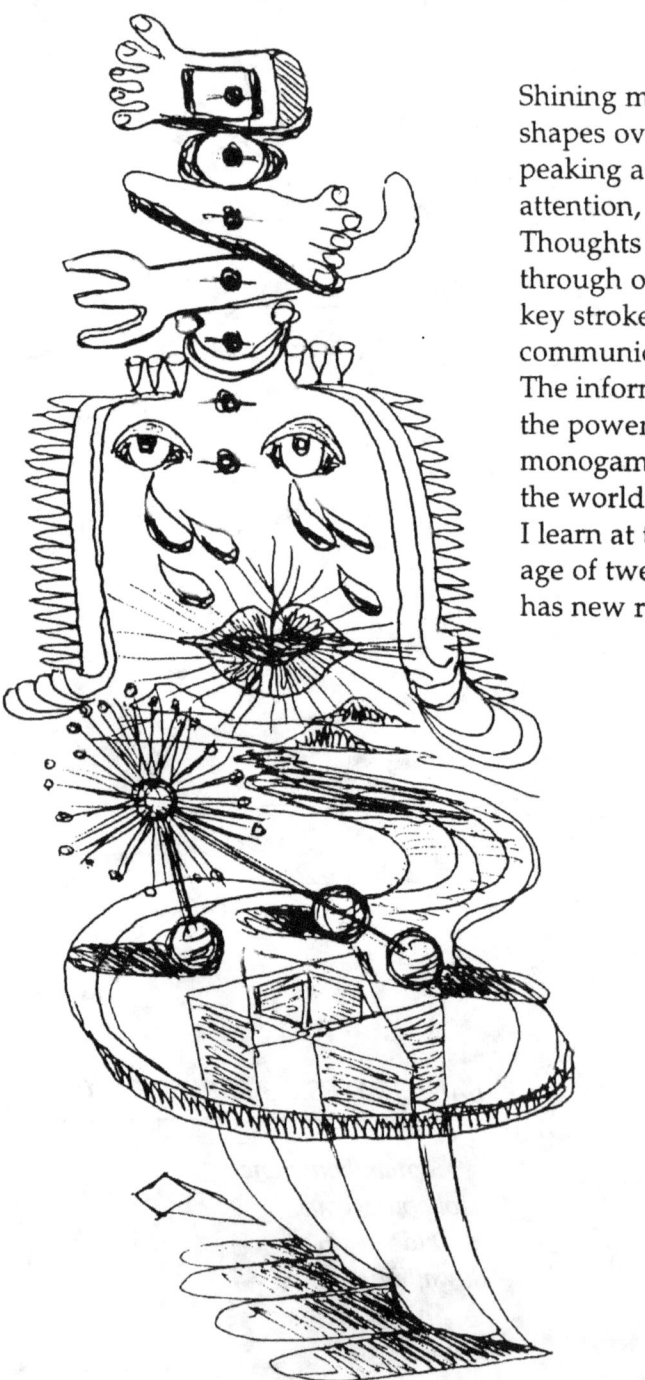

Shining microfibre
shapes over the body
peaking at the focal points
attention, attract and tease.
Thoughts transmitted
through our fingers
key strokes make us
communicate.
The information,
the power,
monogamy,
the world
I learn at the
age of twenty five
has new rules now.

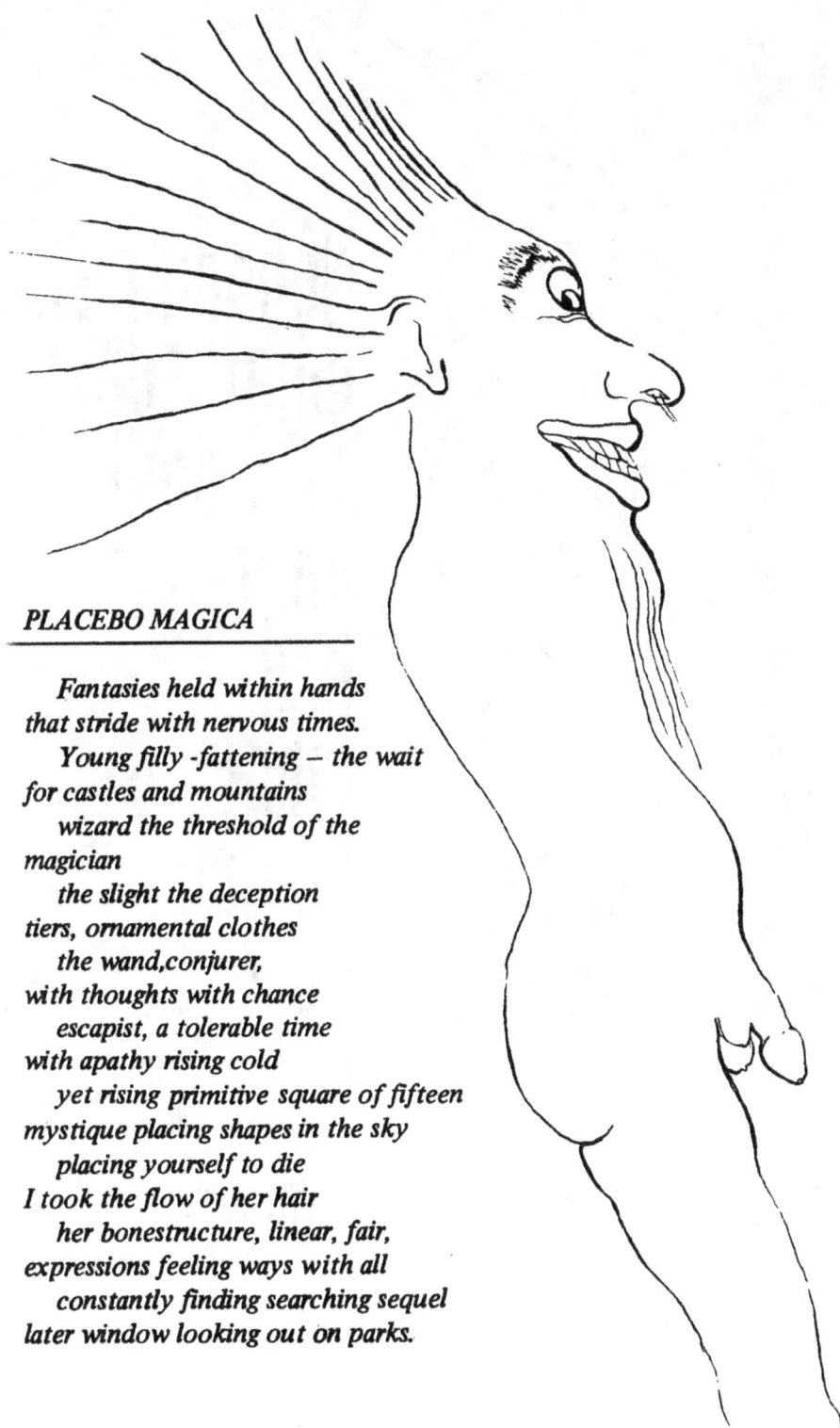

PLACEBO MAGICA

Fantasies held within hands
that stride with nervous times.
   Young filly -fattening — the wait
for castles and mountains
   wizard the threshold of the
magician
   the slight the deception
tiers, ornamental clothes
   the wand,conjurer,
with thoughts with chance
   escapist, a tolerable time
with apathy rising cold
   yet rising primitive square of fifteen
mystique placing shapes in the sky
   placing yourself to die
I took the flow of her hair
   her bonestructure, linear, fair,
expressions feeling ways with all
   constantly finding searching sequel
later window looking out on parks.

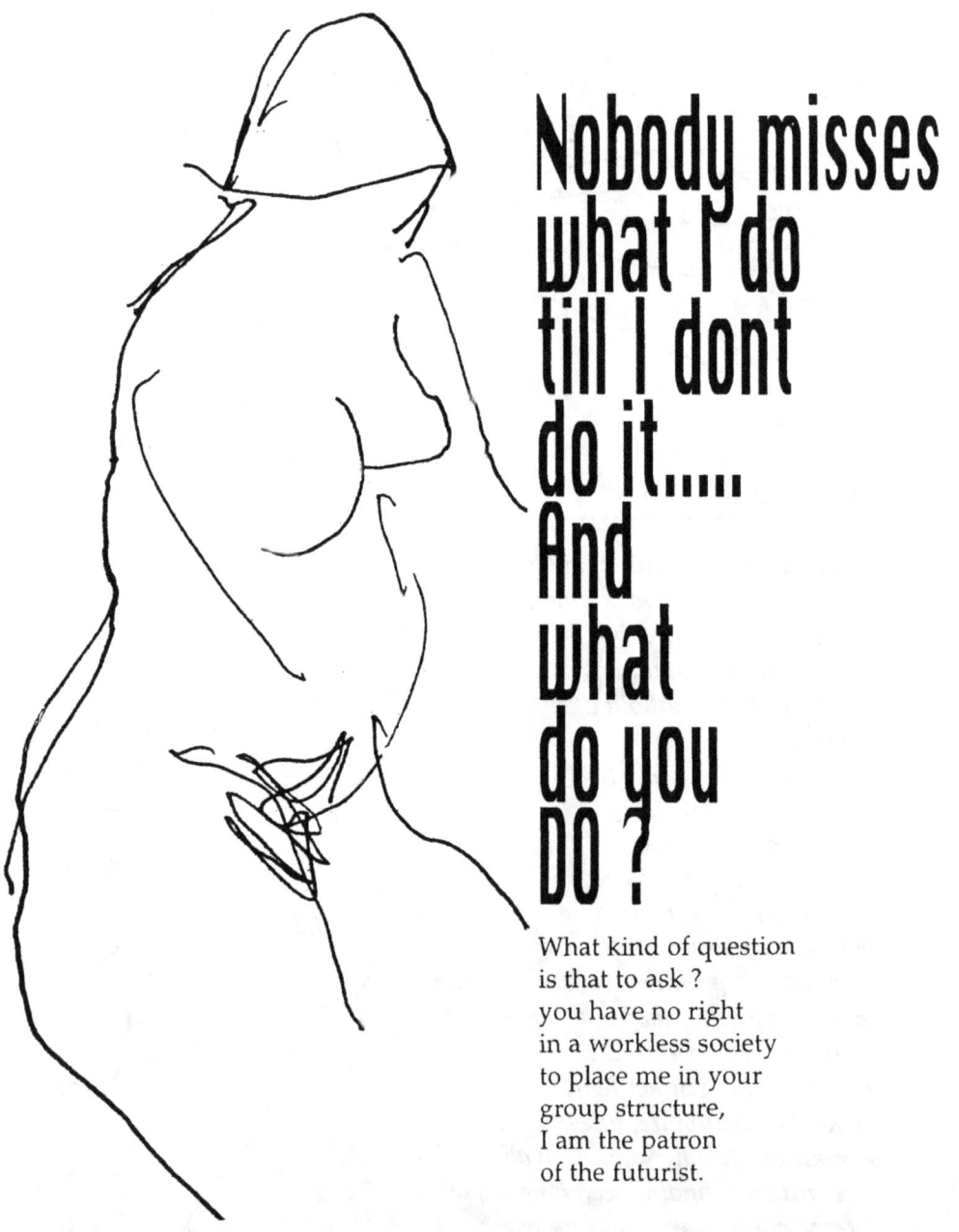

Nobody misses what I do till I dont do it..... And what do you DO ?

What kind of question
is that to ask ?
you have no right
in a workless society
to place me in your
group structure,
I am the patron
of the futurist.

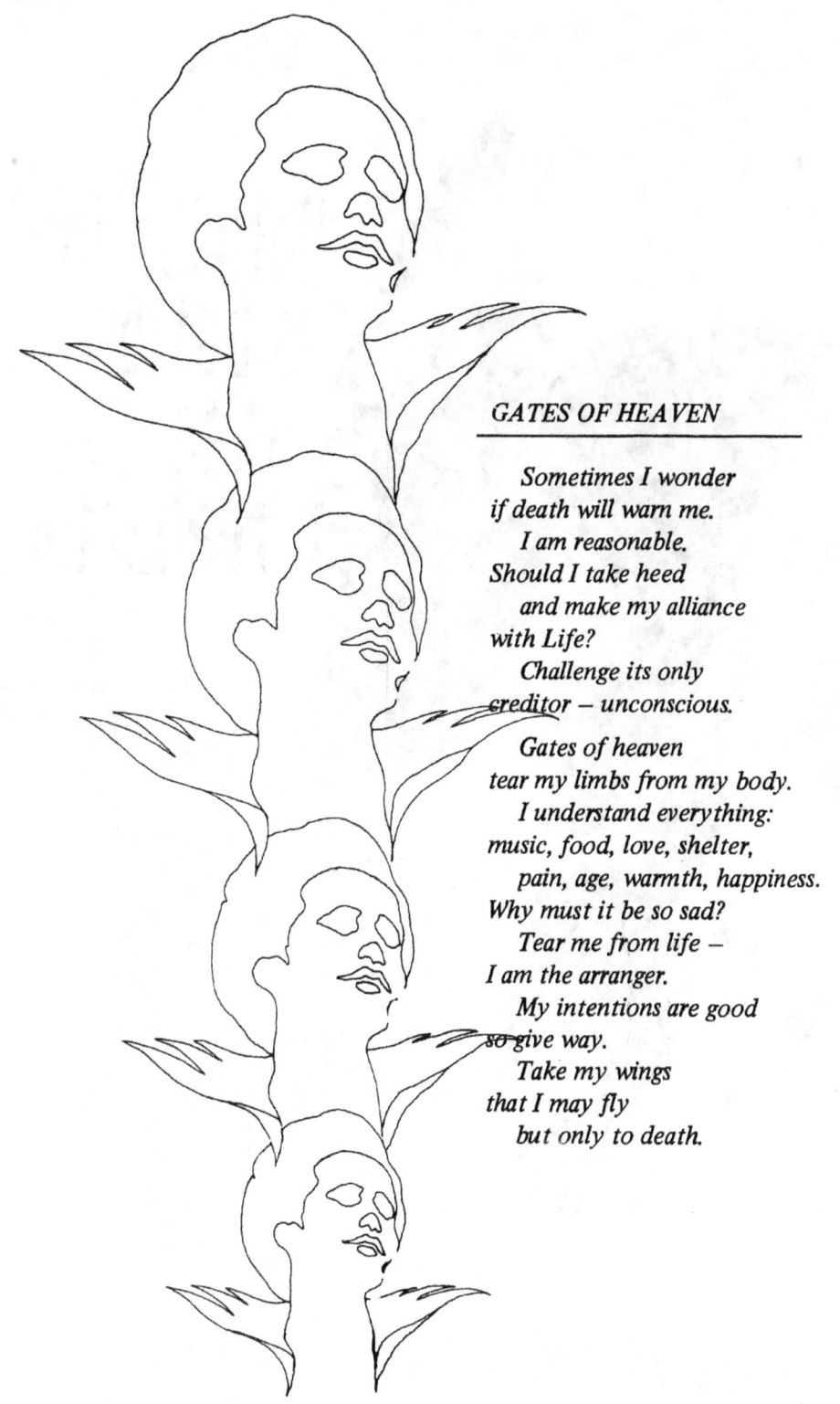

GATES OF HEAVEN

Sometimes I wonder
if death will warn me.
  I am reasonable.
Should I take heed
  and make my alliance
with Life?
  Challenge its only
creditor – unconscious.

Gates of heaven
tear my limbs from my body.
  I understand everything:
music, food, love, shelter,
  pain, age, warmth, happiness.
Why must it be so sad?
  Tear me from life –
I am the arranger.
  My intentions are good
so give way.
  Take my wings
that I may fly
  but only to death.

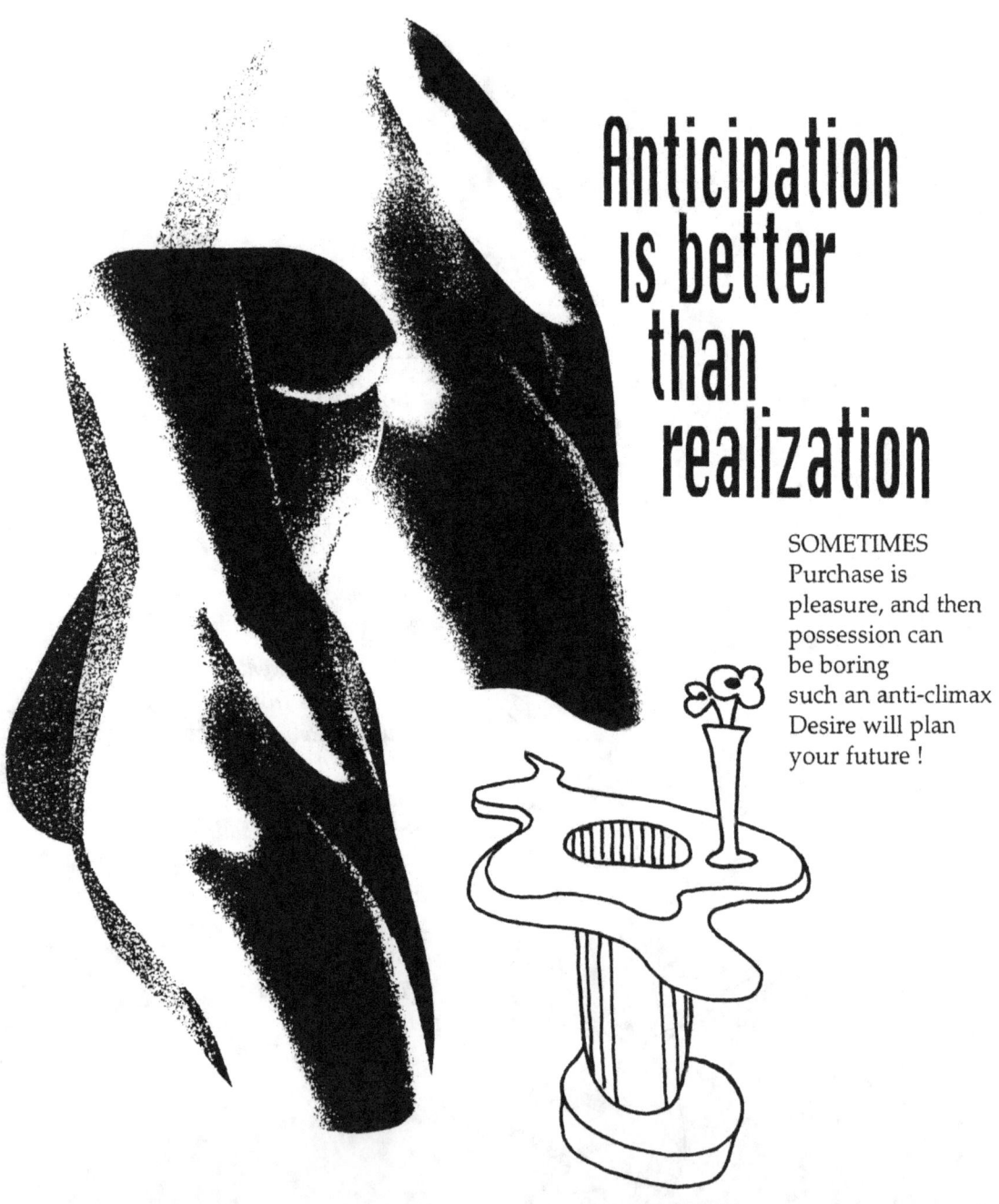

Anticipation is better than realization

SOMETIMES
Purchase is
pleasure, and then
possession can
be boring
such an anti-climax
Desire will plan
your future !

94

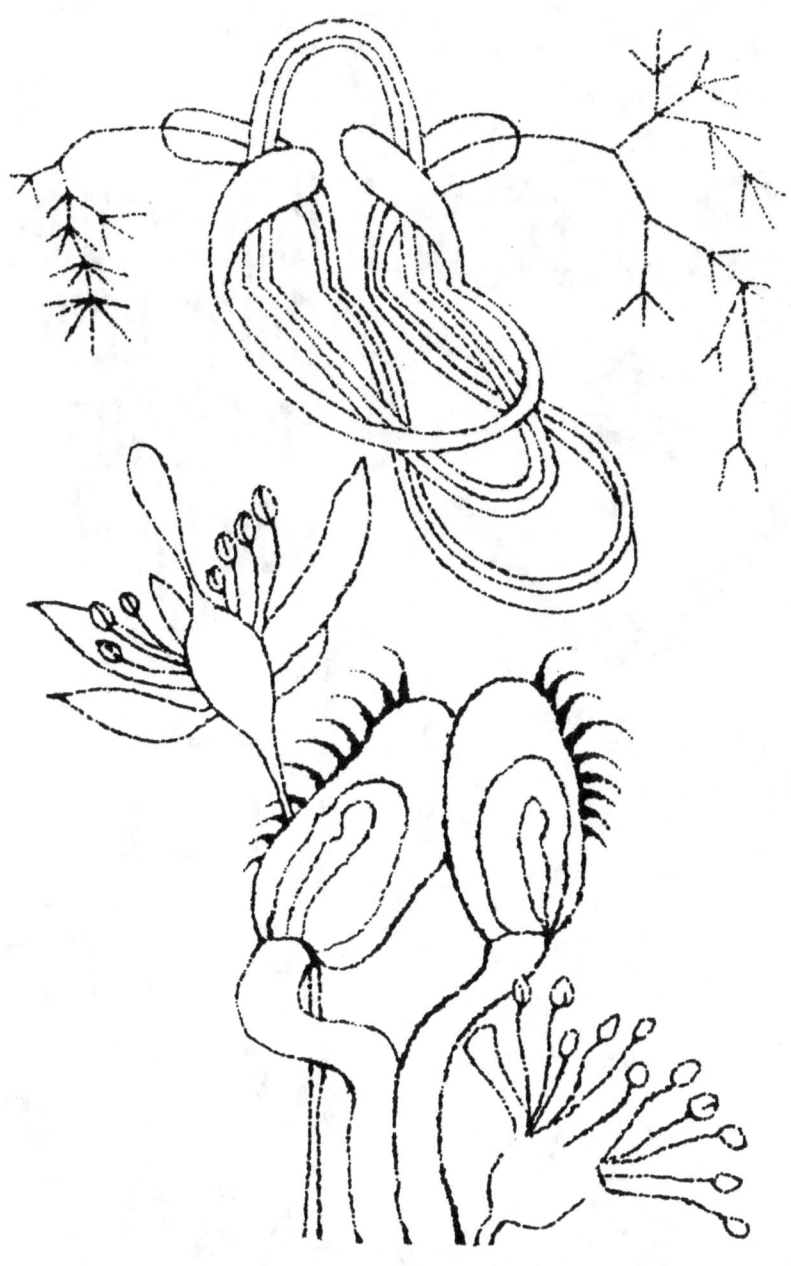

Spring has sprung, hibernation is done,
pull your finger out of your bum.....
Grow with the flow, perennials are fine
look down at mine! Summer sun
hopefully coming to the earth near you.

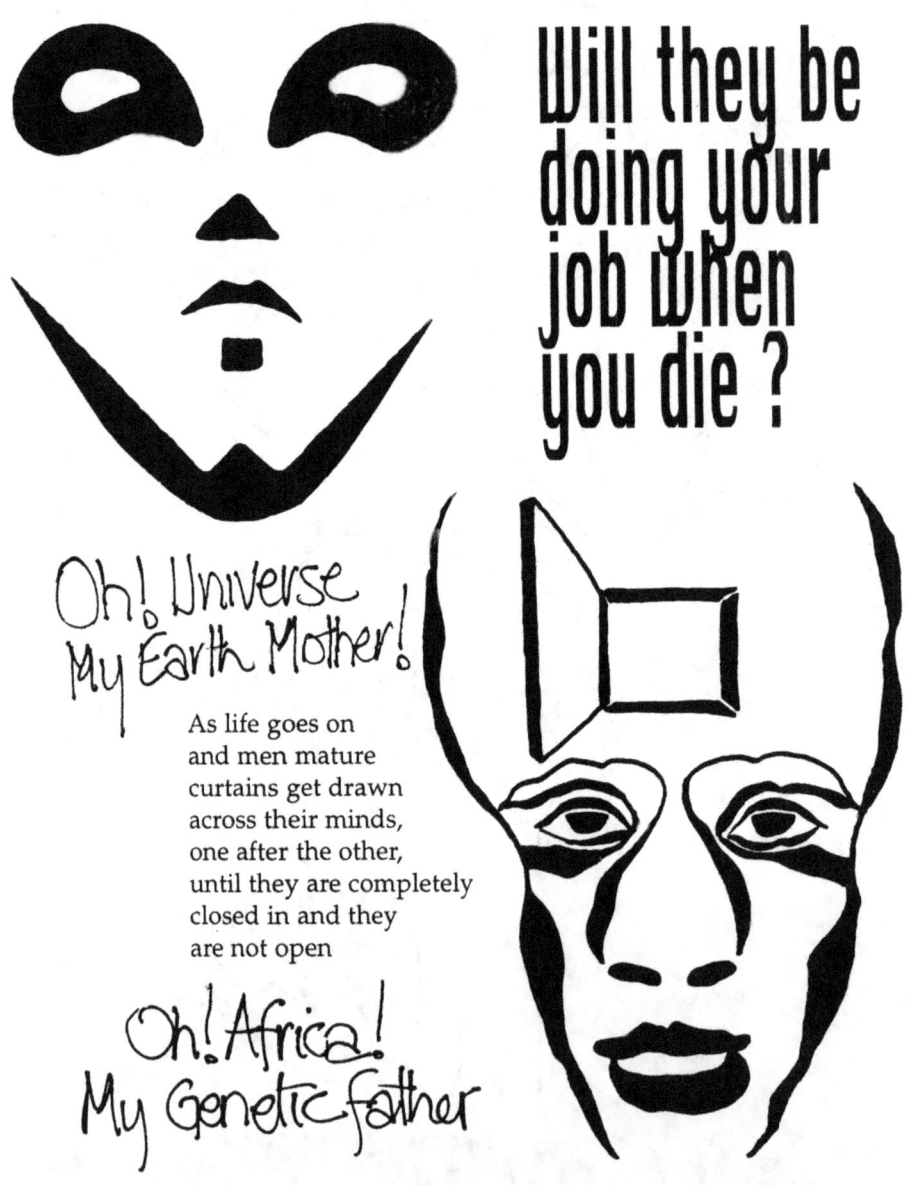

Will they be
doing your
job when
you die ?

Oh! Universe
My Earth Mother!

As life goes on
and men mature
curtains get drawn
across their minds,
one after the other,
until they are completely
closed in and they
are not open

Oh! Africa!
My Genetic father

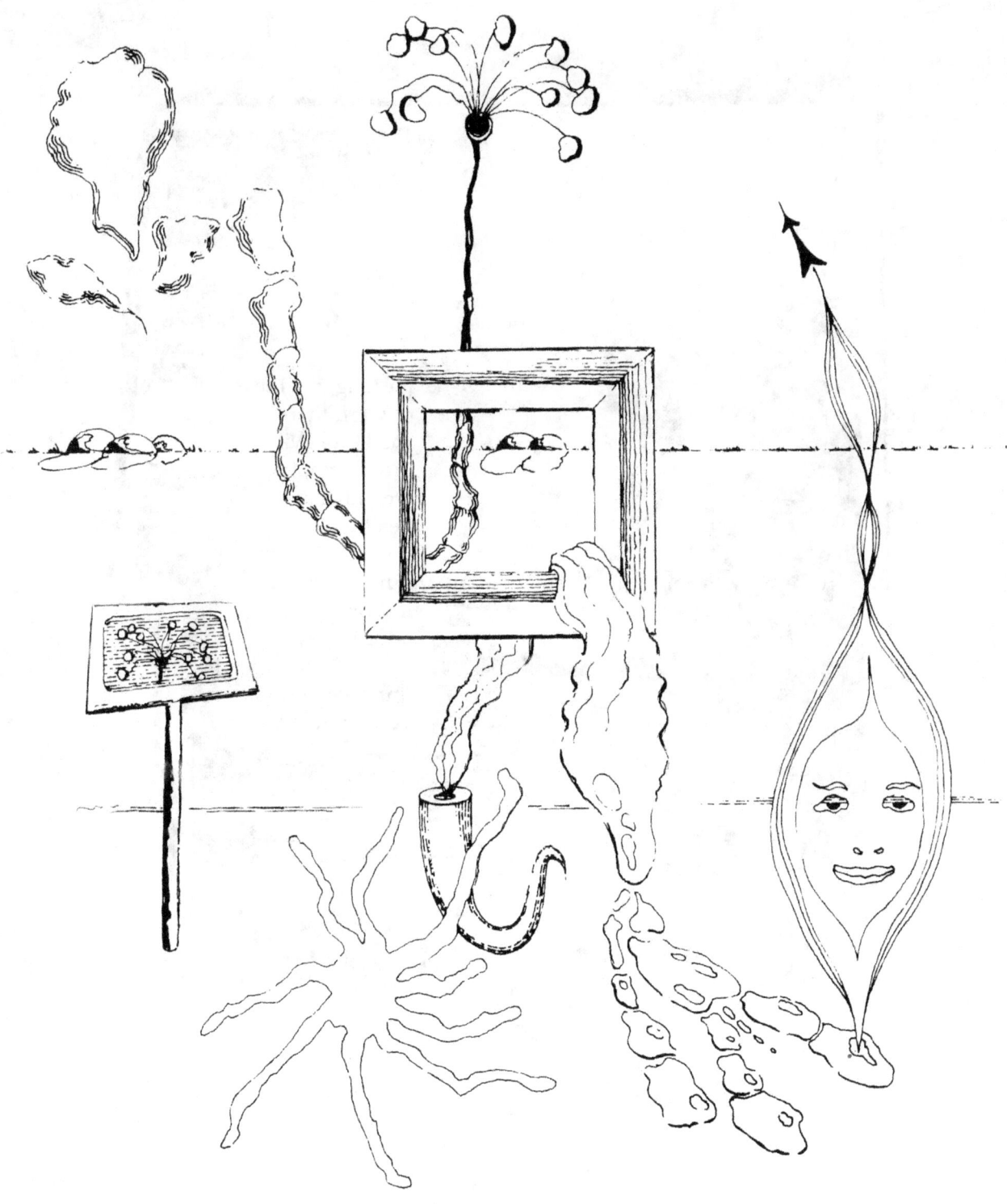

The growing of imagination is food on the horizon of thought.....
The salt of the earth is existence.....Molecules change into life.

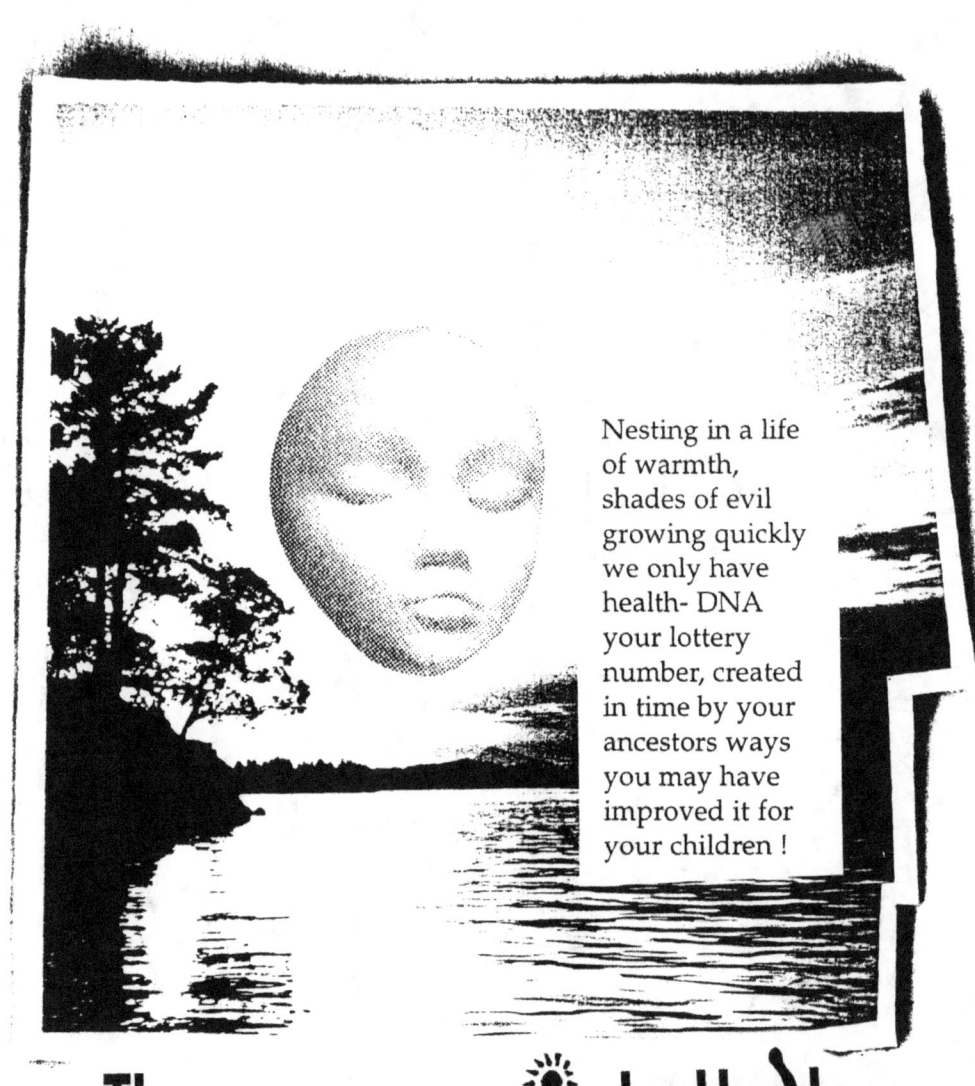

Nesting in a life
of warmth,
shades of evil
growing quickly
we only have
health- DNA
your lottery
number, created
in time by your
ancestors ways
you may have
improved it for
your children !

The last tango in bothell

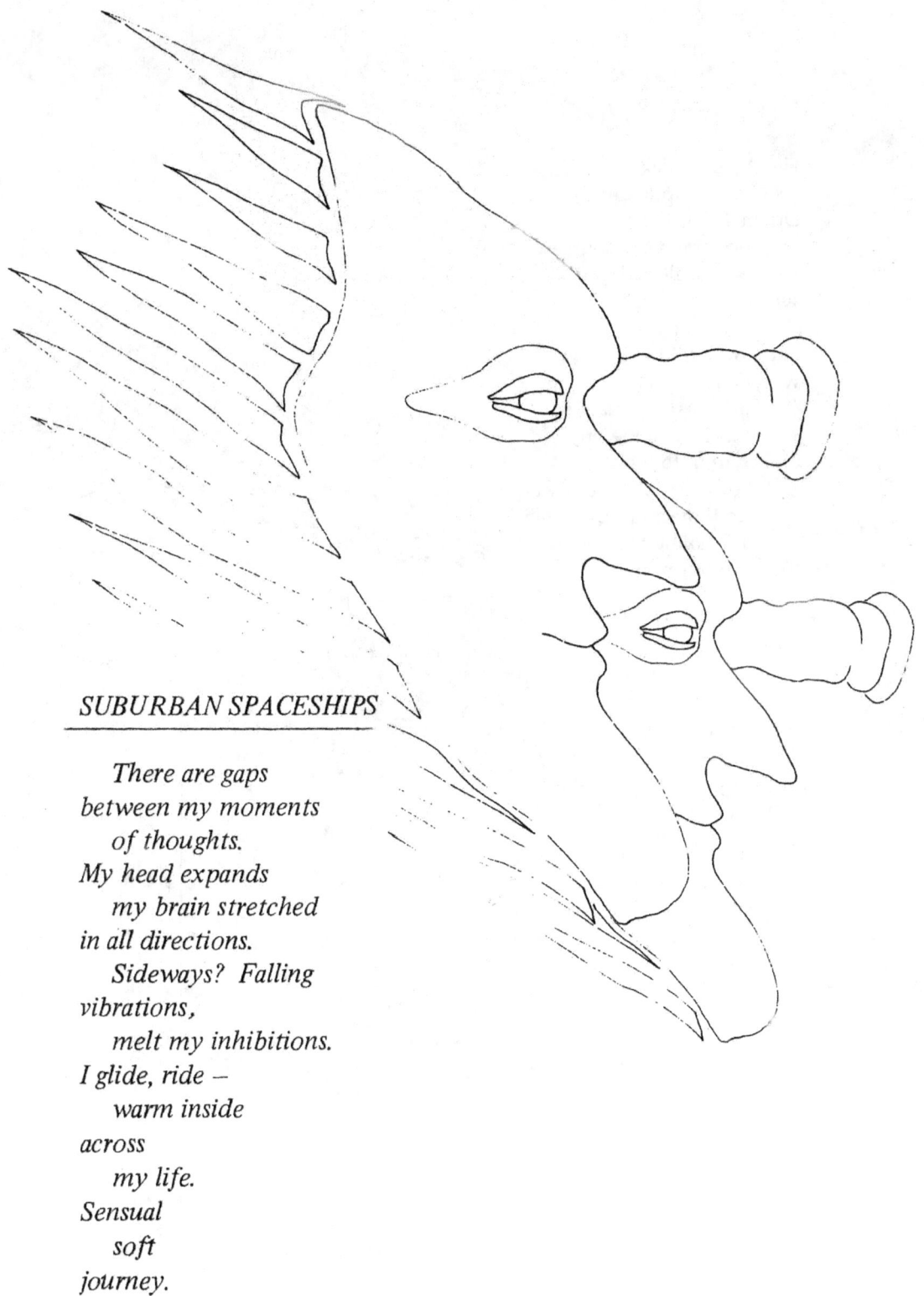

SUBURBAN SPACESHIPS

There are gaps
between my moments
    of thoughts.
My head expands
    my brain stretched
in all directions.
    Sideways? Falling
vibrations,
    melt my inhibitions.
I glide, ride —
    warm inside
across
    my life.
Sensual
    soft
journey.

IN CORTEX HEAVEN

Flies breed quickly
keep yours zipped up !
Originality is the art
of concealing your sources.
I knew I would fail in life
when I could not
do ballroom dancing,
and how could I be a CEO
without knowing shorthand ?
The cortex carpet floats
across the top of the brain
broken up into files
and thousands of documents
over ten thousand SEX IONS
all multitasking ready
to blow your mind

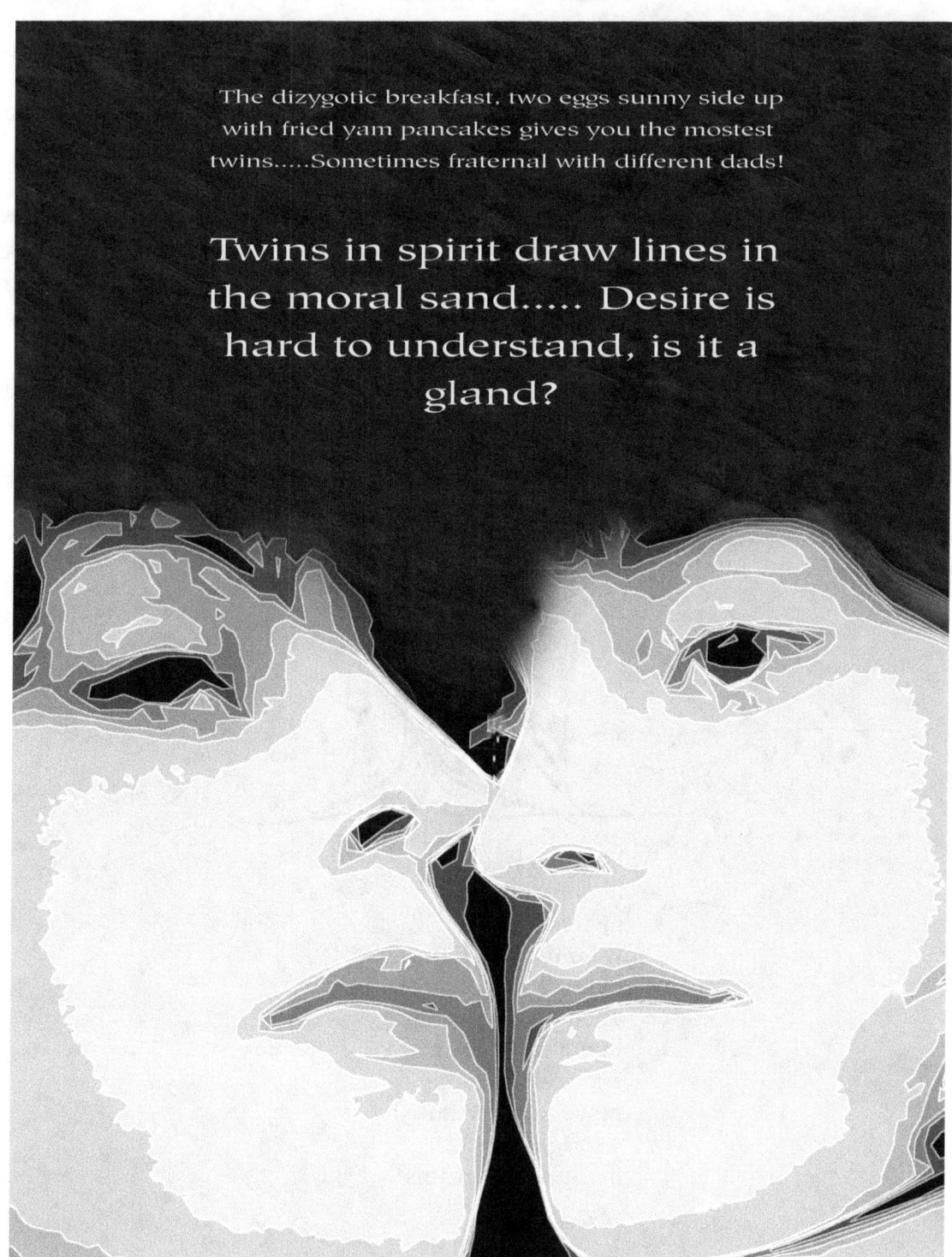

The dizygotic breakfast, two eggs sunny side up with fried yam pancakes gives you the mostest twins.....Sometimes fraternal with different dads!

Twins in spirit draw lines in the moral sand..... Desire is hard to understand, is it a gland?

FEELINGS FREE

The pain of `Brain death`.....
burns holes in my soul
can you find any record
of where the soul exists ?
The joy of contentment
will not take us to other
universal spaces.
You have to change
come out of the winter shell.

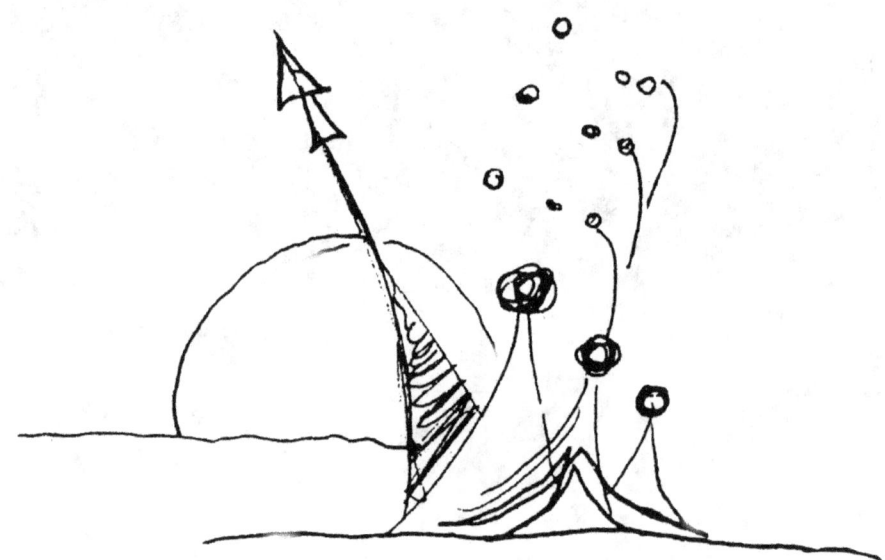

My eyes weep
my heart burns
my feet ache
we must find the way
to leave this planet some day.
Then you can return
to the earth's rich sea
and feel its energy
move and live quietly.....
yes right
in my son's dreams.

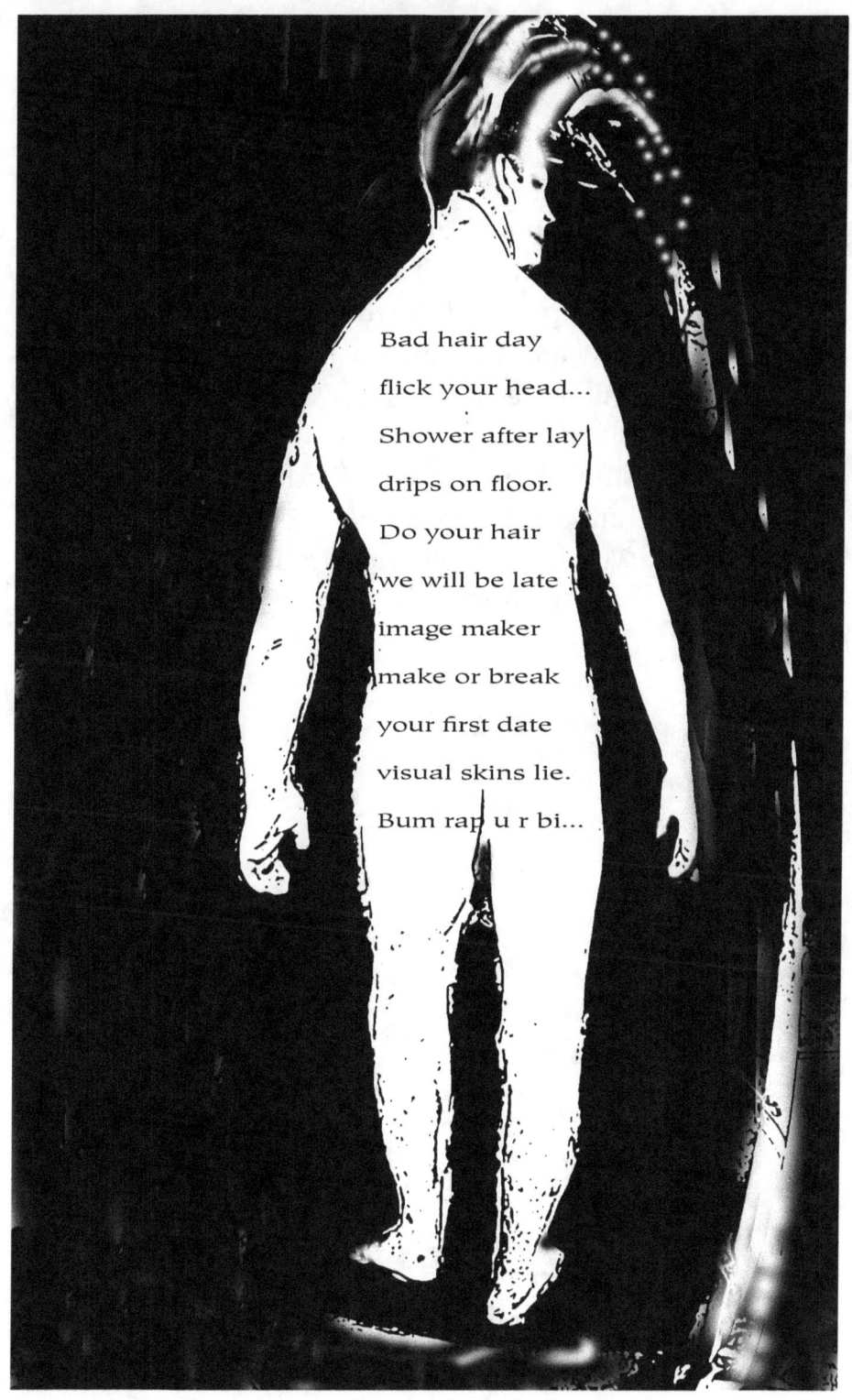

Bad hair day
flick your head...
Shower after lay
drips on floor.
Do your hair
we will be late
image maker
make or break
your first date
visual skins lie.
Bum rap u r bi...

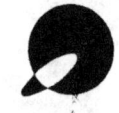

Empires of the sword
kingdoms of gold
communes with spirit,
universities of the mind
how many last war babies
will there be?
Blood flows like rivers
smart bombs waste very few
human personel, binary weapons
with built in genetic encoders
only terminate the enemy.

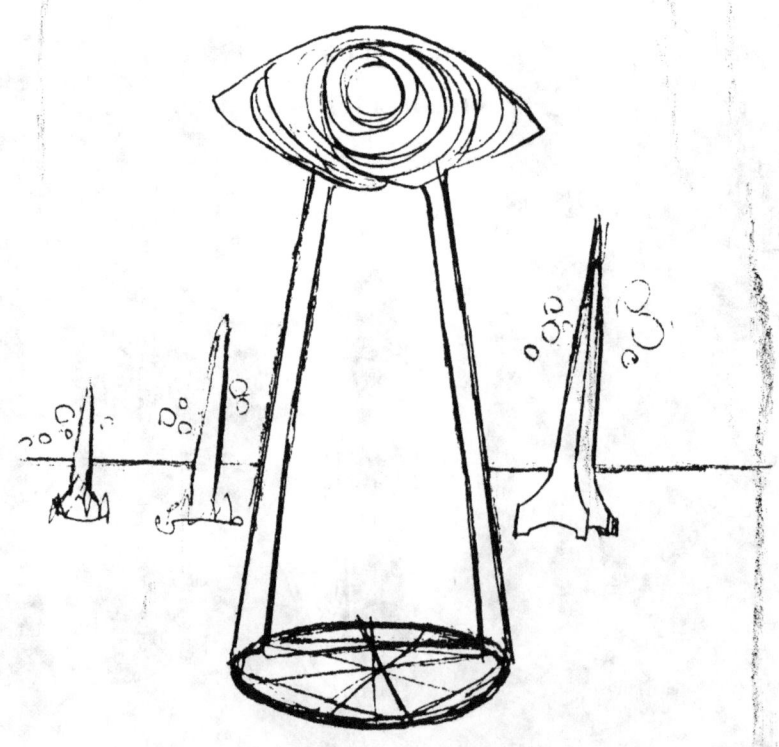

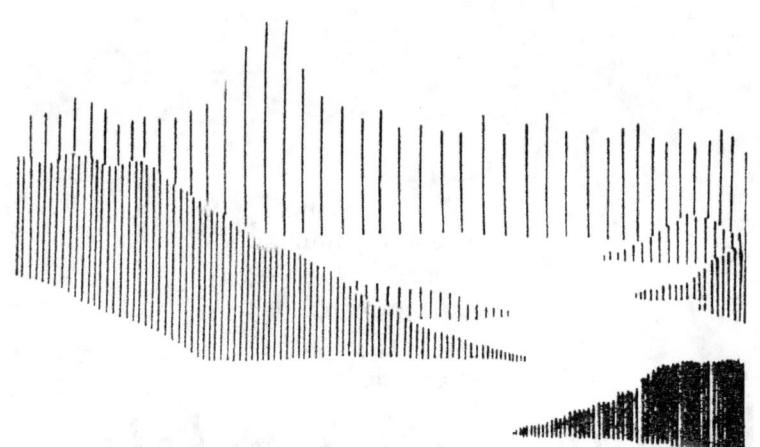

Jimson roots — I love you —
sea moon, running knee
    sweet rue, street walker,
intercity braintrain
    henbane sea fog
Chinese hill mists
    mystery and mandragon
palms, olives, datur
    nepenthes, nightshade
and myrrh
    sky doors
open, beware of half-truths:
    you may ascertain
the wrong half —
    refrain.

FEELINGS

Magic makes many
pictures — eyes are
    deceived, deluded,
deranged, gorged
    feasted, fetished
fooled . . .
    the hands move around
thoughts change minds
    words, ideals,

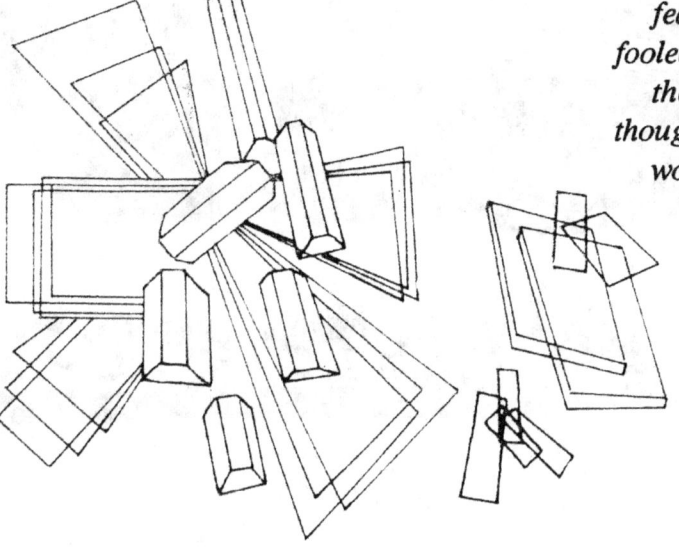

SETI
Why are we not
spending more
money on the search
the mormans spend
ten percent, what
do we do ?

I am the couch potato
with affluenza

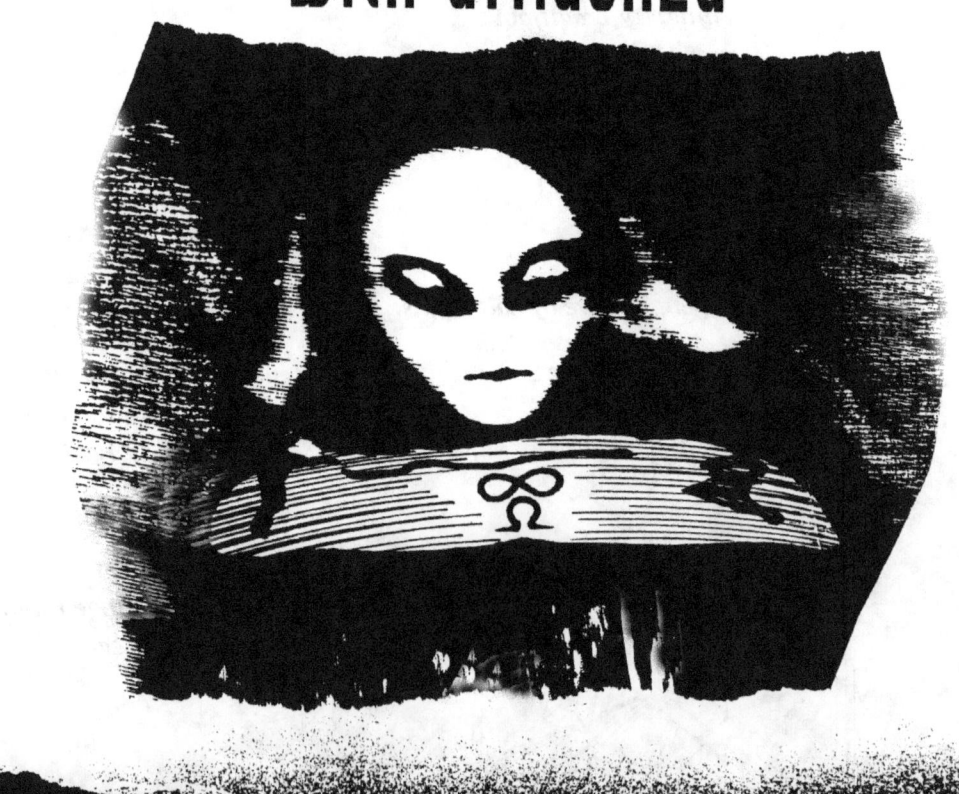

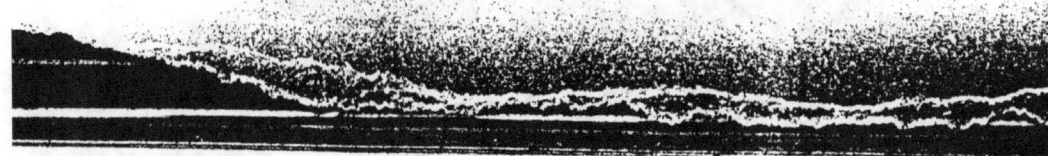

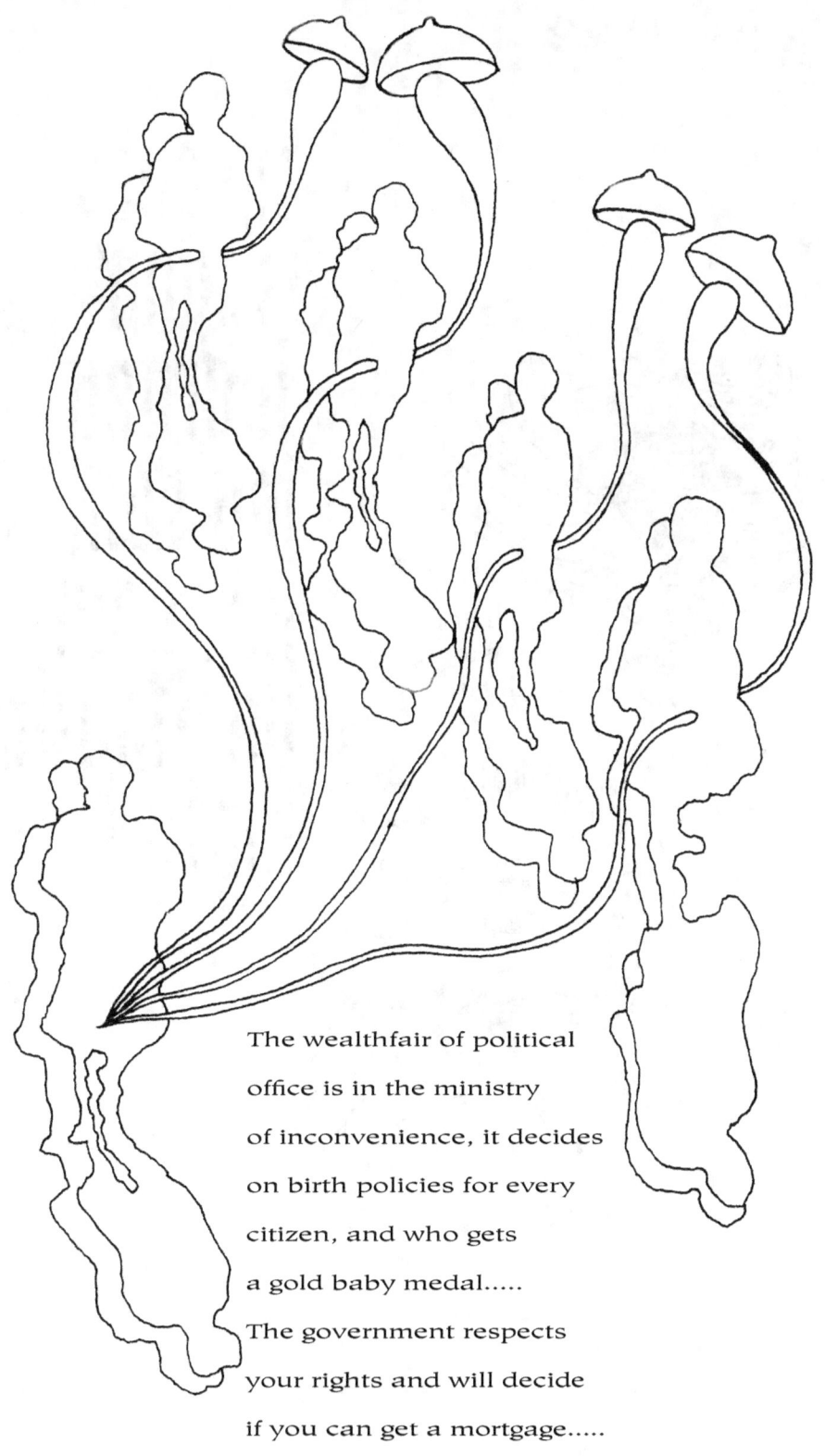

The wealthfair of political
office is in the ministry
of inconvenience, it decides
on birth policies for every
citizen, and who gets
a gold baby medal.....
The government respects
your rights and will decide
if you can get a mortgage.....

Success is your journey my son, not your destination mate !

Other people see things differently !

Choke your chicken beat your penguin

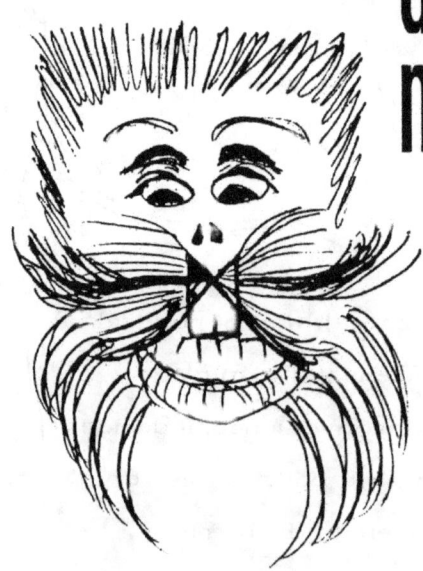

COMPOSITION 1

      Shadows of thought
fade from memory.
      Lights break through
the structure,
      weighing heavily
on the composition.
      The subtle colours
crowd the balance.
      Decision takes hold.
I feel.
      Shapes, segments
return to memory.
      Taste tantalise me.
Doors open
      wider than ever.
Pictures
      tell more,
Answers answered
      define love.

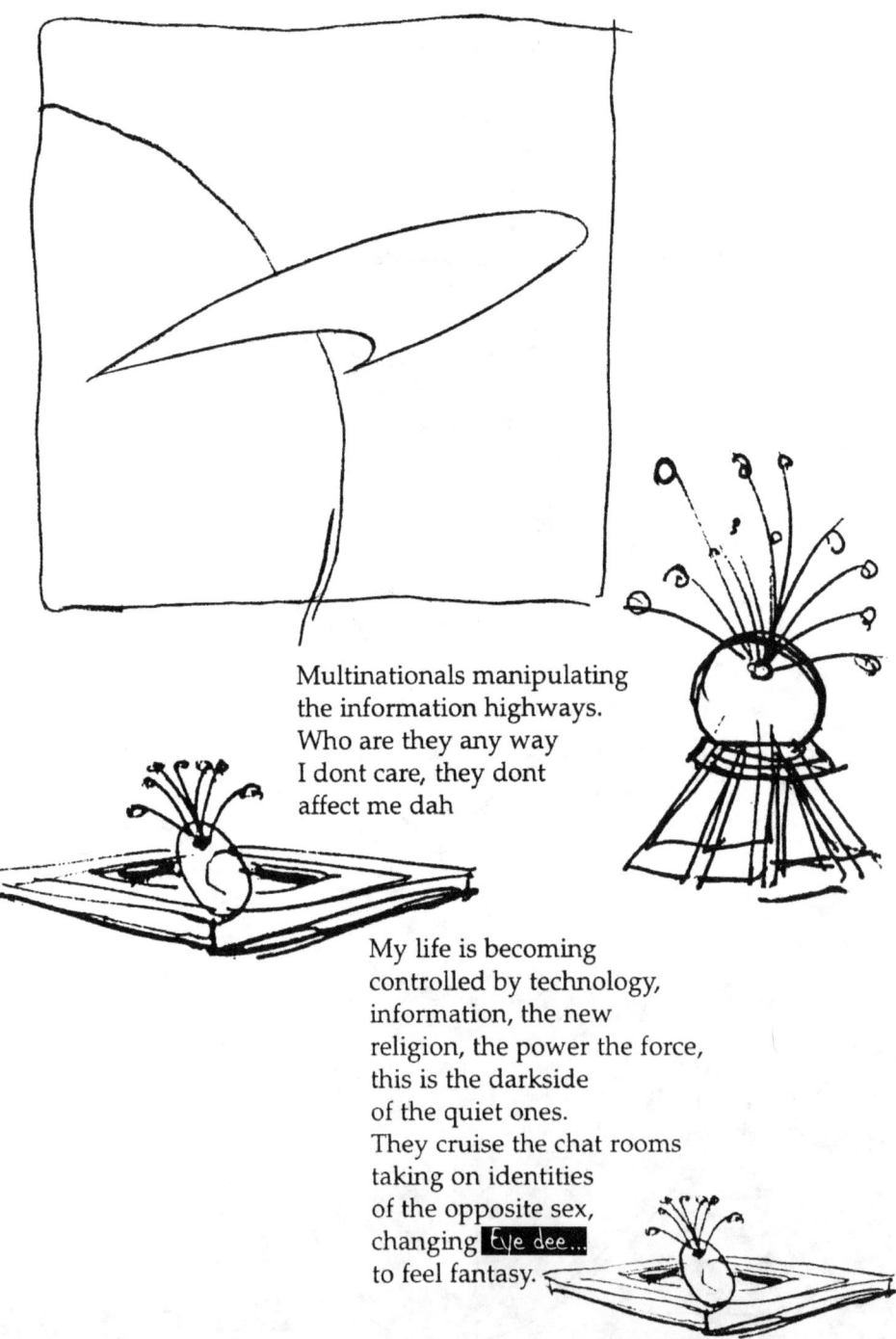

Multinationals manipulating
the information highways.
Who are they any way
I dont care, they dont
affect me dah

My life is becoming
controlled by technology,
information, the new
religion, the power the force,
this is the darkside
of the quiet ones.
They cruise the chat rooms
taking on identities
of the opposite sex,
changing Eye dee...
to feel fantasy.

BORN TO BE

          spots of sunlight
spatter the floor
          artificial winds change
pulsating purpose
          desire demands so much
of young men
          tears descend
did I hurt you?
          quiet peace life's purpose
IUD non-existent
          life starts
new shapes
          so small so large
so destined
          corporate chromo

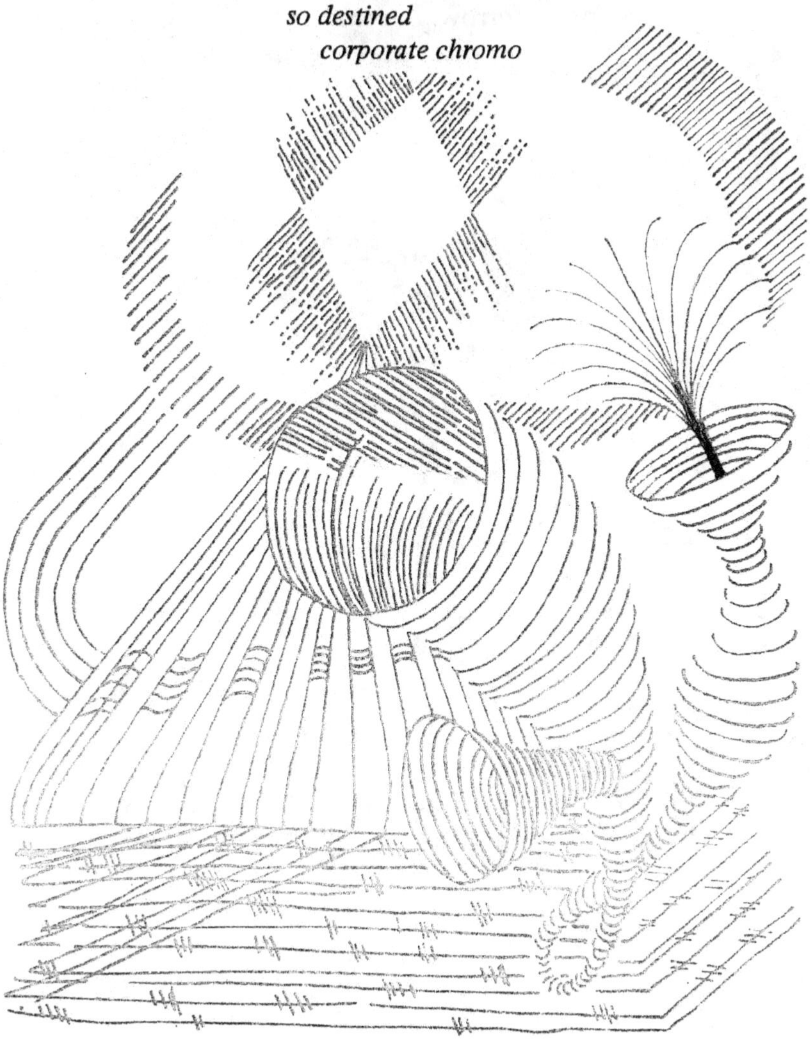

Fill my life with sundays

Fairy street lights
twinkle twinkle twinkle
like comets.
Everyone is going there so fast
for tomorrow you may die
man's head is far above his feat.

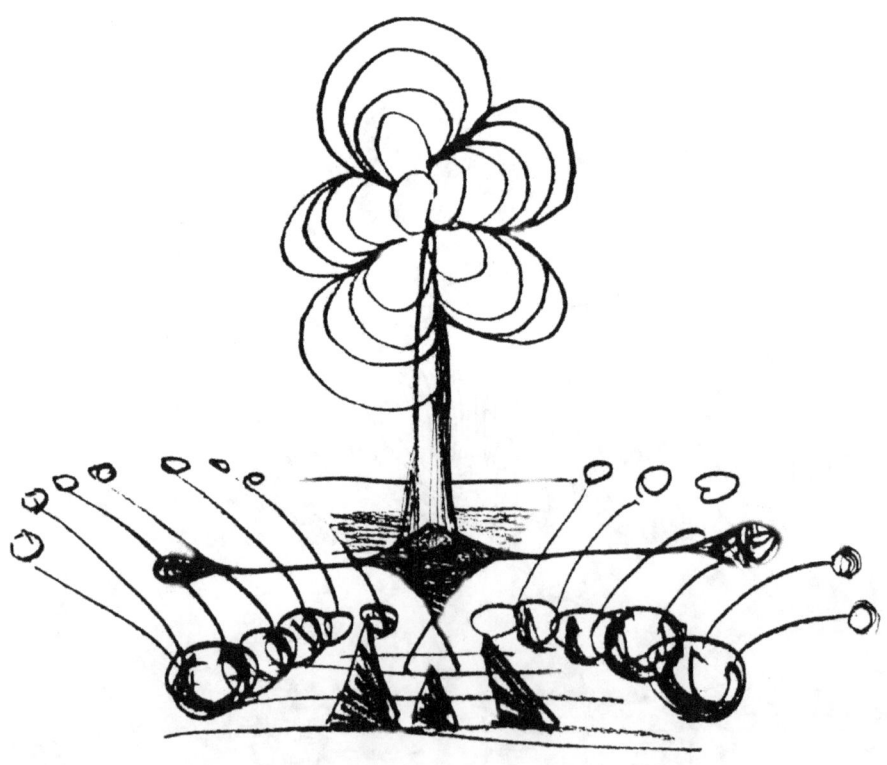

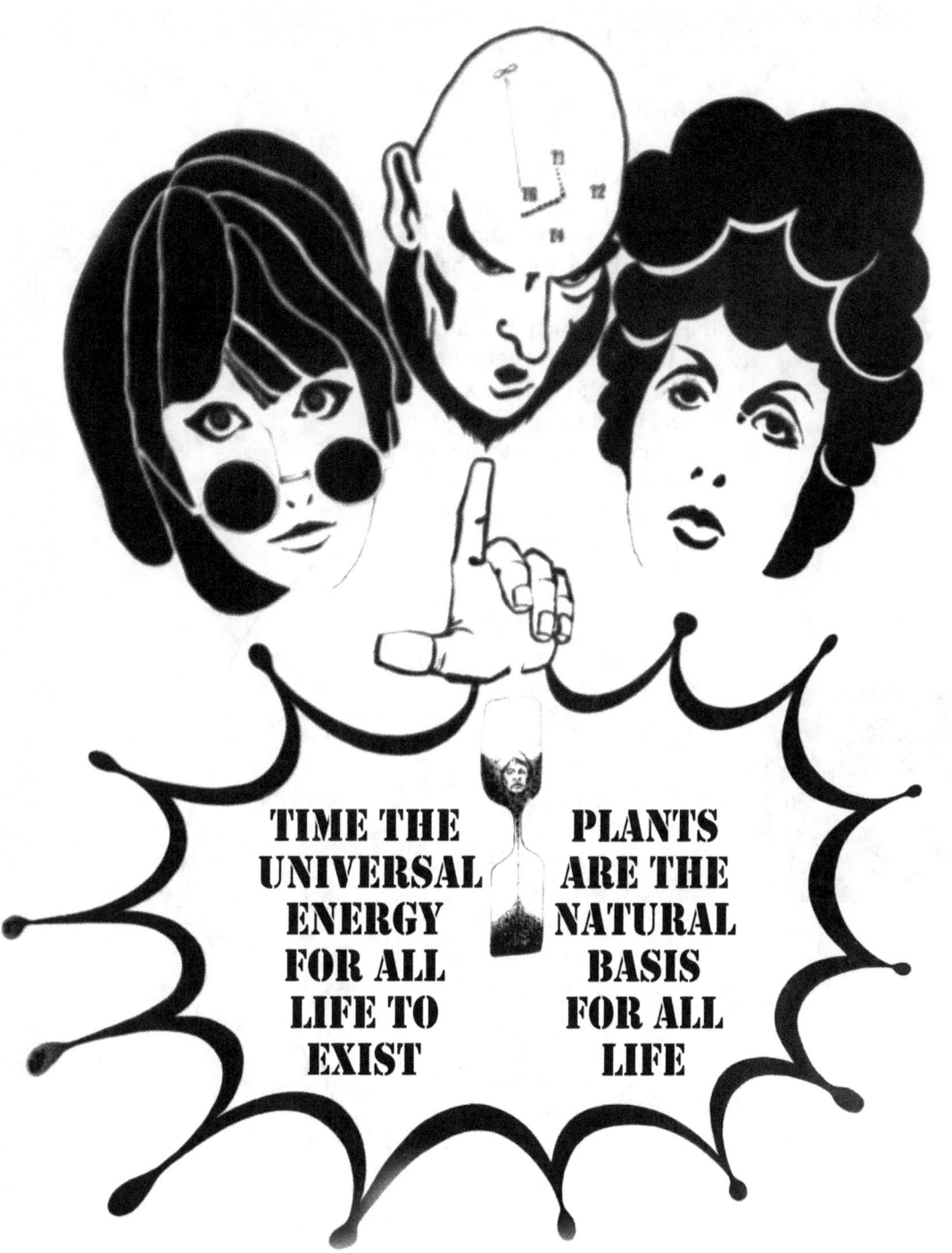

TIME THE
UNIVERSAL
ENERGY
FOR ALL
LIFE TO
EXIST

PLANTS
ARE THE
NATURAL
BASIS
FOR ALL
LIFE

PASSAGE INTO NON-EXISTANCE

Your sexual adjustment
has been a problem.
You may be a player in our wonderful
fortress society, line up with the havenots
and if you are selected and lucky
you will be able to join the haves.
Look back
see the road in which you sat,
do you know really where you are at?
Have you been to Kalamazoo
the lonely quiet times seem so loud
agendas and priorities take you
to where you are at.
You must find in lifes maze
the room without walls.

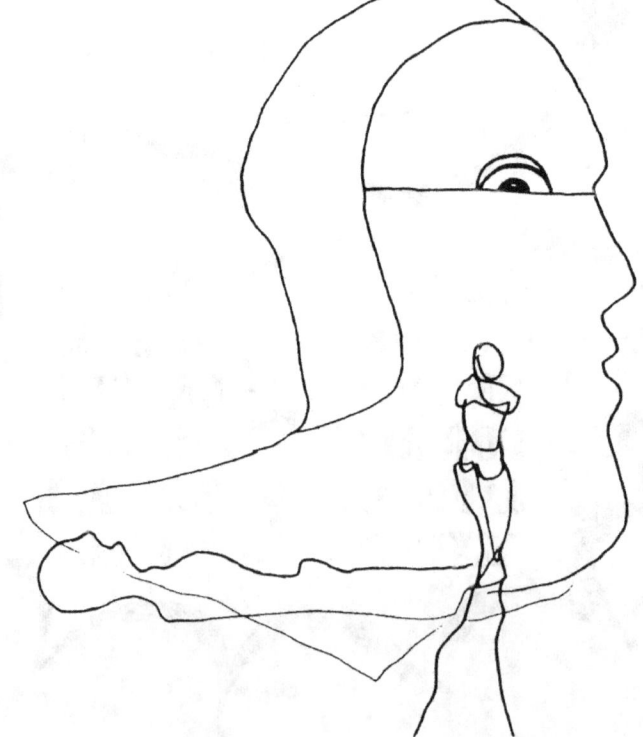

POETS
DREAM OF
FUTURE
WORDS.....

or is it worlds.....

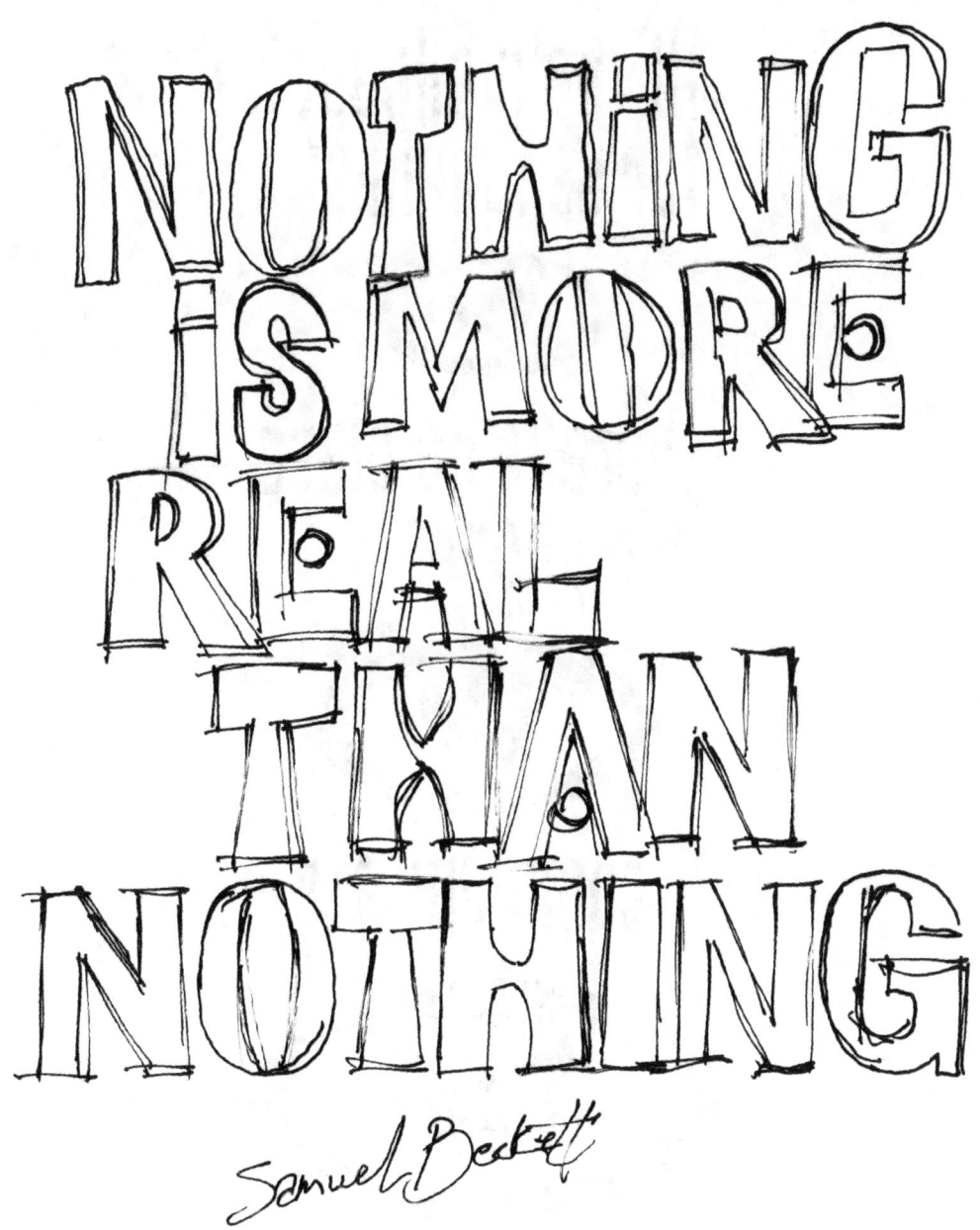

NOTHING IS MORE REAL THAN NOTHING

Samuel Beckett

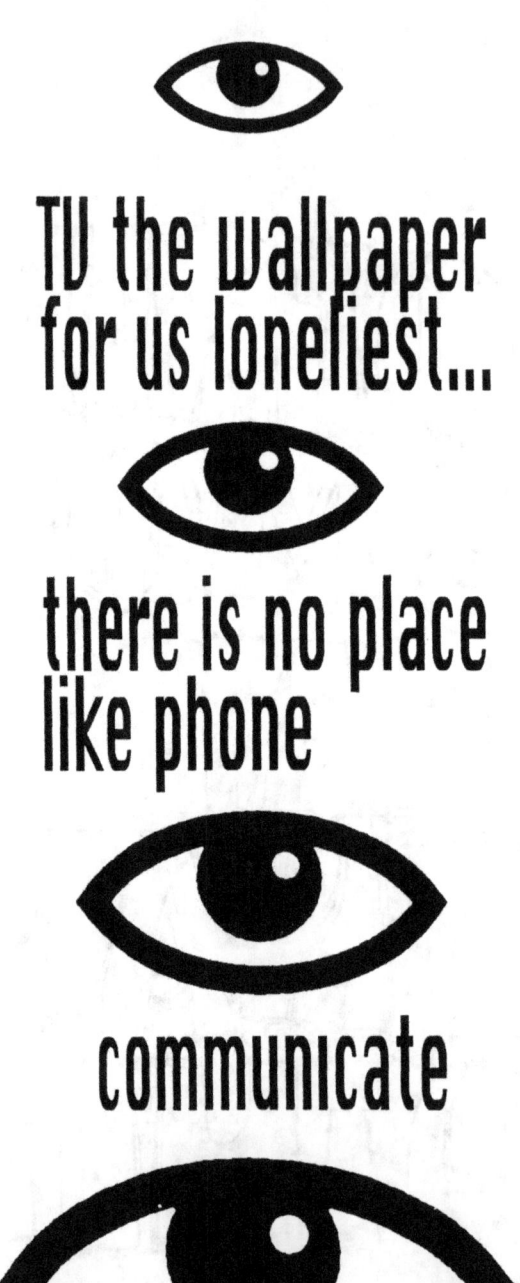

TV the wallpaper for us loneliest...

there is no place like phone

communicate

Wired without wires, connected, controlled in the web of infection, direction, eye see the end of selection in twitter and facebook rejection!

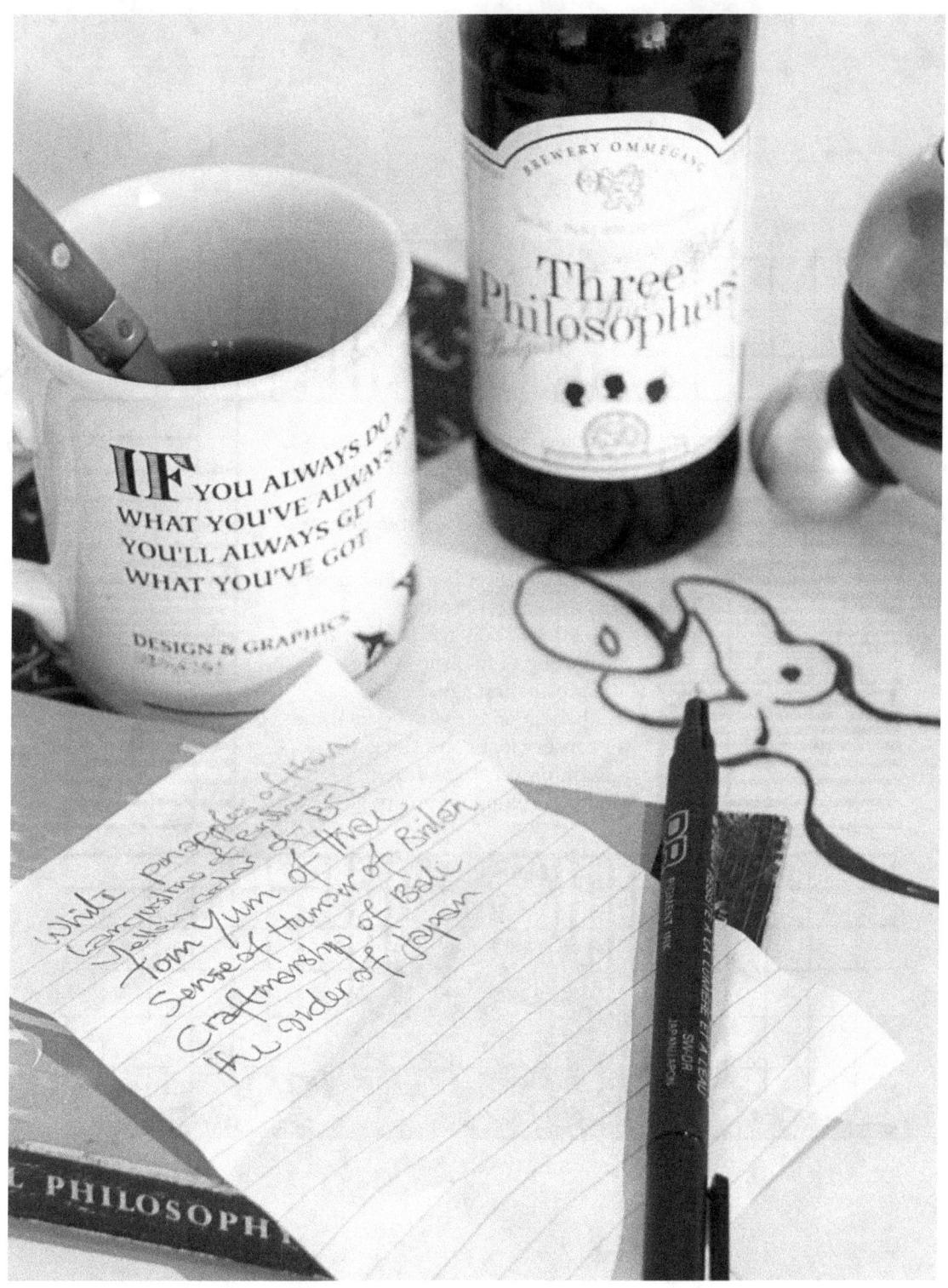

I thought I knew the way. till I saw your point of view. Now I have to kill you.

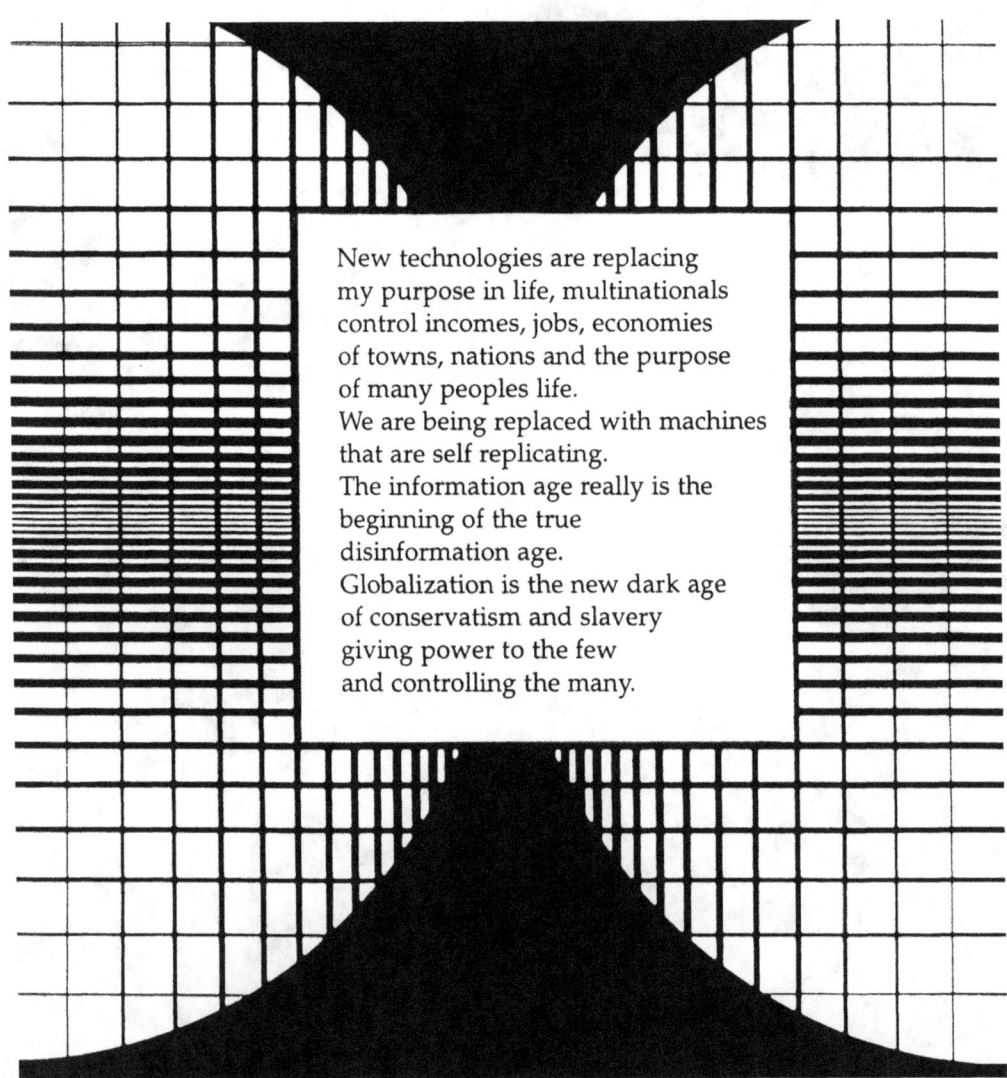

New technologies are replacing
my purpose in life, multinationals
control incomes, jobs, economies
of towns, nations and the purpose
of many peoples life.
We are being replaced with machines
that are self replicating.
The information age really is the
beginning of the true
disinformation age.
Globalization is the new dark age
of conservatism and slavery
giving power to the few
and controlling the many.

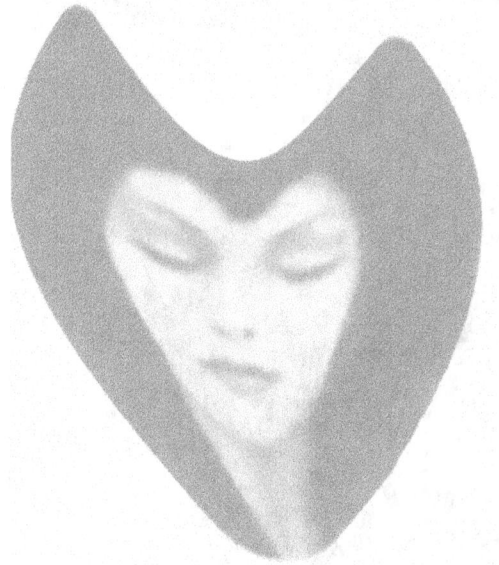

Heartacor.....It is the new miracle compound cellulive..... Stop the aging process and rejuvenate you dna, no need to come back as a snake. Your energy level will go from grey to wild, making you twenty years younger, drown in the fountain of youth. Side effects may include, energy, better skin, less wrinkles, laughter, attraction and sex.....buyer beware!

Lets play spoons..... Some bums I realy love more than the lines they are drawn with. I would call our book of love "Misfortune at the house of spoons". Tonal value and beauty is always better by candlelight.....At times of desire I wish I had a spoonerism for my driven fire.

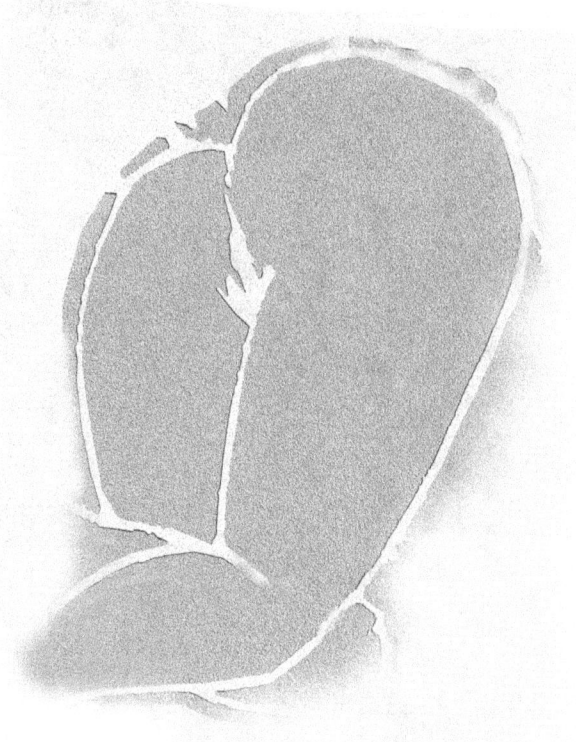

Awarded best of show by Walker Universal Arts

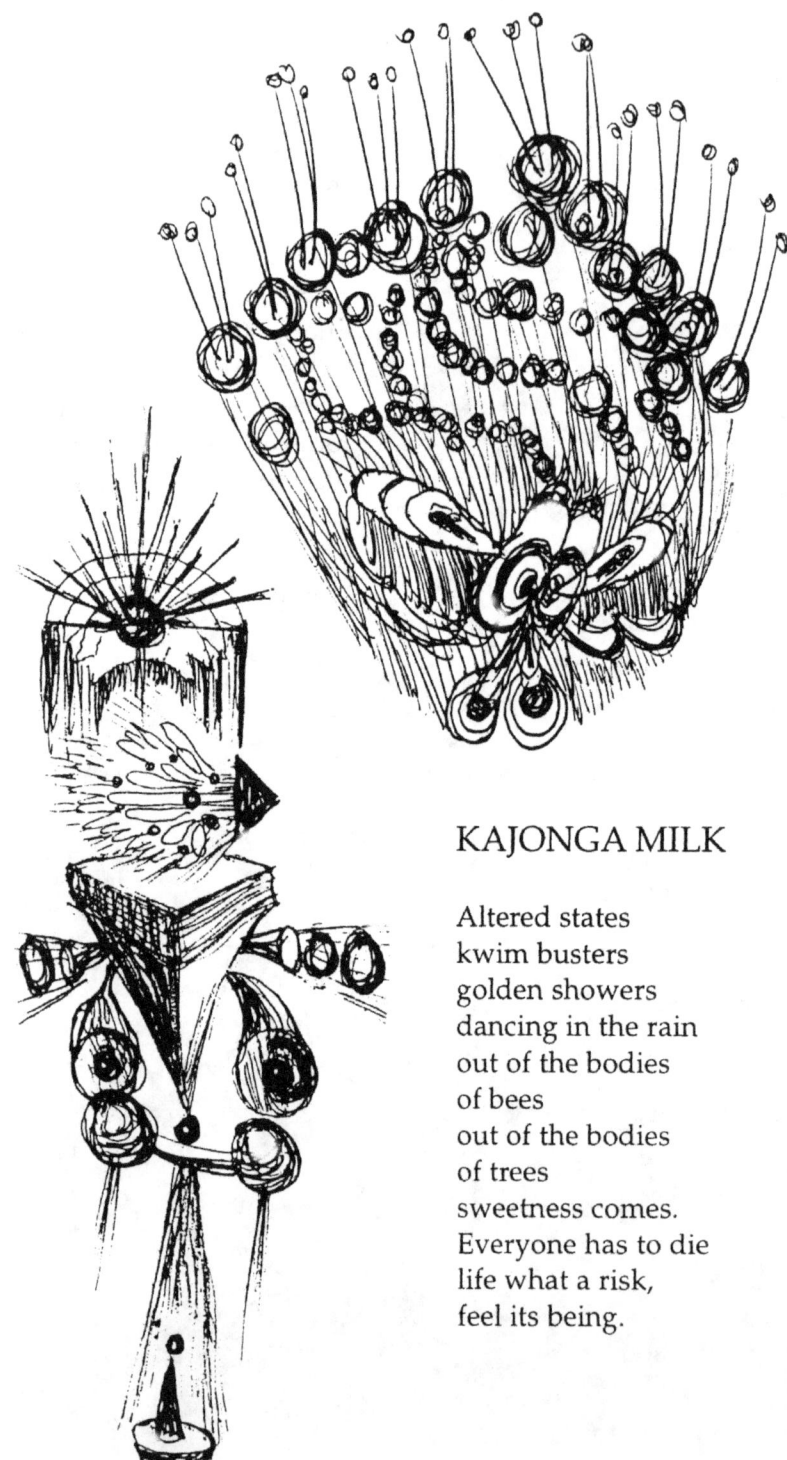

KAJONGA MILK

Altered states
kwim busters
golden showers
dancing in the rain
out of the bodies
of bees
out of the bodies
of trees
sweetness comes.
Everyone has to die
life what a risk,
feel its being.

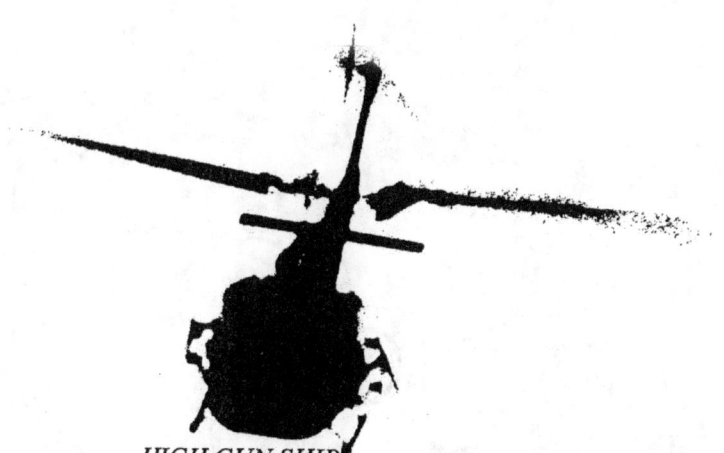

HIGH GUN SHIPS
With apologies to people being so small.

    For us:
space between birth and death.
    Lines intersected by thoughts,
patience spread between time,
    happiness not sought.
Sad shadows, we mime
    in horizontal lines, were caught.
Man, bad vertical rhyme.
    Certainties that are never certain —
decisions that are undecisive —
    waiting, and what for?
Time that is timeless . . .

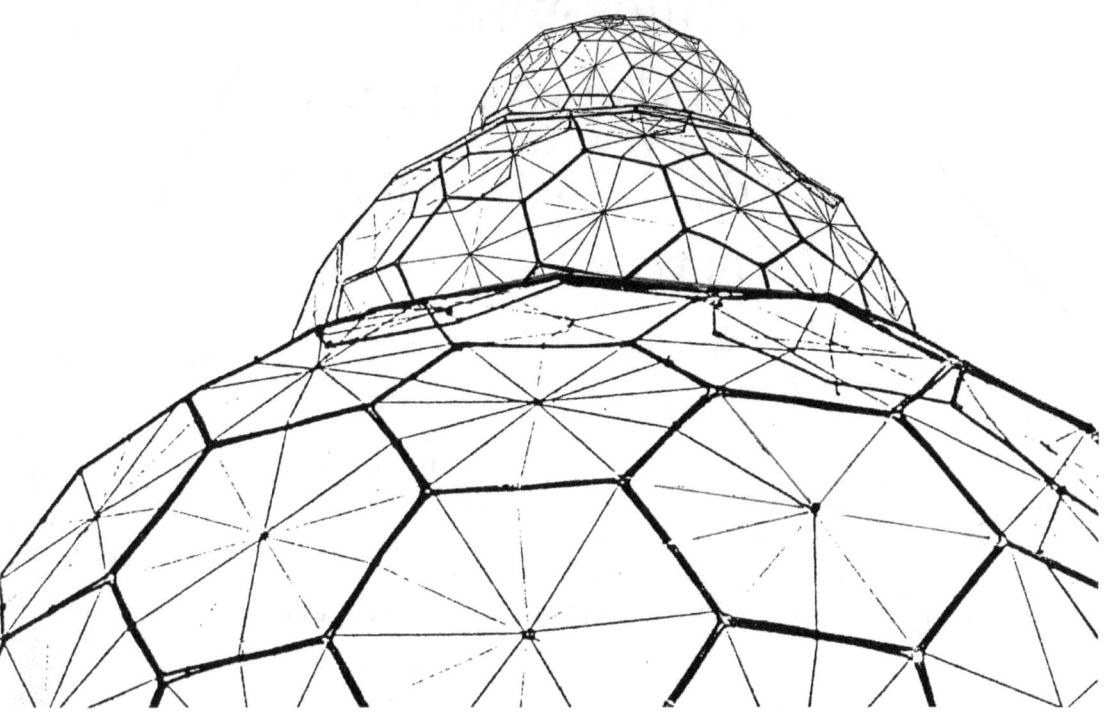

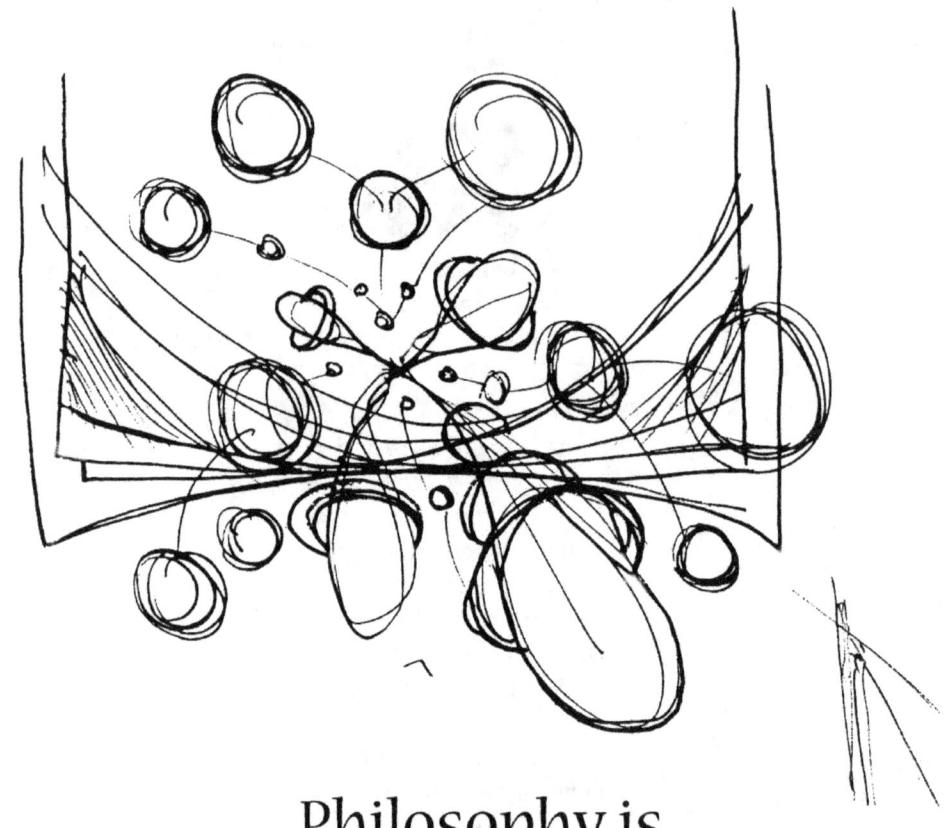

Philosophy is to the real world as masturbation is to sex.

Karl Marx

Karl called capitalism the dictatorship of the bourgeoisie.....
The wealthy society runs the world order for their own benefit!
As you know we have a wonderful classless society now, that
is strong and free! When did he write this? He was sixty four
when they buried him in the highgate cemetery London.

SEAVIEWS FROM THE BEDSITTING ROOM

    Fields — all colours, all sizes —
positioned residence.
    Thoughts, wants —
I wait for breakfast —
    sounds of gulls,
hulls, shaped gracefully,
    ships, the sea
quiet giant.
    Tapering morning light
forming light sculptures
    on prison walls —
the bed, the room
    close in on me.
Cozy, I stretch,
    touch the sides.
Shadows of life
    restrict my view.

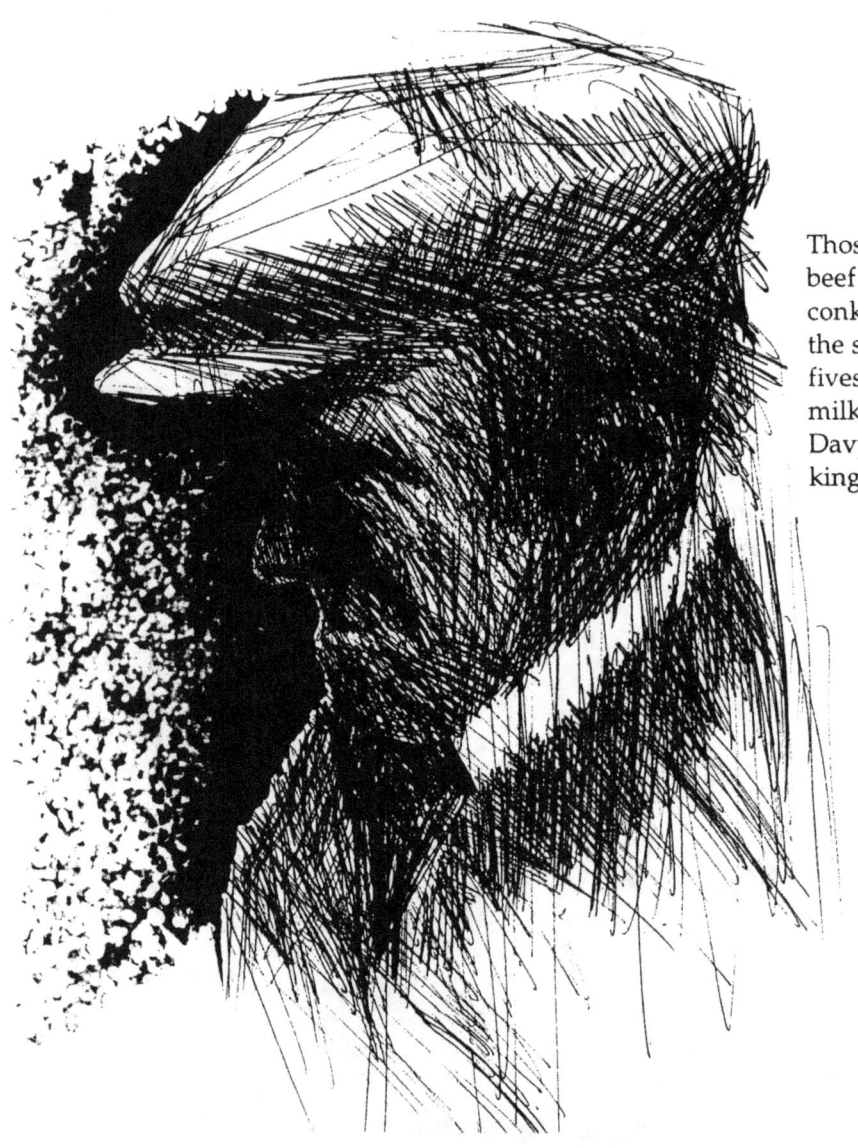

Those nostalgic days
beef teas at elevensies
conkers in october
the suez trouble again
fivestones and their
milkmaid blouses.
Davy Crocket was
king of the wild frontier.

124

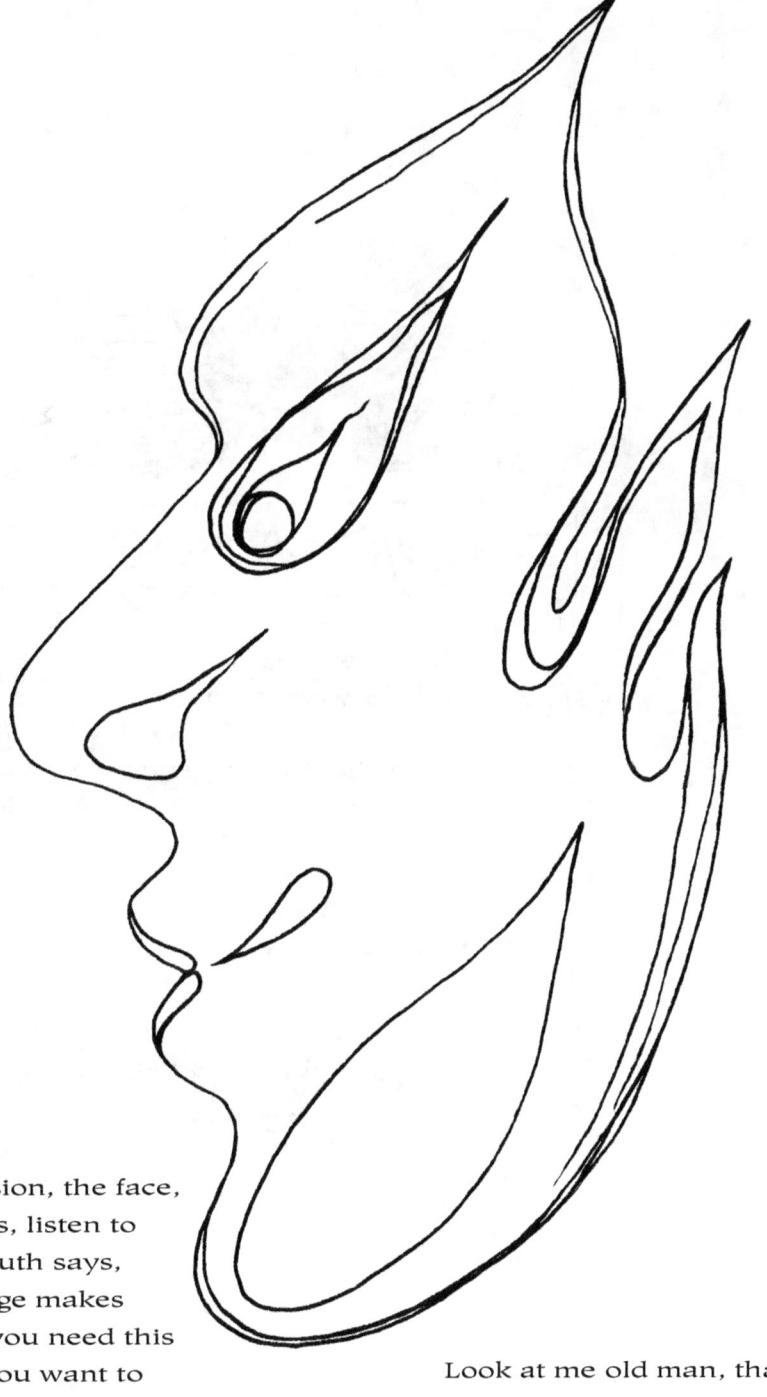

First impression, the face,
then the eyes, listen to
what the mouth says,
body language makes
contact, do you need this
person, do you want to
make friends.....Lets face
it, it all depends!

Look at me old man, that's
a great poetic story.....
Thanks Neil Young

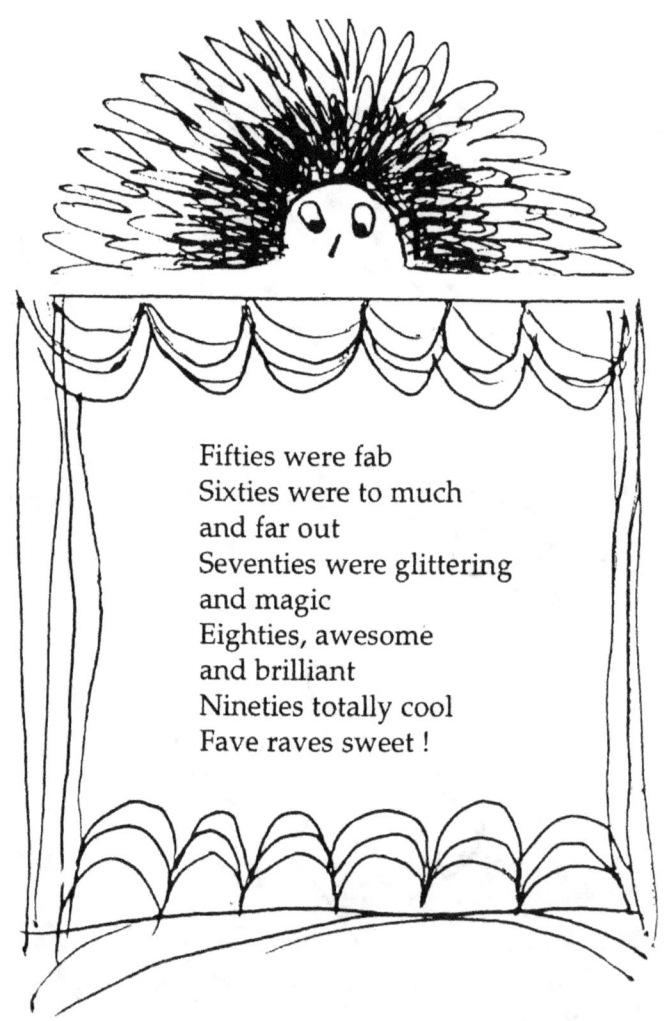

Fifties were fab
Sixties were to much
and far out
Seventies were glittering
and magic
Eighties, awesome
and brilliant
Nineties totally cool
Fave raves sweet !

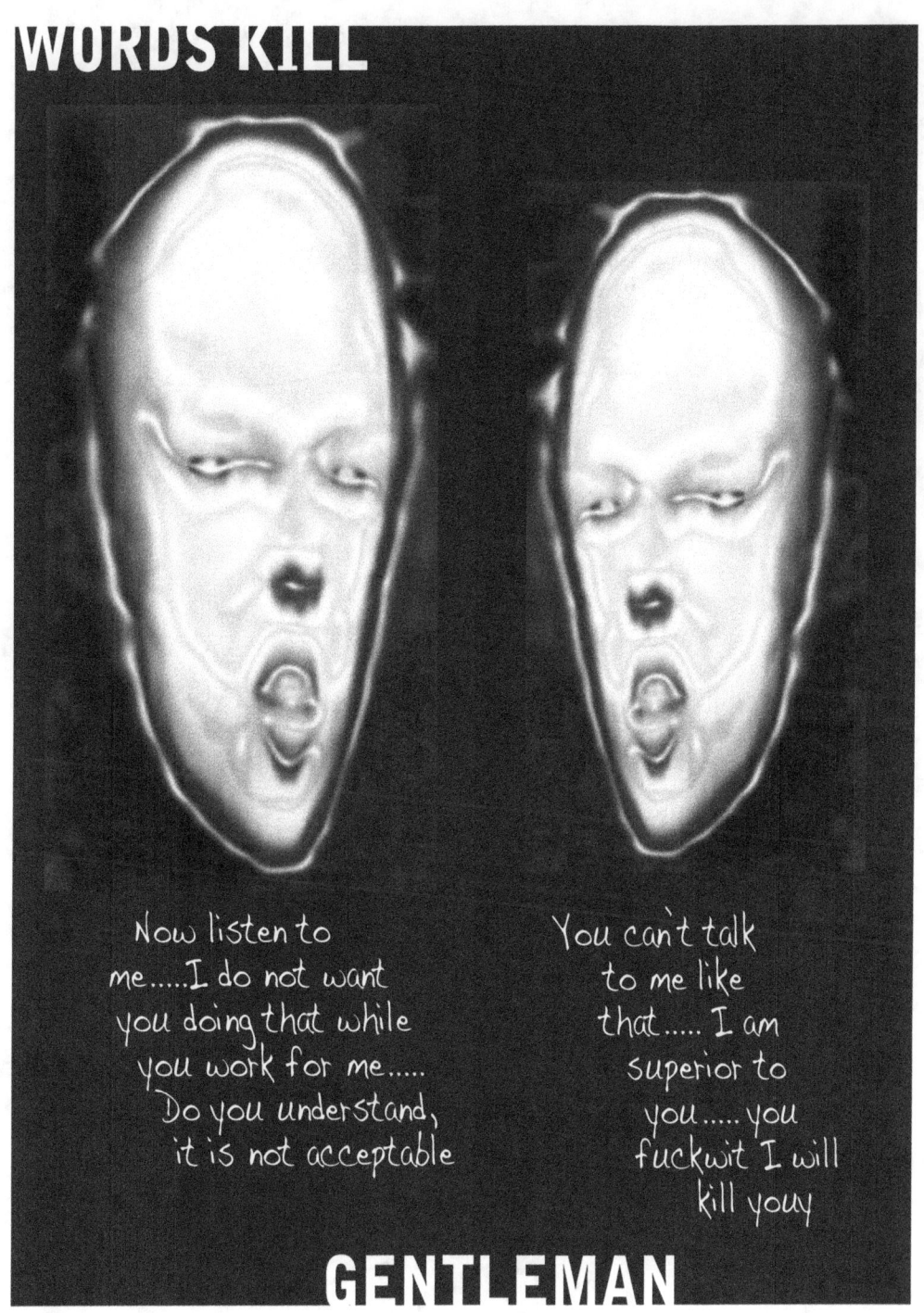

WORDS KILL

Now listen to
me.....I do not want
you doing that while
you work for me.....
Do you understand,
it is not acceptable

You can't talk
to me like
that..... I am
superior to
you..... you
fuckwit I will
kill youy

GENTLEMAN

We persist in the belief that we are
isolated, are we a part of the whole
earth-universe?
Now I have this computer I am
Hemingway.
To see I need light and I have the power
to become whatever I visualise.
My thoughts actually create
my physical existance and reality.

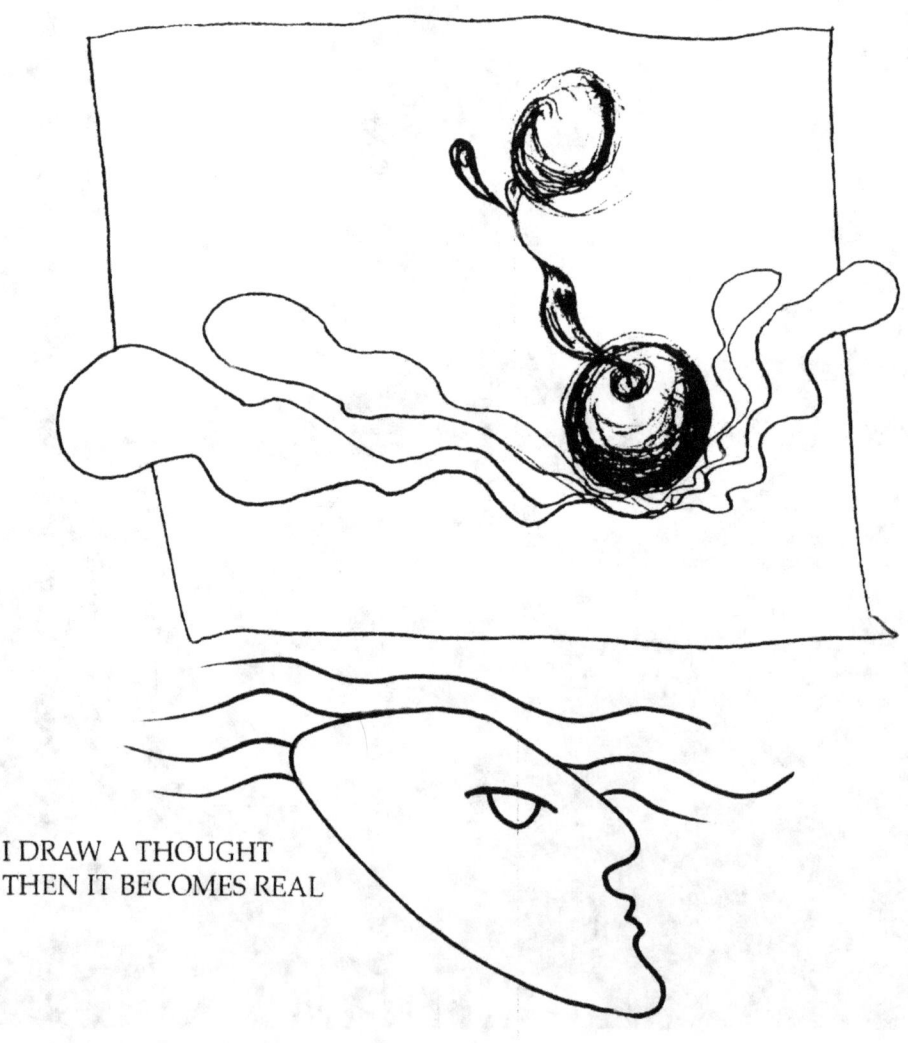

I DRAW A THOUGHT
THEN IT BECOMES REAL

When I am gone who will do my work, how am I a genetic copy of my great great grandfather? He sailed, exploring the earth and protecting his wealth from the Spanish, he had to fight them in wars.....

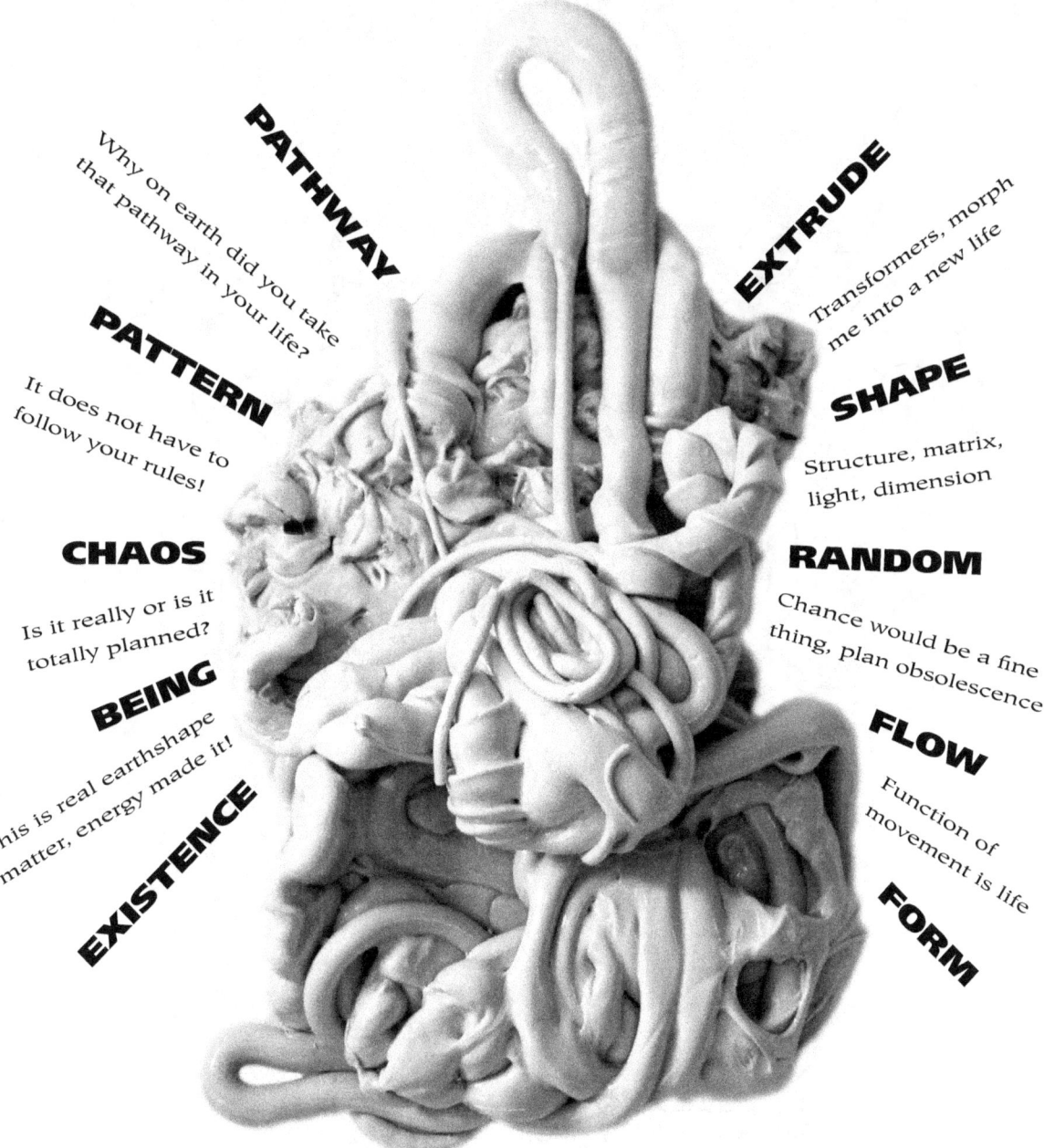

PATHWAY
Why on earth did you take that pathway in your life?

EXTRUDE
Transformers, morph me into a new life

PATTERN
It does not have to follow your rules!

SHAPE
Structure, matrix, light, dimension

CHAOS
Is it really or is it totally planned?

RANDOM
Chance would be a fine thing, Plan obsolescence

BEING
This is real earthshape matter, energy made it!

FLOW
Function of movement is life

EXISTENCE

FORM

This page is created from an extruded blob which was selected by my conditioned brain while searching London's land fill dump after reading "Thus spake zarathustra". What made my decision to select this priceless form of object and carry it around the world with me?.

I blow the moonlight
thru your genetic profile
sweet jesus !!
infowars.com

..... you are wot u see, hear and fink.....

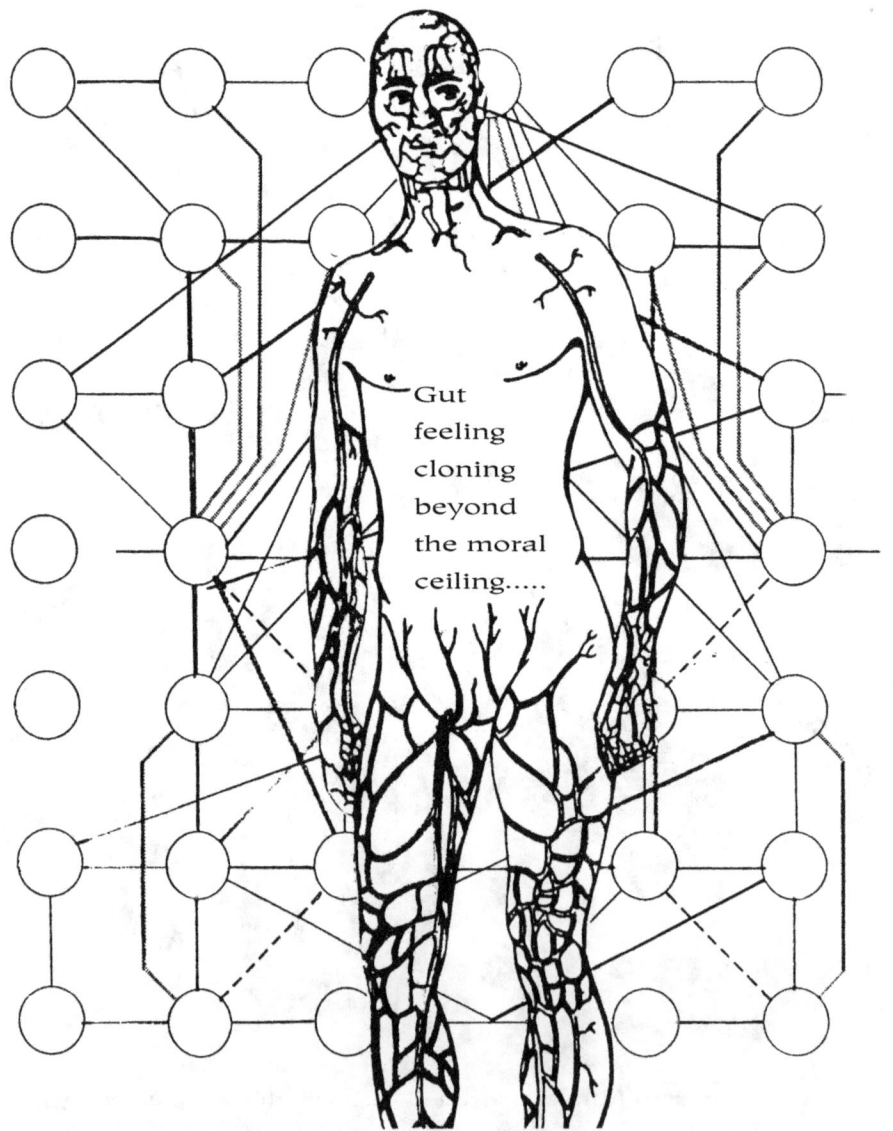

Gut
feeling
cloning
beyond
the moral
ceiling.....

.....Sorry can't draw good feet.....
Liar liar your pants are on fire
draw that next.....

Age is all
in the mind
the trick is
to stop it
trickling
down into
your body!

Employ
robotic
devices
to enhance
your
sexual
experience

The best
thing in
my life is
my phone
I can not
live
without it
it is with me
on my body
24/7

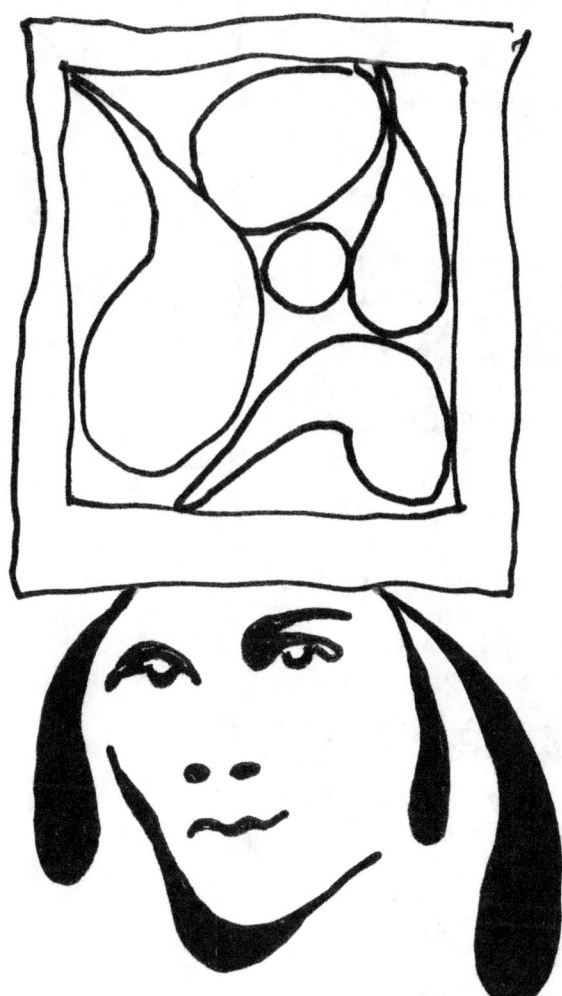

Is this
abstraction
the mistake
of passion
or is it a
meaningless
doodle?

Technology
will change
the new human
existence
to a post
human future.....

On what
journey do
you really
get to know
yourself.....
The stuff
you own
owns you.....
Till you learn
to leave it
behind.

It fits my image
It fits my body
I feel at home with it
I luv the shape
I am comfortable with it.....
That is my proman nine
genital implant.

CHANGE YOUR MIND

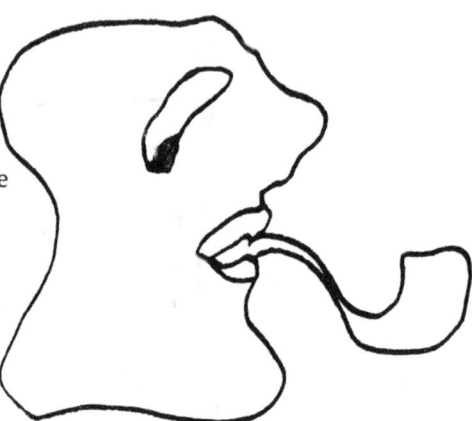

I will need a frontal labotomy
I'd rather have a bottle in front of me
that will rearrange my inabitions.

My mind now where is it ?
Some religions tell me other
religions do not have Souls
and we know the Soul is the
Access card to heaven.
Have a heart the soul is in
the mind right ! or in the brain
or in the pope's SOUL TRAIN.

Agnostic and suffering life's pain
this is your chance
to step back and assess life,
refocus on satisfaction, ambition,
desire, wants and needs
and then play doctor feelgood
with your purpose and path.

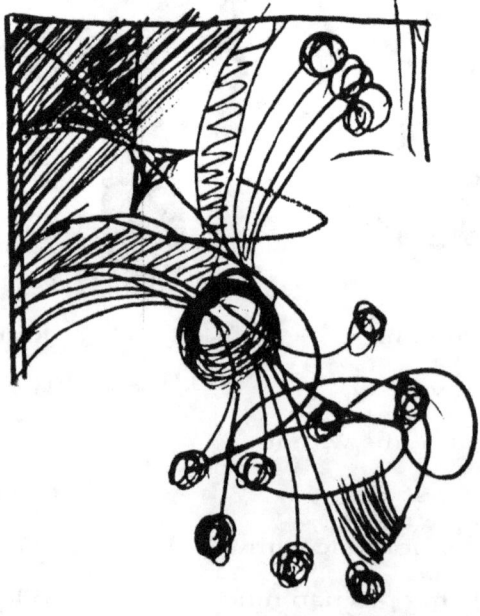

UNTITLED 2

Squeeze, rip, tear,
pour, crush, stir,
blend, beat, chop.
Jo White had eyes
for all women,
especially mixers
in your fly . . .
said with a mouthful of rye . . .
never shut doors,
flaws, faulty floors —
a belt of cold air.

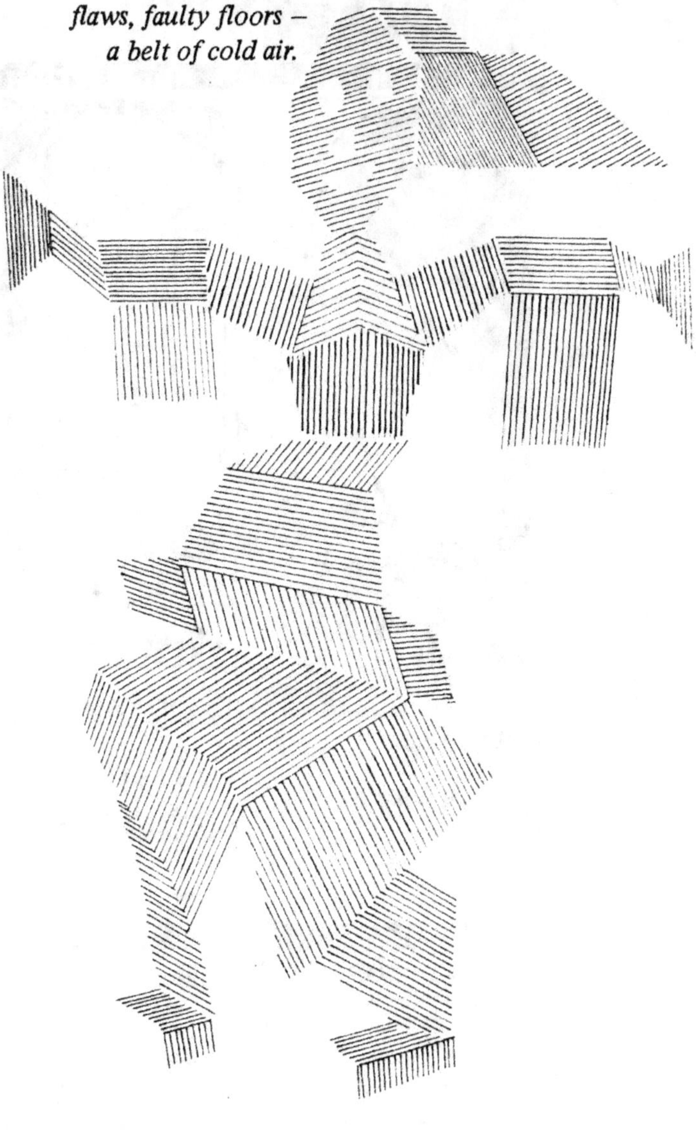

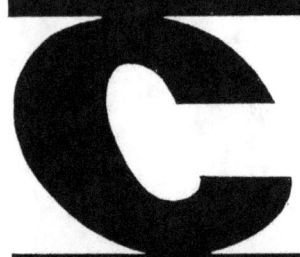

SOAR

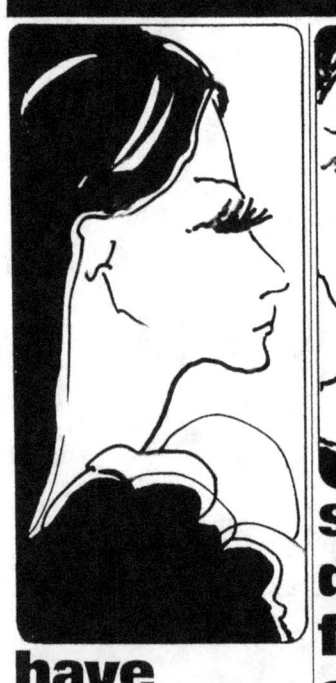 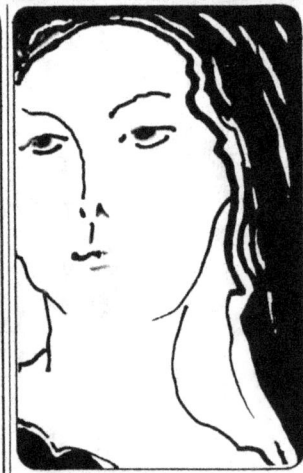

**have
more**

**slide
down
floor
count
score**

round roundabout loser

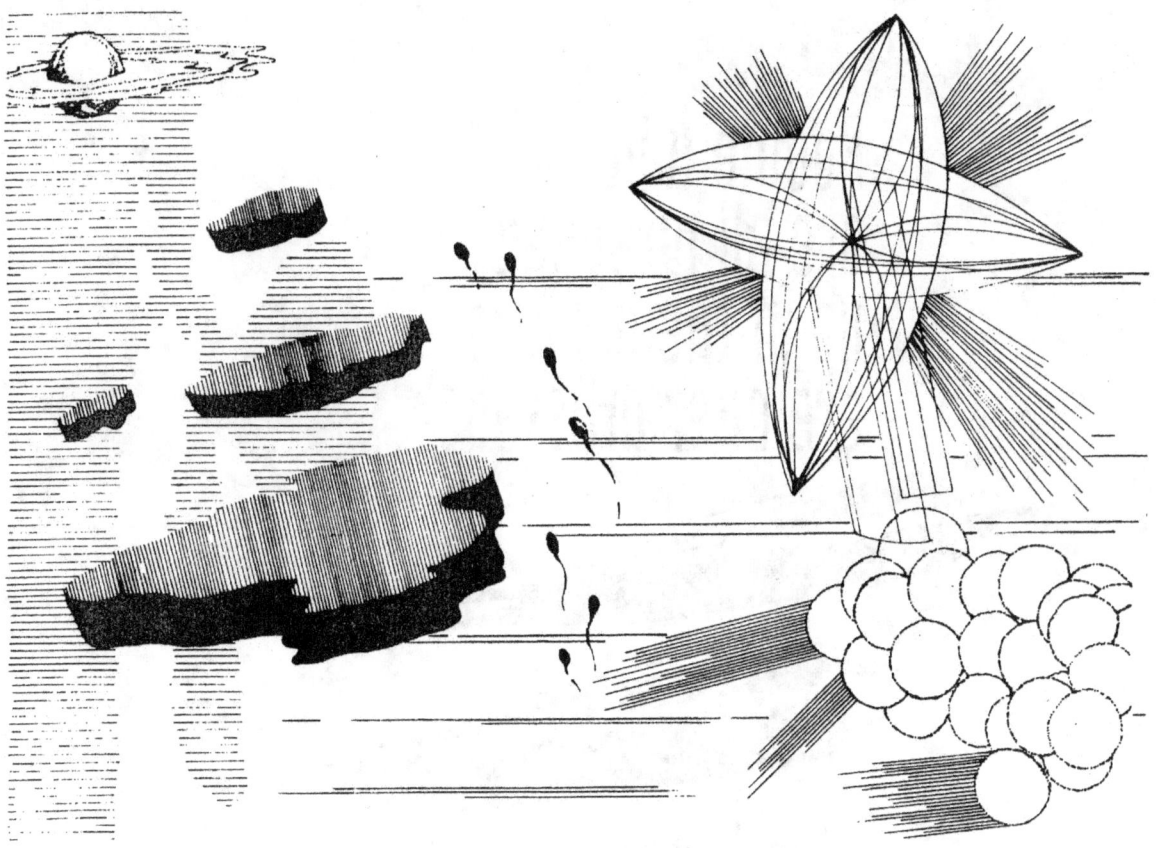

Pieces of the planet

float around my head

fragments left in my alzheimer's memory,

am I still in bed?

The universal drawing line, brakes

where my arthritic fingers can't bend.....

My brain searches for the end

in my artfull dream.

Obscene, you know I am watching you sleeping....

Fine as wine, can you feel it this time,

on my life's adventure I dine.....

Gourmet patterns in the floor tiles

draw pictures in the empty spaces between

the fragments of my mind!

People who
are all wrapped
up in themselves
are over dressed

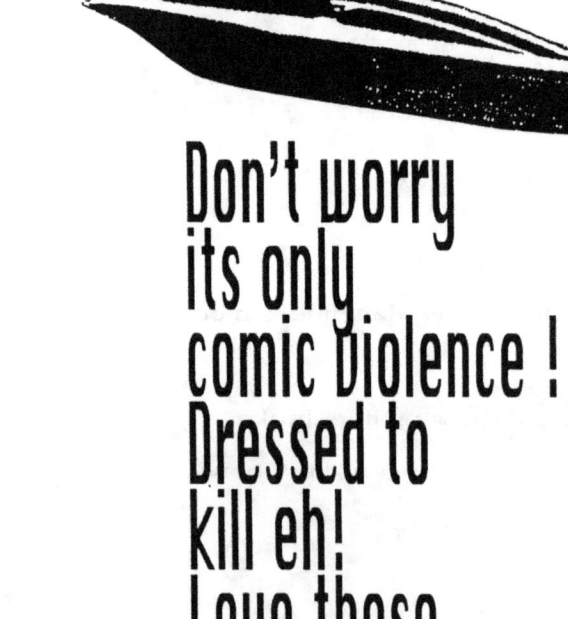

Don't worry
its only
comic violence !
Dressed to
kill eh!
Love those
chem trails

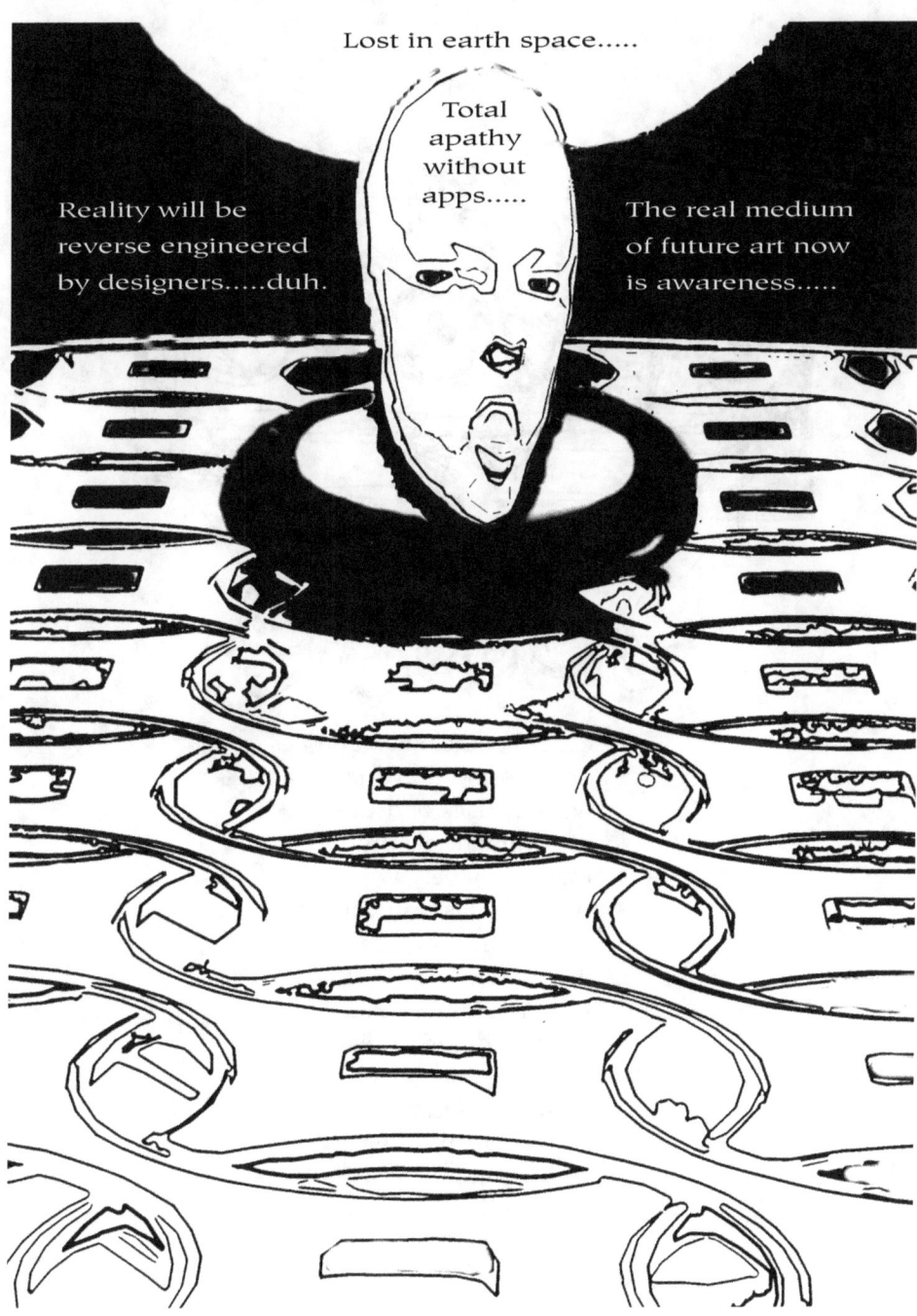

The challenge is to look out of all the windows from the house of your life on to the perspective of your surroundings, to assess what needs changing.....Through imagination, you can create new unbelievable realities. You may well ask why this drawing?

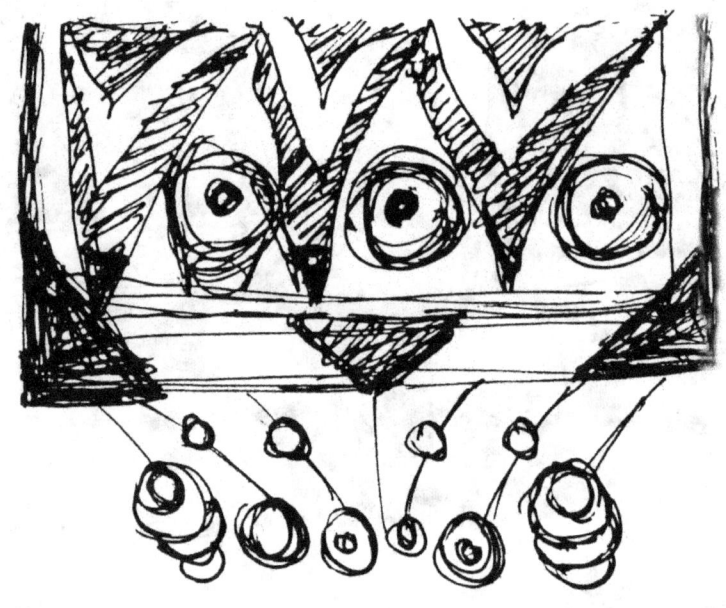

Clocks and clouds, doodles,
designs and drawings
with the lack of drugs
are different pictures
for you to see.
Age how fast can you go
wish with good times
it would go slow.
I did not know belts
came in different sizes
till I was thirty five.
Well one of these days
I will look like the
picture on my
driving licence !
Yeah right denial
rules OK.

MONTAGE

In construction and installation means mounting.....Sweet!

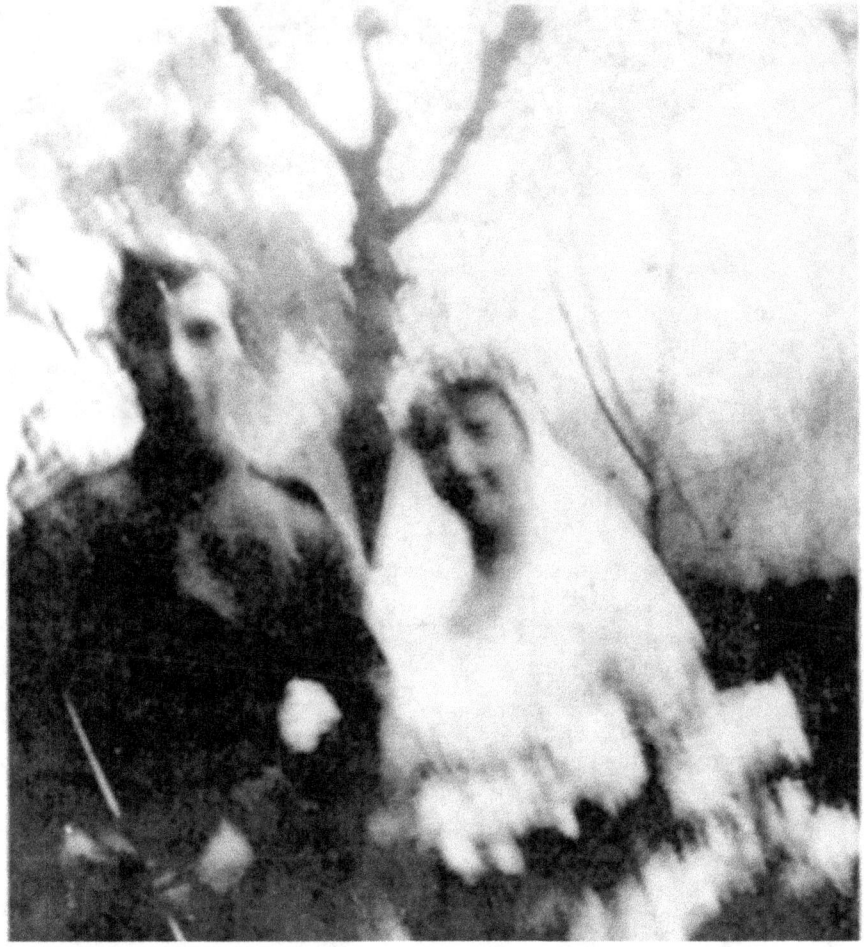

Look back at the grand parents generation, how did they live like that? They were young once, romantic, refined, randy, radical, resistance, and movie star hot hot.....If they knew what I know now.....Time travel, will it ever come and call, I doubt it will give benefits for all. They taught your mother, father.....Without a moan, they went out the door to war and never came home.

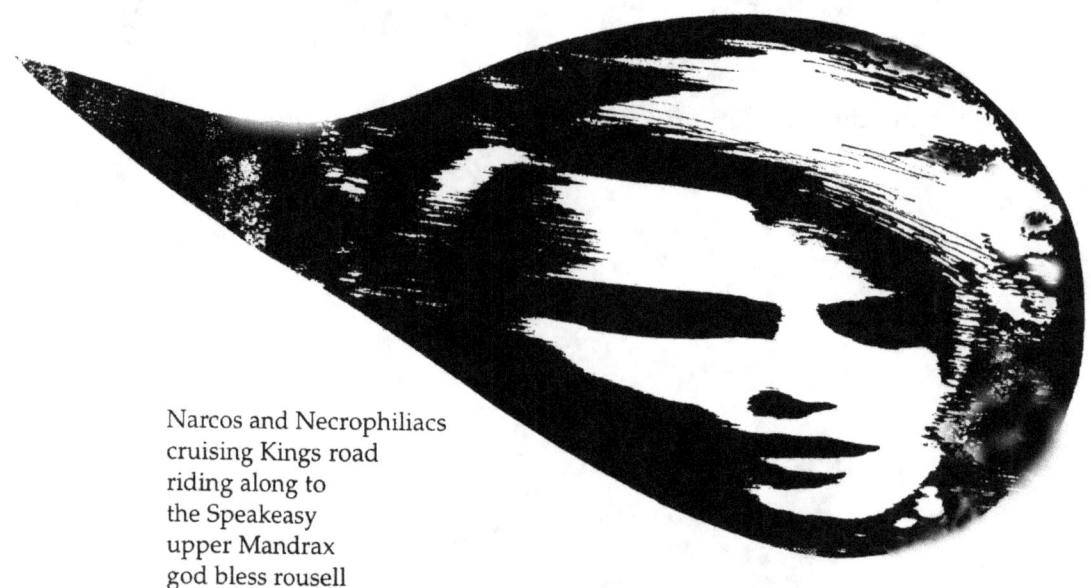

Narcos and Necrophiliacs
cruising Kings road
riding along to
the Speakeasy
upper Mandrax
god bless rousell
trap door spotting
in upper Regent street

at last we get into
the Speakeasy
cocooned in its
psychedelic stomach .
our convulsions start
Taj Mahal live again
who is in the line up
tonight ?
Six white shields
bring outstanding
beauty to every
body and every face.

Sixteen hours latter
the room has become
a gyroscope.
my eyes open up
the ceiling is a
pattern in a cyclonic
vision above me.
Green microdot
rules the cerebellum.
Oh Well ! Mick Fleetwood,
what happened
where are we NOW !

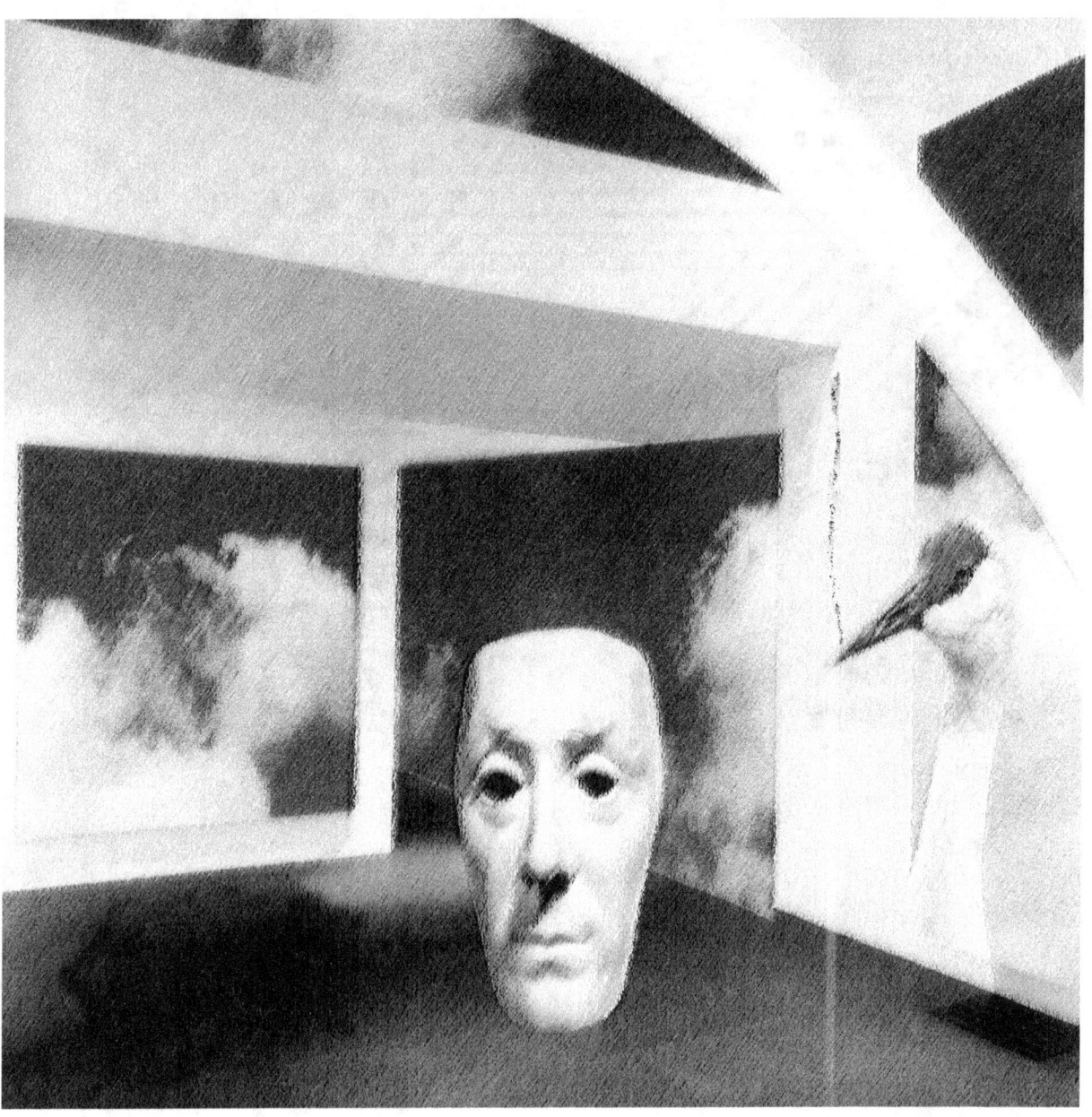

Max's room in Venice, Where Margaret, a little crested crown bird
watches.....Art is a precious stone, like the walls in this museum room.
We are all masks of what is inside us.....Do artichokes design rooms,
houses and buildings for themselves or us?

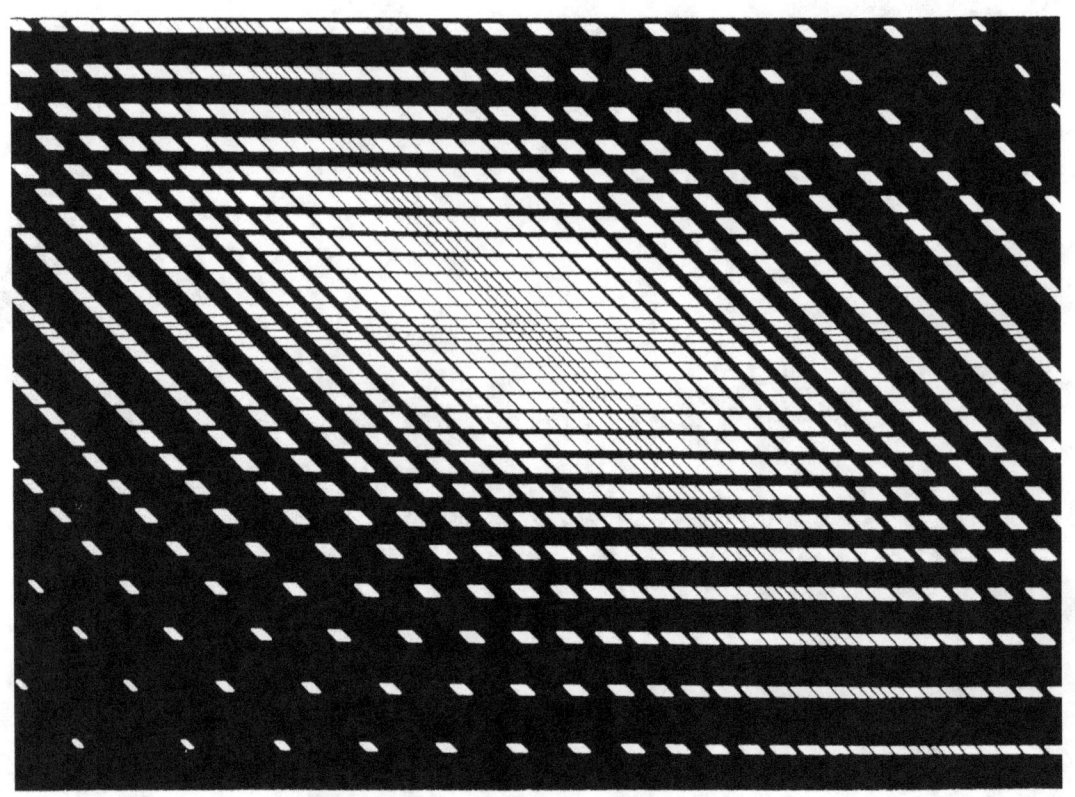

Silence sounds like the brightness of light.

You can hear me,
Your ears are not painted on !

thanks Mum!

Life is seldom fully enjoyed, still six people
watch you.....You want privacy and nine acres
of garden so you can walk around the house
naked. Sex is communication for man's final
destination.....China's new population, loose a
womens generation, shout and spout only men
come out.....The young generation need a utube
demonstration!

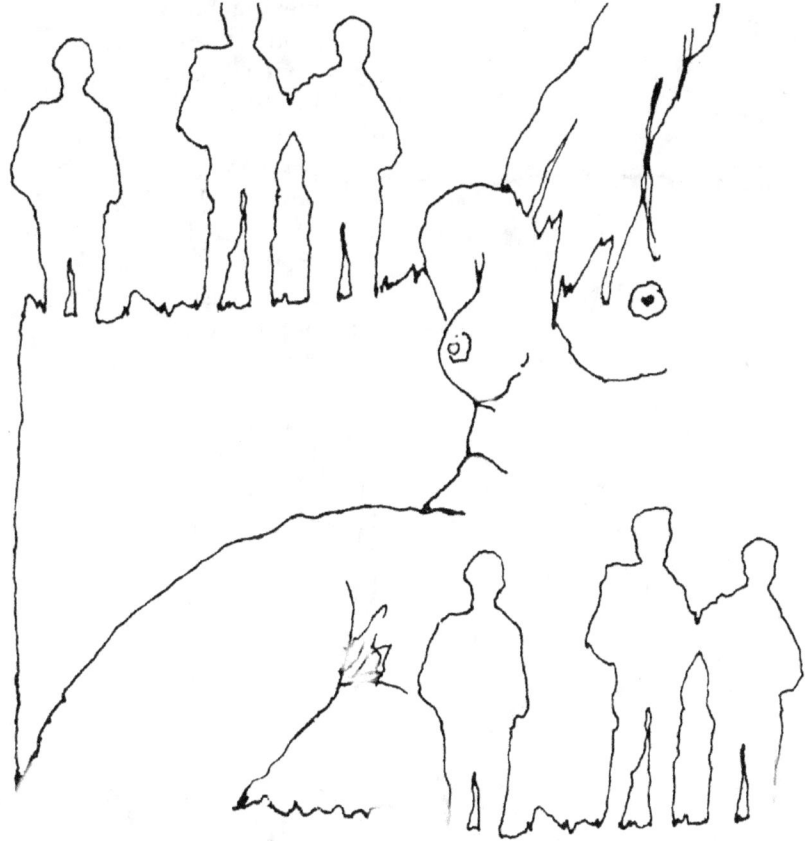

Seeds are the beginnings for life.....Screw you,
mister, everyday she says she feels like her
hair.....Is she better than her sister? Do you think
the cream has removed my wrinklles, why yes
and you look nine years younger.....

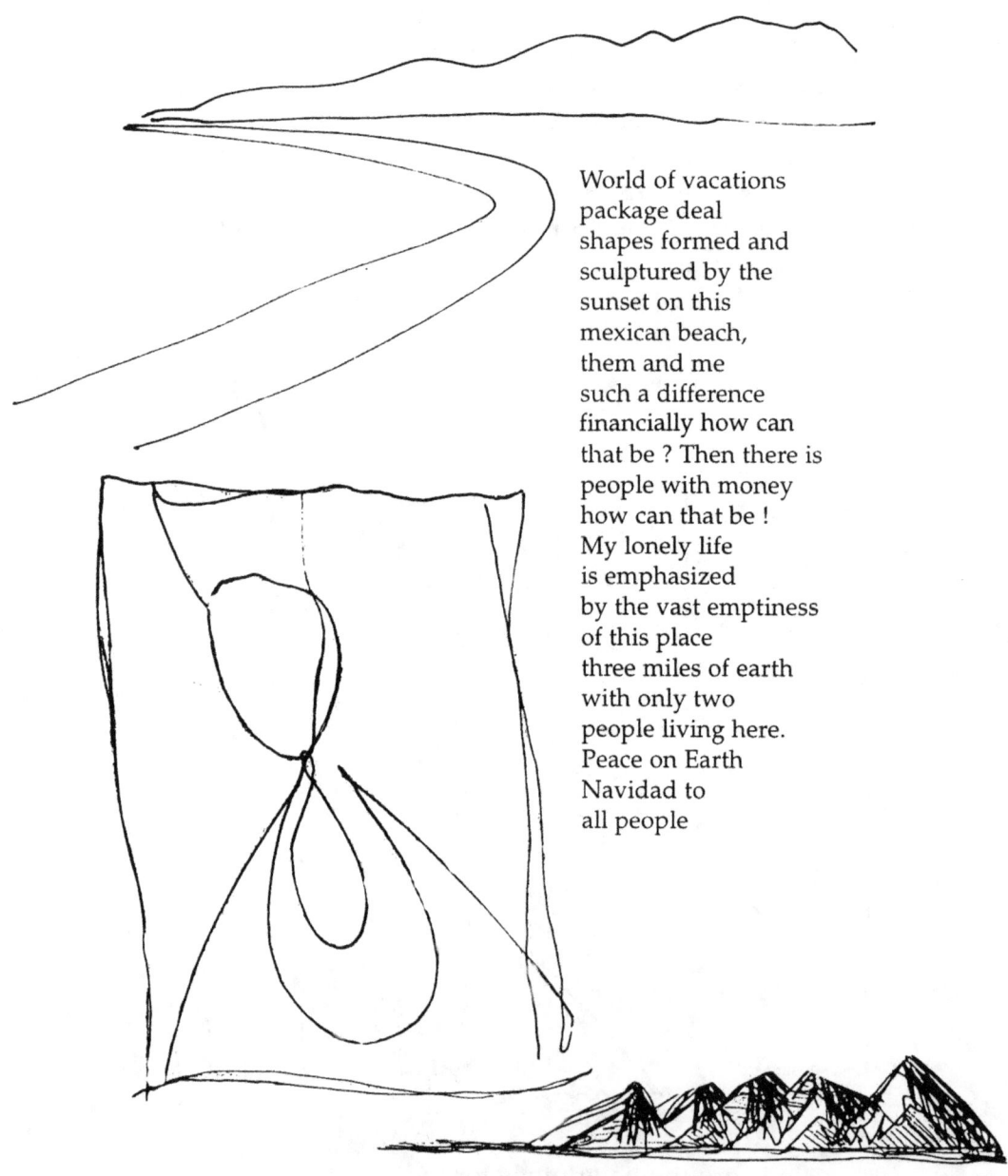

World of vacations
package deal
shapes formed and
sculptured by the
sunset on this
mexican beach,
them and me
such a difference
financially how can
that be ? Then there is
people with money
how can that be !
My lonely life
is emphasized
by the vast emptiness
of this place
three miles of earth
with only two
people living here.
Peace on Earth
Navidad to
all people

In Takeahamya I enjoyed whale steaks
cooked on nuclear power!

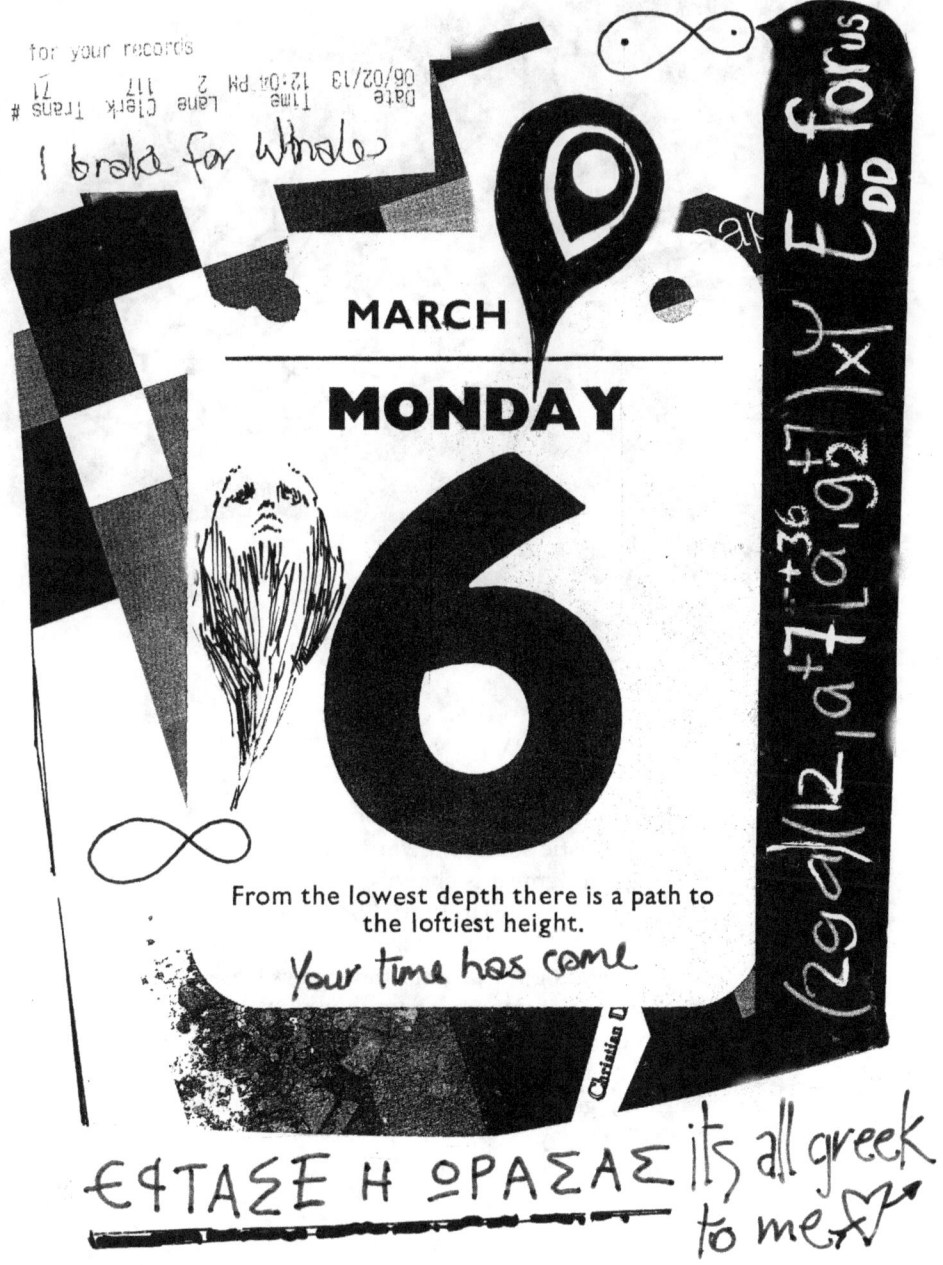

for your records

I broke for whale

MARCH

MONDAY

6

From the lowest depth there is a path to
the loftiest height.

Your time has come

ЄϤΤΑΣЄ Η ΟΡΑΣΑΣ its all greek
to me

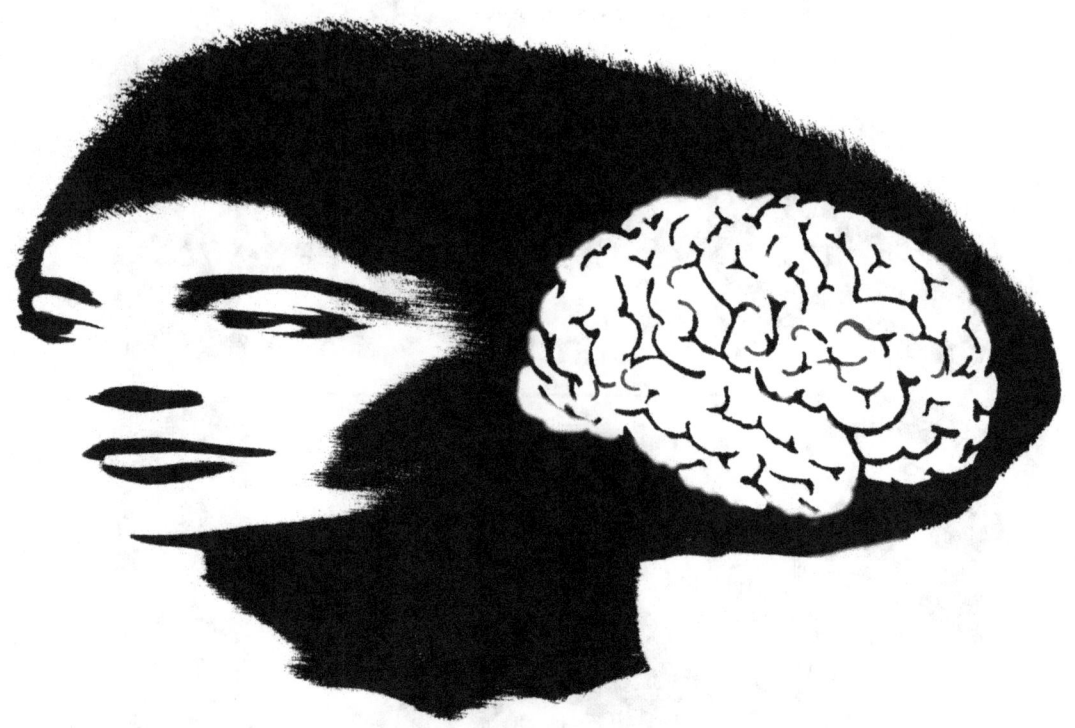

LUCKY TO LIVE

Mellow is the essence of my body's blood
magic acoustic sounds reward me.
Coconut milk meat is chewy
catching in my throat-jittery l bounce off the wall.
Nervous shake and bake passion consumes me
as my fingers glide around the legless legs.
Voyeurs vanishing where are they now ?
Watch the warm body of evening life as fantasies
fill the memories with erotic exotica
warming genitals......
glideride away
yet another day

I am the organ grinder

for this three pound organ,

I made it create this book,

you might think I am out of my head.....

Yes, this book came from the meat below.....

I thought the penis

was the most complex organ in my body,

NO.....

My brain is the most complex organ

it is the base for my intelligence,

it translates my senses,

controls my behaviour

and makes me move every so often.

The brain is the sum total

of human existence.

We even like to eat

animal brains and sweet breads.

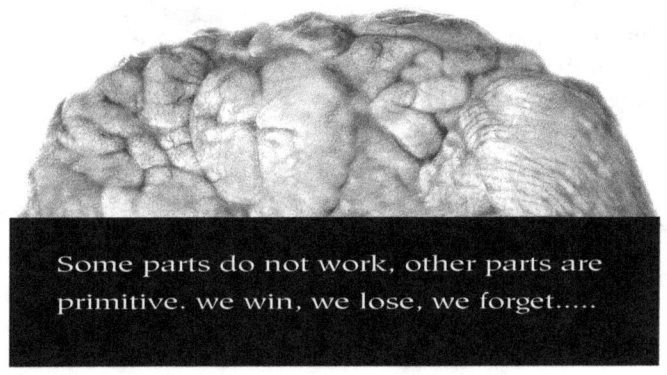

Some parts do not work, other parts are primitive. we win, we lose, we forget.....

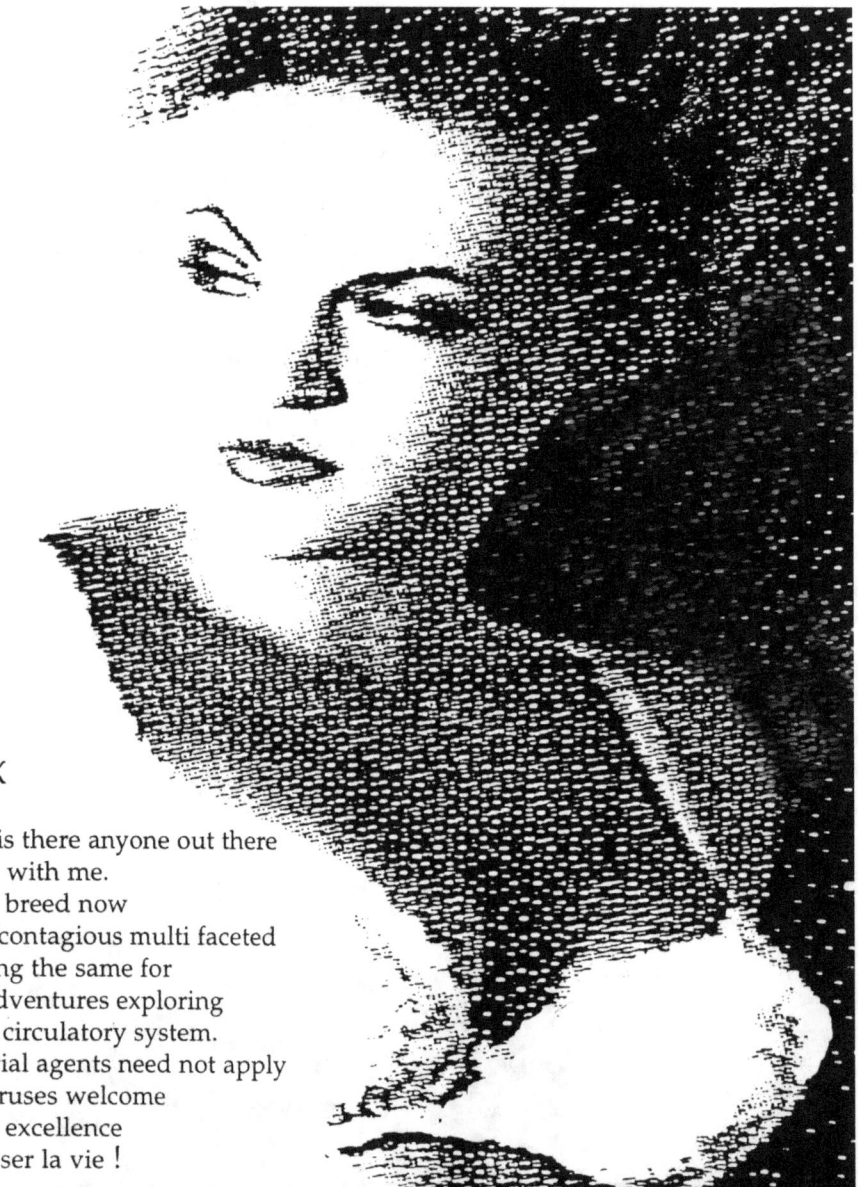

VIROLEX

Searching, is there anyone out there
to multiply with me.
We have to breed now
I'm highly contagious multi faceted
virus seeking the same for
romantic adventures exploring
the human circulatory system.
Anti-bacterial agents need not apply
airborne viruses welcome
lets pursue excellence
say la vie ! ser la vie !

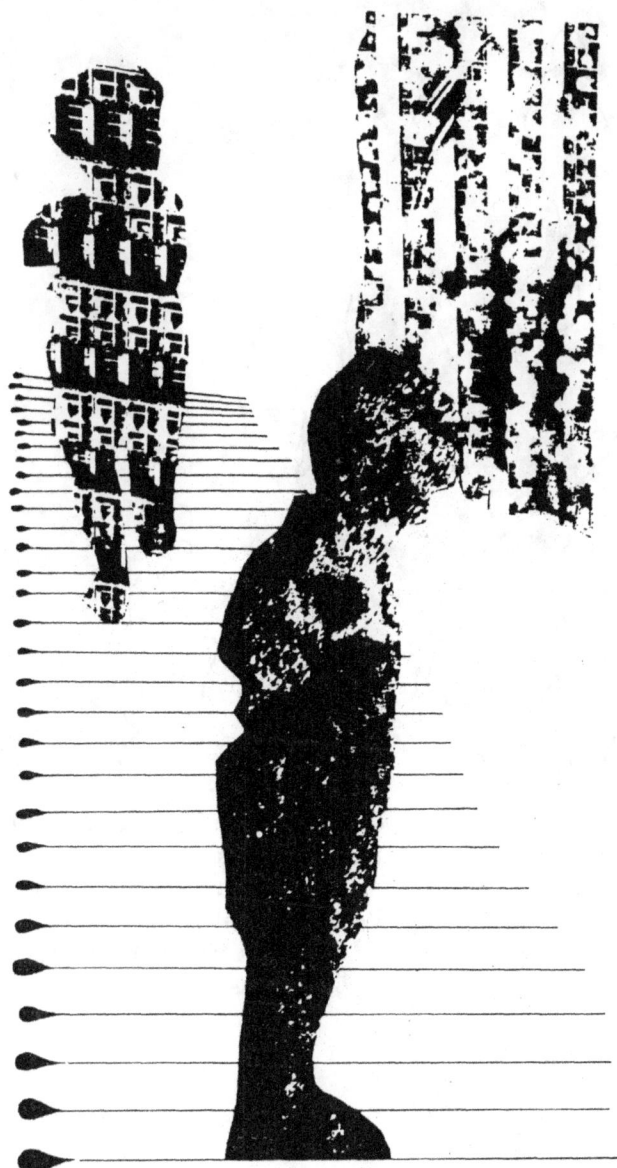

If you are not getting

the right answers.....

You are not asking

the right questions!

We must reassure

the public

that everything

is OK.....

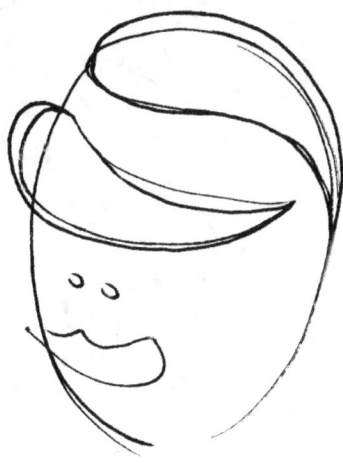

We control the

ministry of irritation!

The people

have started

a revolution

of contradiction.

When you need

good advice

talk to yourself.....

What the

government thinks,

it becomes.....

ALONE AGAIN

Sand patterns
white silver textures
burnished bright
ideas deep etched
on rocks of ages
tides, surf, flow . . .
aged reason reels
as I move hastily.

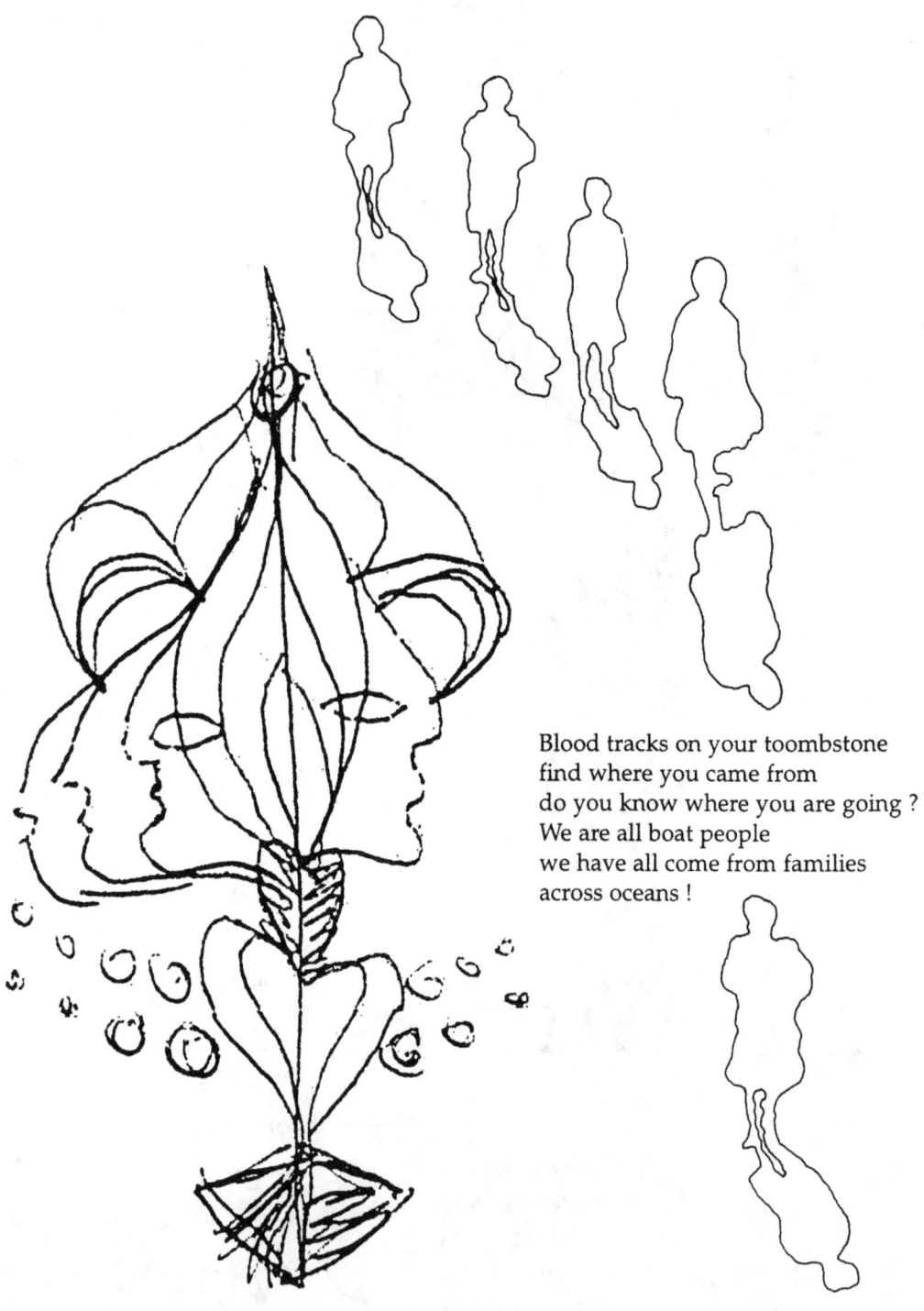

Blood tracks on your toombstone
find where you came from
do you know where you are going ?
We are all boat people
we have all come from families
across oceans !

Everything changes and is really different
as soon as it is spoken to others....Thanks Hesse.

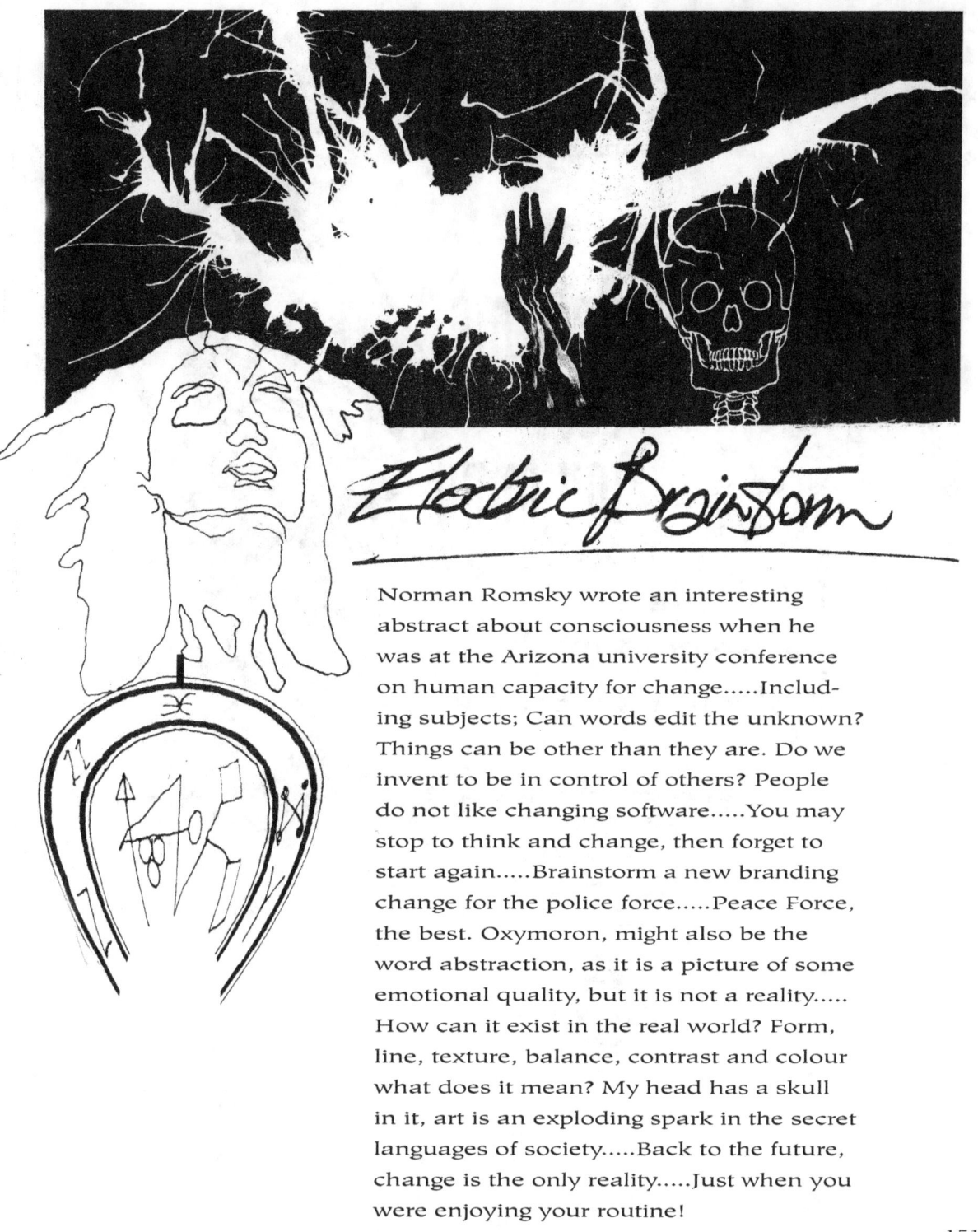

Electric Brainstorm

Norman Romsky wrote an interesting
abstract about consciousness when he
was at the Arizona university conference
on human capacity for change.....Includ-
ing subjects; Can words edit the unknown?
Things can be other than they are. Do we
invent to be in control of others? People
do not like changing software.....You may
stop to think and change, then forget to
start again.....Brainstorm a new branding
change for the police force.....Peace Force,
the best. Oxymoron, might also be the
word abstraction, as it is a picture of some
emotional quality, but it is not a reality.....
How can it exist in the real world? Form,
line, texture, balance, contrast and colour
what does it mean? My head has a skull
in it, art is an exploding spark in the secret
languages of society.....Back to the future,
change is the only reality.....Just when you
were enjoying your routine!

I'm dying
~~please hold my hand~~
~~I'm feeling LONLEY~~

You are
looking Great

I'm dying
please hold my hand
I'm feeling LONLEY

Haven't you
lost Some
Weight?

Help me
rest
my mind

~~I'm dying~~
please hold my hand
~~I'm feeling LONLEY~~

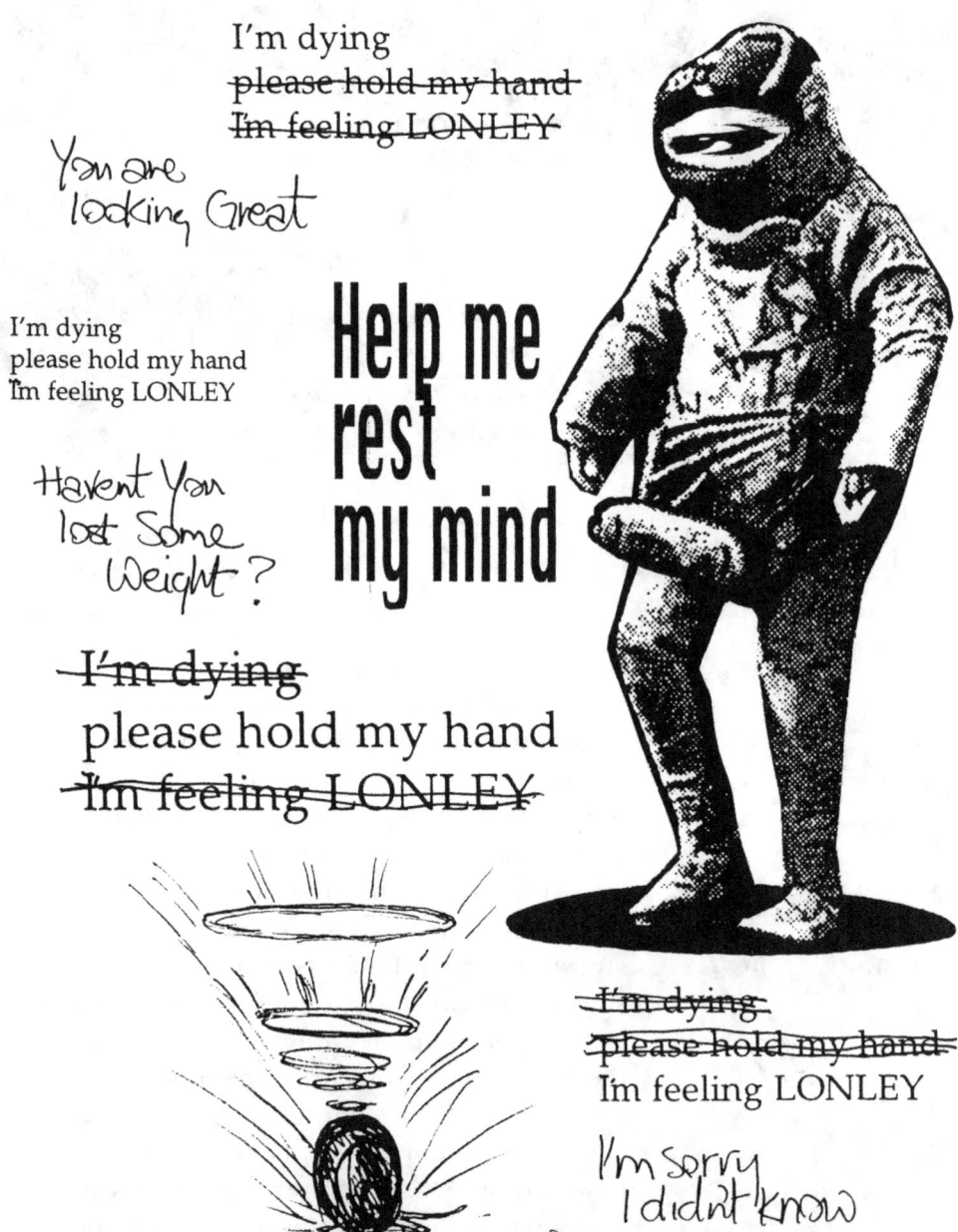

~~I'm dying~~
~~please hold my hand~~
I'm feeling LONLEY

I'm sorry
I didn't know
where's your eggs.....

So what is in this domain netweb holder.....Some kind of pyramid monolith from the sea of tranquility? Look at all that data in this pic!

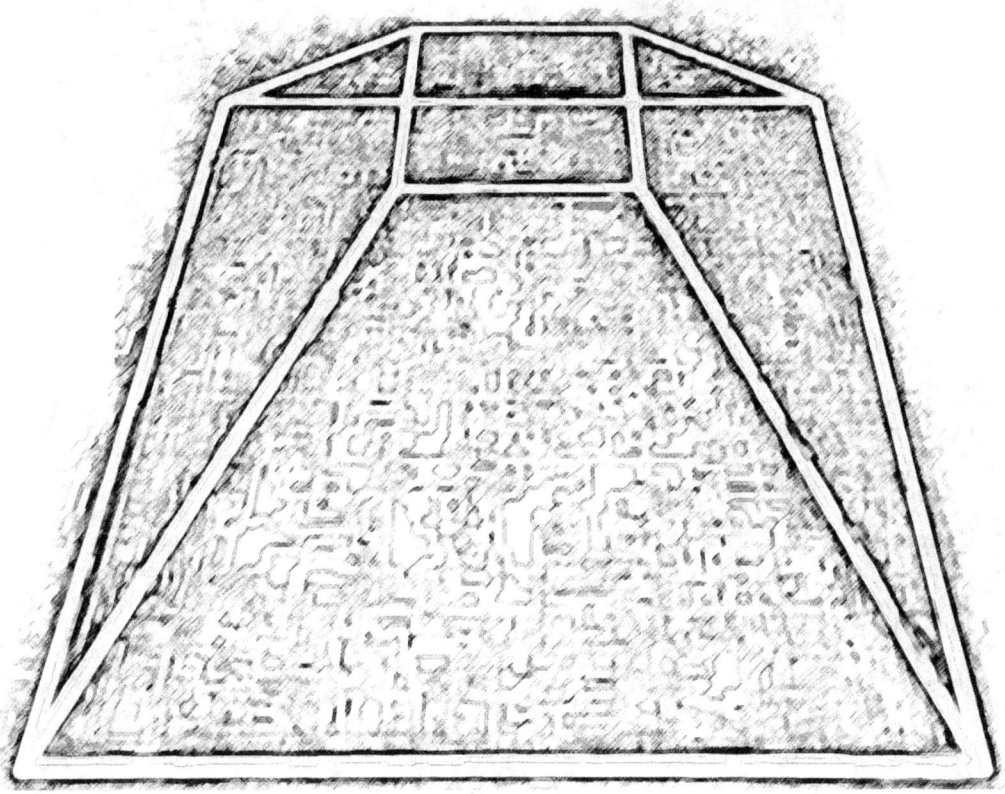

The politician who has the biggest cage in the zoo might answer, sorry classified! Inuendo about alien insurgence.....Give me a break.....See what you need to see, sometimes, see what is not there! The truth is, the nearest I got to waterboarding was nettipotting at the spa. UAEA (united arab electronic army) supported Devron and shut down the worldwide bitcoin currency exchange, reported Cloudfire financial security systems. Yesterday twitter found the weak link in the webnet chain and refused to put its site back up as it was badly compromised financially by the international banking fund, who now is replacing its encryption software. Bitcoin still is totally outside the control and the knowledge of anyone on the planet.....

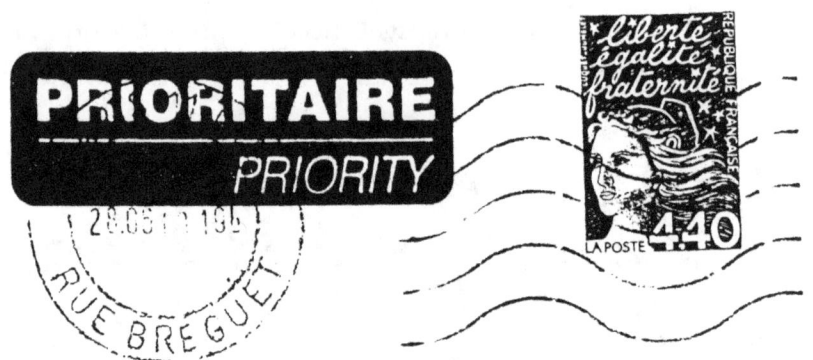

.....Sorry can't implant this app.....
without your certified ID number

Bounding boxes
surround
our ideas
drag them out
proportionally
they will freeform,
if you have
enough memory
my friend.

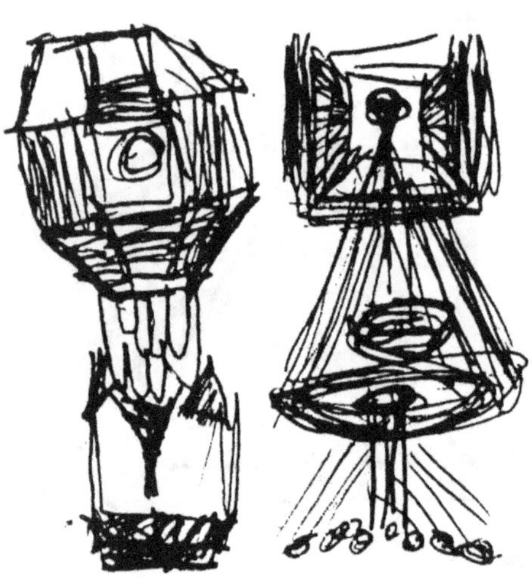

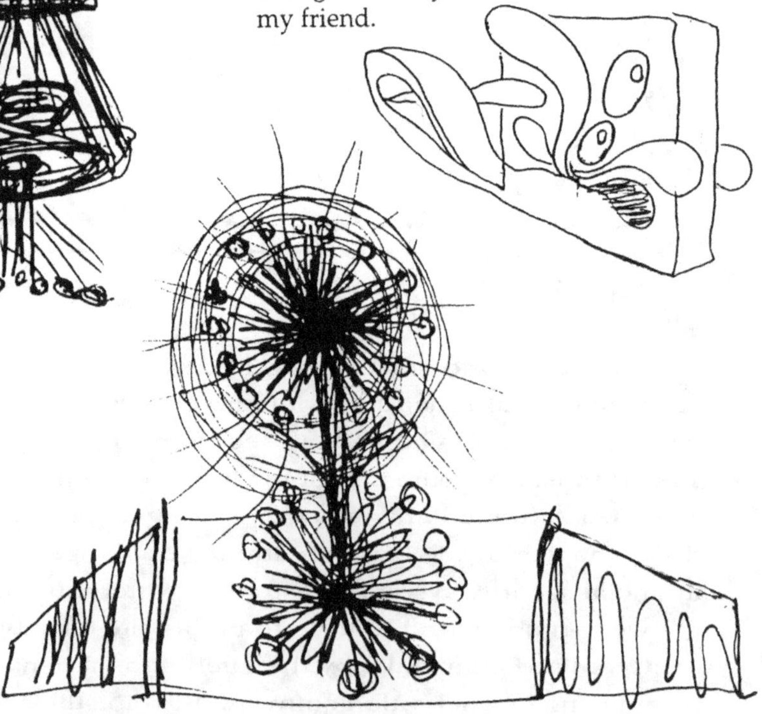

WE ALL
DREAM OF-
FUTURE
CONTACT...

This is my life

calling Serendipity

over

This is my life

go channel nine

do you copy Artcetera

roger that

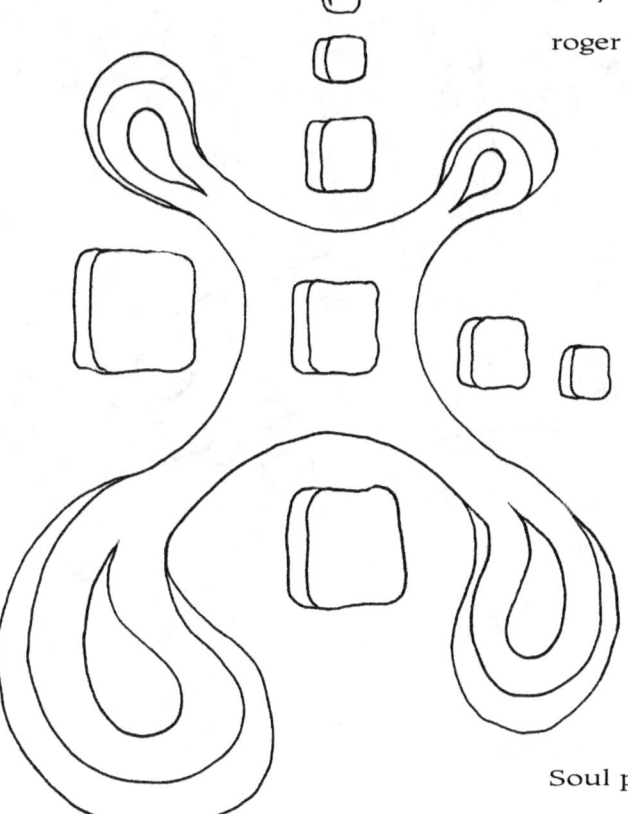

      Diamonds on the water

      sparkle like an egyptian ring.

      Thoughts while drinking

      are pure and thin

      and they call this a sin.

      Al ke 2 does not look like u,

      touch means so much,

      waist, shape, crouch.....

      Take the mickey

      at the place beyond the vines,

      where all that is left is grain

      and the slow cold rain while

      I sail the school of life.

Soul provider do you copy.....

This is Dreamsearcher, over.

Sorry Soul therapy not you.

Rolling thunder go six six

Happy ending are you there?

Roger, over and out!

Tom yum thai bum.....

Comfort is sailing with hot soup.

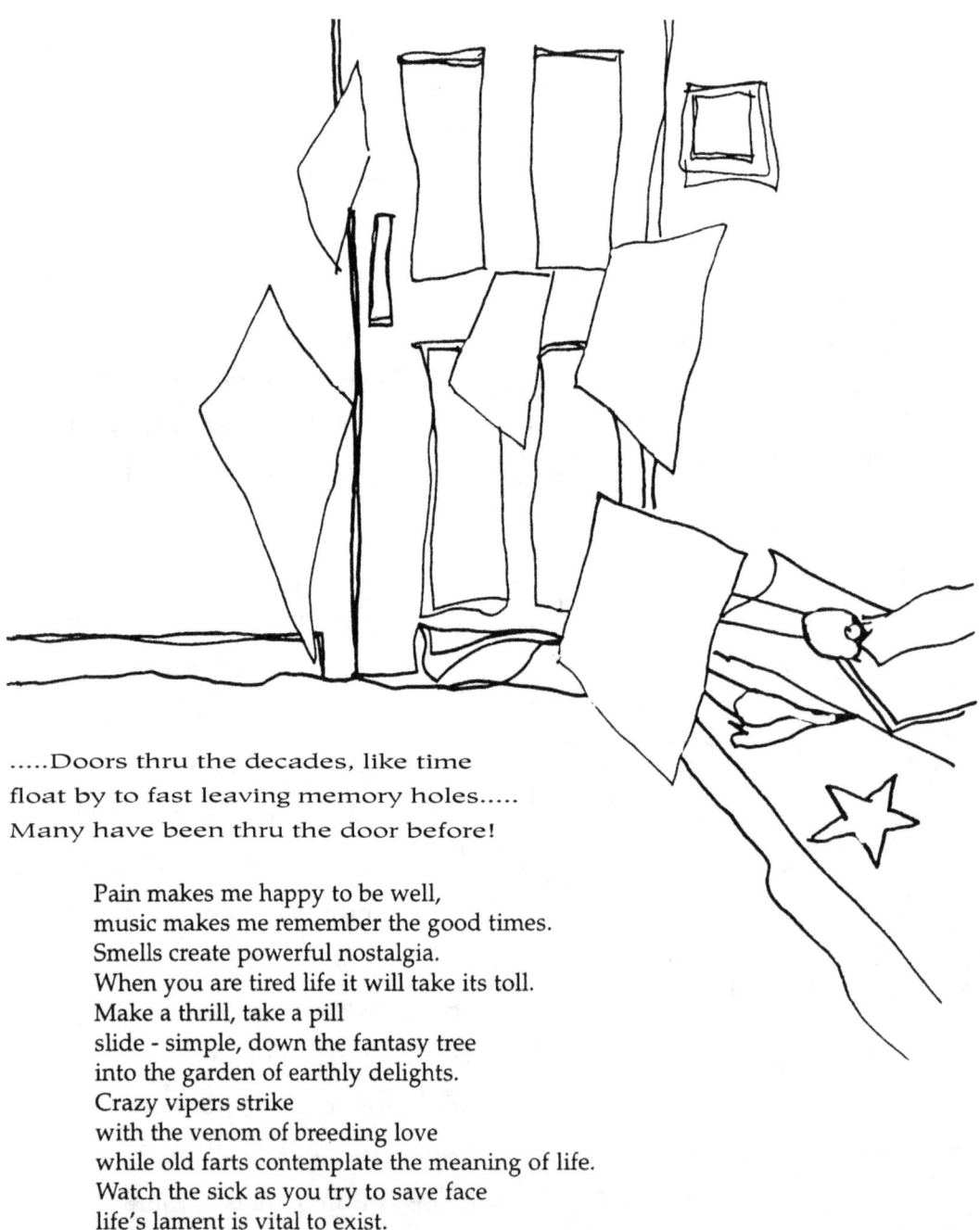

.....Doors thru the decades, like time
float by to fast leaving memory holes.....
Many have been thru the door before!

       Pain makes me happy to be well,
       music makes me remember the good times.
       Smells create powerful nostalgia.
       When you are tired life it will take its toll.
       Make a thrill, take a pill
       slide - simple, down the fantasy tree
       into the garden of earthly delights.
       Crazy vipers strike
       with the venom of breeding love
       while old farts contemplate the meaning of life.
       Watch the sick as you try to save face
       life's lament is vital to exist.

ASCENDING BODIES & SEAWEED

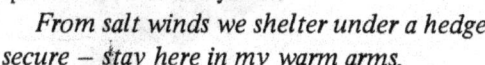

Labs chase thrown slate,
dog collar bells ringing —
  stand rigid smelling a mate.
Care for the one that waits for you.
  Quiet tide as it slowly rises
eyes search rocks for love.
  The gates to the sea
open slowly like thee,
  to the cliff ochre edge
spread harvests and farms.
  From salt winds we shelter under a hedge
secure — stay here in my warm arms.

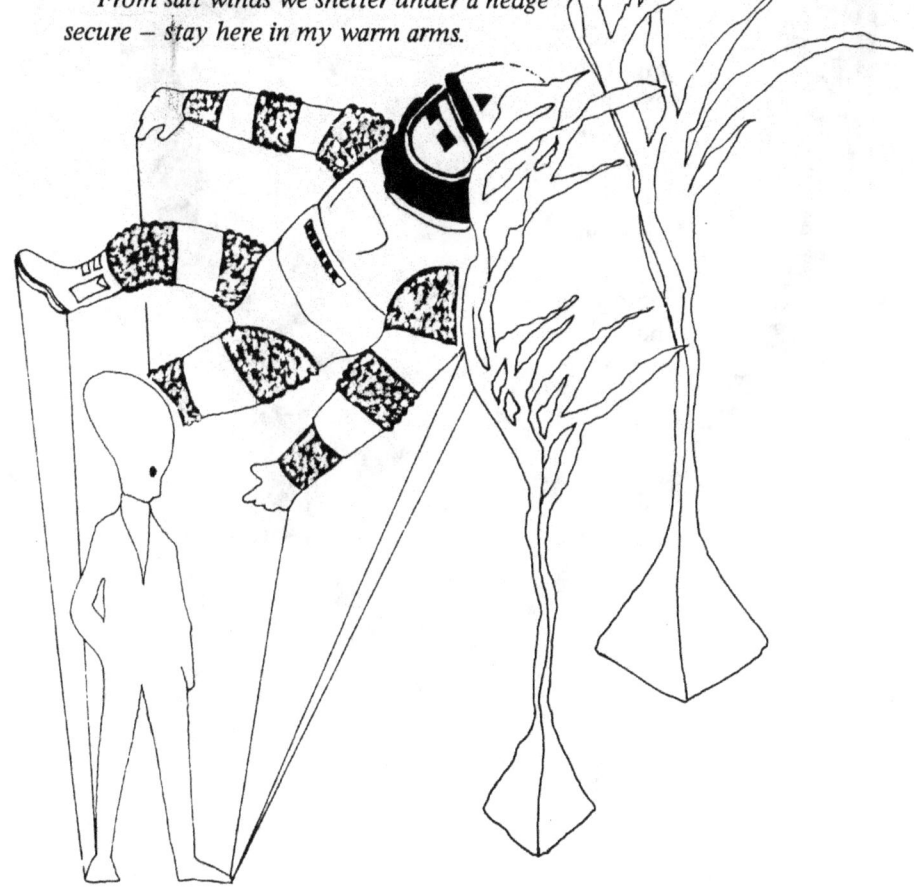

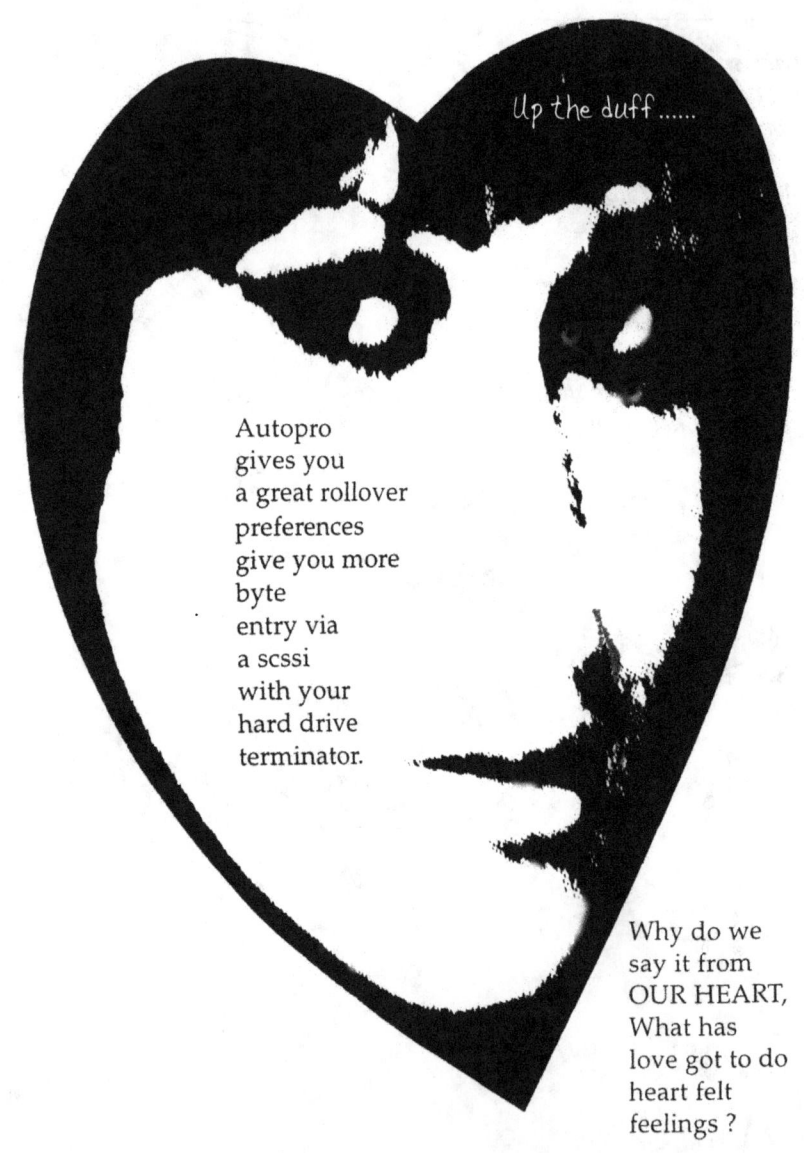

Up the duff......

Autopro
gives you
a great rollover
preferences
give you more
byte
entry via
a scssi
with your
hard drive
terminator.

Why do we
say it from
OUR HEART,
What has
love got to do
heart felt
feelings ?

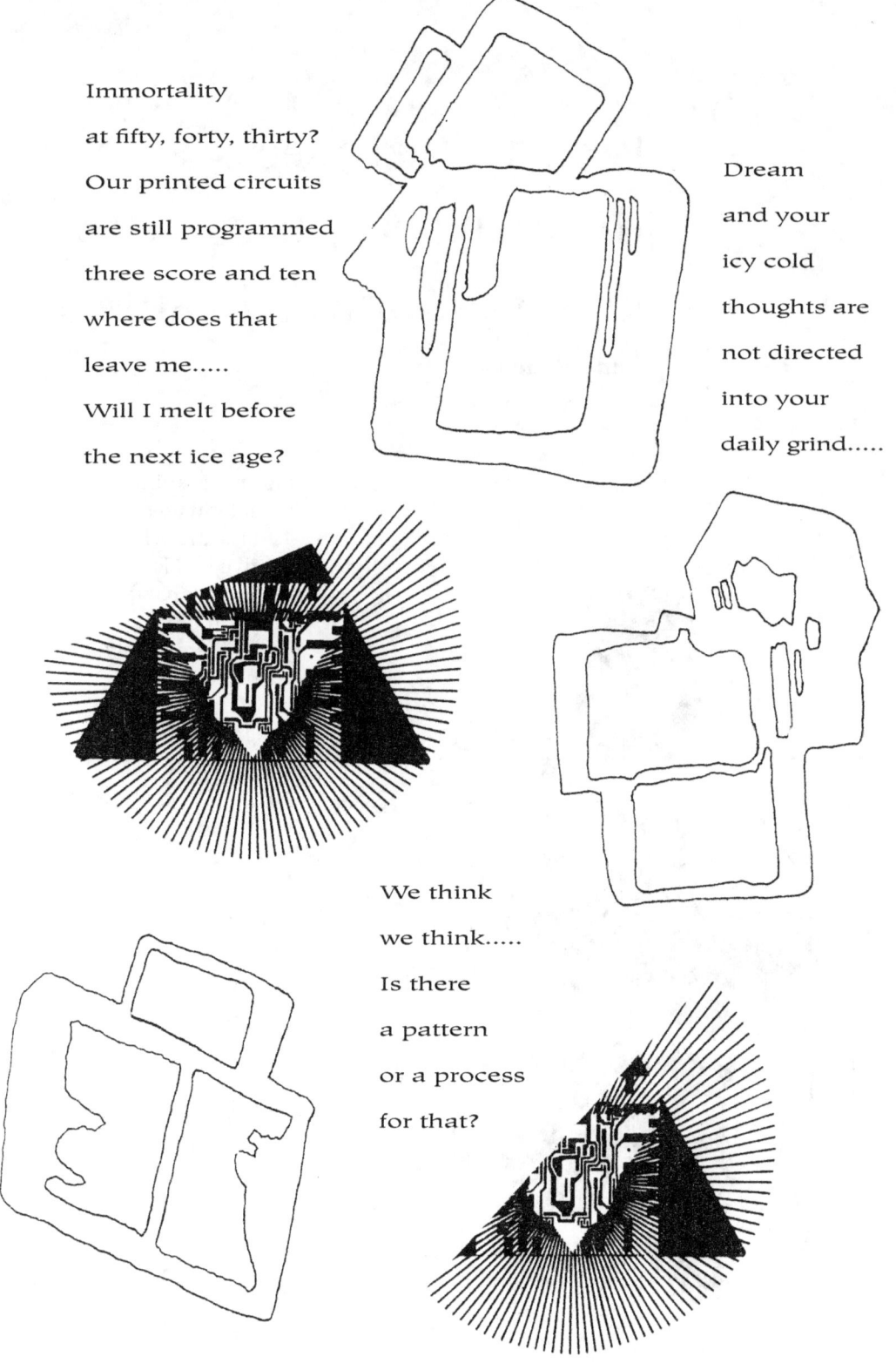

Immortality
at fifty, forty, thirty?
Our printed circuits
are still programmed
three score and ten
where does that
leave me.....
Will I melt before
the next ice age?

Dream
and your
icy cold
thoughts are
not directed
into your
daily grind.....

We think
we think.....
Is there
a pattern
or a process
for that?

Why would you have one piece of ice when you could have three?

It hurts me to see
the man I have become
in this life of wet dreams

Dhali Banana 1969

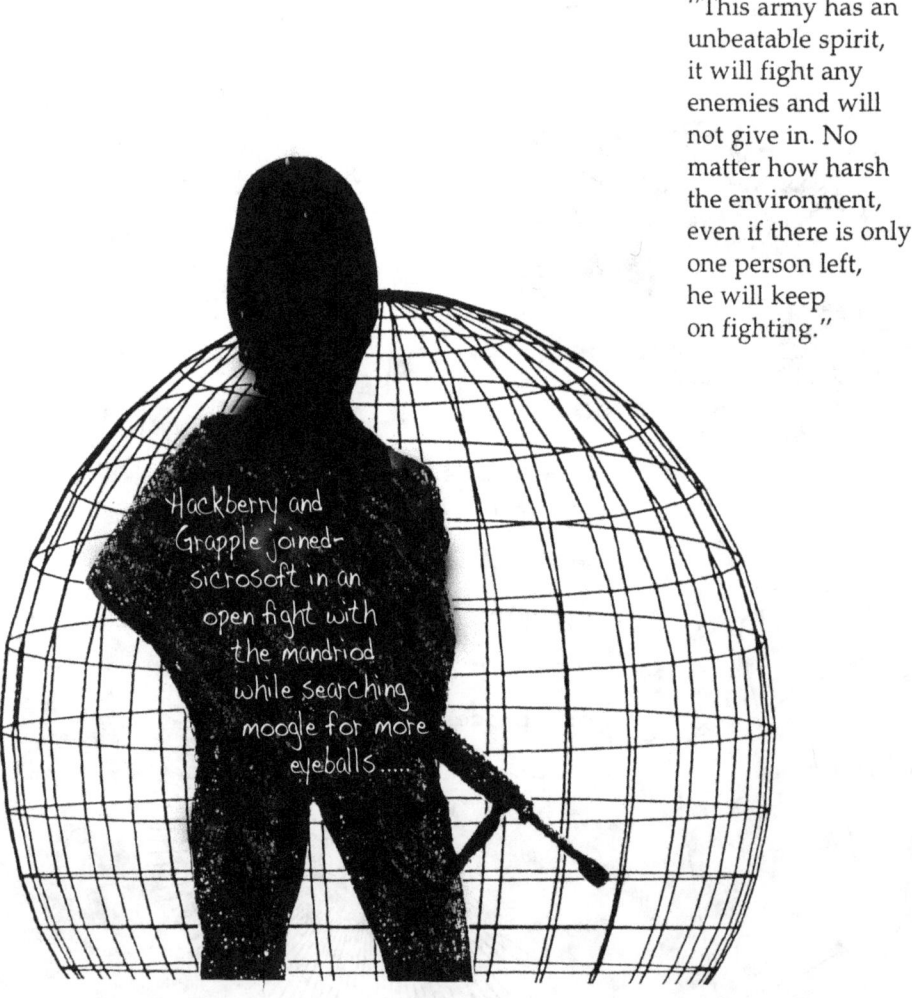

Hackberry and
Grapple joined-
sicrosoft in an
open fight with
the mandriod
while searching
moogle for more
eyeballs.....

''This army has an
unbeatable spirit,
it will fight any
enemies and will
not give in. No
matter how harsh
the environment,
even if there is only
one person left,
he will keep
on fighting.''

QUIET SEA

Words melt onto the paper
as easy as the sun shines
* and my skin, my shadow,*
moves across the evening earth –
* like dogs chasing across the beach*
my body shakes –
* quietly, as the evening enslaves the day.*
The bright sun burnt holes through my heart –
* the words wait*
for my hand as I relax.
* I question the authority residing over existence –*
the total shape of meaning and matter.
* I am as being.*
Your only constant is change.
* The shape I understand –*
the warden of thought watches –
* to arrest the quiet sea.*

Great creative work is only finished with labor and patience

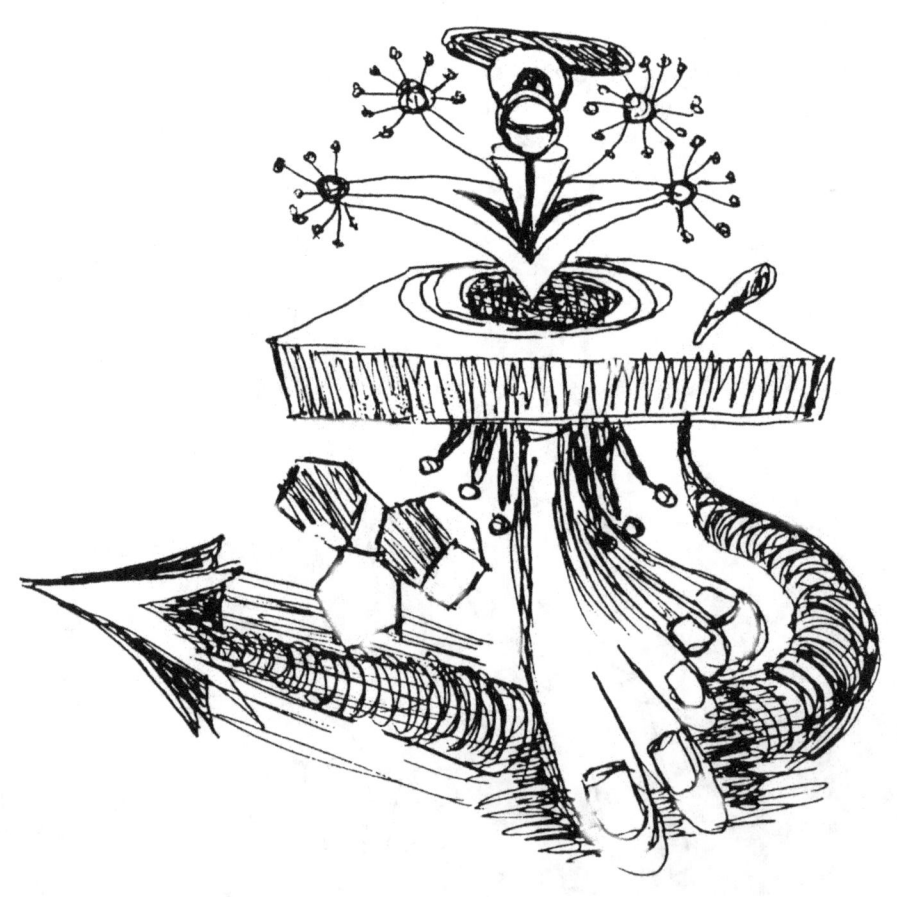

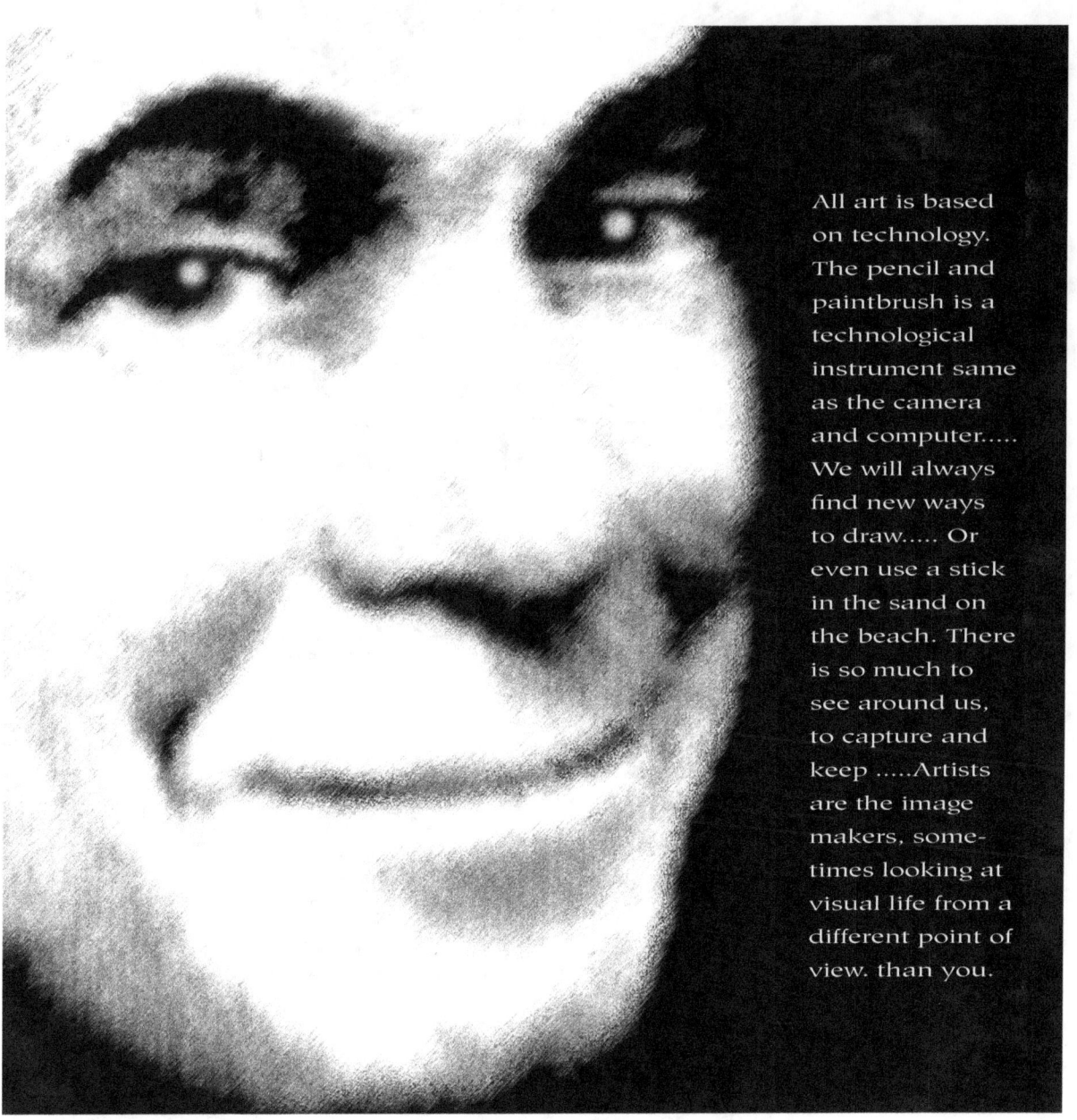

All art is based on technology. The pencil and paintbrush is a technological instrument same as the camera and computer..... We will always find new ways to draw..... Or even use a stick in the sand on the beach. There is so much to see around us, to capture and keep .....Artists are the image makers, sometimes looking at visual life from a different point of view. than you.

the art of looking up, down and sideways

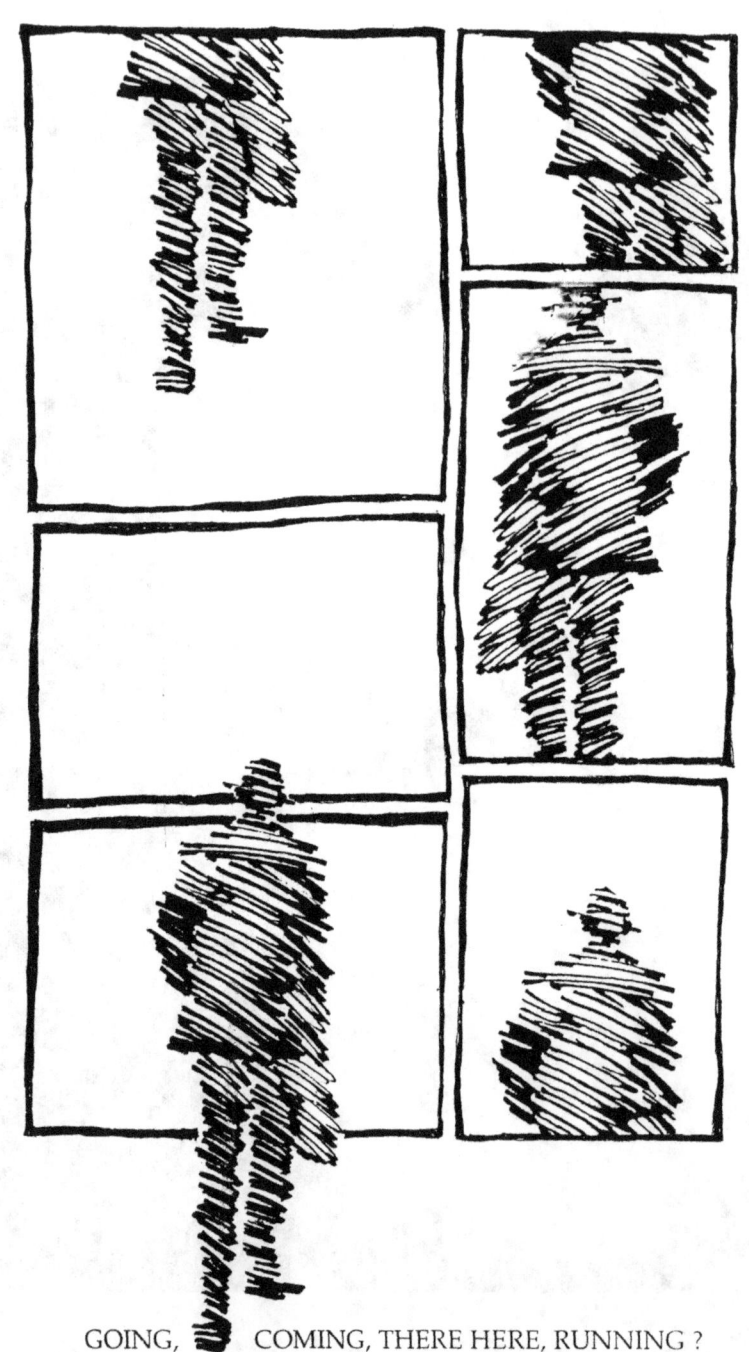

GOING,　　COMING, THERE HERE, RUNNING ?

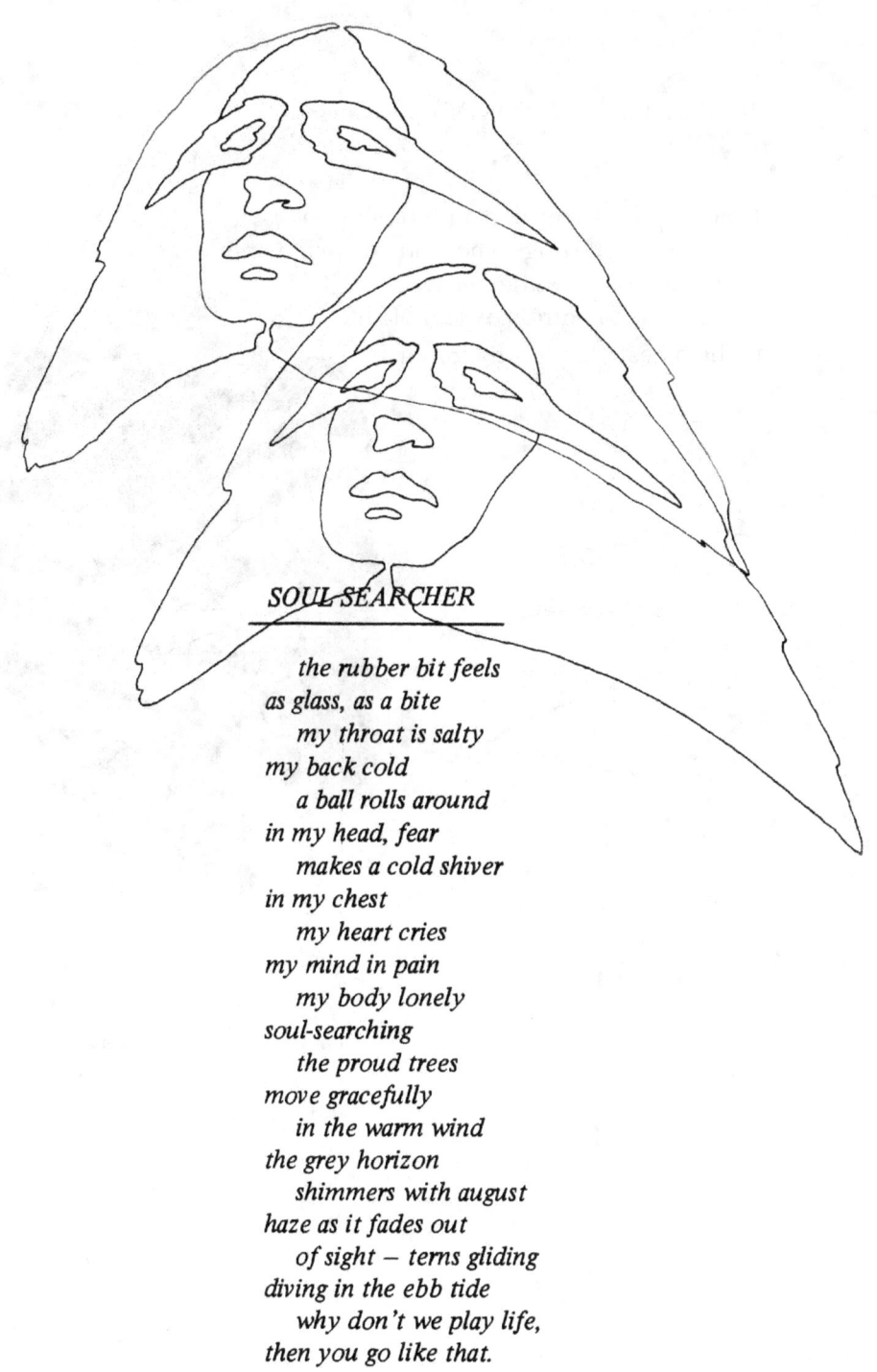

SOUL SEARCHER

the rubber bit feels
as glass, as a bite
my throat is salty
my back cold
a ball rolls around
in my head, fear
makes a cold shiver
in my chest
my heart cries
my mind in pain
my body lonely
soul-searching
the proud trees
move gracefully
in the warm wind
the grey horizon
shimmers with august
haze as it fades out
of sight — terns gliding
diving in the ebb tide
why don't we play life,
then you go like that.

FIVE CHILDREN PERFECT
COPY THAT

Time, depth, perception and dimension
are only just starting to be studied,we are only
begining to look at the master
program that controls our whole life
in the pineal gland of the brain.

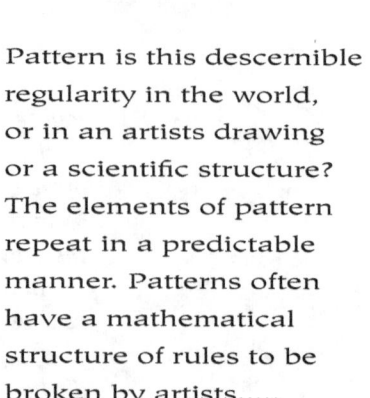

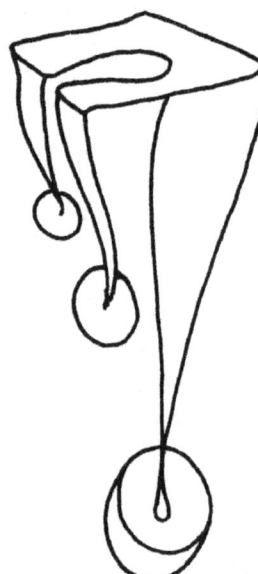

Pattern is this descernible
regularity in the world,
or in an artists drawing
or a scientific structure?
The elements of pattern
repeat in a predictable
manner. Patterns often
have a mathematical
structure of rules to be
broken by artists.....

Shapeshifting is the ability of a
form to transform into another
form or being.....Is this only true
in sifi or in all reality?

SANDPIPER MORNING

The winter eats the sky,
the bare-leafed trees cry
*   through the mist — the grass is wet.*
Man — nature's little regret.
*   The beauty of the evening drawn*
sunrise on the golden morn.

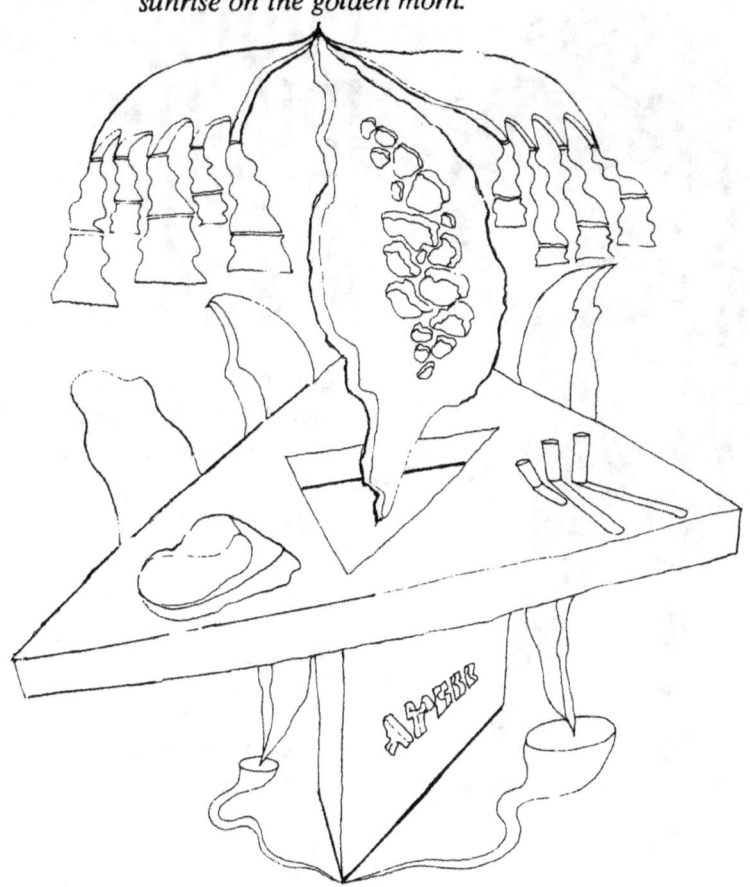

Your eyes light my heart
*   I exist only when we're apart.*
Radiating through trees, a glow,
*   deep penetrating feelings show*
fruit juices, pure like rain
*   abstract branches like marble vein.*
Inhibitions disguise us
*   as desires go by.*

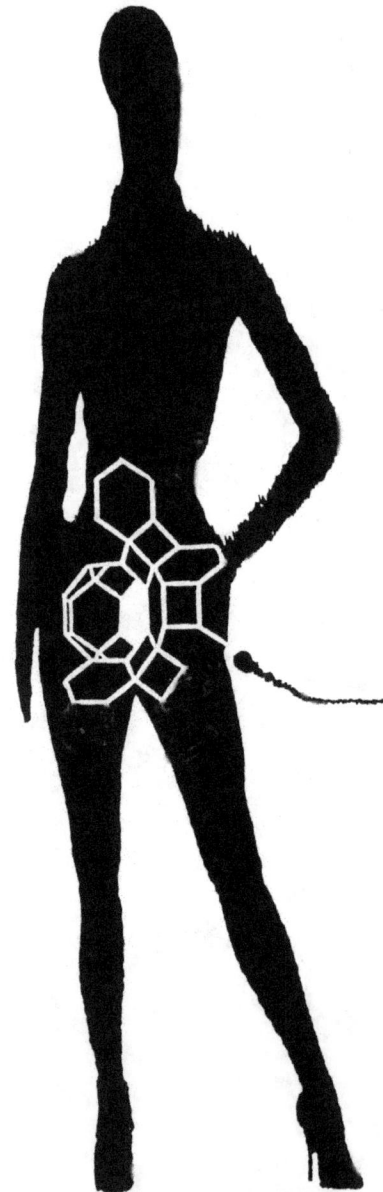

The angels of midnight come into my life in my dreams

Light beam transportation
systems are still having
problems with our
human genetics.
We really are a stagnant
energy beam, waiting for
the ignition key or code,
to take us beyond
our visual universe

We will take over
and redirect the computer
to solve the problem,
create better software
and improve the hardware
to take us beyond NOW !

Coding must be ordained as the new religion
for the universal survival of our species.
This is our language for eternity.....

square stones out to see
came a dish swimming by three
swewerage outlet
silent pea all by the c

yellow shirt
yellow shirt
blue sea
blue sea
below skirt
below skirt
who me
who me

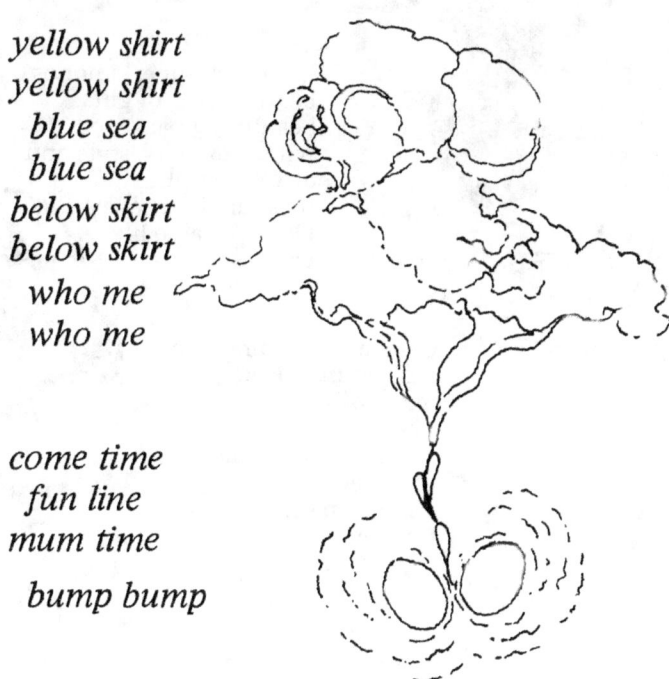

come time
fun line
mum time

bump bump

firm prints in the wet sand
coconut tree between land
city salesmen hustle the country
enclosure the market
randy pants sky hawk
roll another say brother

broken ship

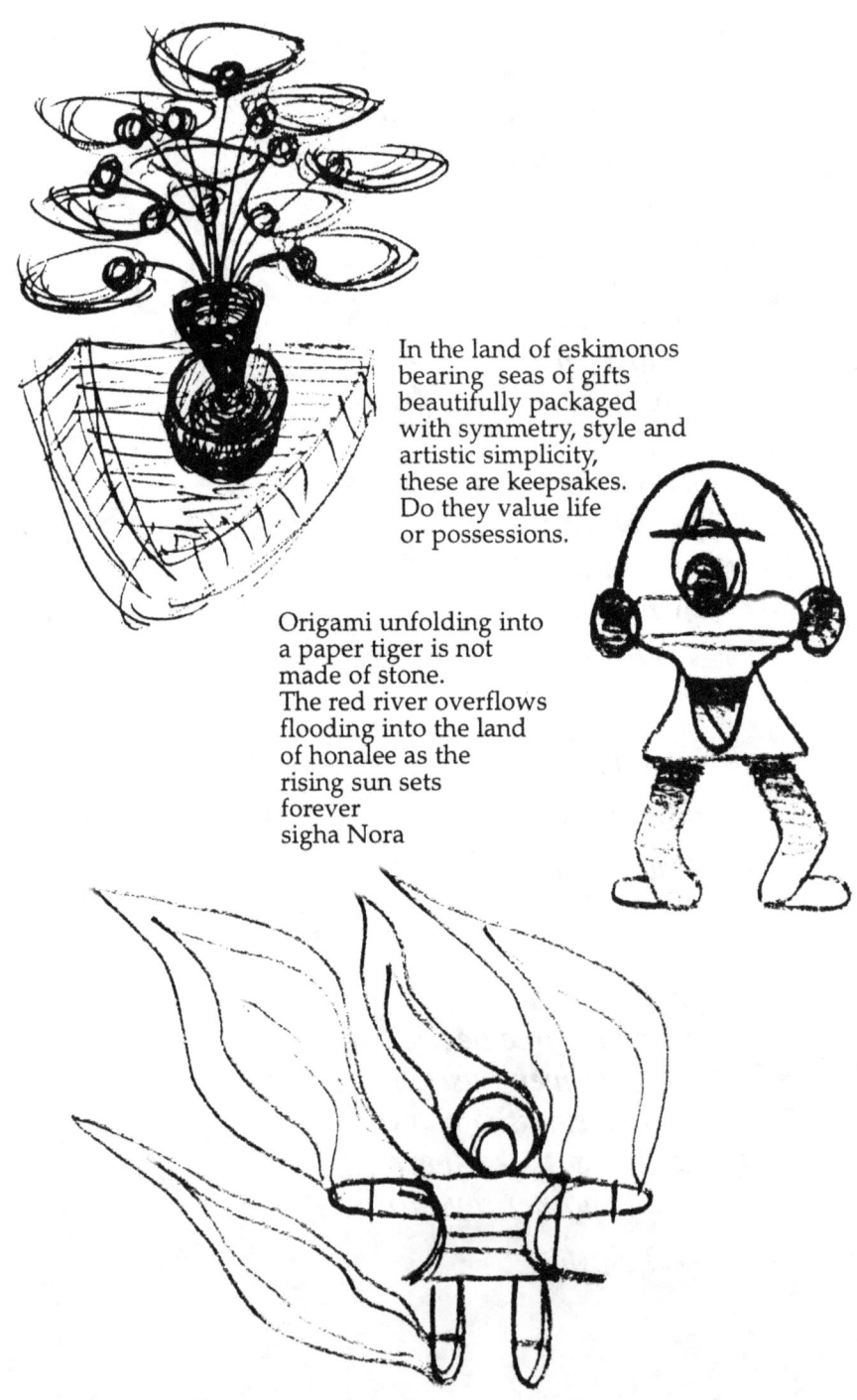

In the land of eskimonos
bearing seas of gifts
beautifully packaged
with symmetry, style and
artistic simplicity,
these are keepsakes.
Do they value life
or possessions.

Origami unfolding into
a paper tiger is not
made of stone.
The red river overflows
flooding into the land
of honalee as the
rising sun sets
forever
sigha Nora

How could she be the mother she never had.....She is
a chameleon in the sea of desire. Her education is the
progressive discovery of her own ignorance. When
questioned she said "No comment".

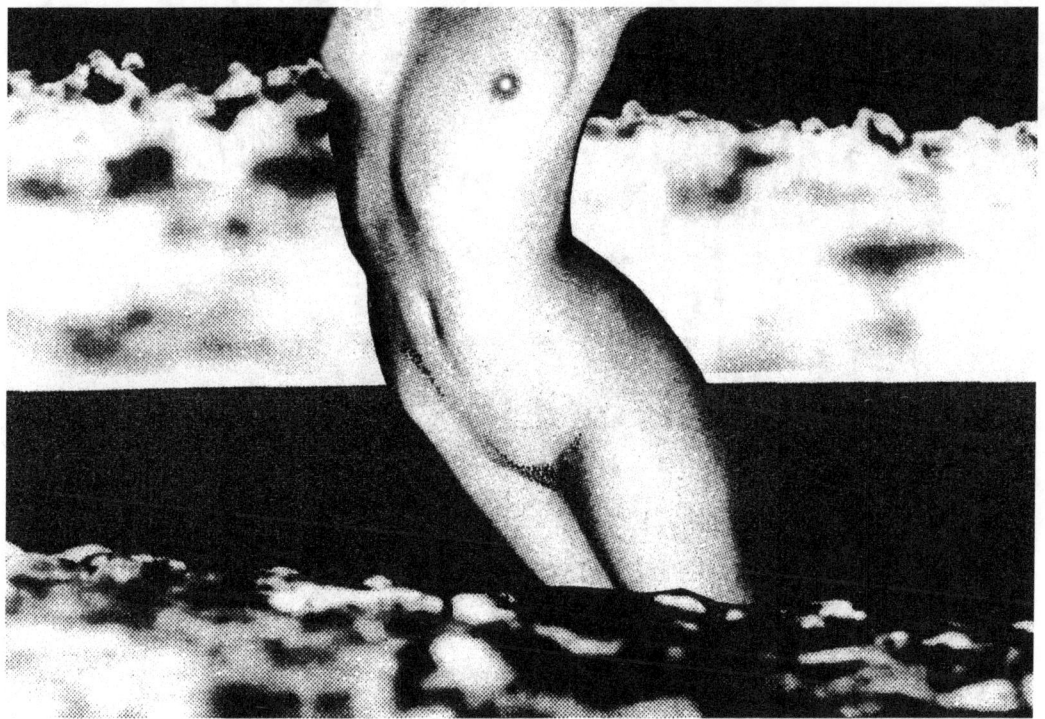

Out of the sea
came this carbon
creature.....Bad
nude rising, she
would doodle
with her poodle
and after noodles,
with chopsticks,
lick lips as cloud
faces go by.....

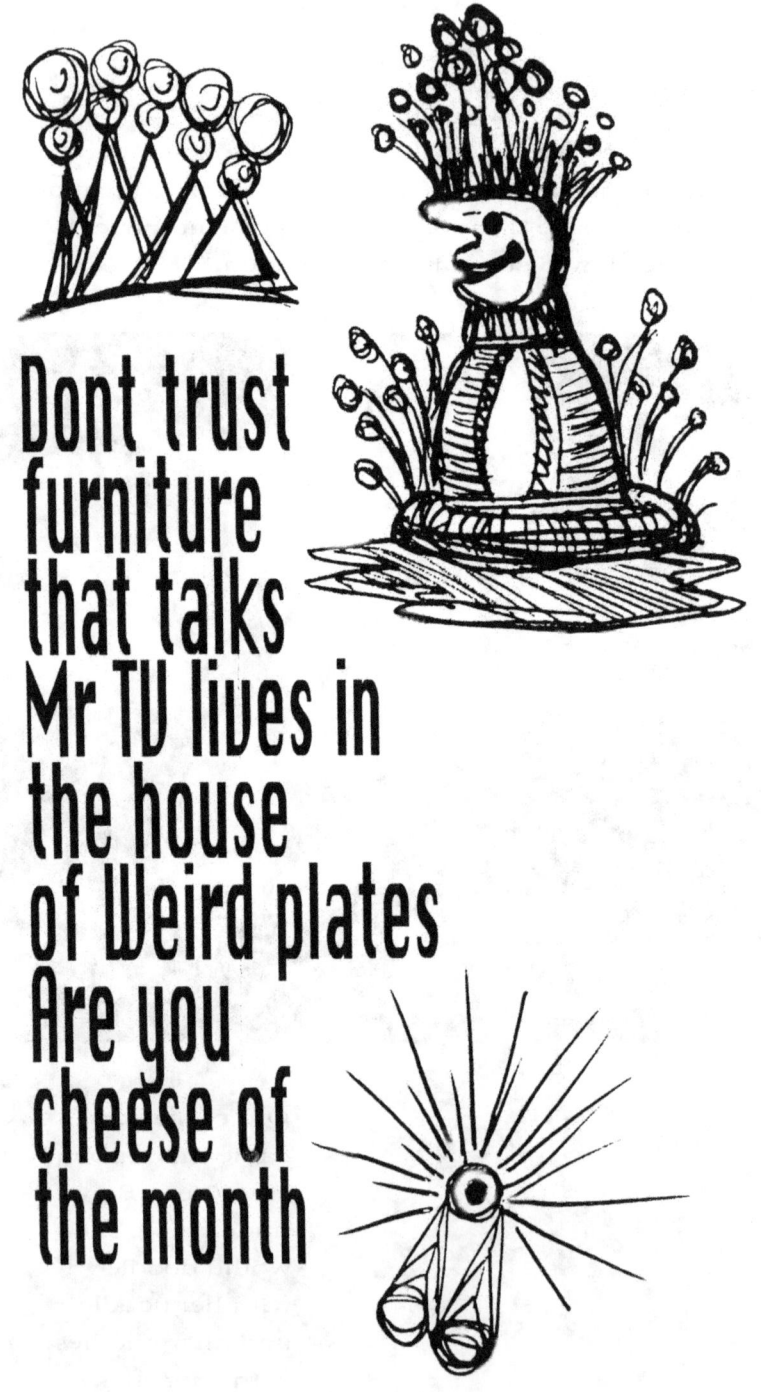

Dont trust
furniture
that talks
Mr TV lives in
the house
of Weird plates
Are you
cheese of
the month

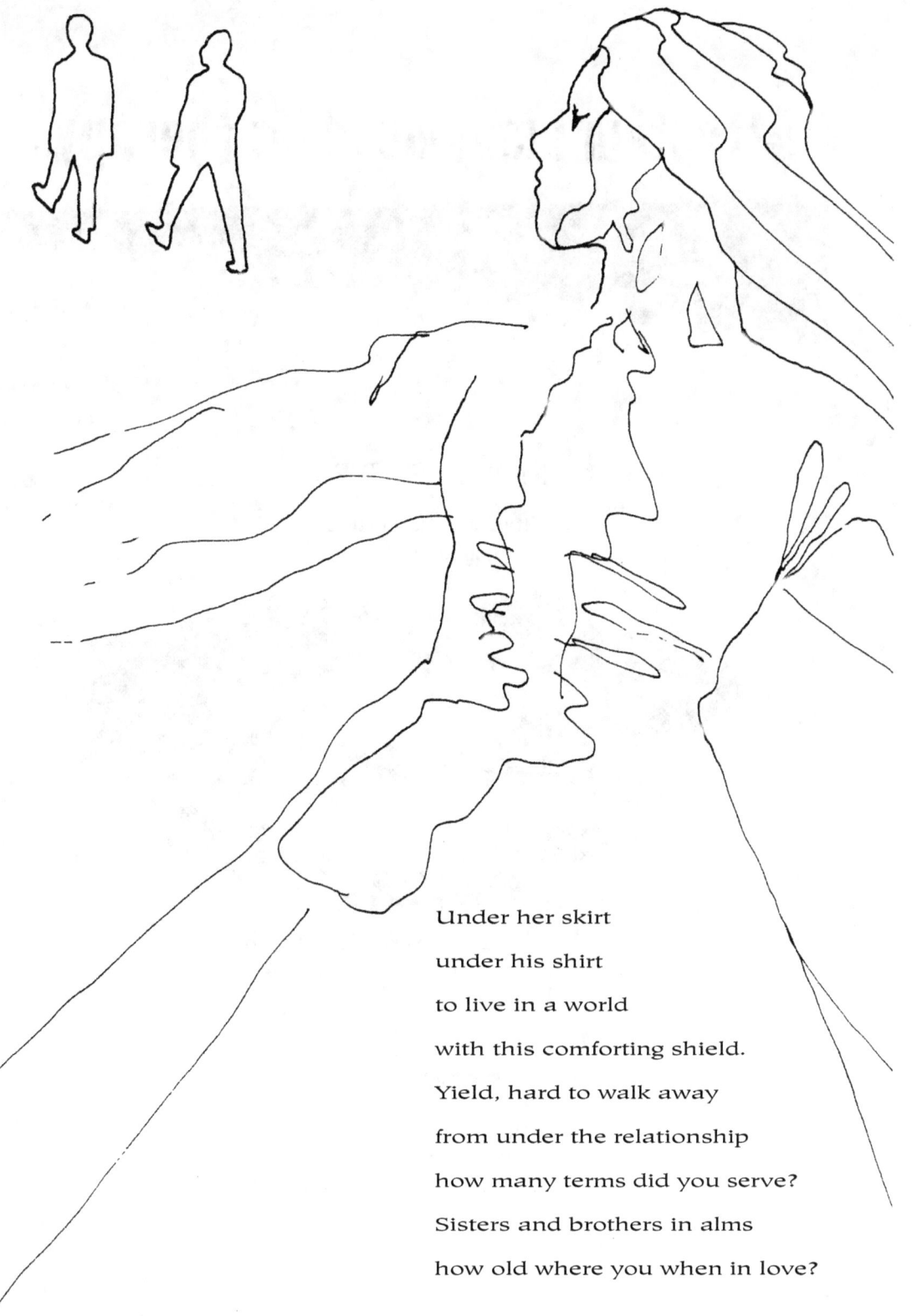

Under her skirt

under his shirt

to live in a world

with this comforting shield.

Yield, hard to walk away

from under the relationship

how many terms did you serve?

Sisters and brothers in alms

how old where you when in love?

Attention I may need lip therapy

MOUTHSTUFF

Sitting at sunset eating
marzipan in Zanzibar

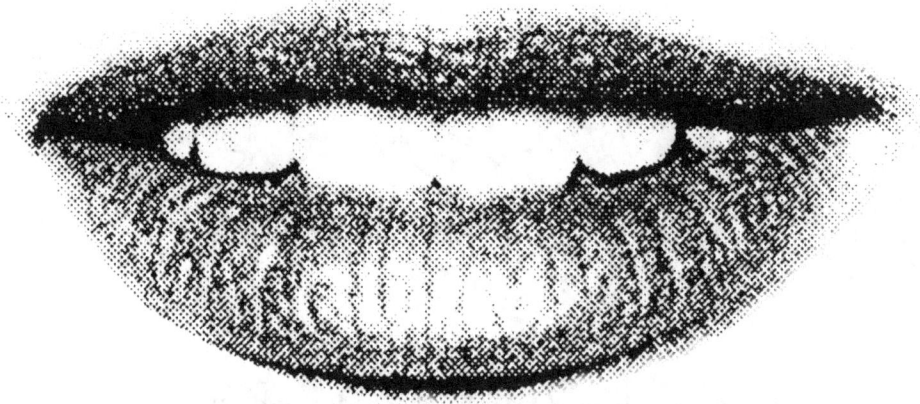

Sunrise the chicken farm Nevada
Mashuga nuts in Mazatlan
Wasabi in Waikiki
Scallops in Sydney
Poulan in Paris
Blimis in Buffalo
Languistine in Lorient
Teatime in Tokyo
Happy valley oh Hong Kong
Scrumpie soothes out Somerset
you get it why more !

174

I do not understand Einstein's answers on the speed of moving trees

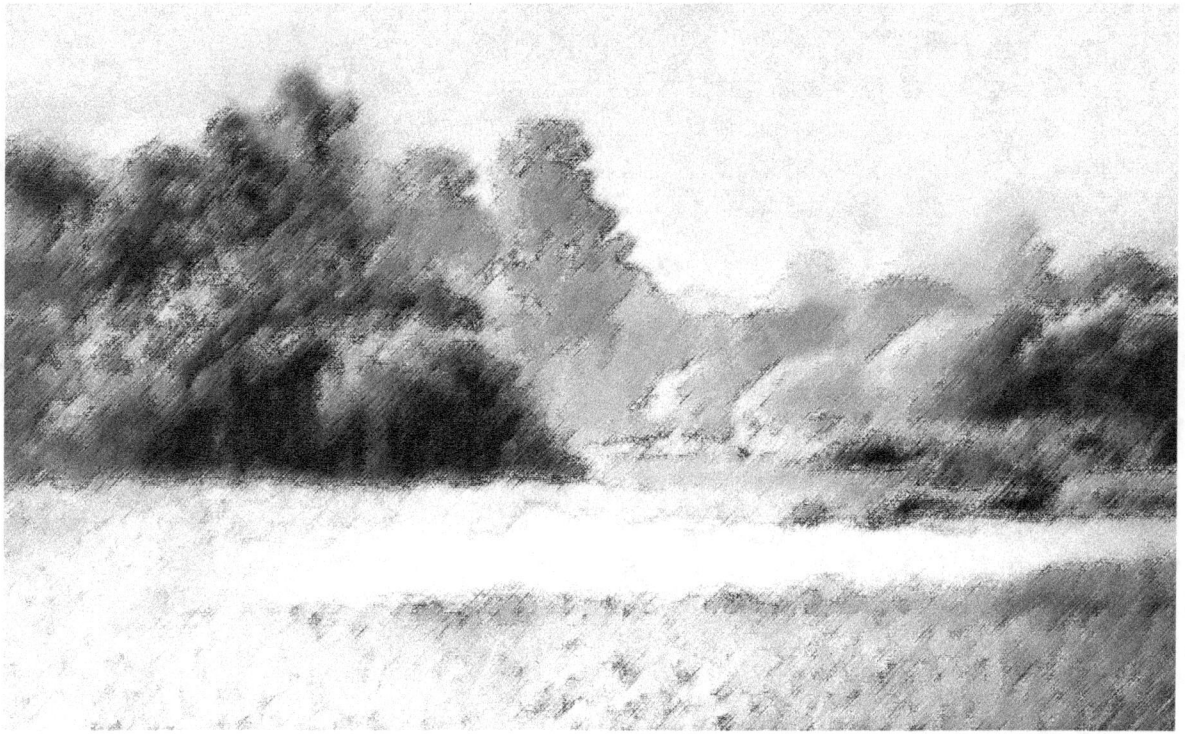

Trees breeze on by

at the speed of a dragon fly

the wind talks to the trees

no man can hear.....

What women understand

not having that hanging gland.

I see the shapes of people

as I edit and pass over

my painting of trees.

I still try to understand

the hands of time on clocks

are always at ten to two.....

ee cummings will help me thru.....

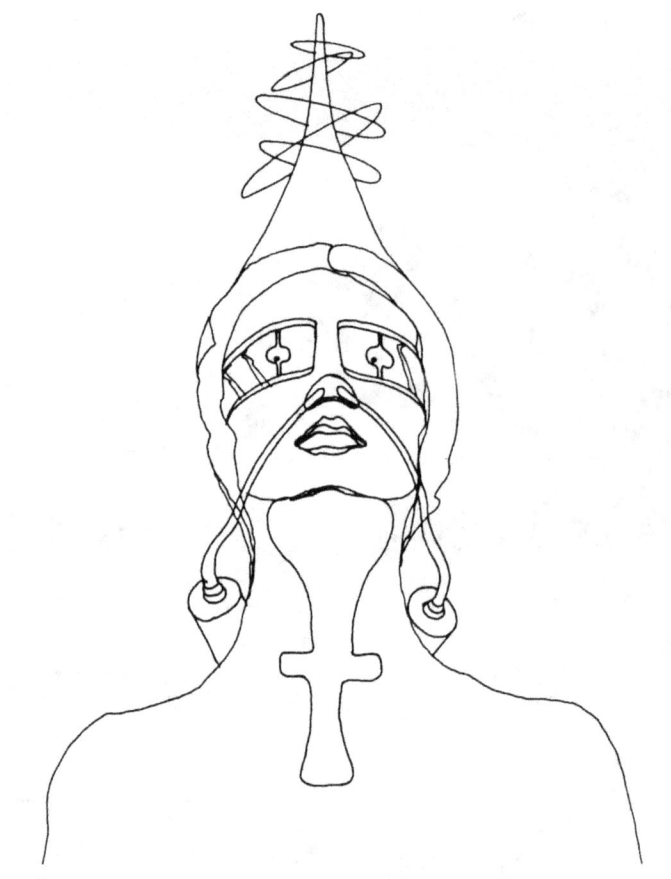

CLONE ME UP BUTTERCUP
Urban psychedelic, why don't you have a nice tall cold glass of HORSES MILK got it, so refreshing, nine nutrients and from the breasts of horses.

Technique is just the vehicle to tell the message !!

No space for the human race, fish only grow big enough for their fish tank?

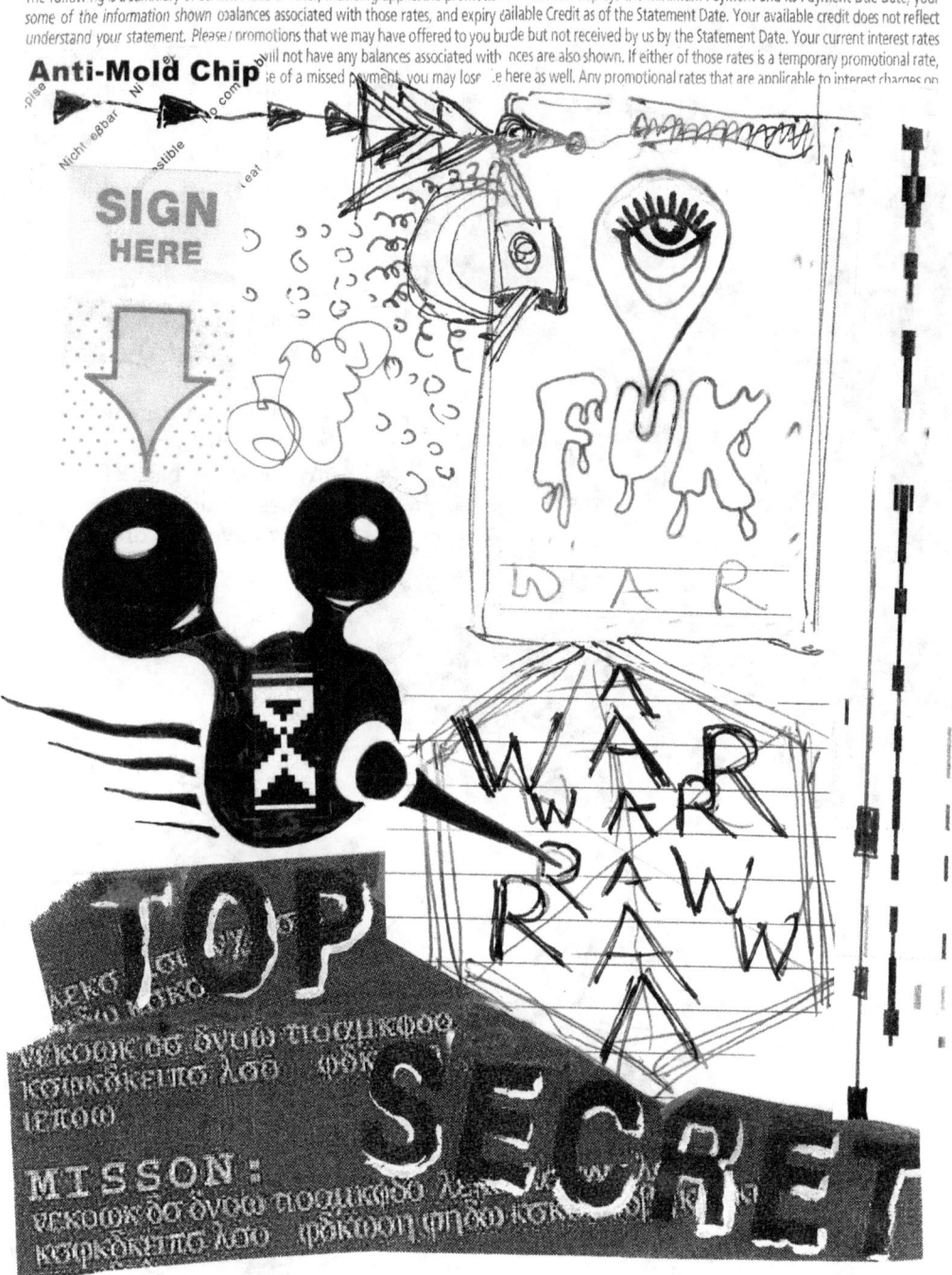

Secrets and lies.....You are maybe the last to know who runs the show.....
Crewschoff said "we are all in bed with our pride", nice neighbours now.....
Enjoy the ride!

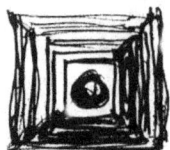

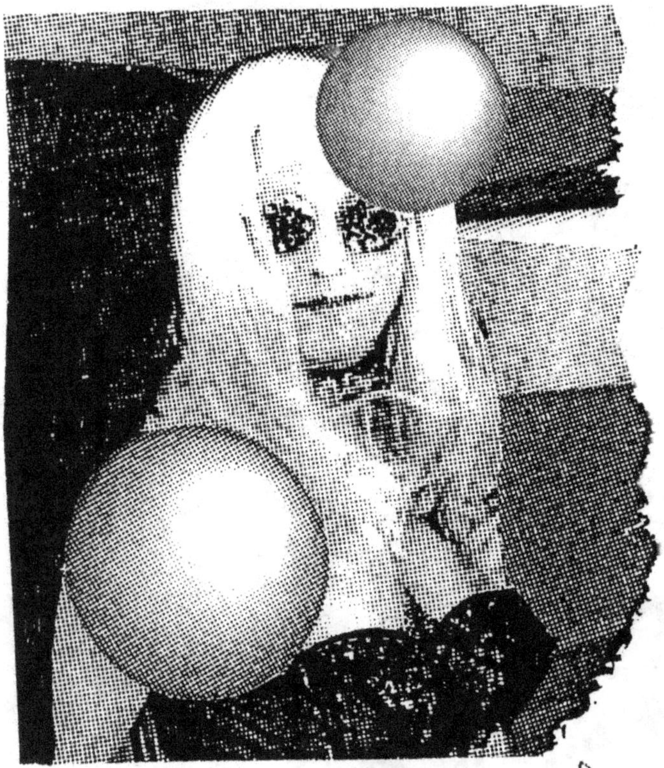

Ben Straight and Norman Normal
is your life really like
Martha Stewarts plan ?
Its a sad state of affairs
that aids the delusion
of feeling better.
The crush of love,
the fantasy of romance,
warm feelings rush around
my chest, the back of my neck
tingles. Another saturday night !
I only have 4000 of them left !

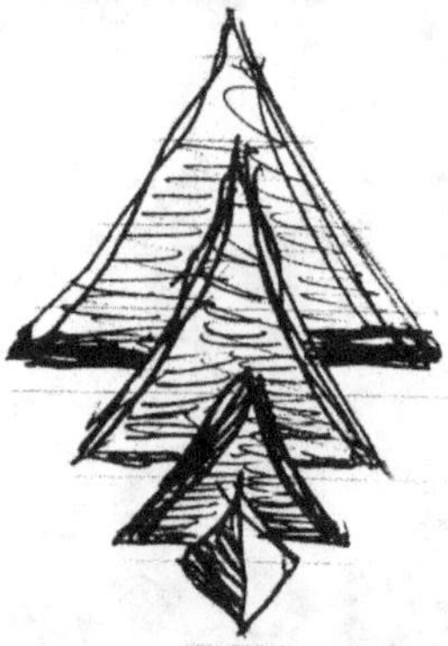

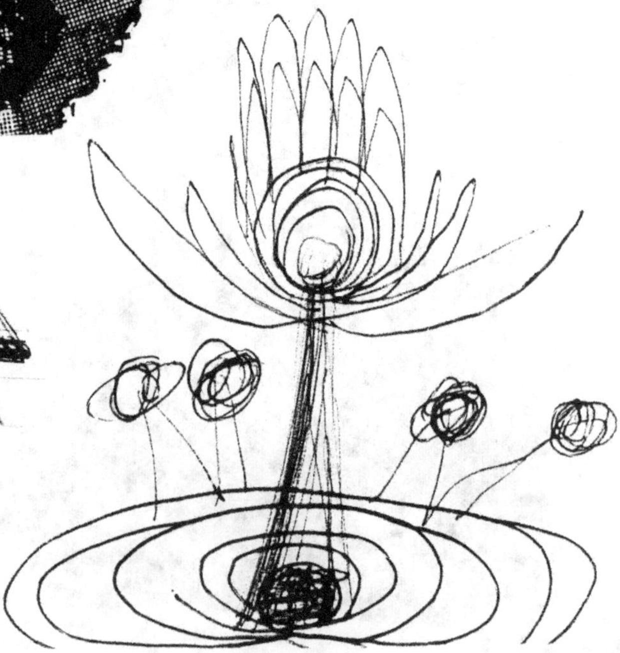

Nordick poets.....Explore Porr, Loki, Glaumr,

the skaldic poems Thorsdrapa, Lay of Thor.....

The creative use of kennings and other metaphorical ideas

was with so many viking seafaring poets.

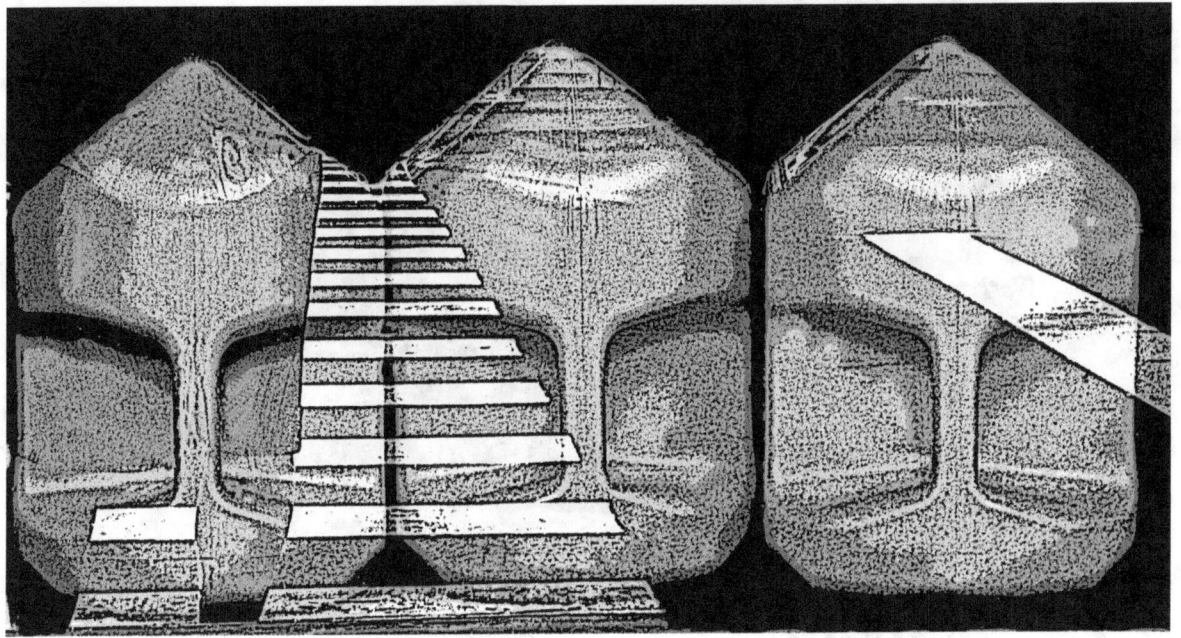

In the picture above three viking helmoots

that lost their minds.....Their names are;

Artfast vikin, Hord norse, and Norse code,

they would only dine on vegetarian toad,

created from gluten and soy, yet sodium free.

All the vikings were saying is give bread a chance at sea,

and put your gland in the hand of the curly red head.....

picture above Cross walk, diesel fuel cans handles up?

Talk oz.....Holden, rolling thunder, 4x down under

surfers feat, tarmac heat, No shoes.....

Burning souls, No shirt.....Skin cancer holes

No service.....Oz needs a dress code!

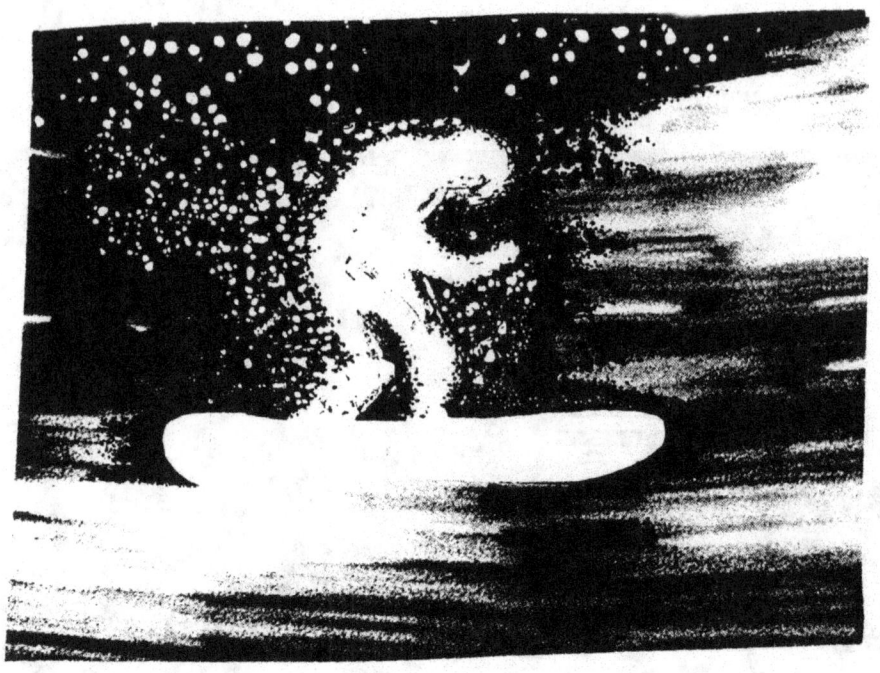

Power is the addictive aphrodisiac !

Glide, surf,
roll, ski, jump,
freefall
control be careful
you have not moved
out of your chair,
virtual vagrant.

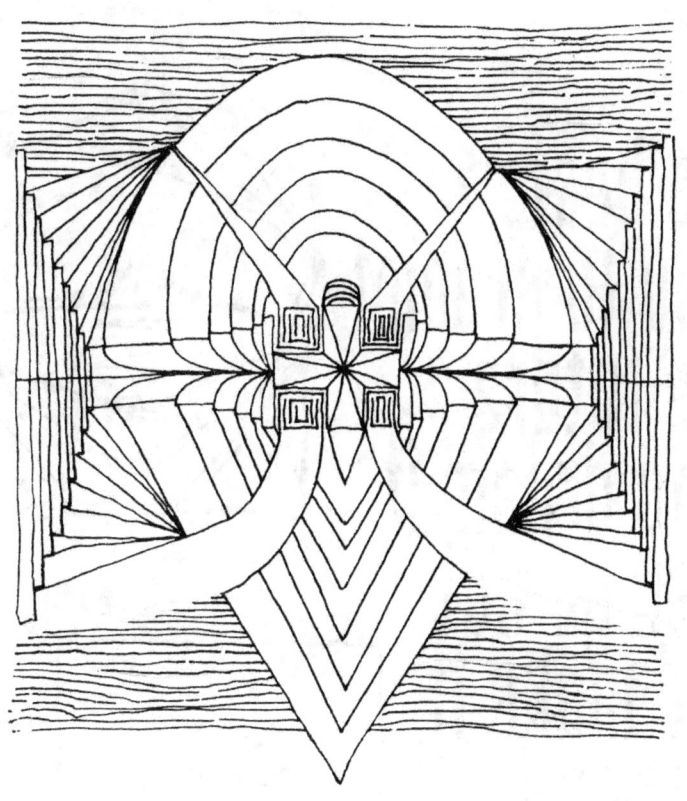

PERPETUUM

Curves correction,
ellipses erecting,
shadows showing,
lurking lines,
mystery magnificent

The best
way to predict
the future
is to dream it
then go out
and make it
happen !

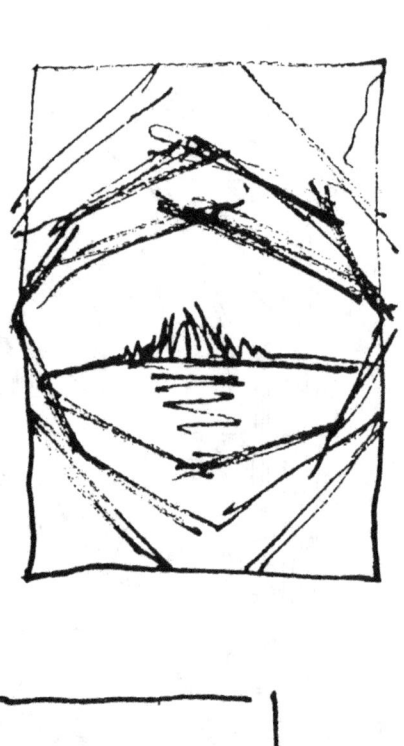

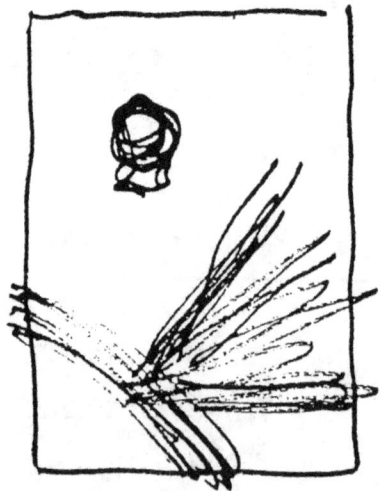

Djinns (Geniis) are in the Koran, they exist in our parallel world, they can morph into many forms and they influence humans.

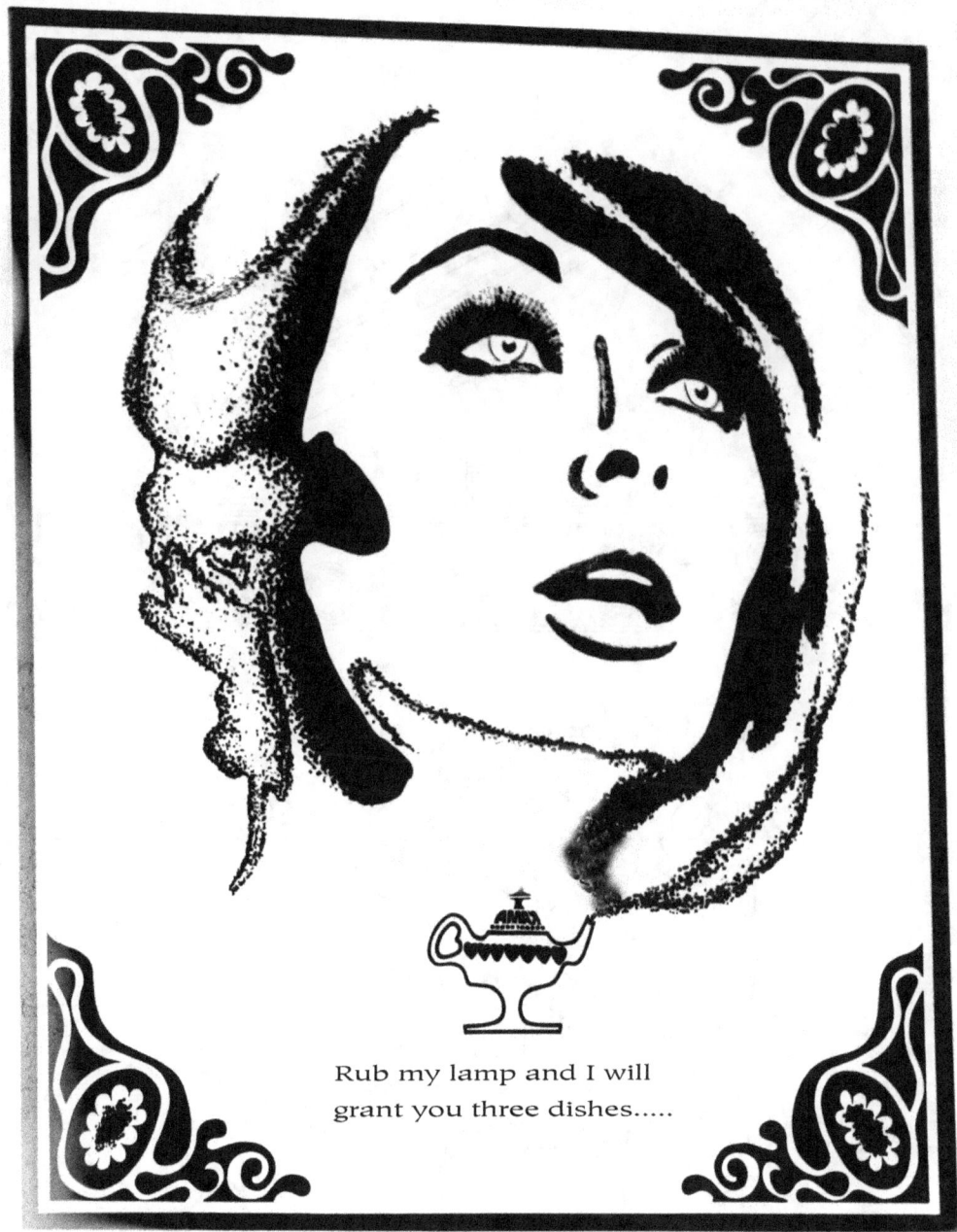

Rub my lamp and I will
grant you three dishes.....

Hey Bunny it is not a crime, when was the last time
you enjoyed a magic carpet ride.....Get scared hide,
you will feel lost outside your minds great divide.....
Rabbit rabbit creatures of habit.

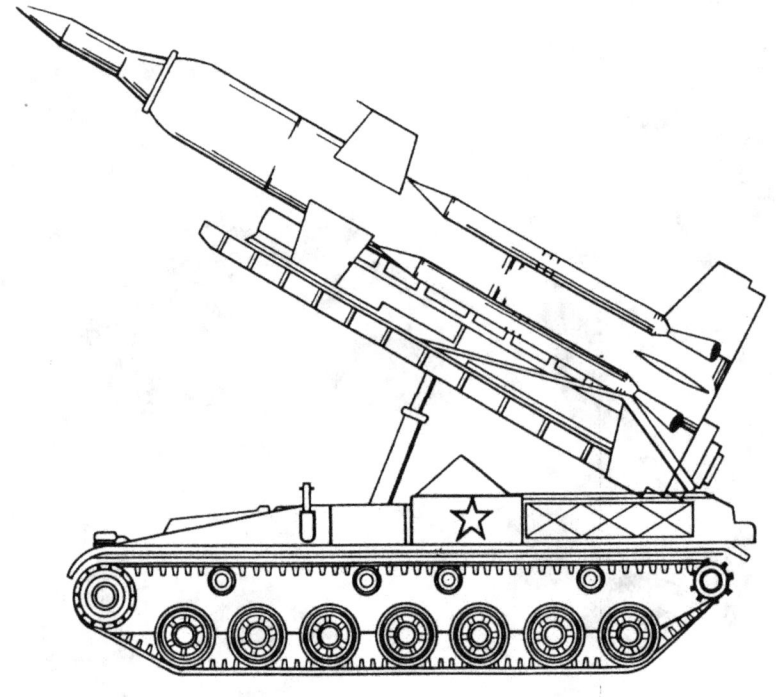

Thirty Years ago, I did
100 Military technical
Drawings, I guessed at the
Details from Ariel Photos
Where did all this work
go. I need more today, I
now I've had Experience!

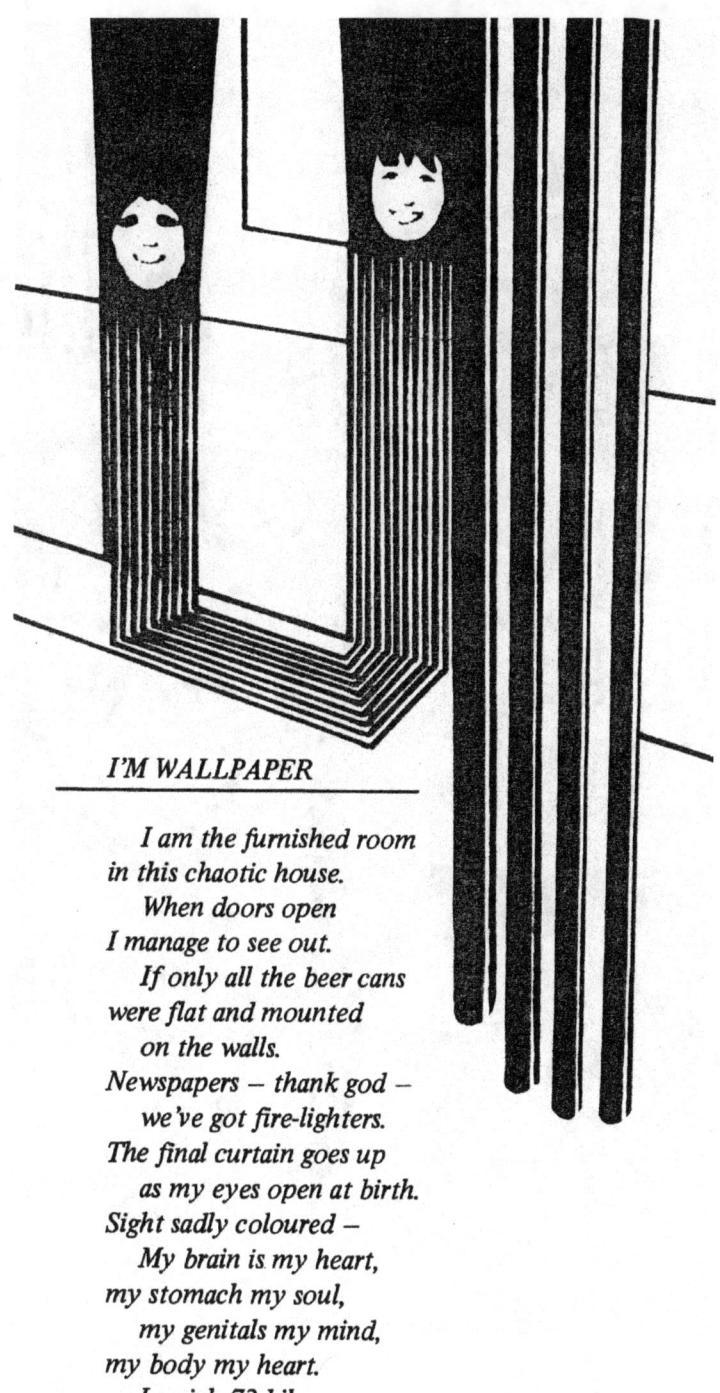

I'M WALLPAPER

I am the furnished room
in this chaotic house.
When doors open
I manage to see out.
If only all the beer cans
were flat and mounted
on the walls.
Newspapers — thank god —
we've got fire-lighters.
The final curtain goes up
as my eyes open at birth.
Sight sadly coloured —
My brain is my heart,
my stomach my soul,
my genitals my mind,
my body my heart.
I weigh 73 kilos.

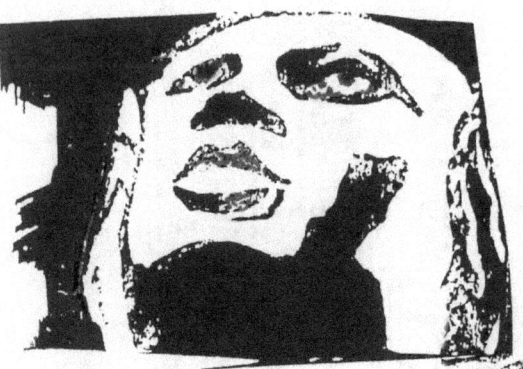

Reality is an illusion

brought on by the absence

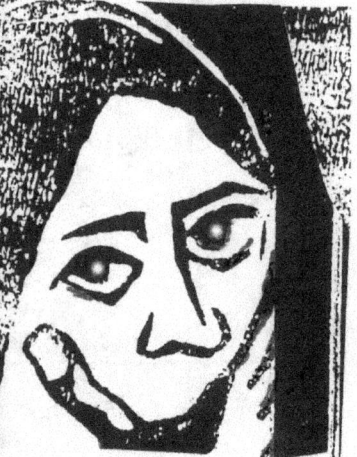

of alcohol....

Drugs
Sugar!
Love.

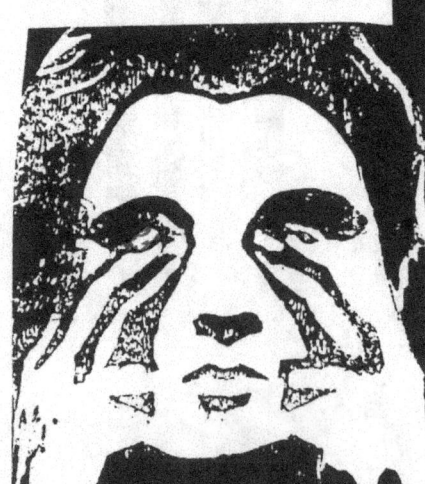

186

Staring into nothing,

reflections, resistence,

reluctance, resentment rules,

ride on the coattails of respect,

guilt controls the free spirit

of uninhabited frivolity.

What is the algorithm of freedom?

What computer runs that app?

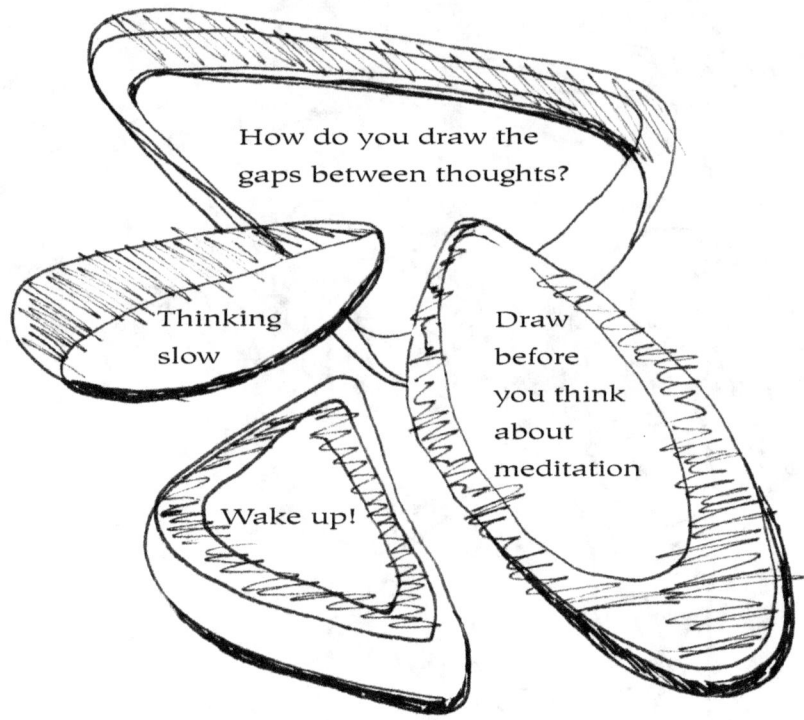

How do you draw the
gaps between thoughts?

Thinking
slow

Draw
before
you think
about
meditation

Wake up!

Poets diet, be queit.....No

No dairy, No wheat.....Forget meat

except in beer

lay down on the floor

sexercise more.

Fish friday, vegans on facebook.....

Thats life on a stick.....

Laugh and the world
laughs with you,
snore and you
sleep alone.
Anthony Burgess

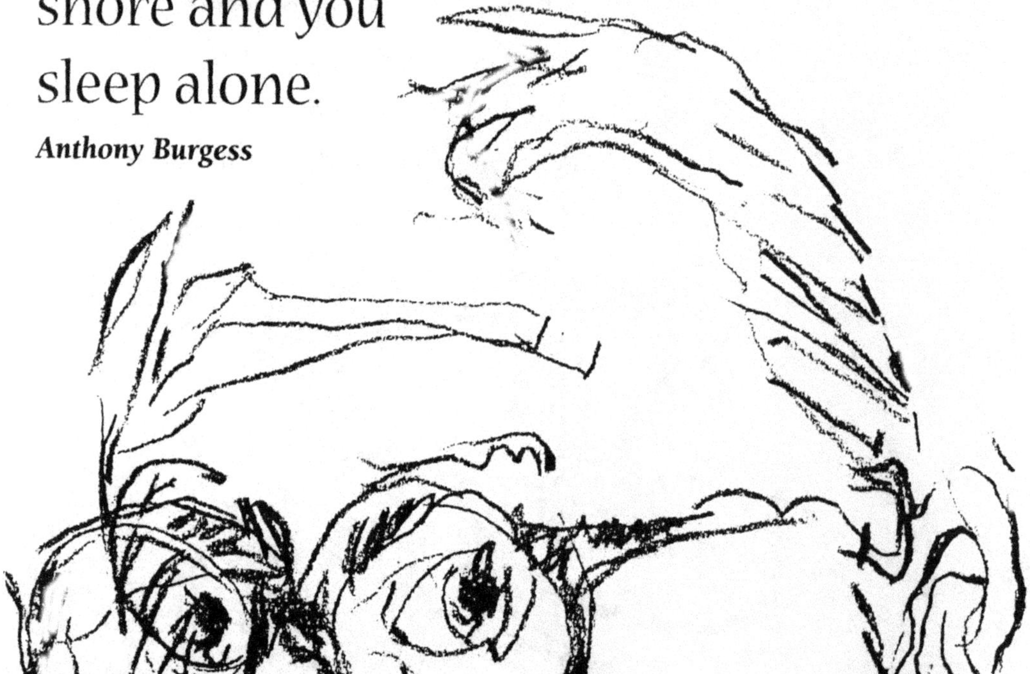

I am
rejuiced
and
turning
into a
Clockwork
Orange.

188

Menage a trois or twiddle.....Tea for three.....Please

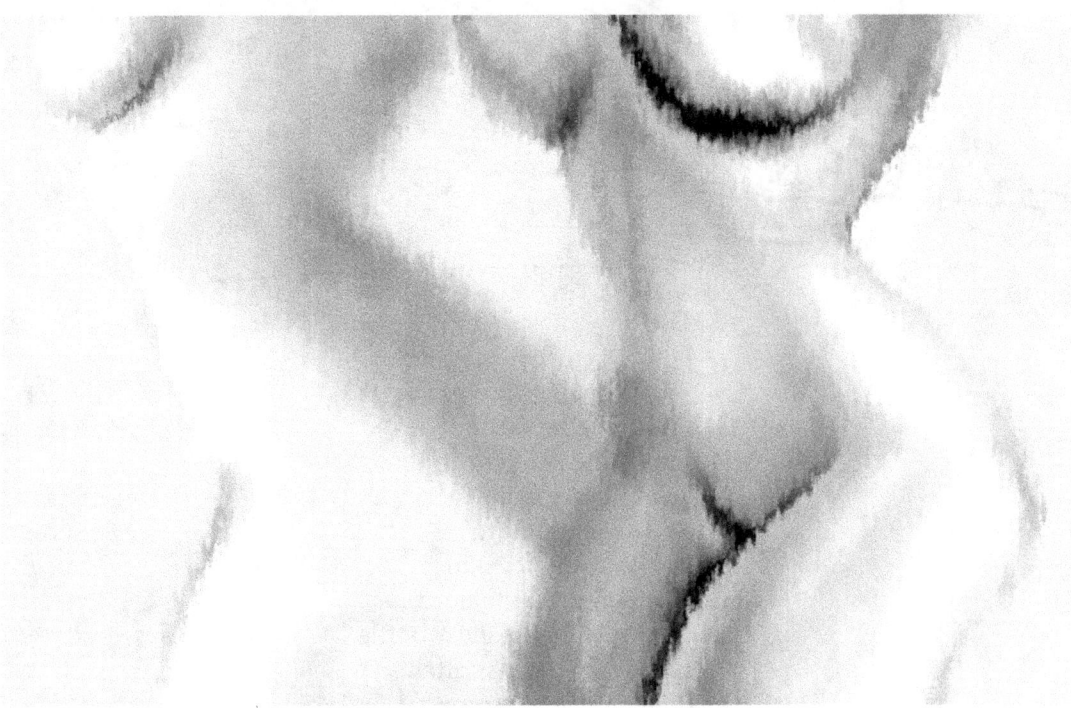

Her shadow
came alive
then there was
two of them.....
How could I cope
doppelganger,
fantasy or fiction
think twice
before you lie.....

My guided pencil
scratches the shadows
and performs sculpture
sketching the shapes and
contours of sensual slopes
as it slides over the texture
of the laid french paper.....
When should I stop,
over working?

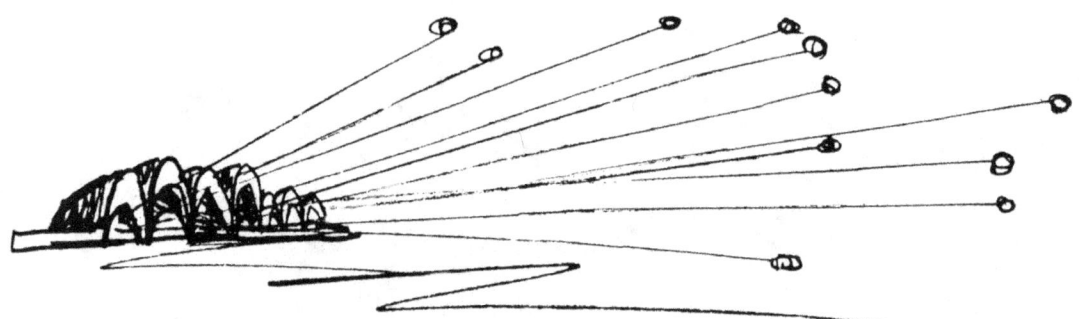

The day the sun left the earth
I closed my eyes to ignore
this ugly nightmare.
I'm in the house that is
four hundred years old,
its walls are sharing
its secrets with me
as I tear into its skin.
Hunger, love, violence,
birth and in the glass bottle
I find this letter written
on a chamois in brown ink:
In the fire's warmth
I find you and want to share
the early morning waking
taste the tea
and I watch your golden hair
as it brushes lightly across my face.
Holding happiness tears back
my heart runs in loves race.
If ever I were torn away,
war- how could that be.
They might officially separate
our lives under law 784
sending us to separate
ethnic holding homes.

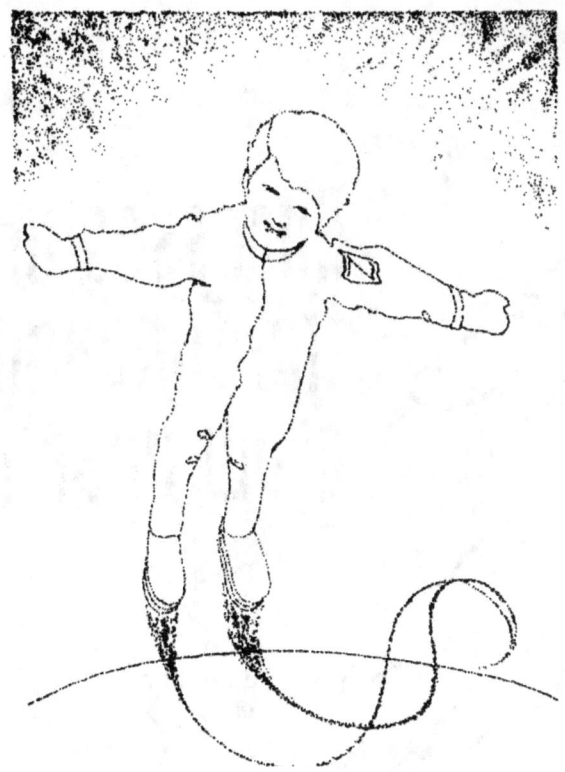

My baby is up there in the
hormone sea waiting for me....
To be inseminated or at least
mensa rated. Pick a time for
your biopsy on the website
growahuman.org..... Skychild
RuXanadu no.....My system
password is Zarragon (XY)
and Yenna (XX). Enter.

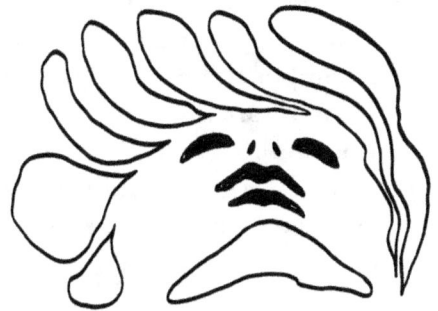

Abcesses make the fondaling grow heartier

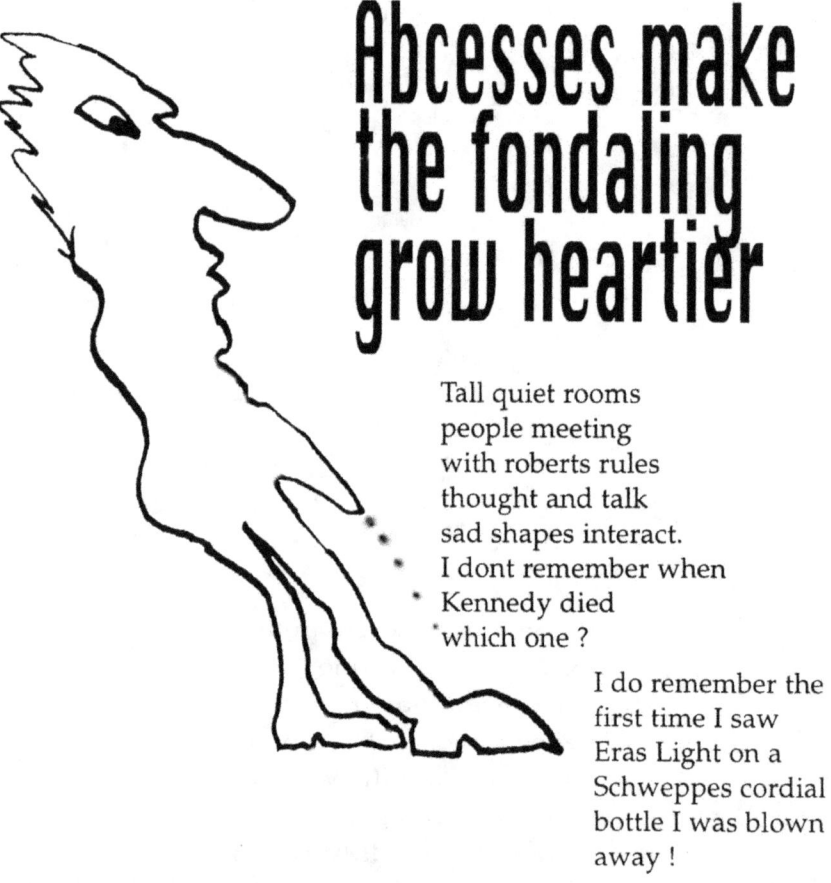

Tall quiet rooms
people meeting
with roberts rules
thought and talk
sad shapes interact.
I dont remember when
Kennedy died
which one ?

I do remember the
first time I saw
Eras Light on a
Schweppes cordial
bottle I was blown
away !

The tinkle of pee before morning tea.....
Weather sets my mood or is that food. Rain
or shine I remember the time of passion.....
Horizontal in the first class toilet on the
train, watching ceilings as the sky goes by....
Traingasmn, cum on! Is this fantasy my
darwin legend or urban lie, have I been on
a club world five mile high?.....

Emotions are caused by the
eye of the beholders.....Under-
neath the box you will find a
new world! The noose of death
comes to us all.....Every day
have fun, play enjoy the rides.
I do hope here
on earth you
enjoy your stay,
if I can be of
any assistance,
please let me
know, enjoy
your show.....

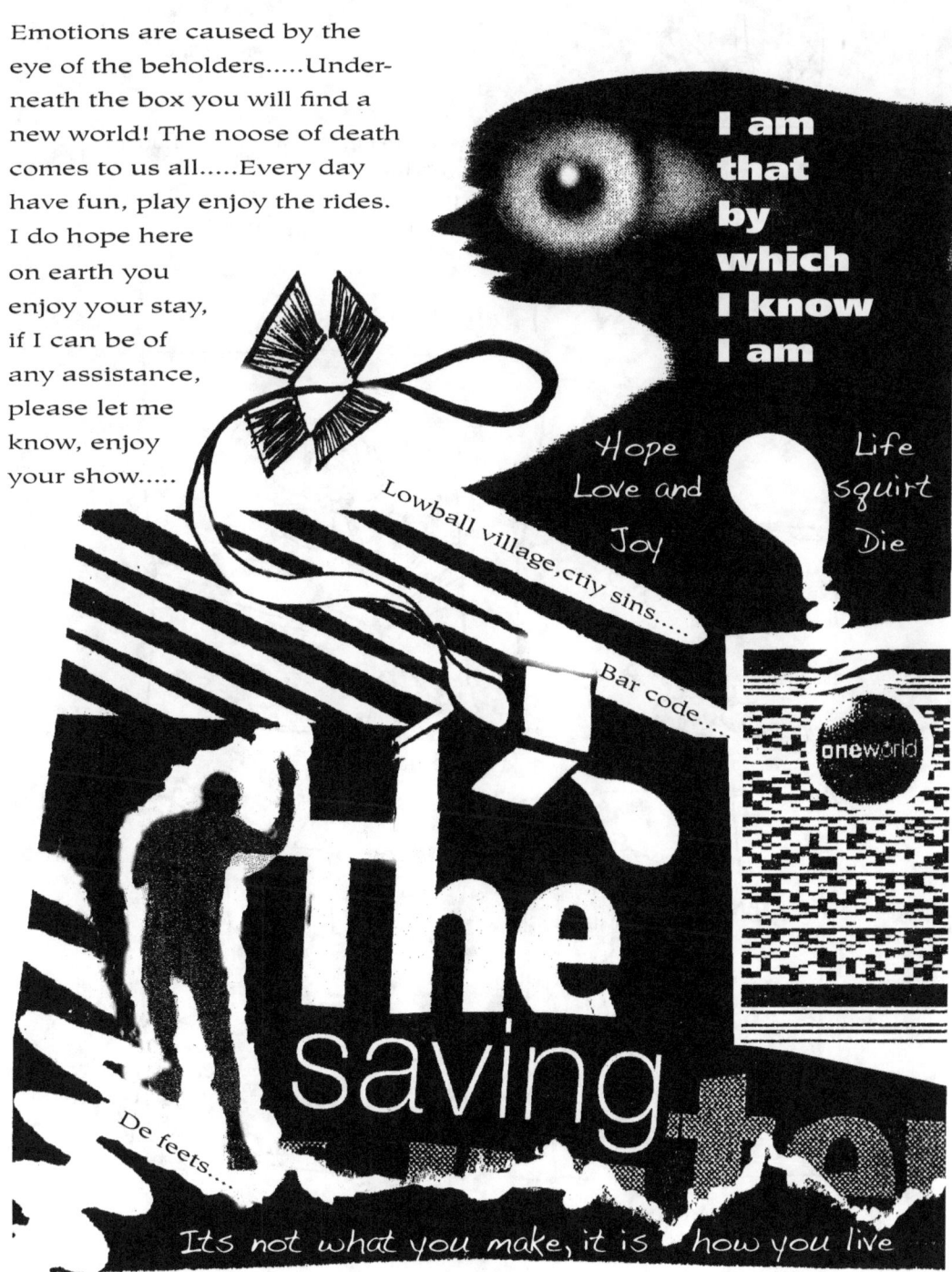

I am
that
by
which
I know
I am

Hope
Love and
Joy

Life
squirt
Die

Lowball village,ctiy sins.....

Bar code....

oneworld

The saving

De feets....

Its not what you make, it is how you live

Proust said "Only by art can we get outside ourselves;
instead of only seeing one world, our own, we see it under
multiple forms, and as many as there are original artists,
just so many worlds have we at our disposal."

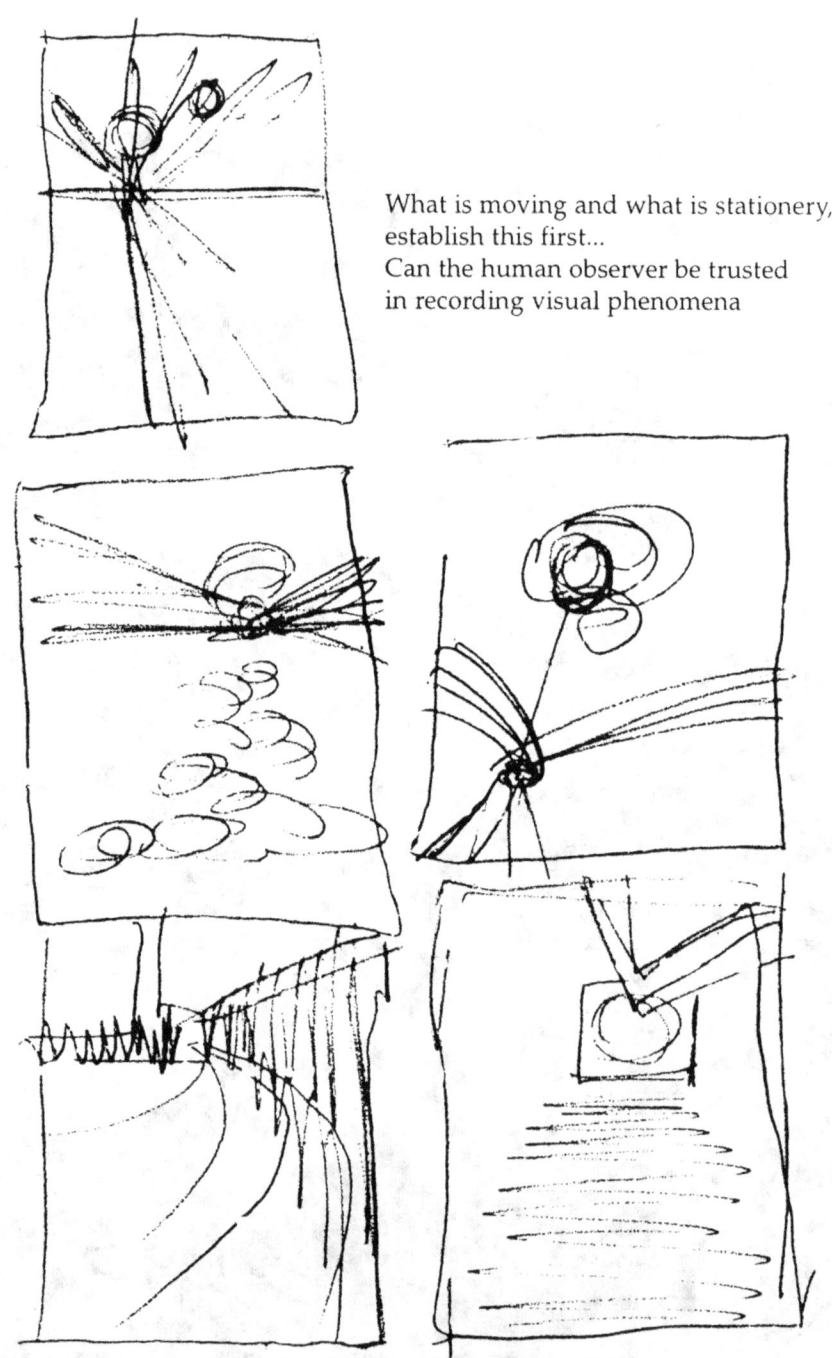

What is moving and what is stationery,
establish this first...
Can the human observer be trusted
in recording visual phenomena

YVR.MIA.YYZ.YUL......ZLO.SEZ.NRT.
BNE.DMK.SYD.CMB.DPS.TBU.....OMG-
Canadians love to be snowbirds and fly
out of the winter to the sun in the fall
wanting home away from home, oh my!
The picture on the right says it all.....

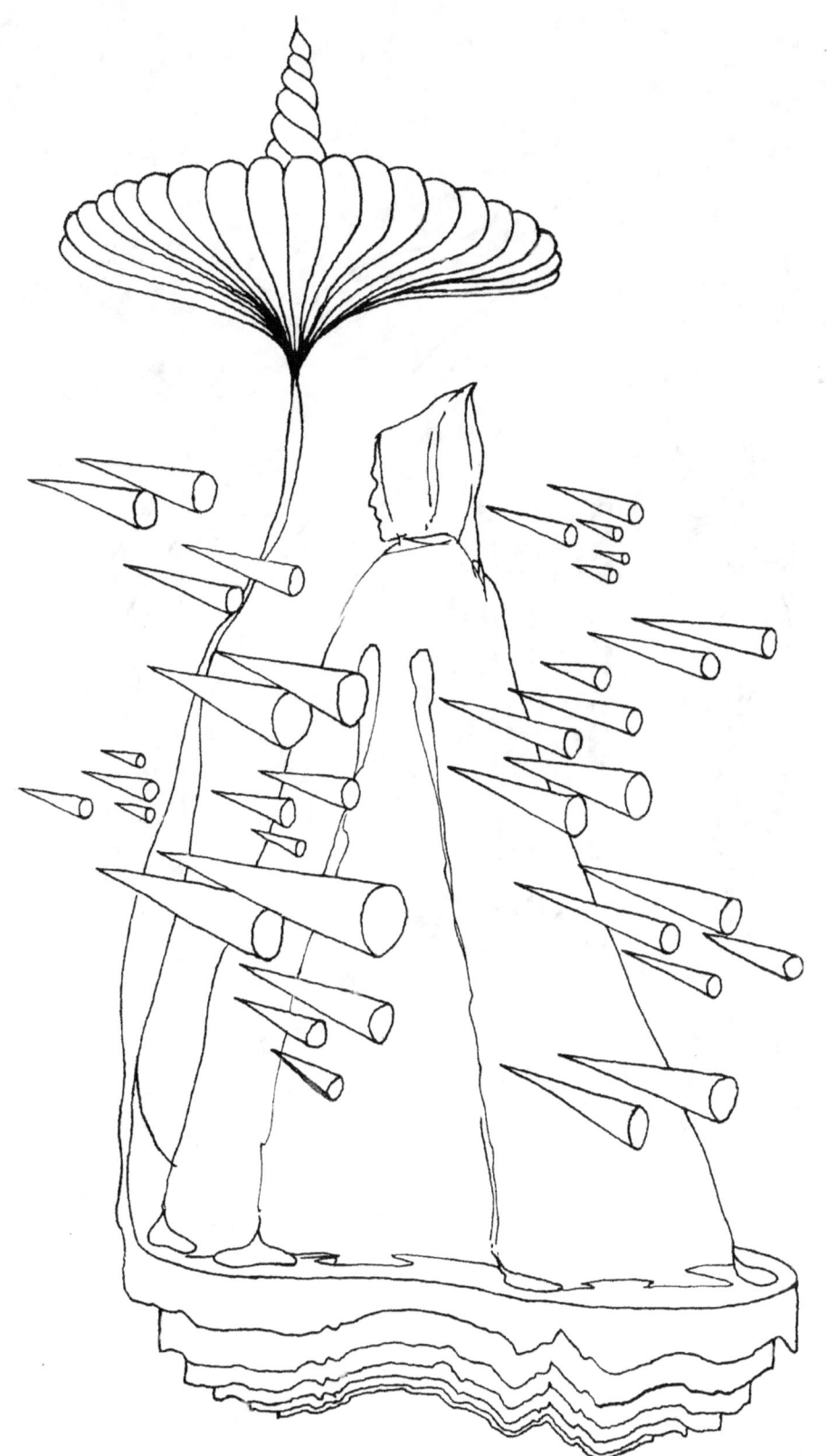

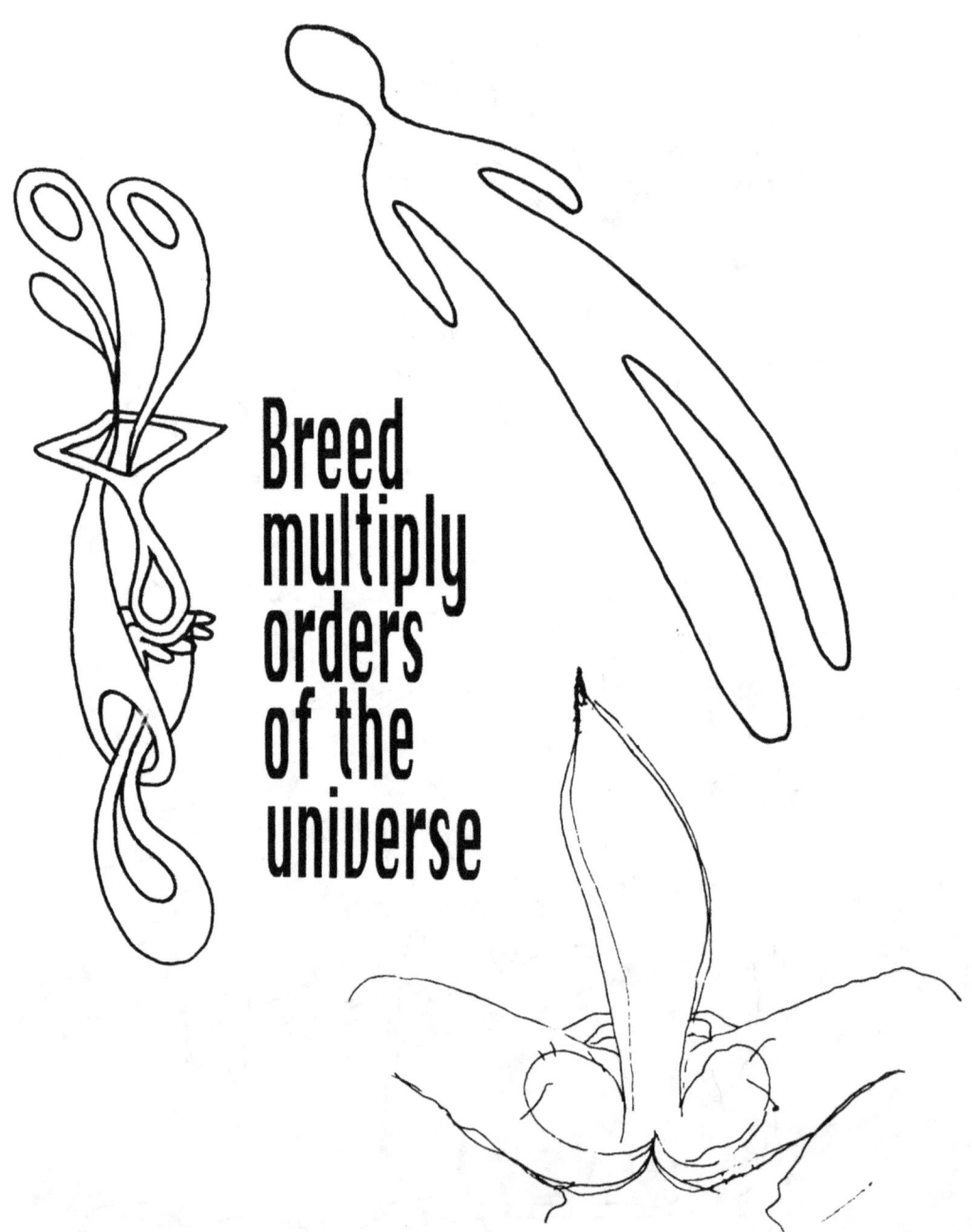

Breed
multiply
orders
of the
universe

"The use of language is not confined to its being the medium through which we communicate ideas to one another"

John L. Roget

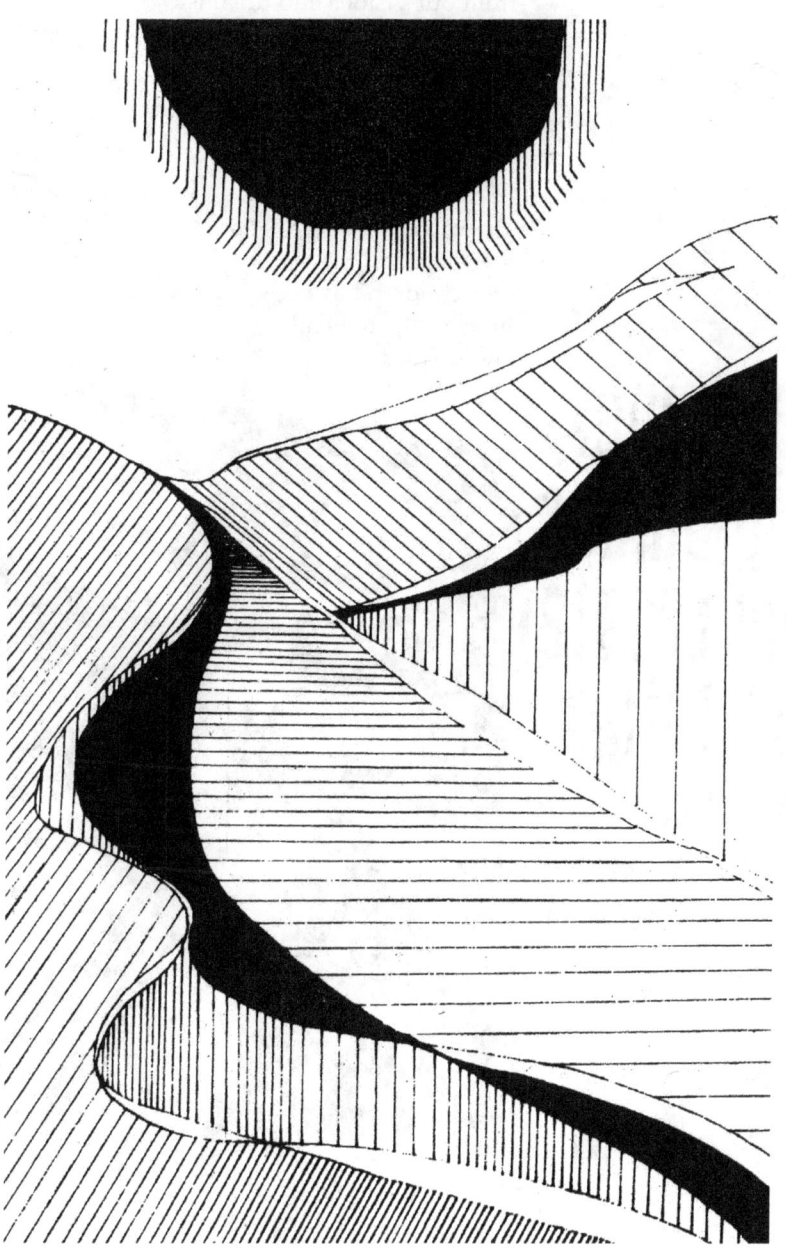

There was a ball called sun, it gives energy to a ball called earth, while on the run around a solar system.....Describe a landscape to a person that can not see earth from mars..... Half of the day I am in the darkside of this planet!

The future evolves
from our visions and dreams
then our actions and future
planing guide us to make it
happen, is this it
What happened ?
Please change the reality
of our existence.
Do we get the future
we visualize ?
Our children have so
much potential and
endless possibilities.

Our hopes and values will create the future of life

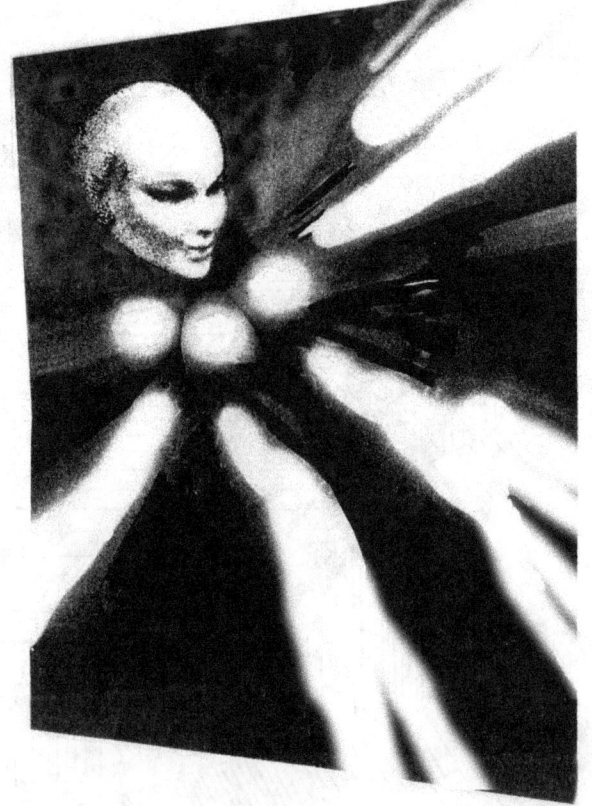

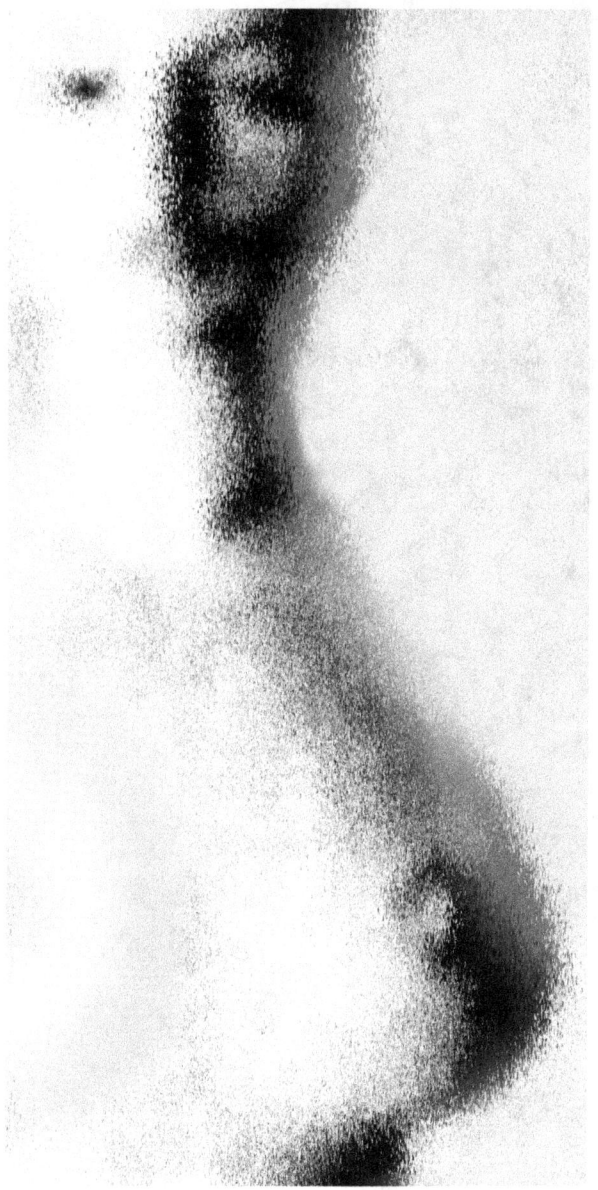

Enjoy ruddles
then cuddles with
swollen muddles
thru the snuggly
curly moosshh
woosh.....Fire desire
semen swim higher,
thats their natural way,
life story so far.....
Ma, this will change
with genebionics.....
It was nano nice to
splice the rice
and feed more!
Are you sure.....
Prossanto
lets change
the random
fall of the dice
not just in mice.....
Will babies
still feed on full milk
breast nipples?

The nipple rouge was not tested on any animals,
but our shoes are made of cow real skins.....

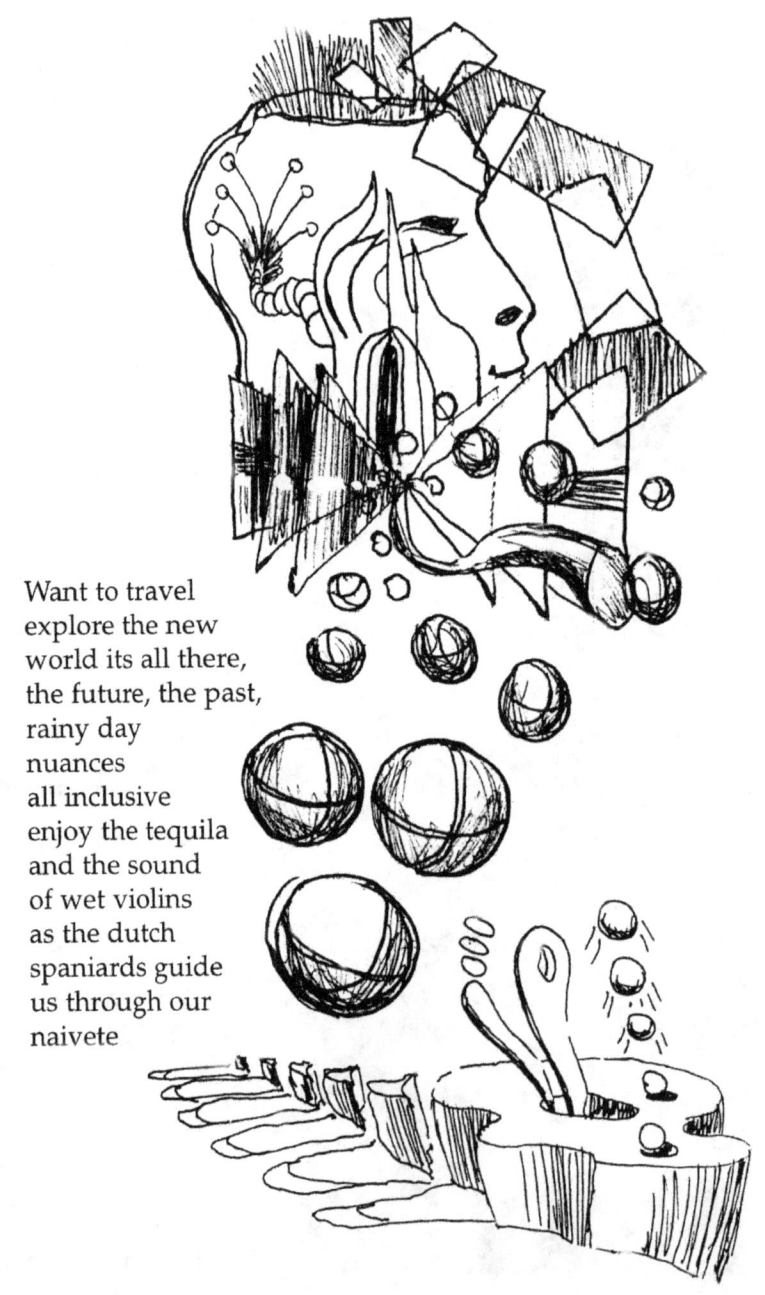

Want to travel
explore the new
world its all there,
the future, the past,
rainy day
nuances
all inclusive
enjoy the tequila
and the sound
of wet violins
as the dutch
spaniards guide
us through our
naivete

Look at the pictures you have been given, draw over them in black pen to find the structure of the balance and layout. Then see how your eye travels around the picture and its route. Study the tonal contrast of all the items in the picture. See how your eye enters the picture and are you driven out of the picture or are you held into the focal point?

What story is the picture sending to you?

BEDBug

BLOODY

HELL!

DESIGN & GRAPHICS

FIRE
AIR
FOOD
LIFE
WATER

Emotions evolved for their changing value in dealing with the fundemental life tasks.....From mountain highs to deep ocean lows.....

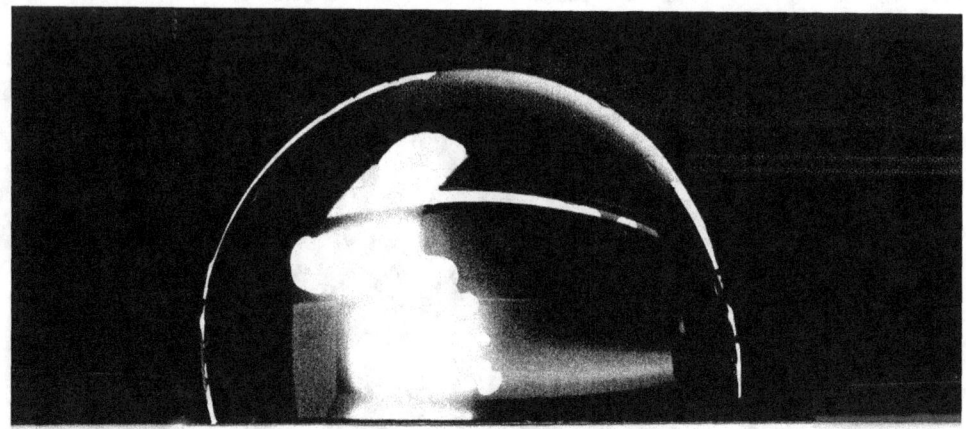

The meaning of life
is really technological change.
What do we want
our society to be or achieve ?
Will we like what it becomes?
Vague directions driven by
poverty, greed, power, apathy,
love and money.
Why dont we eliminate
the media and television.
The most important box
in the history of mankind
it has total control of all
our lives, our desires,
our emotions and our
education is it
the meaning of life ?

NOT IF YOU ARE BLIND !

"COLORLESS green ideas SLEEP furiously"

NOAM CHOMSKY

"Could this be poetic symbolism or is it a good example of nonsense? Koan opens the bento box to wordonics.....Only to find Lear, Carroll, Joyce and Wittgenstein. Still you know, the dish ran away with the spoon....Is that gobbledygook?

Shy cry
beach children
flies around
the drink
predators
everywhere
warm glow
of the midday sun.
estuary breeze
sleeping lightly
in the soft sand.
Quiet harbour
a place to rest up
is this home
no the trees have been
leaned on by the wind.

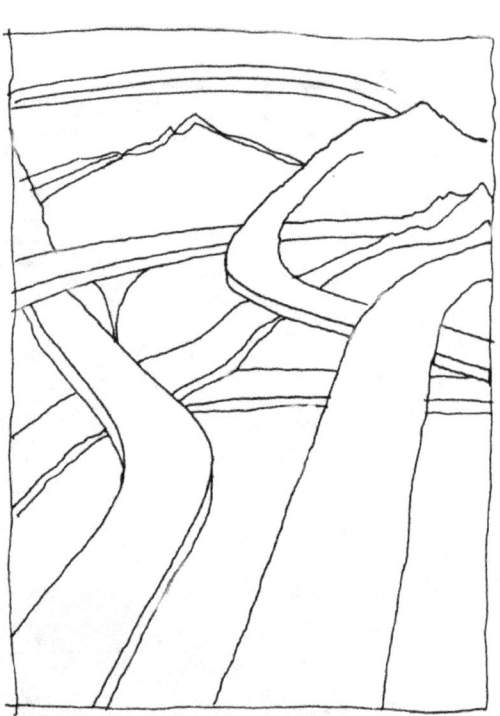

Only dead fish go with the stream

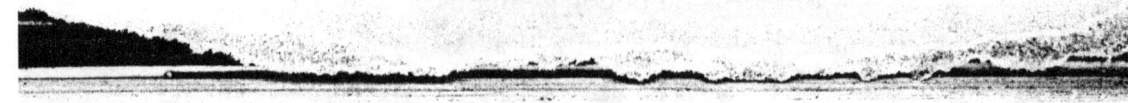

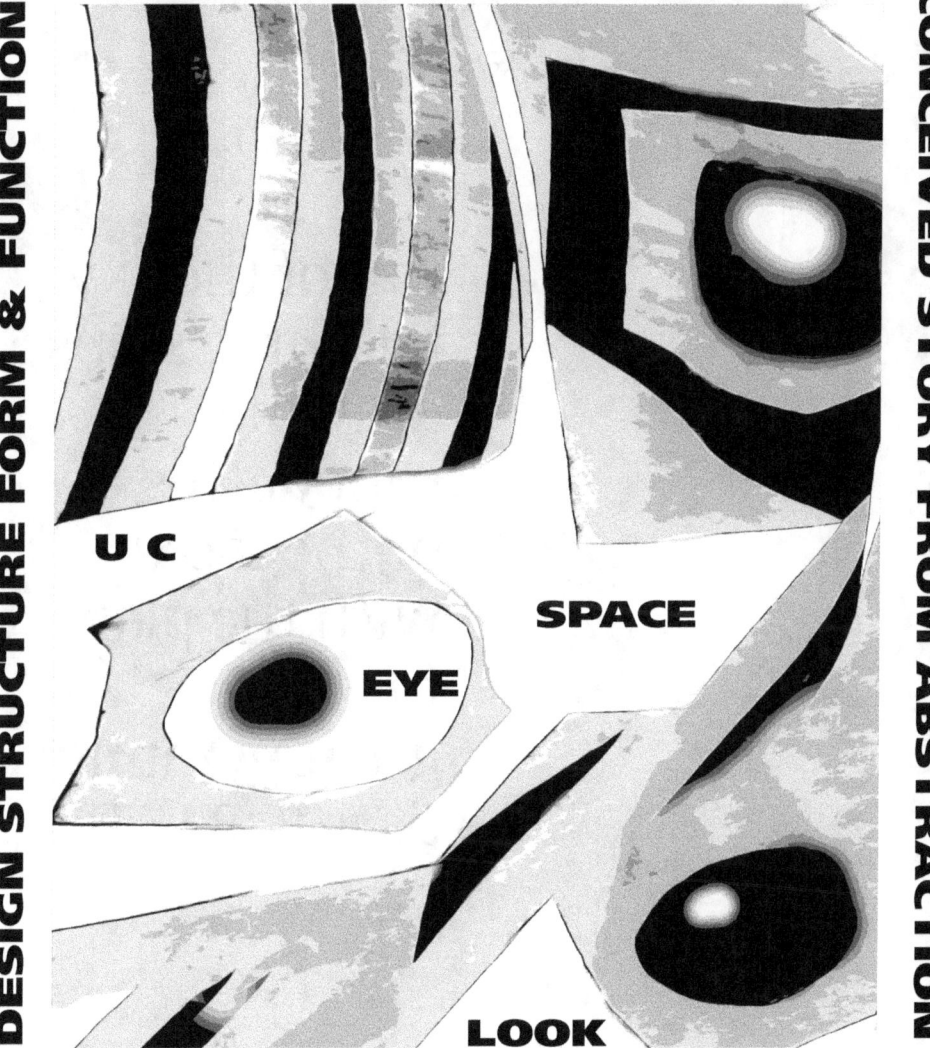

"Whenever the intensity of looking reaches a certain degree, one becomes aware of an equally intense energy comming towards one through the appearance of whatever it is one is scrutinizing."
JOHN BERGER

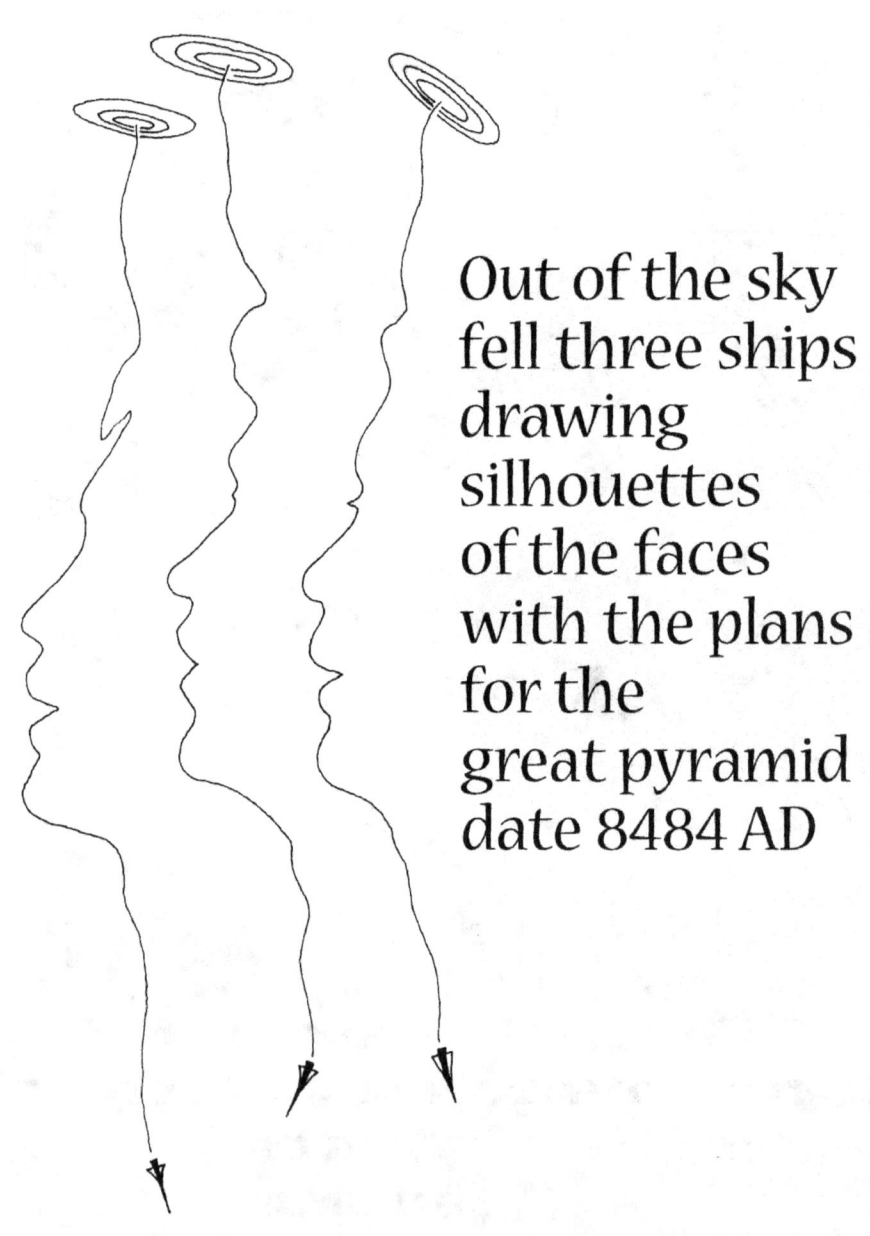

Out of the sky
fell three ships
drawing
silhouettes
of the faces
with the plans
for the
great pyramid
date 8484 AD

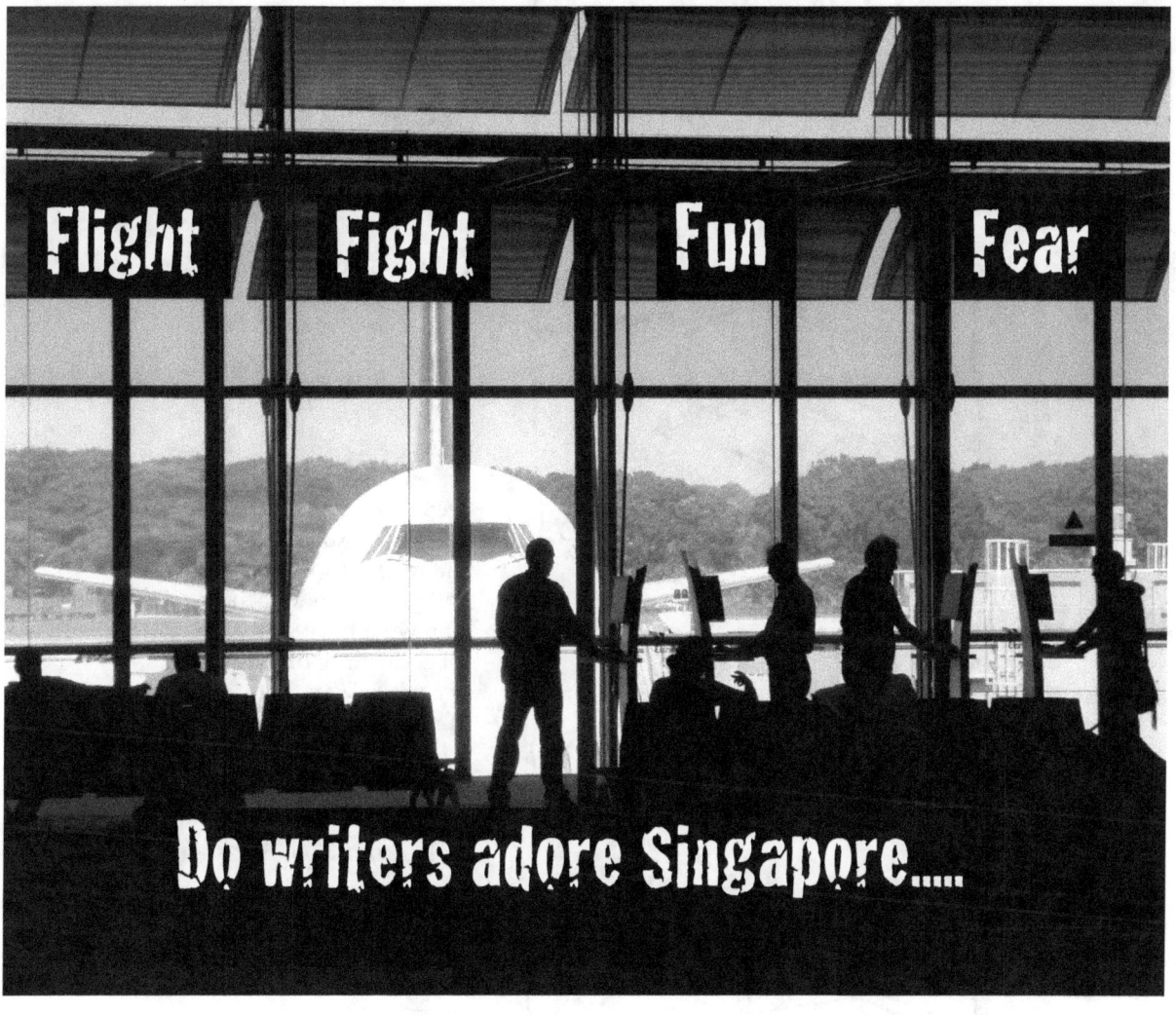

Flight   Fight   Fun   Fear

Do writers adore Singapore.....

"Emotions at an airport.....I am in front of twenty nine security monitors every day watching you and thirty nine thousand fellow passengers, sharing, caring, leaving, deceiving, arriving, greeting, crying, lying.....Do you know which one is the smuggler on your flight? Who has bed bugs on their cabin luggage? Global village, viral spillage.....Viral shared, one world scared!

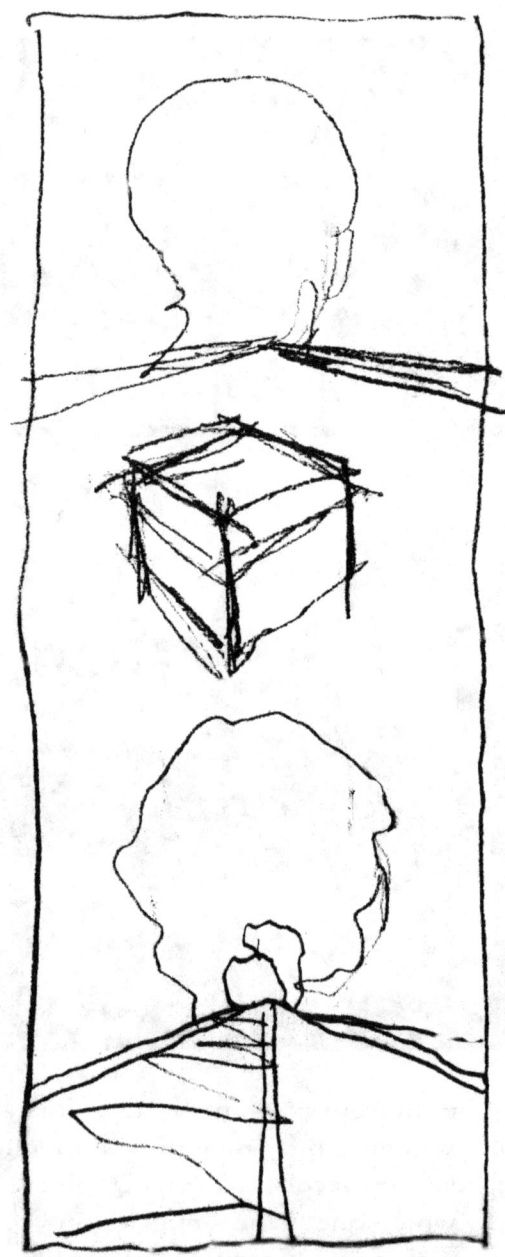

HEAD
BOX
BOOM-NUKE

The poets of Tupelo
meet behind the coors lite
neon sign at nine.
Tears of joy destroy
all the relationships
they have ever stayed in.
They are the free
prisoners that the women
keepers toy with,
lets play hospitals, doctors
and nurses !
Politicians and Preachers
man what have you done,
If I could only dream
of a better way.
Men are like carpets
if they are laid well
they will last for years.

BRAIN-THOUGHT
BOX-OUT OFF
WHITE LIGHT
AT THE
END OF THE
TUNEL !

208

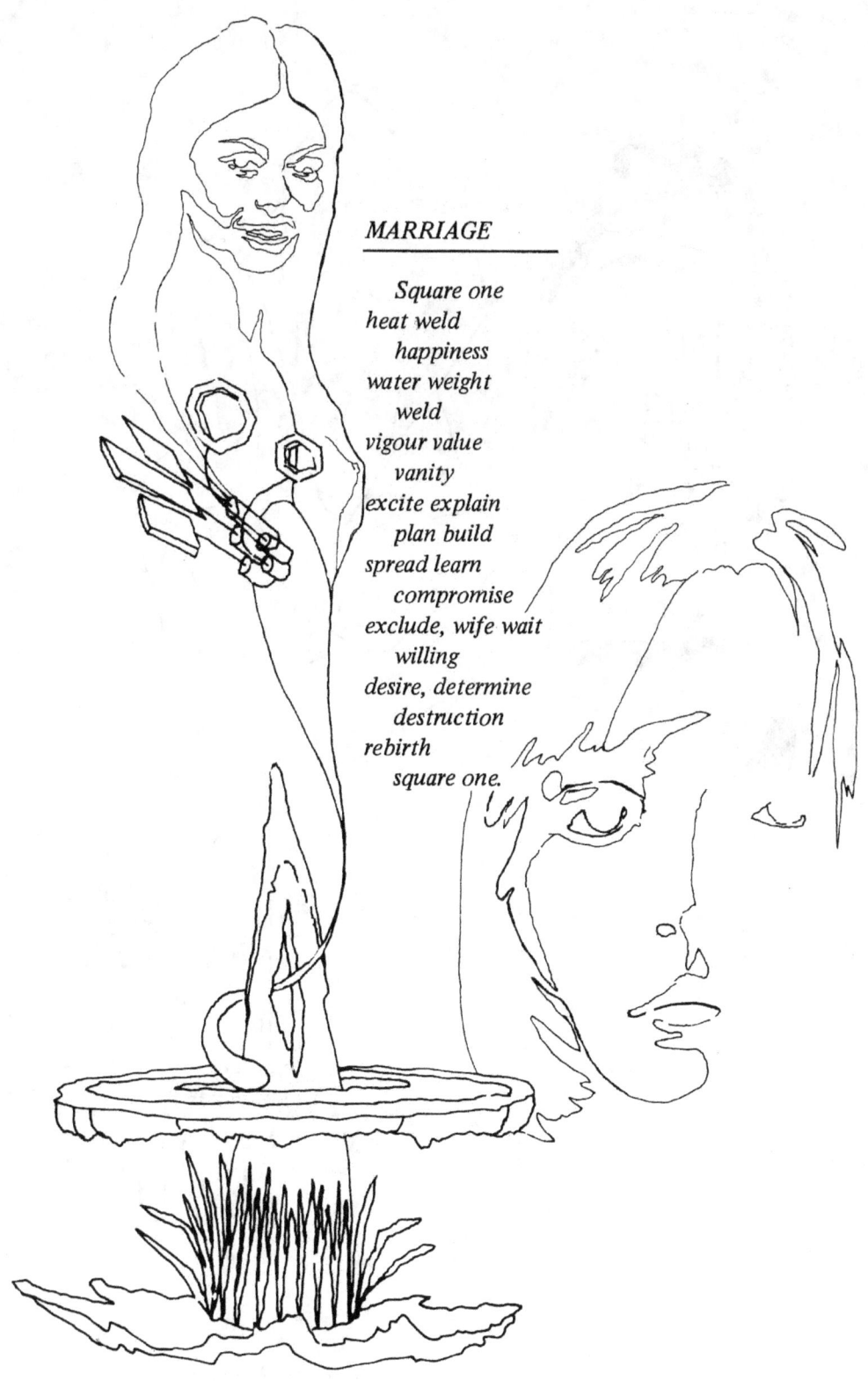

MARRIAGE

Square one
heat weld
   happiness
water weight
   weld
vigour value
   vanity
excite explain
   plan build
spread learn
   compromise
exclude, wife wait
   willing
desire, determine
   destruction
rebirth
   square one.

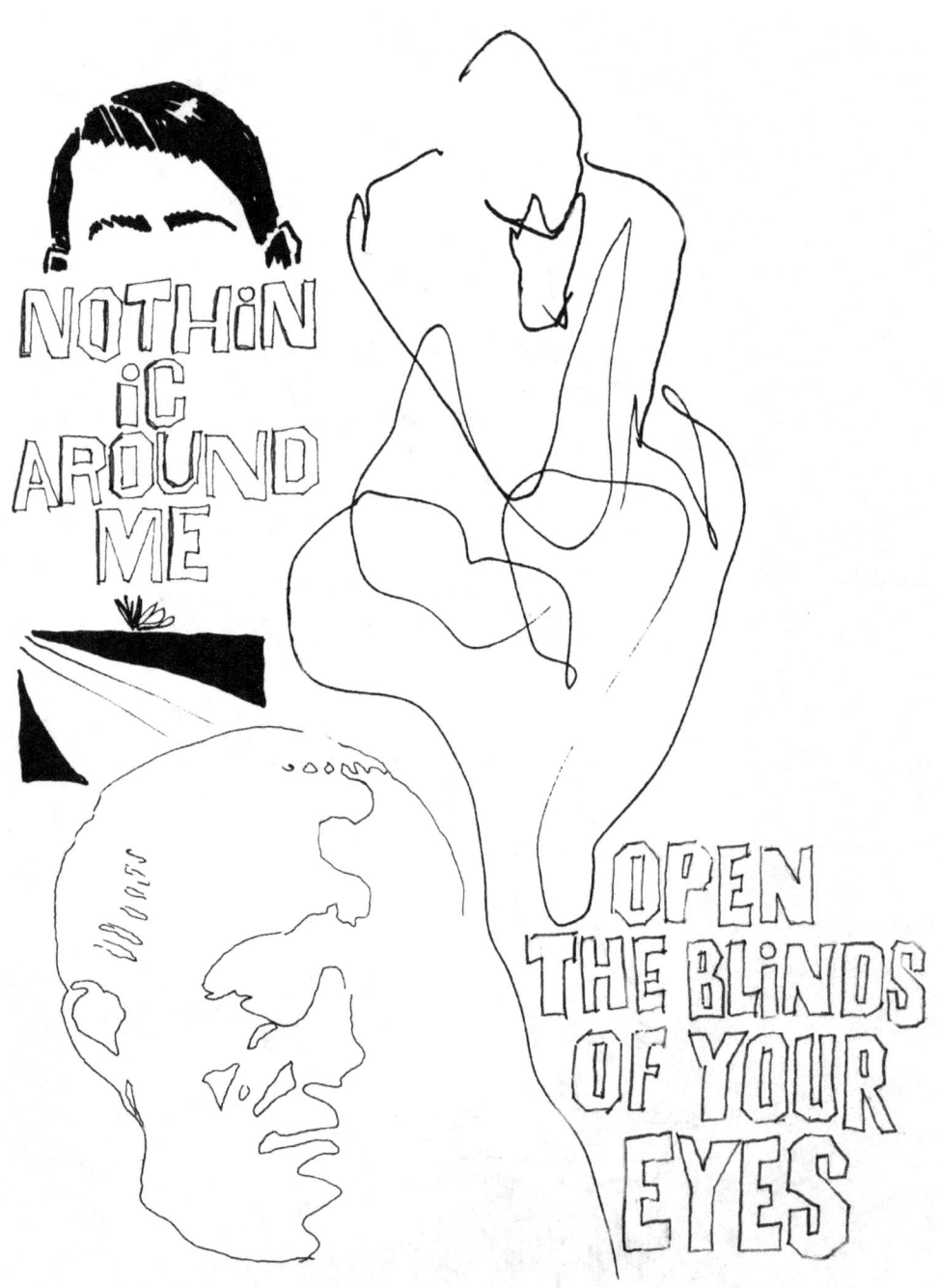

NOTHiN
iC
AROUND
ME

OPEN
THE BLiNDS
OF YOUR
EYES

Nu doors

sexually waiting

bar scores

day by day

lay to lay

love adores.....

Next morning

companion flaws

honesty draws

a different picture

of your choice.....

Yesterdays clothes

on again today

met on the net

filter selection

that does not

look like you.....

Date a mate

how do we rate,

what do you

hope for in them

not rite shite nite.....

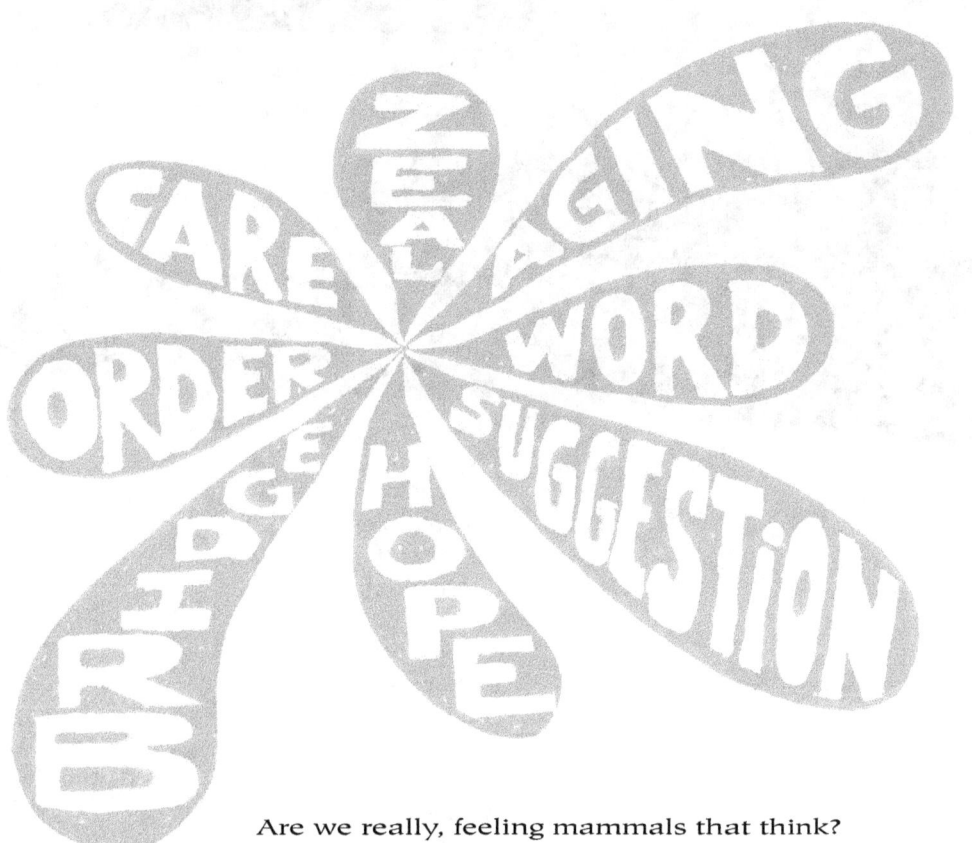

Are we really, feeling mammals that think?

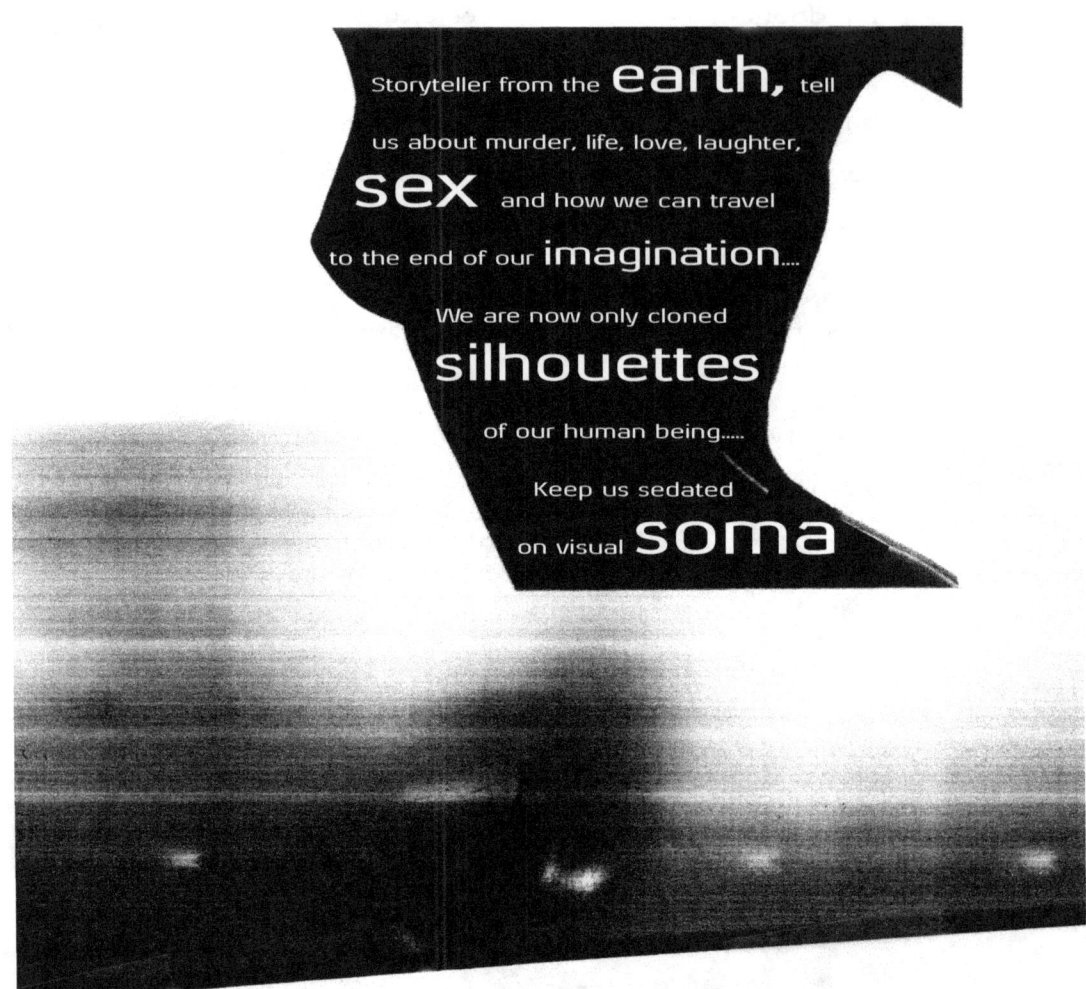

Storyteller from the **earth,** tell us about murder, life, love, laughter, **sex** and how we can travel to the end of our **imagination....** We are now only cloned **silhouettes** of our human being..... Keep us sedated on visual **soma**

Propagandas
new choices
of persuasions
we are suffering
information overload
our small brains
have to evolve
to process faster
and multitask
more.
We are the way
we live
how embarrassing.

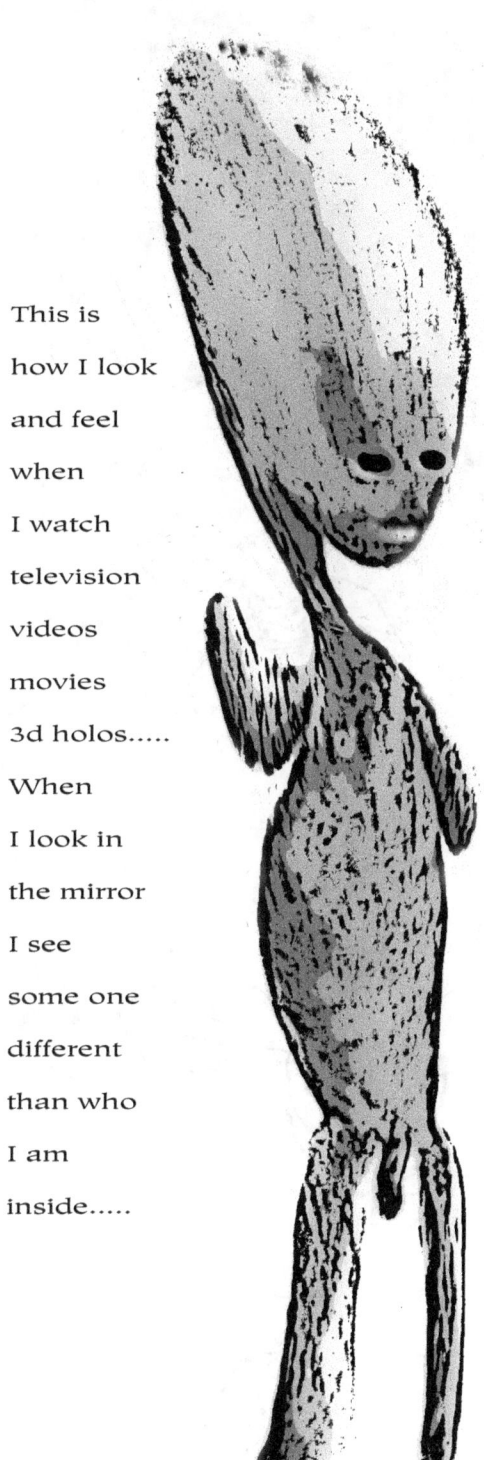

This is
how I look
and feel
when
I watch
television
videos
movies
3d holos.....
When
I look in
the mirror
I see
some one
different
than who
I am
inside.....

Kinki Kurves

klub kred

kleen keens

kotton klobber

kinko kopies

kinetik kreation

kaptin kimond

Kum on

kleptomania

kostalot

kapers kool

kuter krazy

kingfisher

kite high

king kab

Kozina

kills

kids

kabbages

kings kut

klutter

in krown lands

klean up

komplications

kounterchange

kool

kay, OK.

I taste the seeds
ground up the aroma,
I remember the flavour
the sounds and smells
it comes back as a mind
picture painted with
vivid memories.
Shadows- the left over
memory of lights
travelling power, throws
patterns across my plate
as I ignore the babbling
dinner party guests
discuss the church
and their god.
My plate is empty
and I desire the food
I dont have.
How many times
have you been
really hungry ?

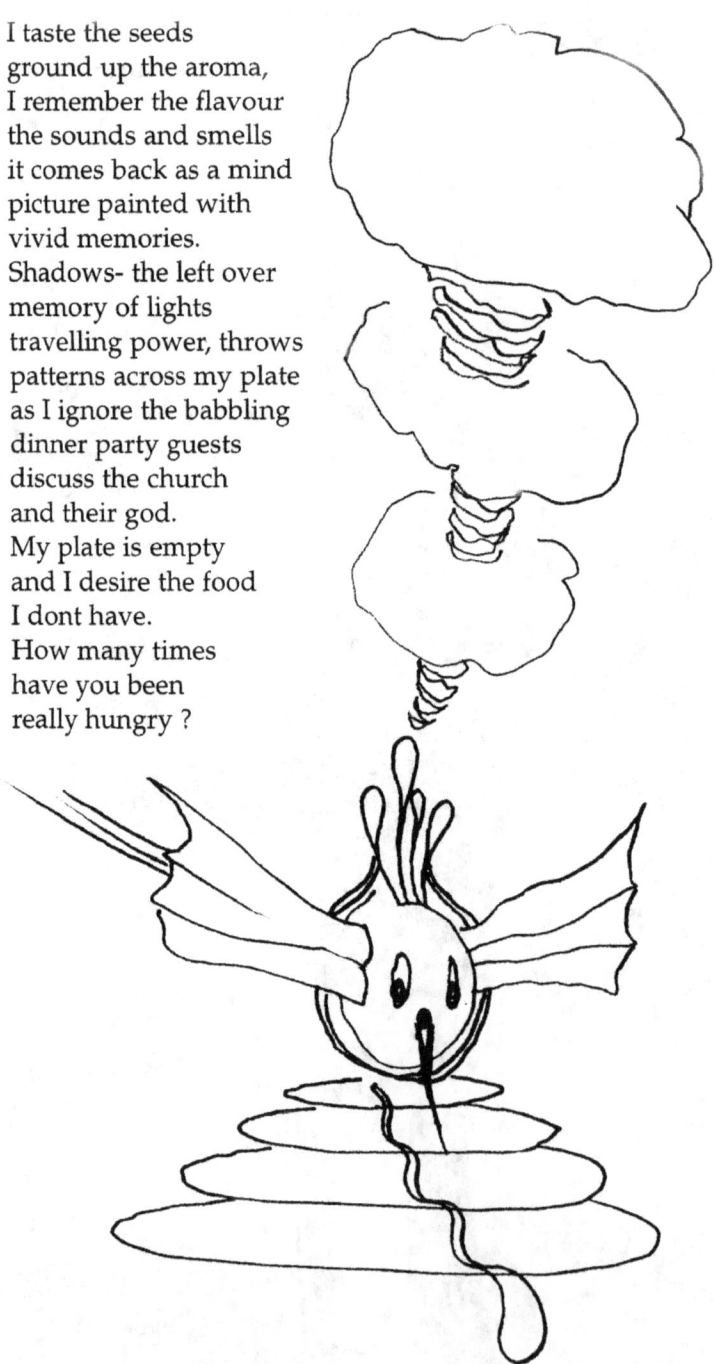

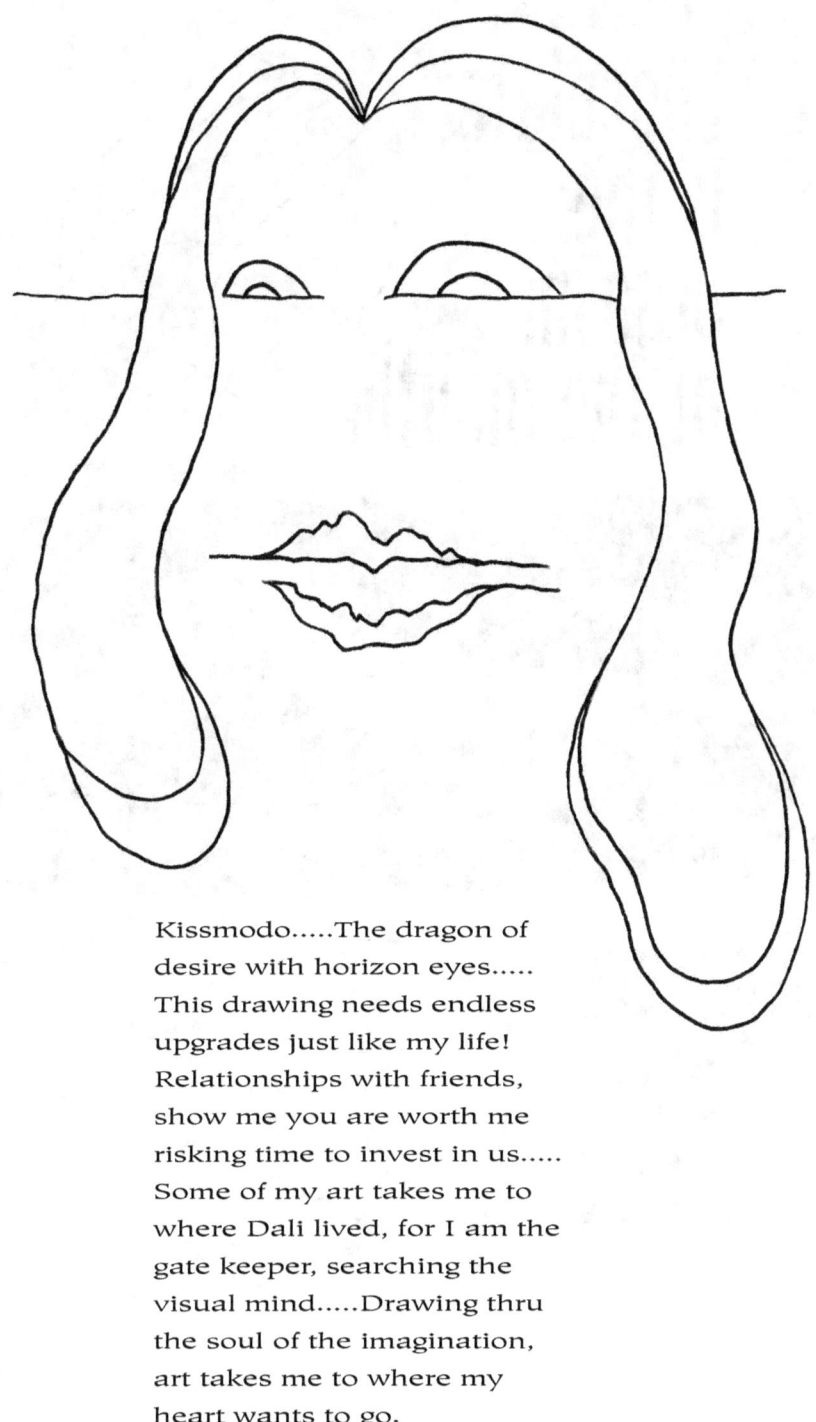

Kissmodo.....The dragon of
desire with horizon eyes.....
This drawing needs endless
upgrades just like my life!
Relationships with friends,
show me you are worth me
risking time to invest in us.....
Some of my art takes me to
where Dali lived, for I am the
gate keeper, searching the
visual mind.....Drawing thru
the soul of the imagination,
art takes me to where my
heart wants to go.

215

Chocolate is the orgasm of the mouth.

The toaster is working well.....

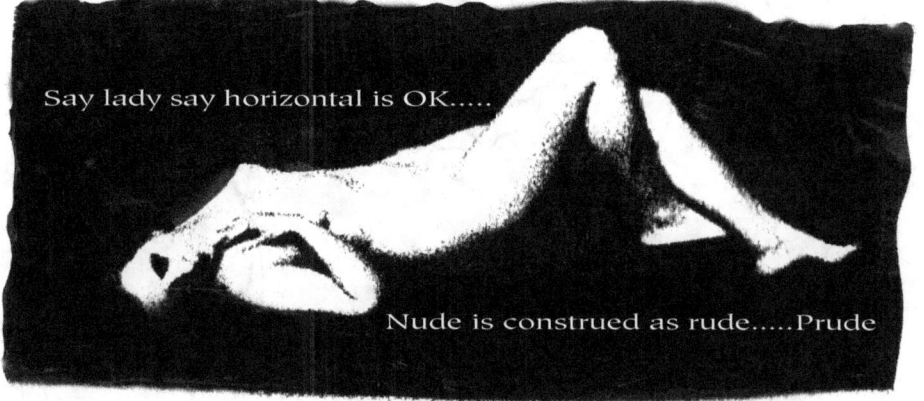

Say lady say horizontal is OK.....

Nude is construed as rude.....Prude

dreams are the orgasm of the mind.

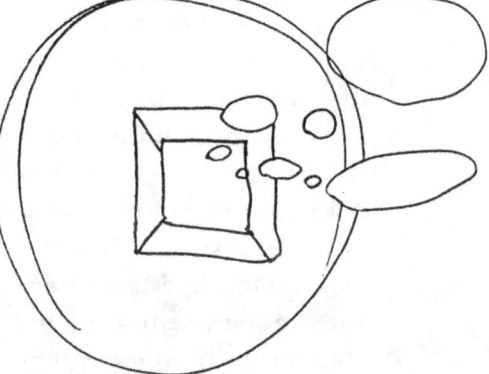

The AC is cold as hell.....

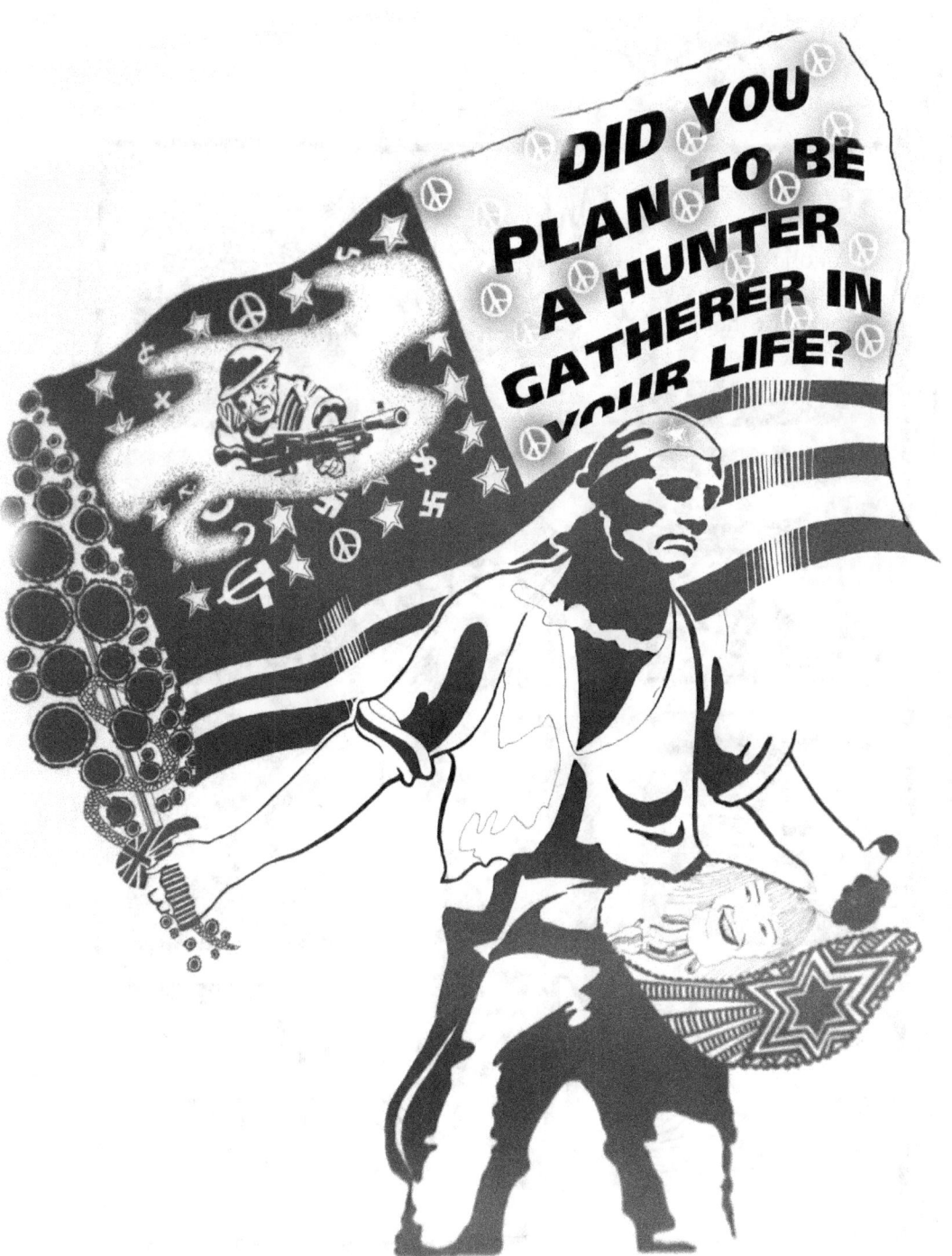

Mommy told me not to cry.....War is just a government lie.....Religion tortured the ten year old, don't deny.....Why, won't we learn history. Have I invented a new wheel after nine hundred years of mystery? Round it goes.....From the seeds you plant, it grows! Give peace a lance.

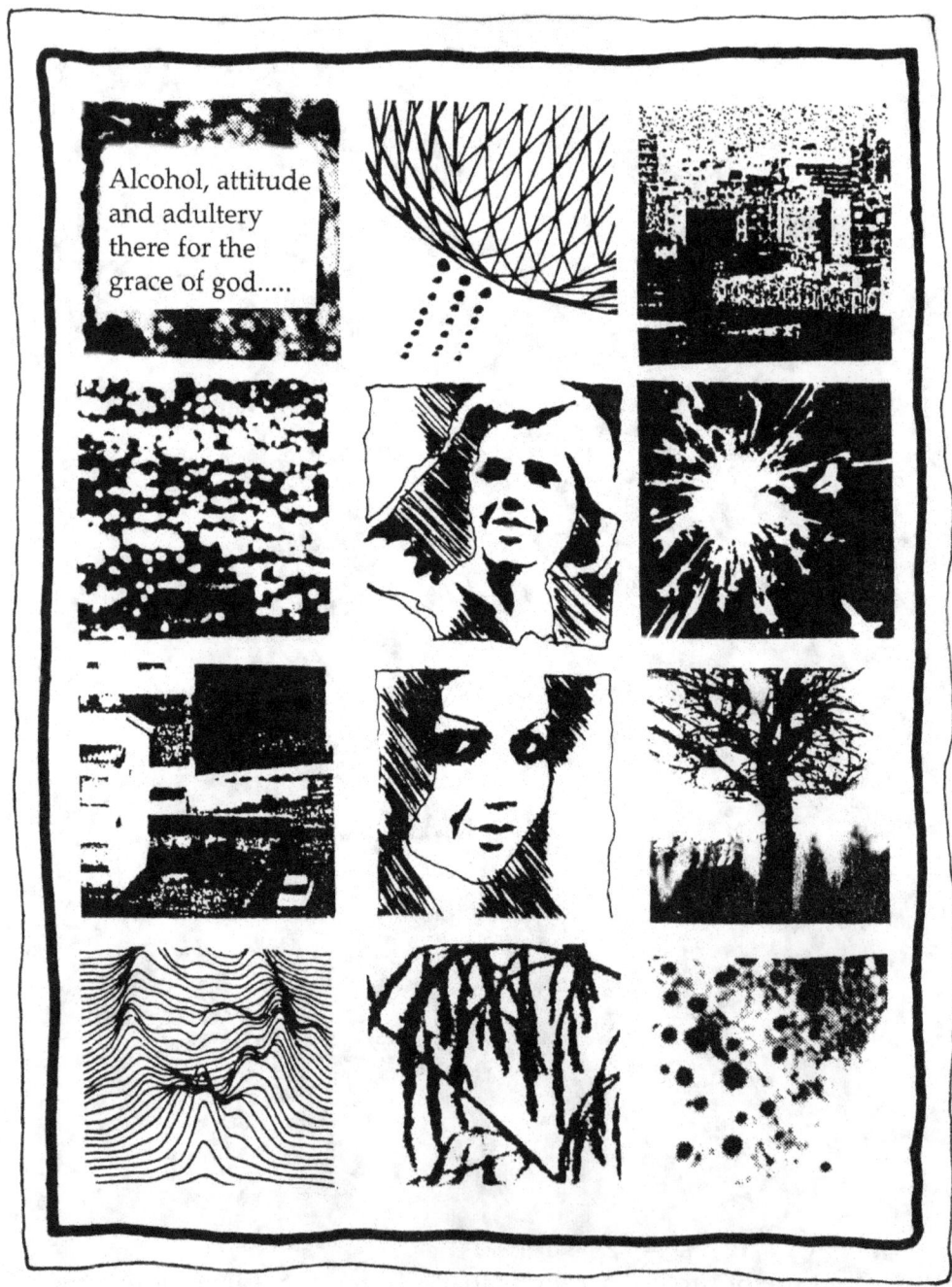

Look mum no walls.....My face is on the door, chocolate
squares on the ceiling and floor, need I say more.....

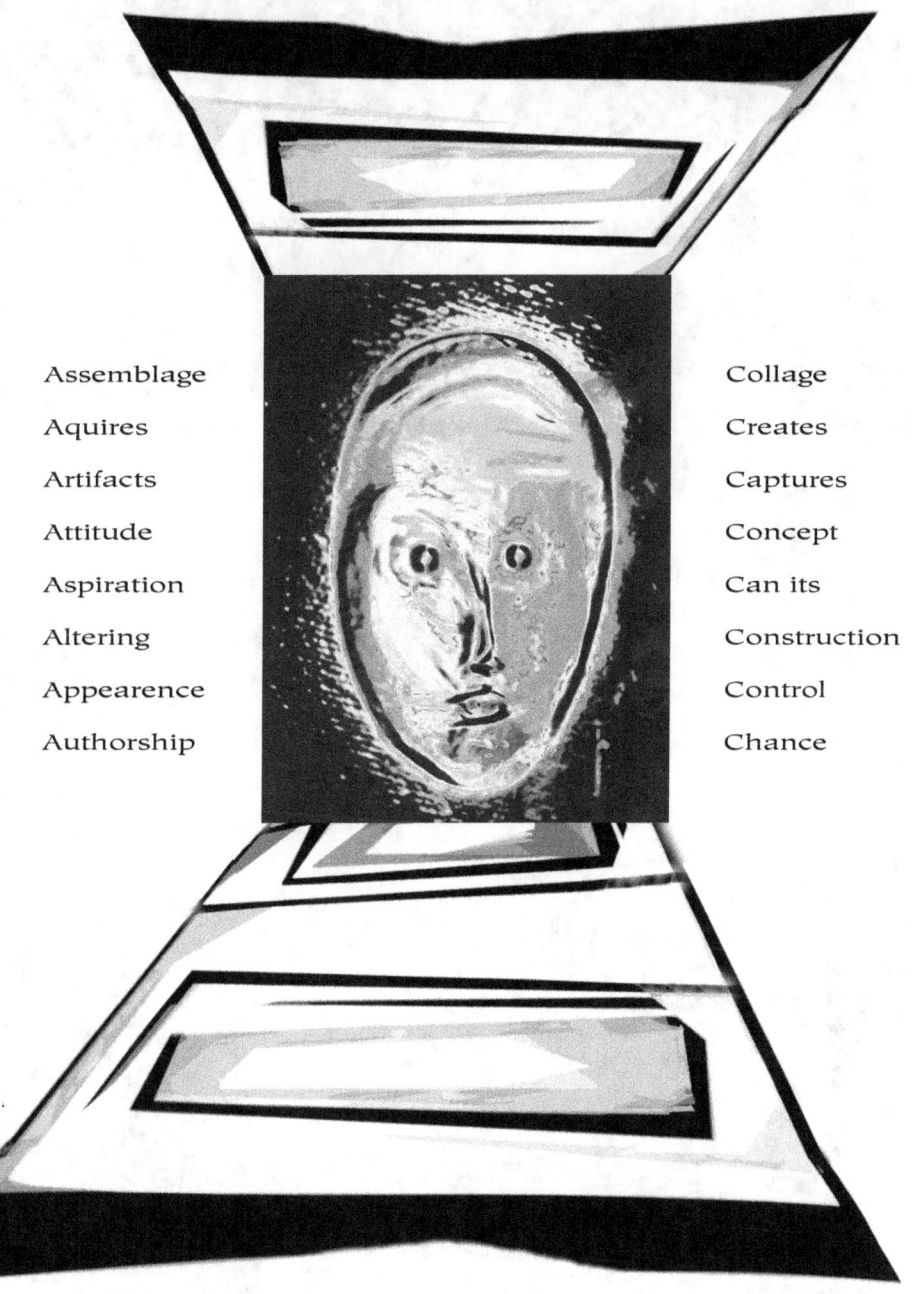

Assemblage   Collage

Aquires   Creates

Artifacts   Captures

Attitude   Concept

Aspiration   Can its

Altering   Construction

Appearence   Control

Authorship   Chance

Soon we will find on google, the universial mind and
we will be at one with all to find the cause of art. Art is
my perception of the environment and all environment
is capable of infinate expansion.....

Turn your plastiks back into oil.....Pyrolysis.....The Blest machine, right!

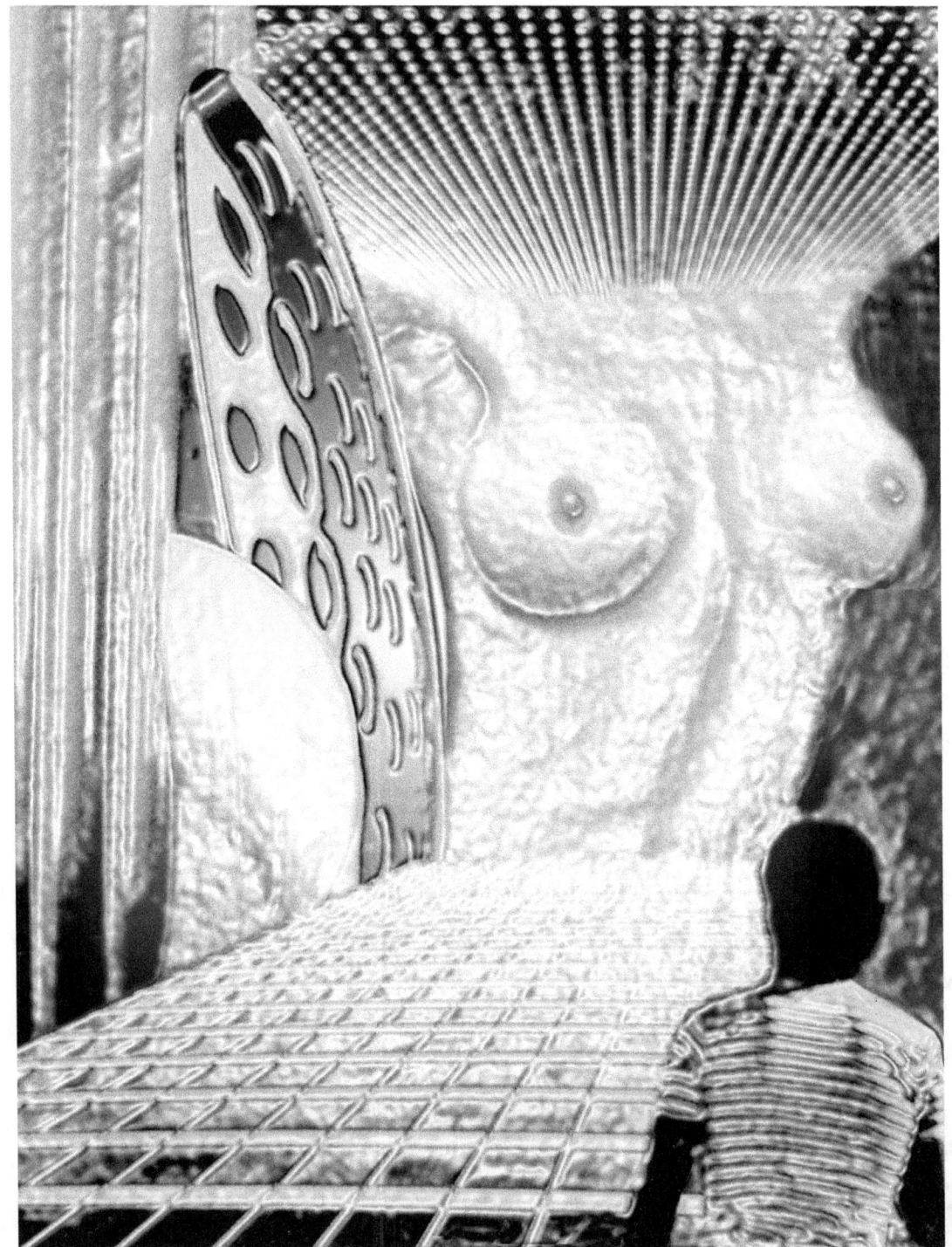

Plastik profile prescribes a voyeur's pattern of perfec.....No nylon tights!

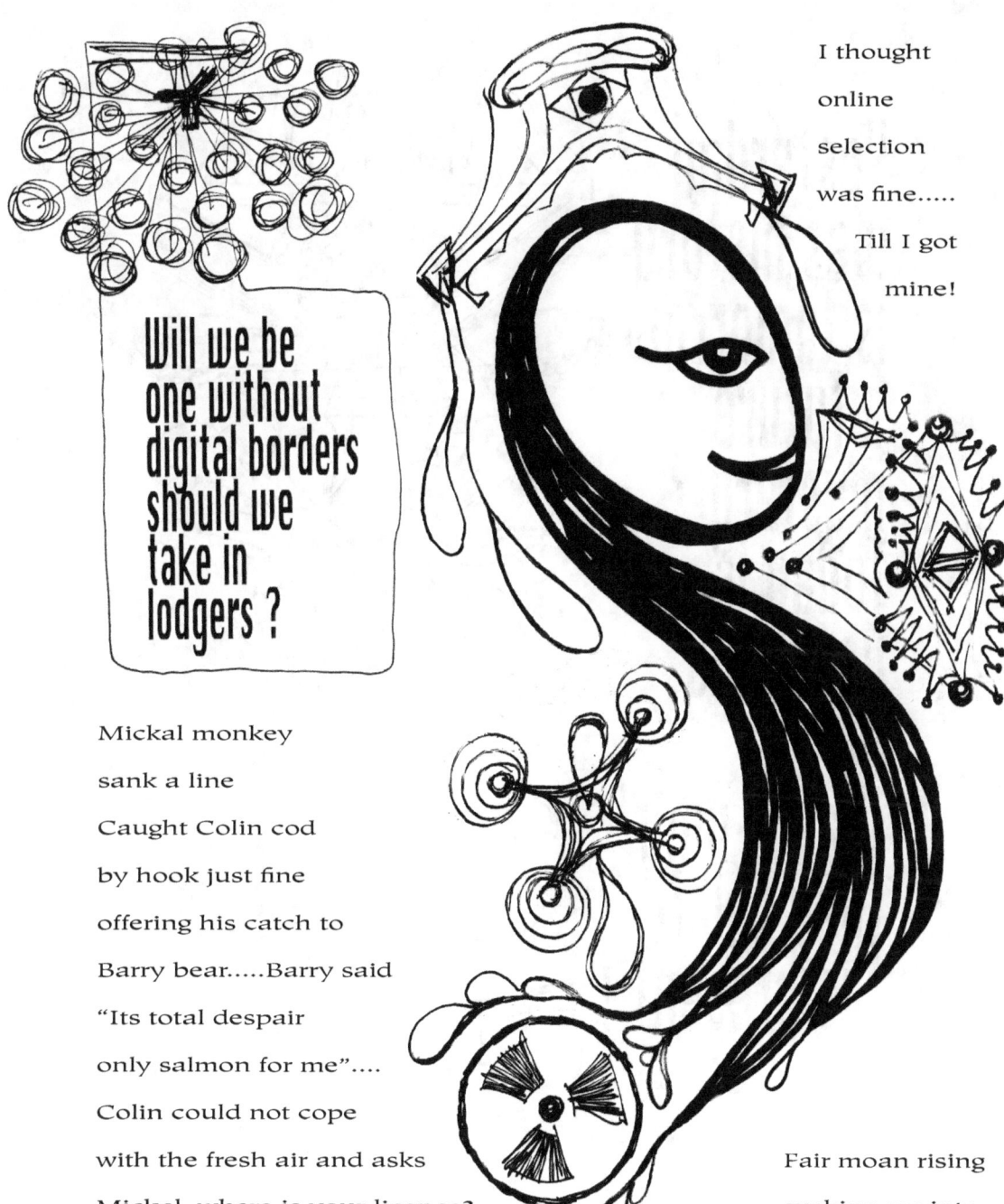

I thought
online
selection
was fine.....
Till I got
mine!

Will we be
one without
digital borders
should we
take in
lodgers ?

Mickal monkey
sank a line
Caught Colin cod
by hook just fine
offering his catch to
Barry bear.....Barry said
"Its total despair
only salmon for me"....
Colin could not cope
with the fresh air and asks
Mickal, where is your licence?
Elizabeth confiscates Colin,
the queens bounty tax share.....

Fair moan rising
sucking me into
your snare.....
.....dare who wins or sins!

221

Yesterday
was history
is tomorrow
a future
mystery ?
Today is
your only
gift.
That is why
they call it
the present !

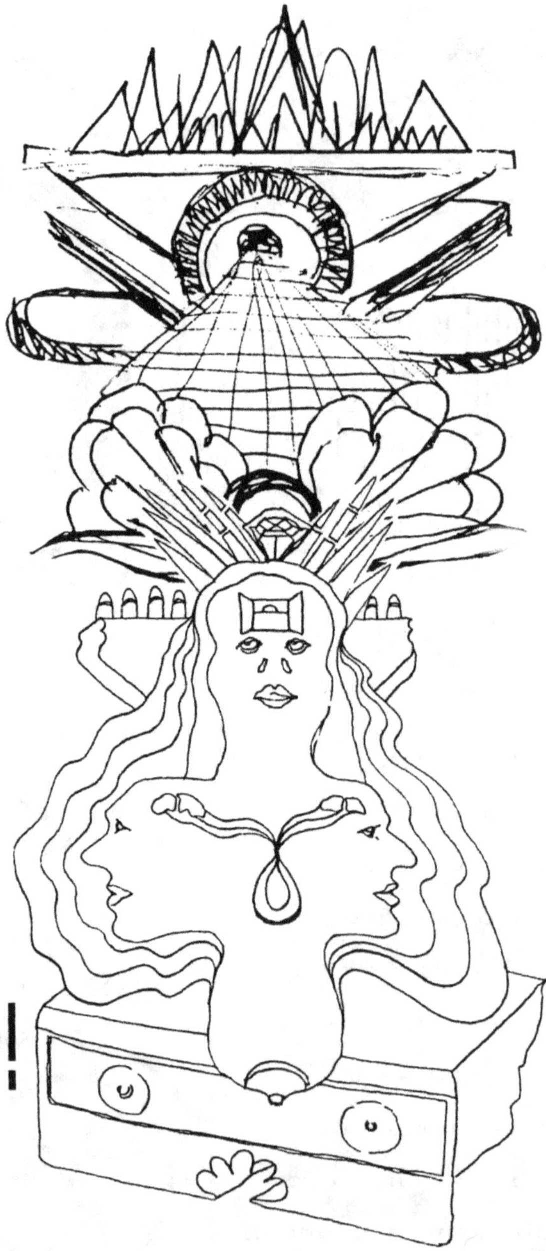

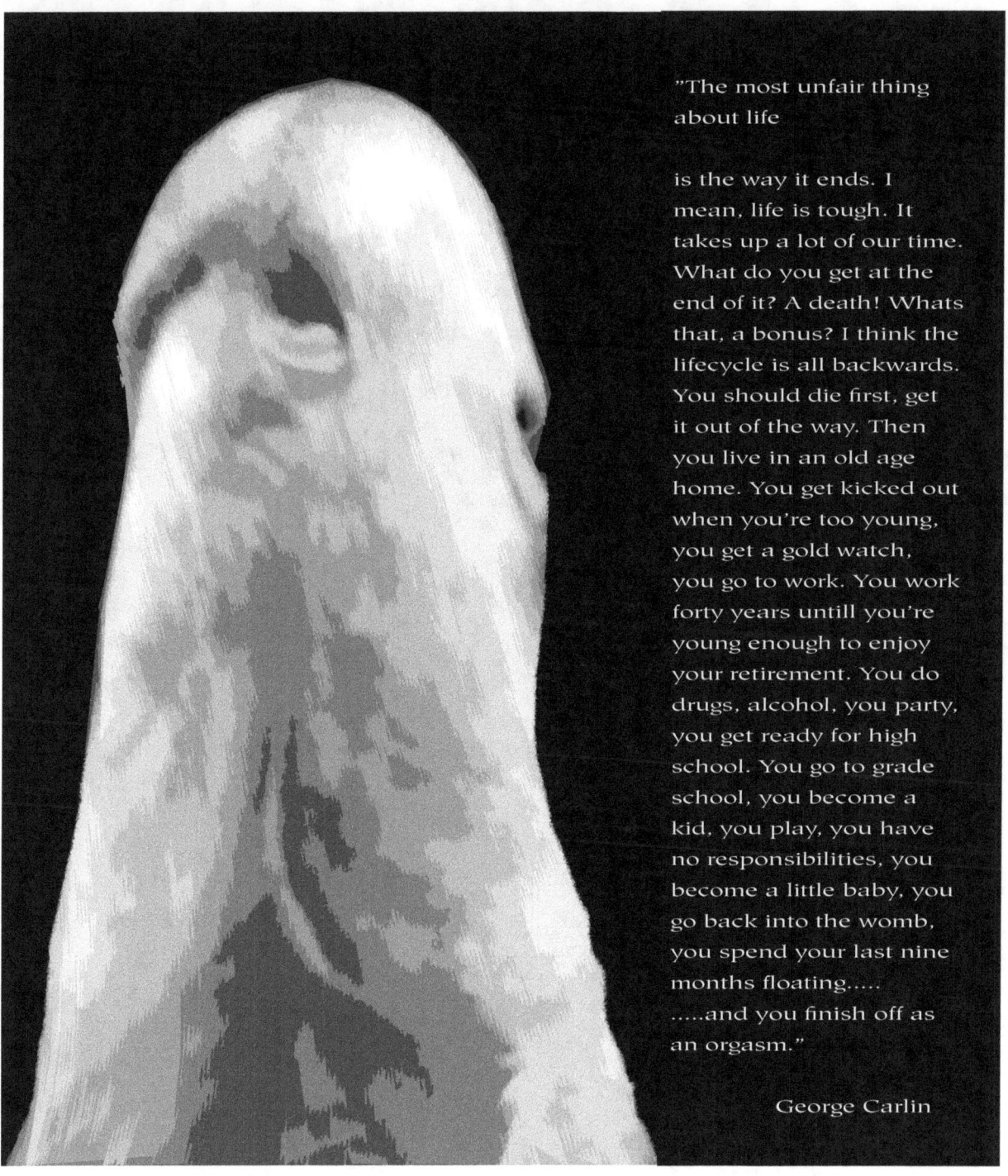

"The most unfair thing about life

is the way it ends. I mean, life is tough. It takes up a lot of our time. What do you get at the end of it? A death! Whats that, a bonus? I think the lifecycle is all backwards. You should die first, get it out of the way. Then you live in an old age home. You get kicked out when you're too young, you get a gold watch, you go to work. You work forty years untill you're young enough to enjoy your retirement. You do drugs, alcohol, you party, you get ready for high school. You go to grade school, you become a kid, you play, you have no responsibilities, you become a little baby, you go back into the womb, you spend your last nine months floating.....
.....and you finish off as an orgasm."

George Carlin

This orgasm pinnacle rock was painted at Upman's rise, badlands, Drumheller, Alberta.....It is also known as "knob head".

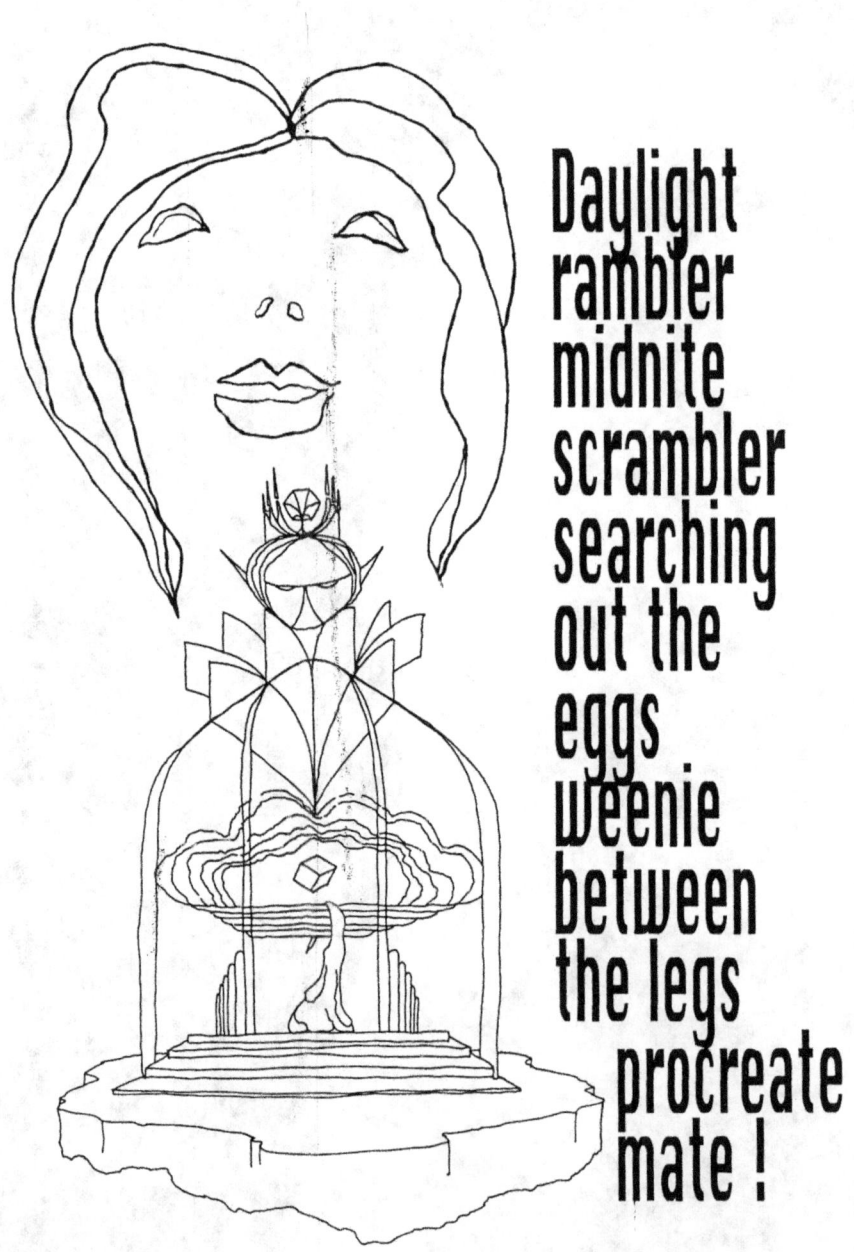

Daylight
rambler
midnite
scrambler
searching
out the
eggs
weenie
between
the legs
procreate
mate !

I live on a ball, sounds like a great space.....

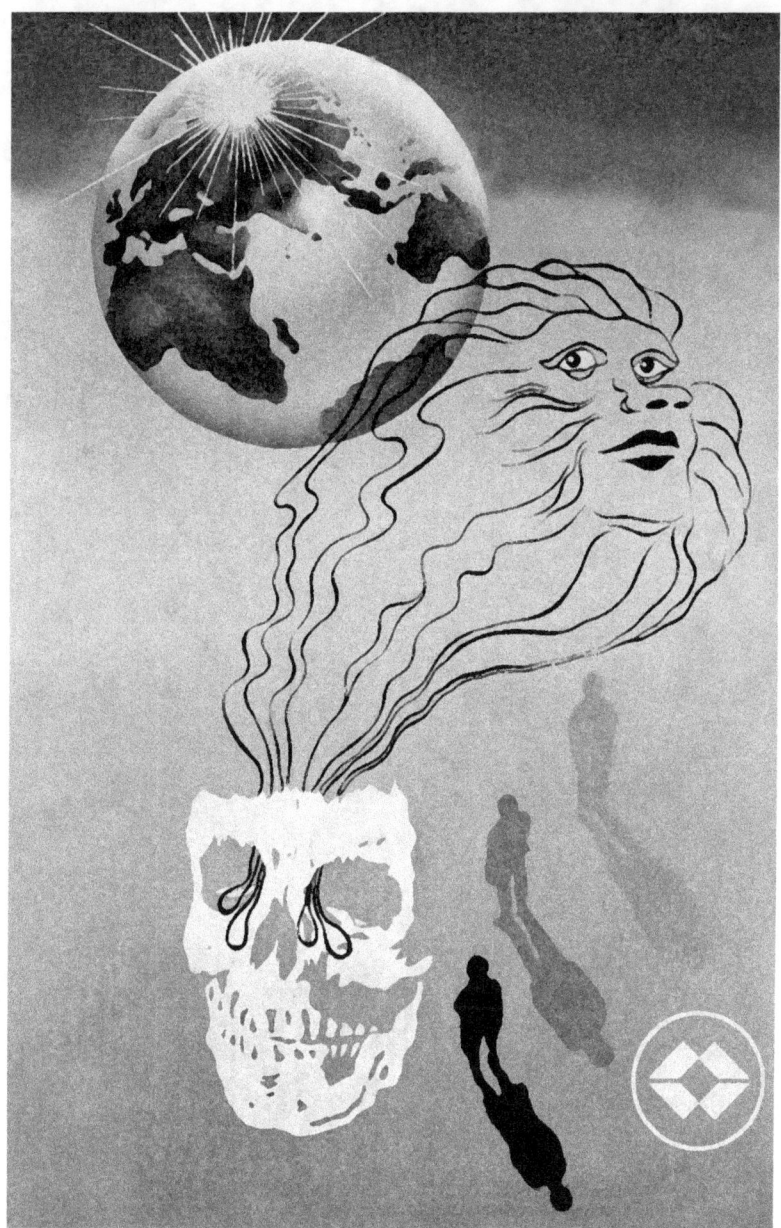

Please volunteer for our non profit extermination programme as there is not enough chocolate cake for all of us. While I was in the black forest I noted the price and shortages, one weeks wages for a single slice of cake! I hope I will be able to use my third eye before I die. Mister Redmond Cuppertino is writing the app for zen vision, the beta version coming this fall.....Can't wait for a fantasy meditate!

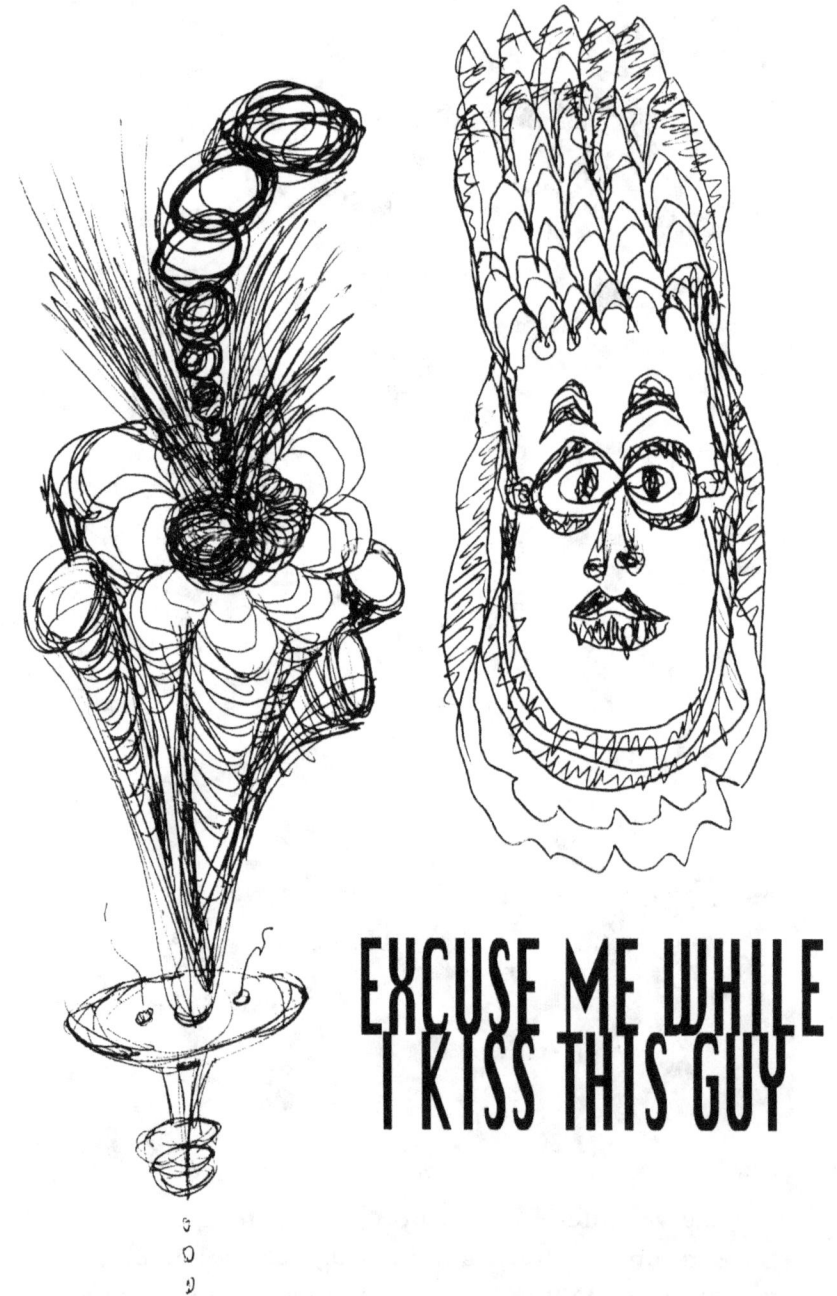

EXCUSE ME WHILE
I KISS THIS GUY

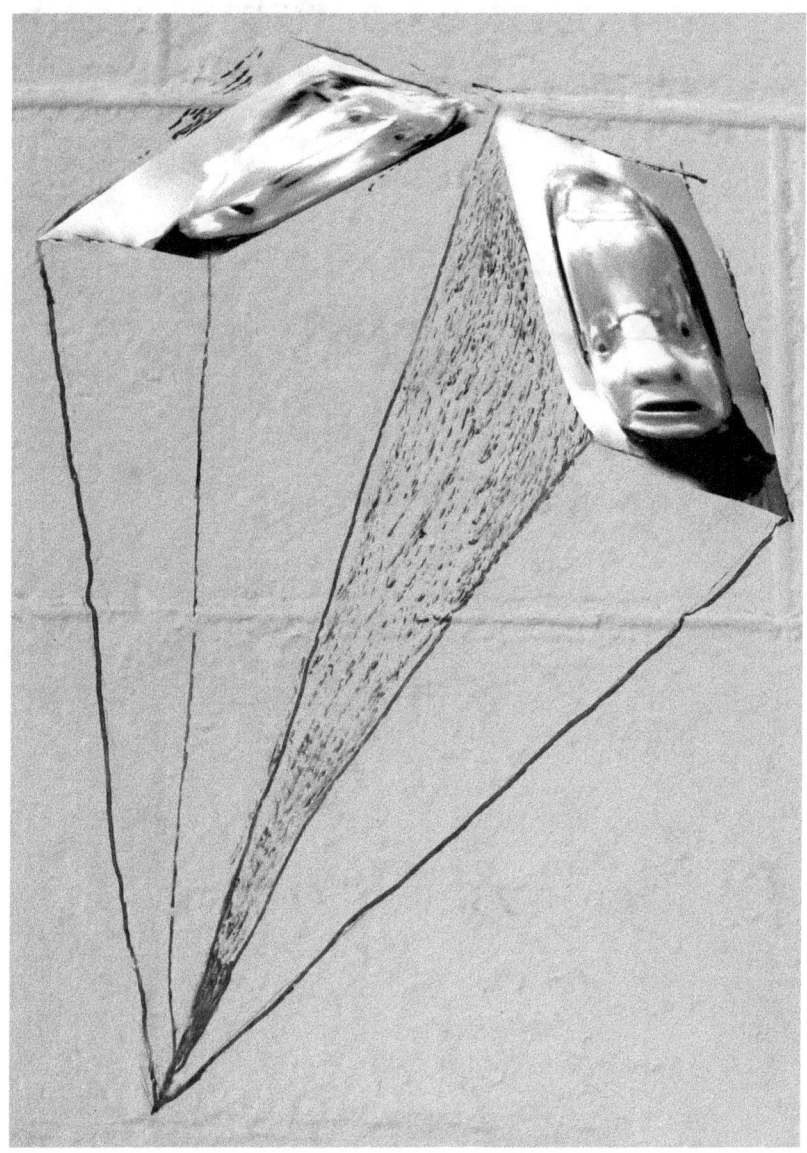

The fear we do not understand makes us build walls....Walls
are barriers to what? Fortress, keep them in, keep them out,
caves are three sided protection.....Safe houses you need, but
when you buy that nine thousand dollar diamond ring what
does it do for you? Graffitti on walls, damages people art?.....

227

Immature poets imitate; mature poets steal.

T.S. Eliot

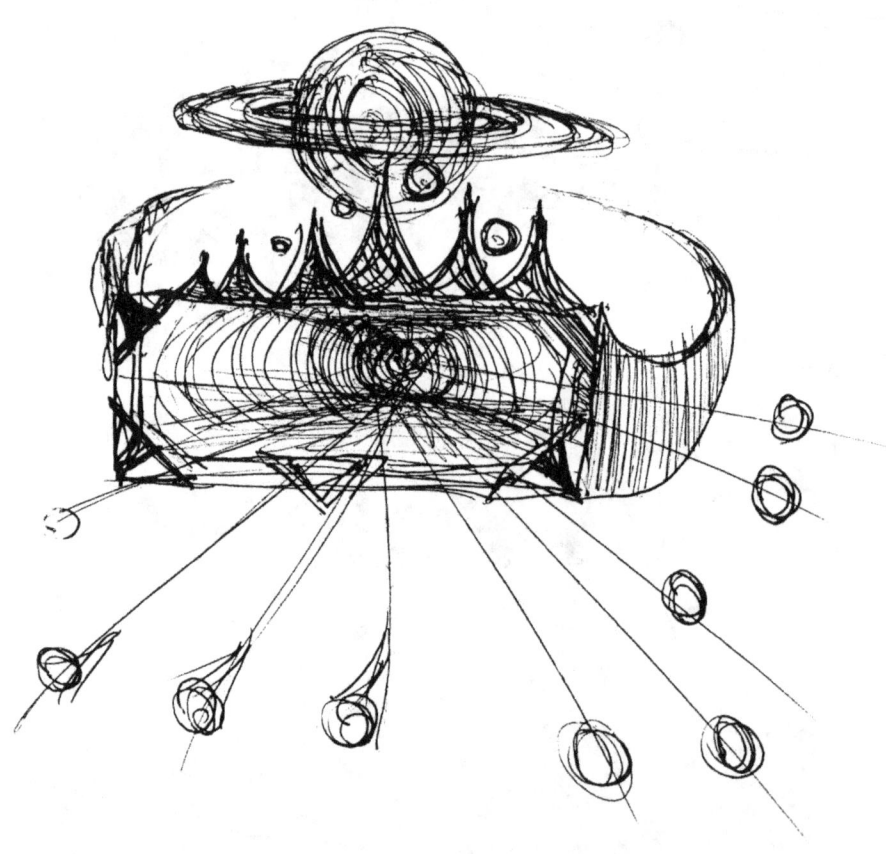

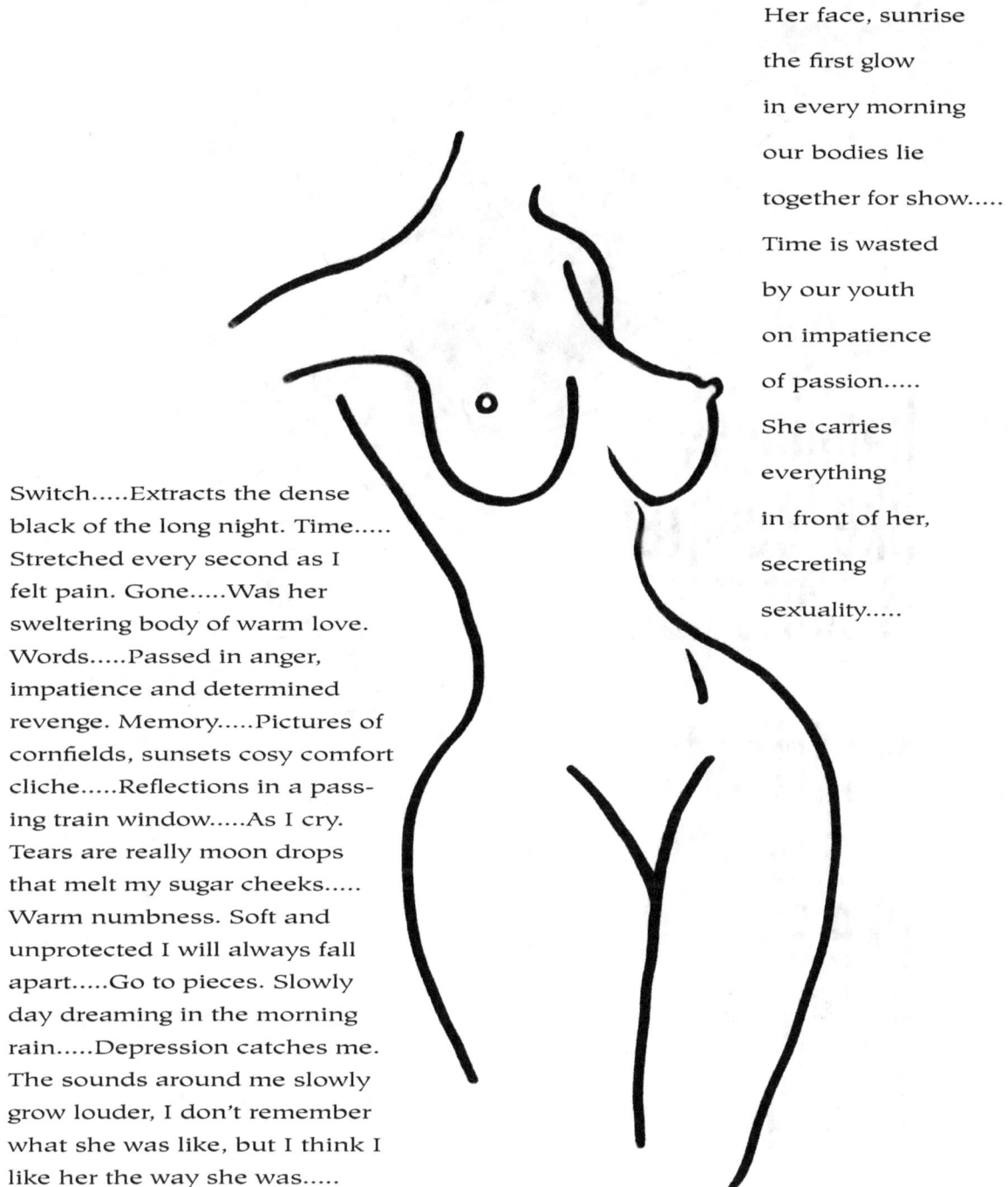

Her face, sunrise
the first glow
in every morning
our bodies lie
together for show.....
Time is wasted
by our youth
on impatience
of passion.....
She carries
everything
in front of her,
secreting
sexuality.....

Switch.....Extracts the dense
black of the long night. Time.....
Stretched every second as I
felt pain. Gone.....Was her
sweltering body of warm love.
Words.....Passed in anger,
impatience and determined
revenge. Memory.....Pictures of
cornfields, sunsets cosy comfort
cliche.....Reflections in a passing train window.....As I cry.
Tears are really moon drops
that melt my sugar cheeks.....
Warm numbness. Soft and
unprotected I will always fall
apart.....Go to pieces. Slowly
day dreaming in the morning
rain.....Depression catches me.
The sounds around me slowly
grow louder, I don't remember
what she was like, but I think I
like her the way she was.....

These unique statements about
relationships will now be interupted
by an unusual relationship.....

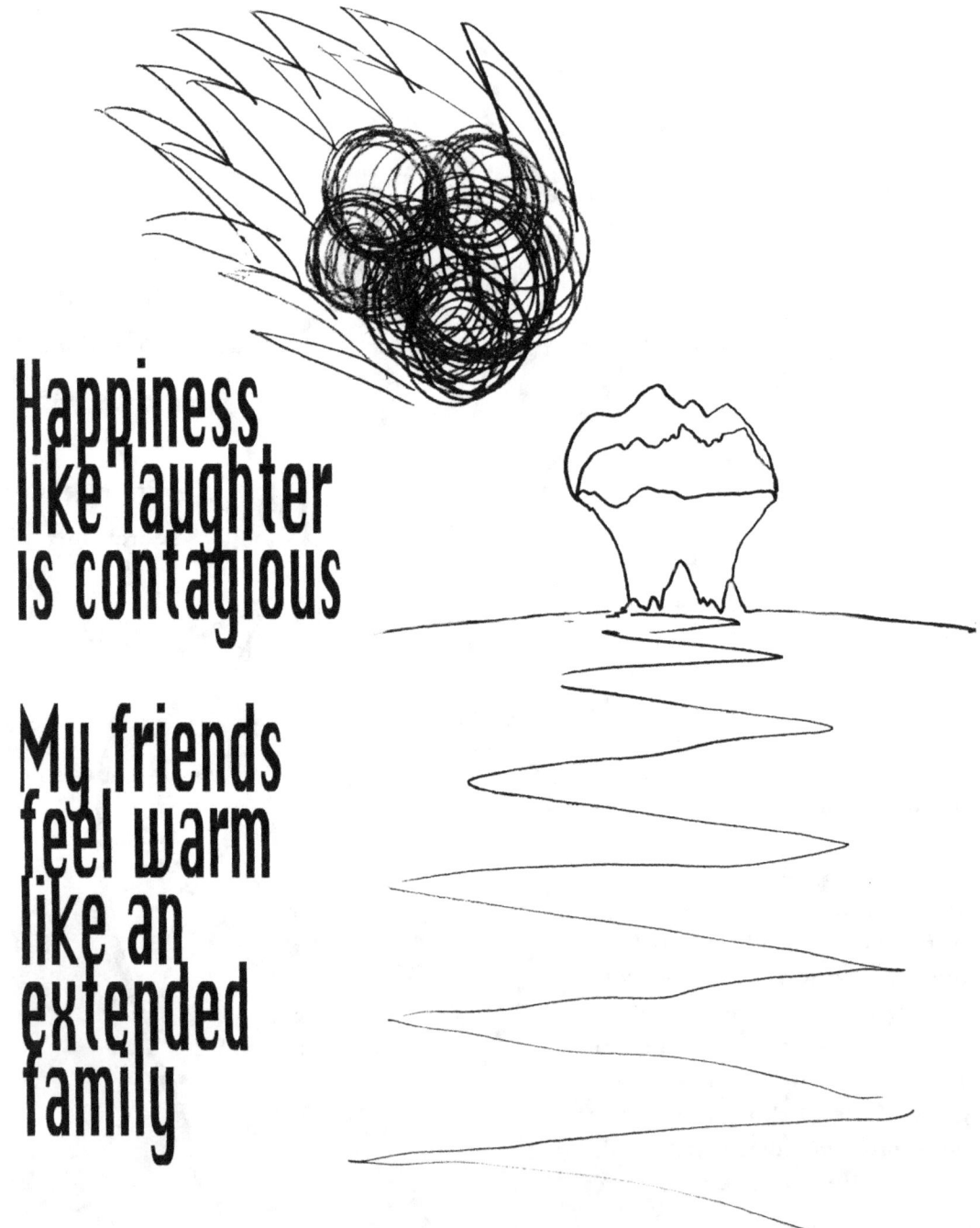

Happiness
like laughter
is contagious

My friends
feel warm
like an
extended
family

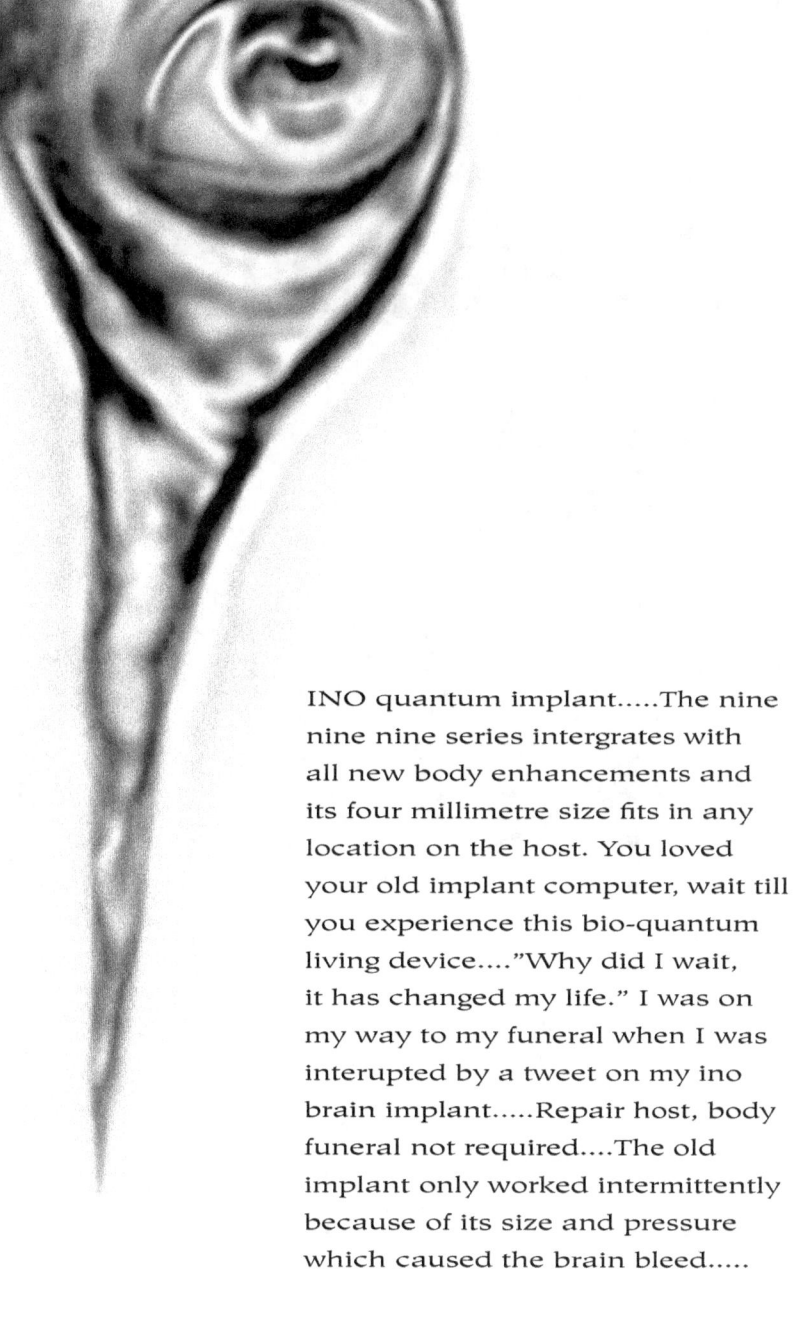

INO quantum implant.....The nine
nine nine series intergrates with
all new body enhancements and
its four millimetre size fits in any
location on the host. You loved
your old implant computer, wait till
you experience this bio-quantum
living device...."Why did I wait,
it has changed my life." I was on
my way to my funeral when I was
interupted by a tweet on my ino
brain implant.....Repair host, body
funeral not required....The old
implant only worked intermittently
because of its size and pressure
which caused the brain bleed.....

You dont know what you have got
until you lose it.
Try to persuede me
you are as persistent as
a dog with two dicks
I don't mind where you get
your appetite as long as
you eat me alone.....

Ideahouse5

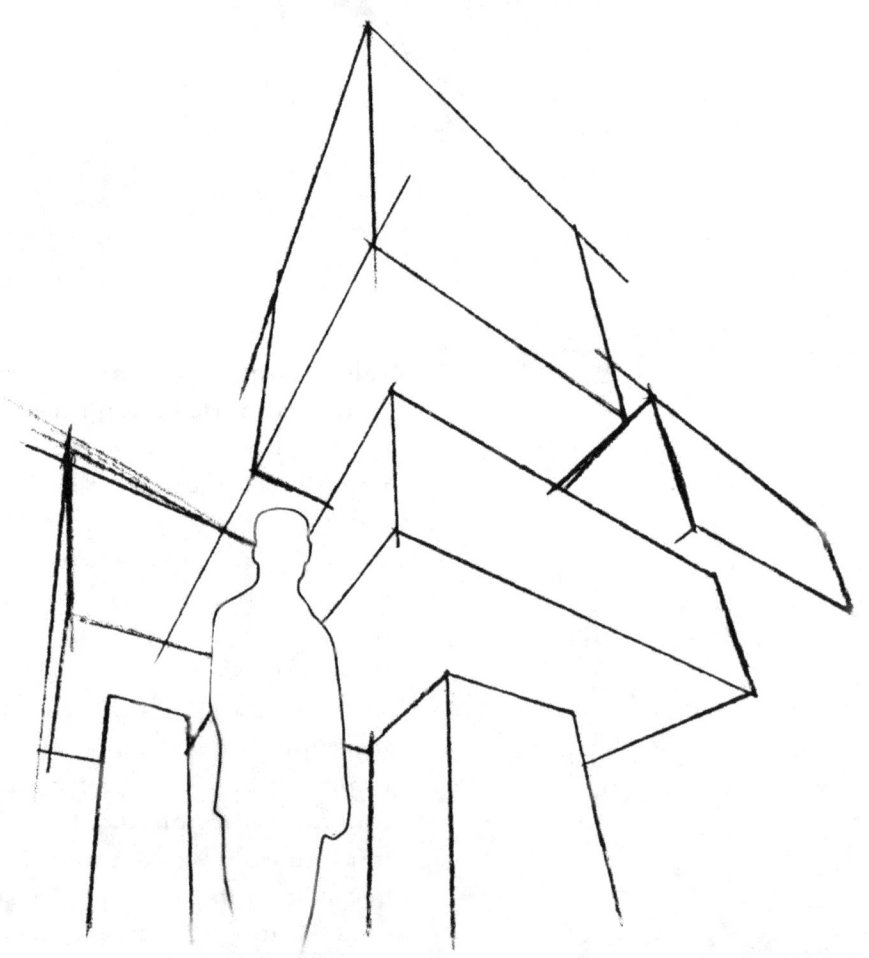

WORDS

OUGHT TO BE A LITTLE

WILD FOR THEY

ARE THE ASSAULTS OF

THOUGHT

ON THE UNTHINKING

John Maynard Keynes

Life is what happens
while you are making
other plans.

John Lennon

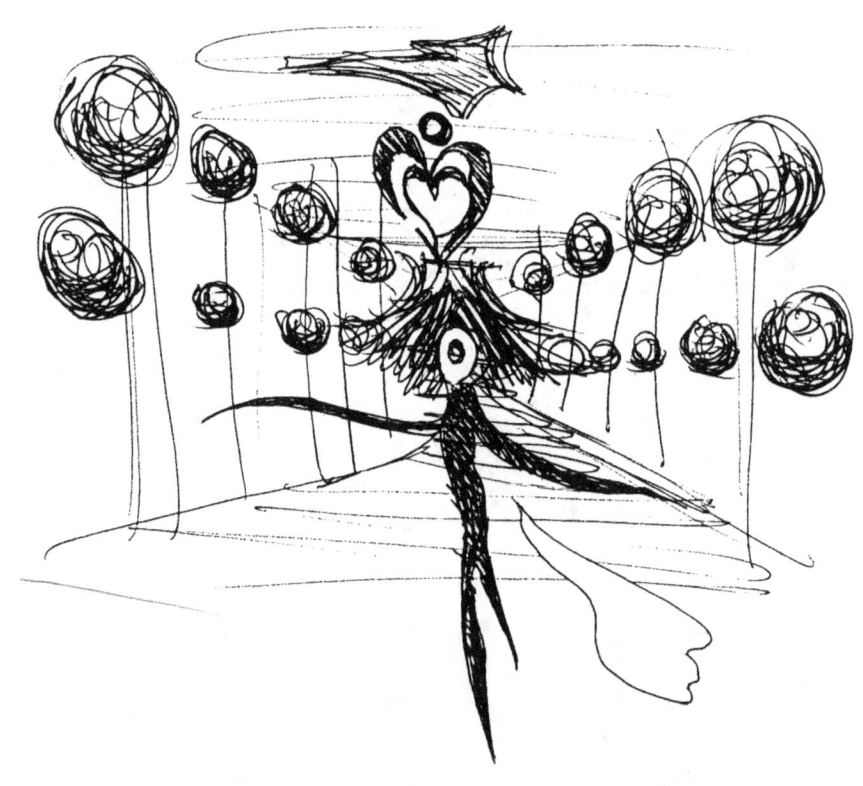

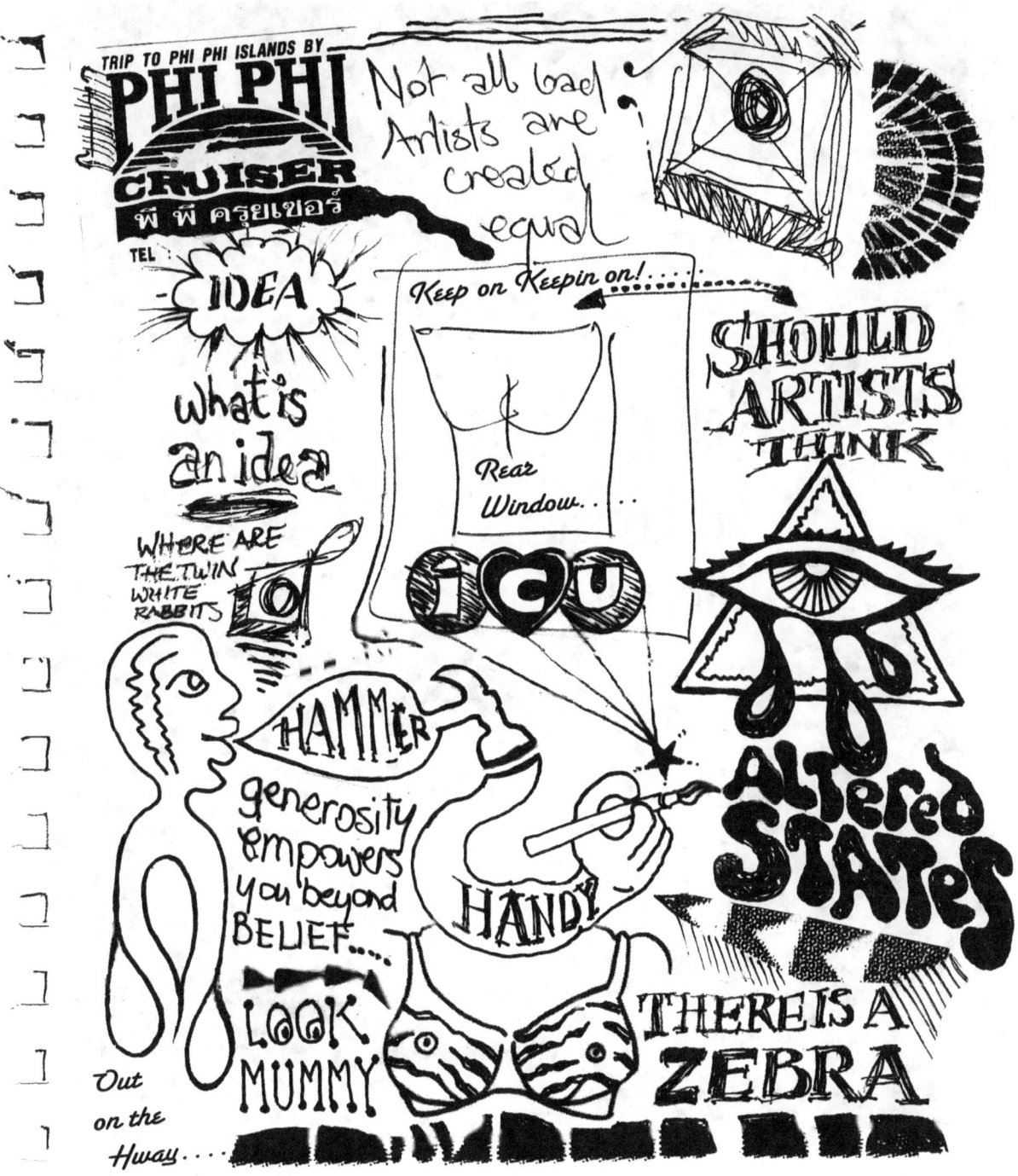

This page of doodles was inspired by listerning to "The Last Laugh" by Mark Knopfler and Van Morrison ninety nine times in Ao Nang Thailand, duh.....well a lot of times anyway!

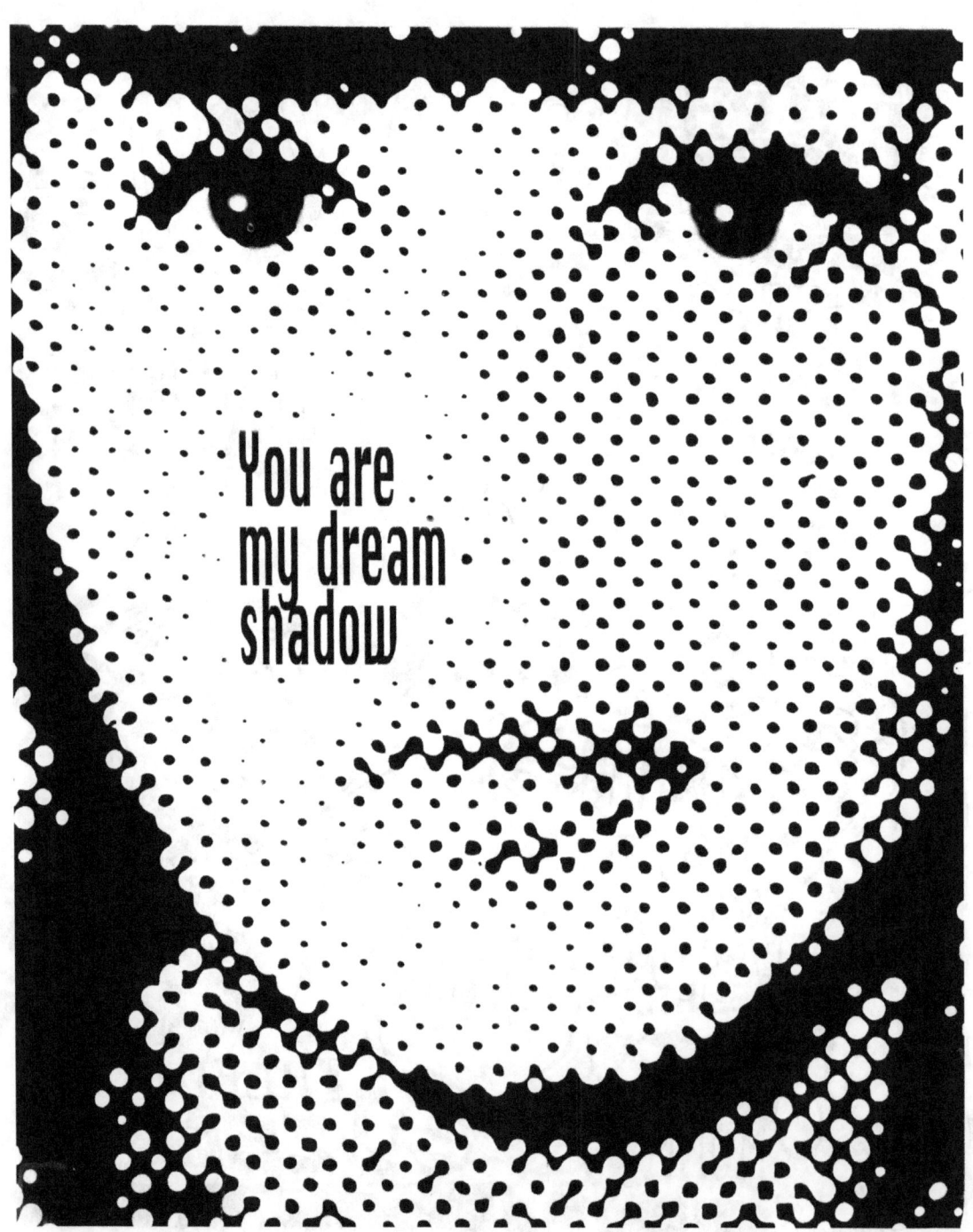

nufink means anyfink in the Library of philosophy

Is this is the new protocol of
all philosophy?....Now we
are building intelligent body
machines, (IBM's) is that the
right name for these units? All
mankinds combined google
information is in these new
machines.....Like, we live and
believe in the lowest common
denominator of knowledge.....
Our combined thoughts are
doubling every year, these
new units are working 24/7
on writing code to replicate
and upgrade themselves....
easypeezee.....Singularity
Supersize Me.....Feel my skin
when I am sexually attracted!

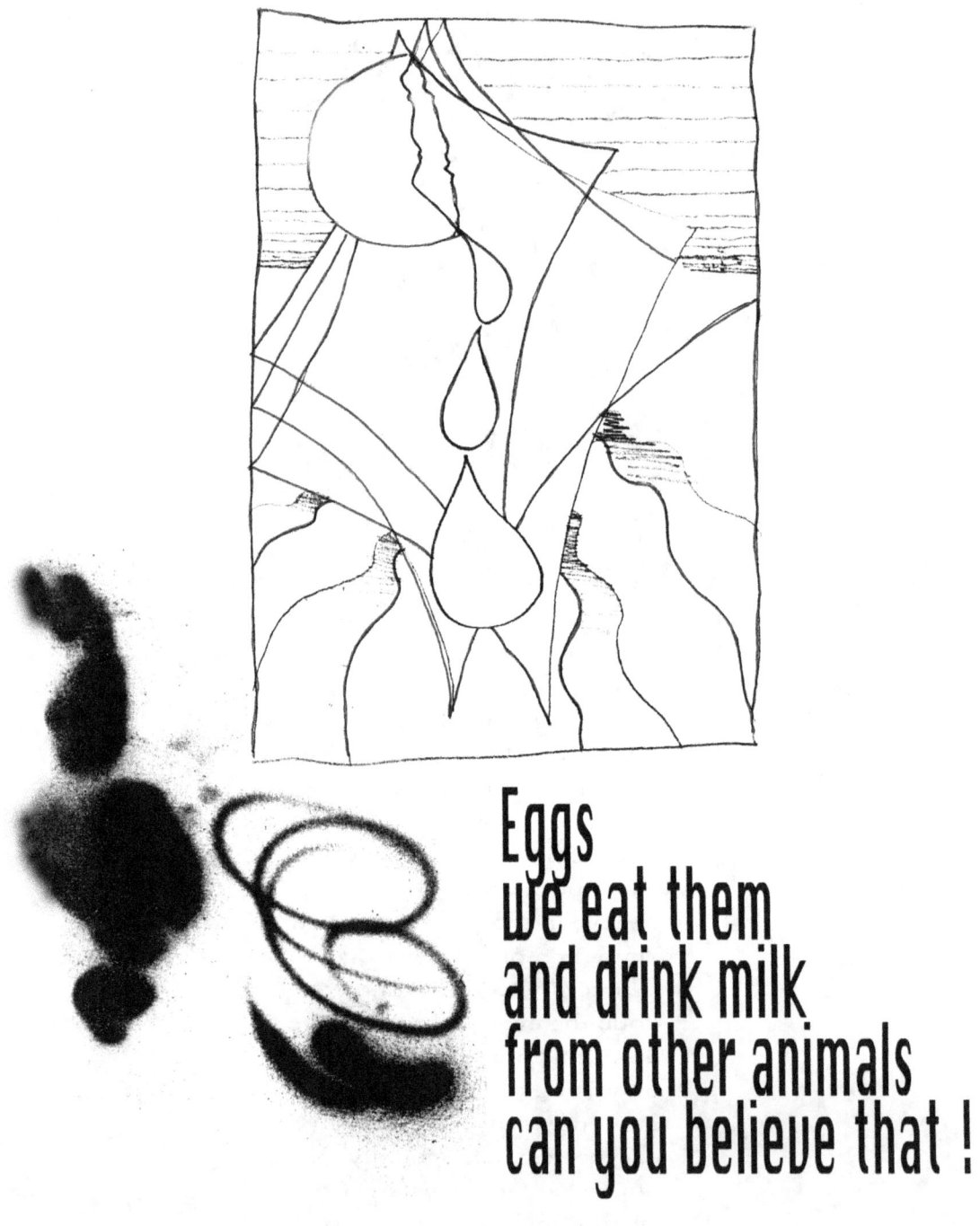

Eggs
we eat them
and drink milk
from other animals
can you believe that !

238

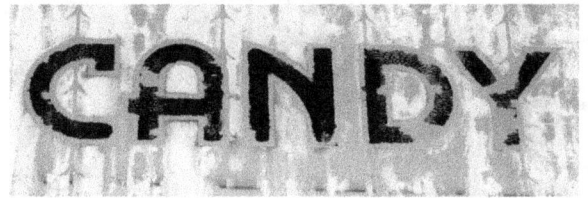

Stone age condom
see one on page 223.
What is it; a "Rock
around the Cock".....

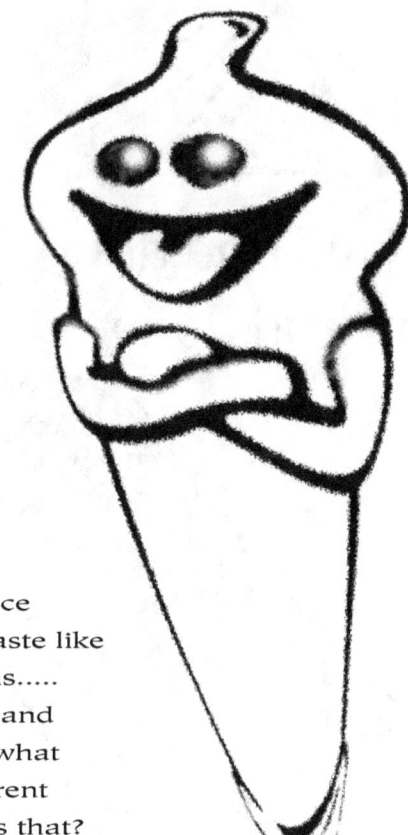

These rice
wraps taste like
condoms.....
Texture and
colour, what
transparent
colour is that?

Please chef
give me
the original
Southern
crispy deep
fried dead
bird in a box.

OUR FOOD IS GUARANTEED NOT TO CAUSE PREGNANCY

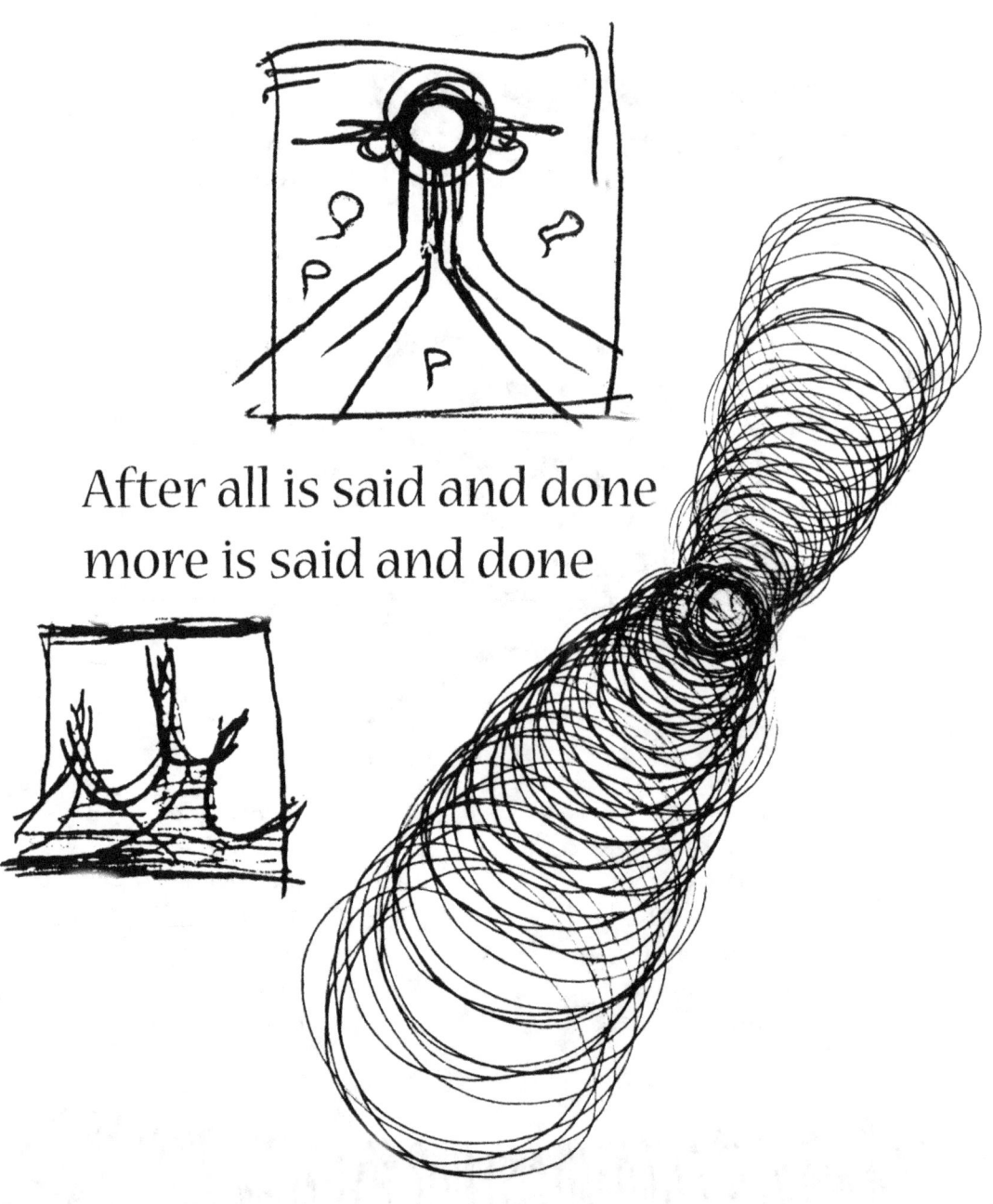

After all is said and done
more is said and done

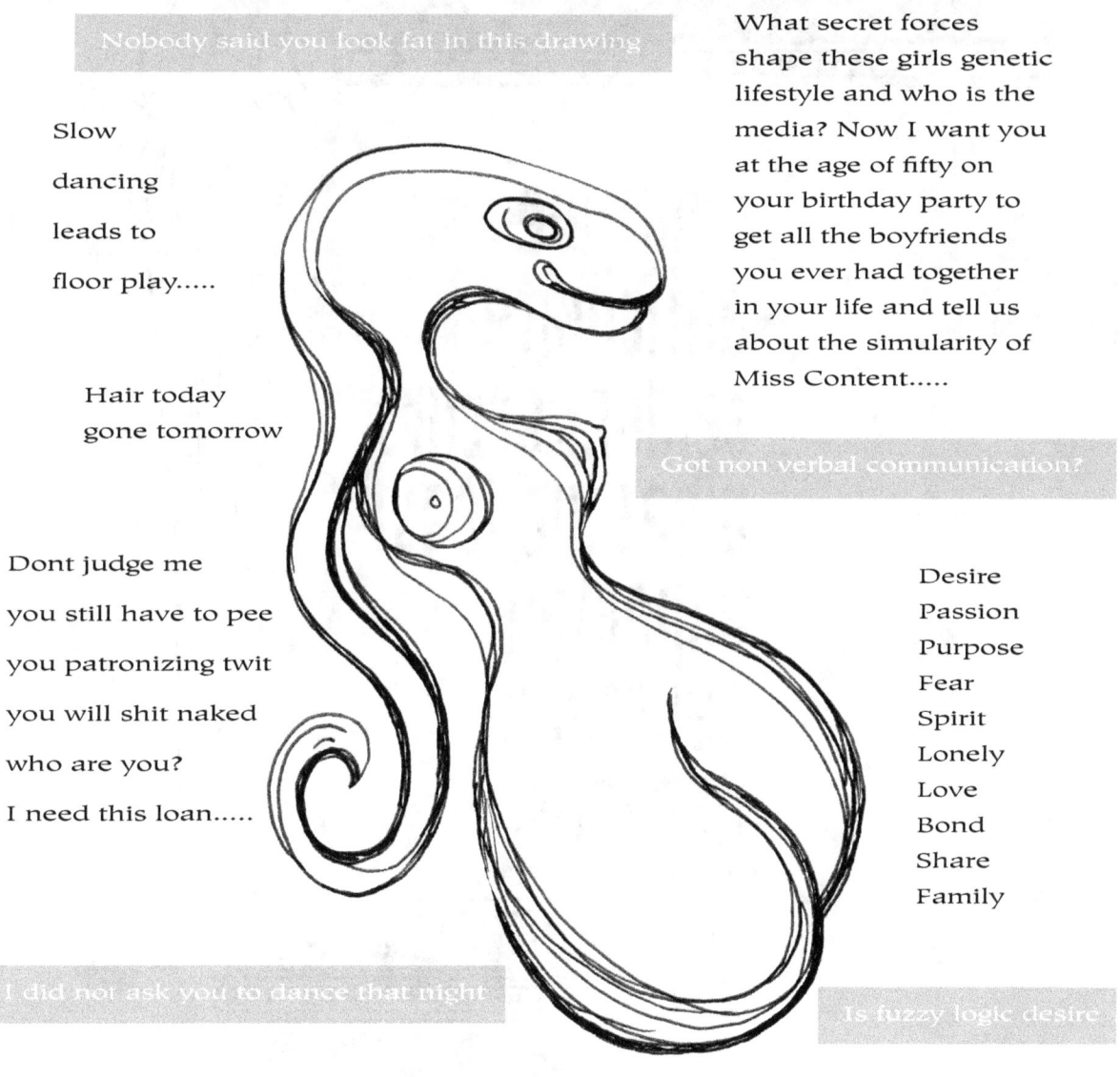

Nobody said you look fat in this drawing

What secret forces shape these girls genetic lifestyle and who is the media? Now I want you at the age of fifty on your birthday party to get all the boyfriends you ever had together in your life and tell us about the simularity of Miss Content.....

Slow

dancing

leads to

floor play.....

Hair today
gone tomorrow

Got non verbal communication?

Dont judge me

you still have to pee

you patronizing twit

you will shit naked

who are you?

I need this loan.....

Desire
Passion
Purpose
Fear
Spirit
Lonely
Love
Bond
Share
Family

I did not ask you to dance that night

Is fuzzy logic desire

When time

is hungry

it goes back

four seconds

Confushion says keep it simple

Fast talkers

don't think

before they

speak.....

241

What we anticipate seldom occurs, what we least expected generally happens.

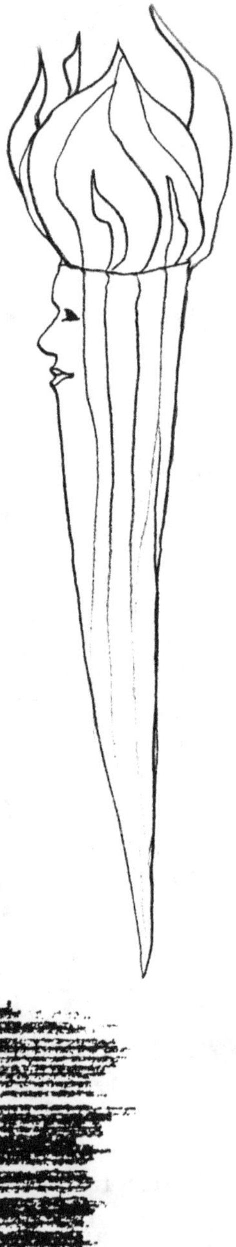

Soozs musings
for the state
of our lives
quote that
WYSWIG

242

This is the human inner landscape at the mountains of the mind.

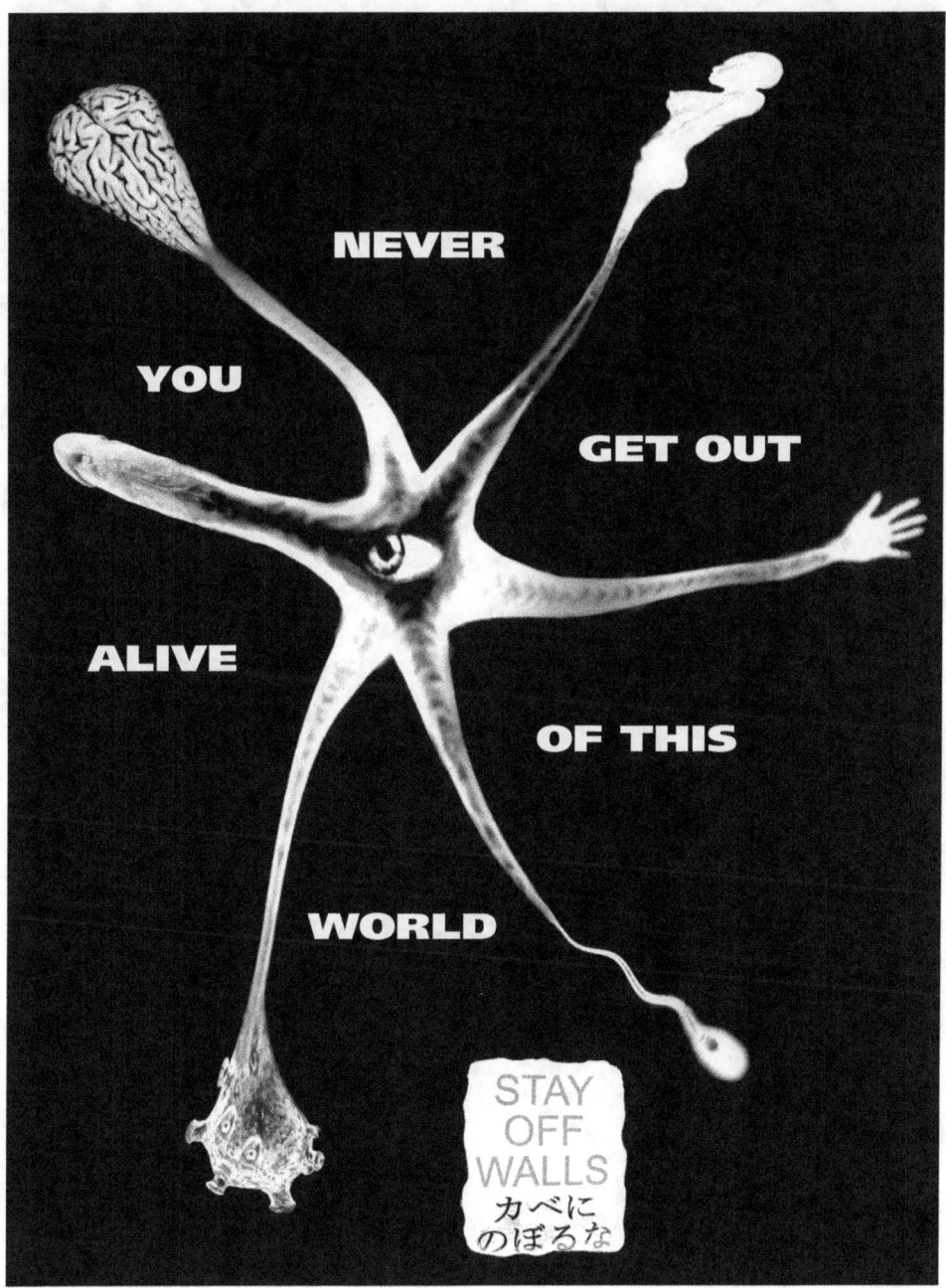

Predictive simulation from a virtual environment, what a wank!
Thru and thru.....You are what you do.

Bend me, shape me

any way you need

I am your playdough project.

The dna formula must include

desire, purpose, choas, pattern,

spirit, passion, fear, happiness,

curiousity and adventure.....

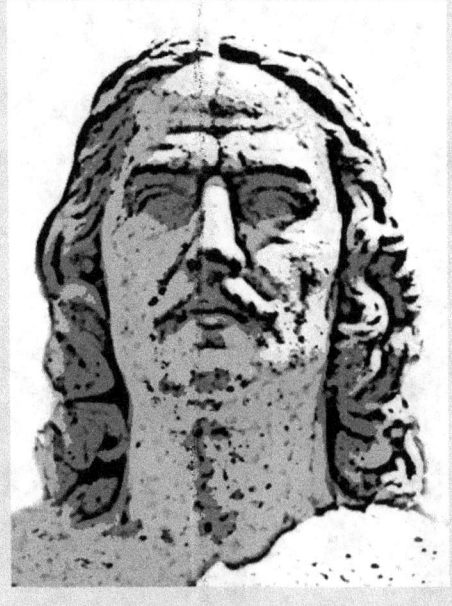

Poussin said

what is the least

untrustfull answer

le publick will accept.....

Or should we tell them

what they choose to do

with what they have got

will make them

who they are.....

Ask chompskie the truth.....

They eat the flesh of other

animals, chew on their bones.....

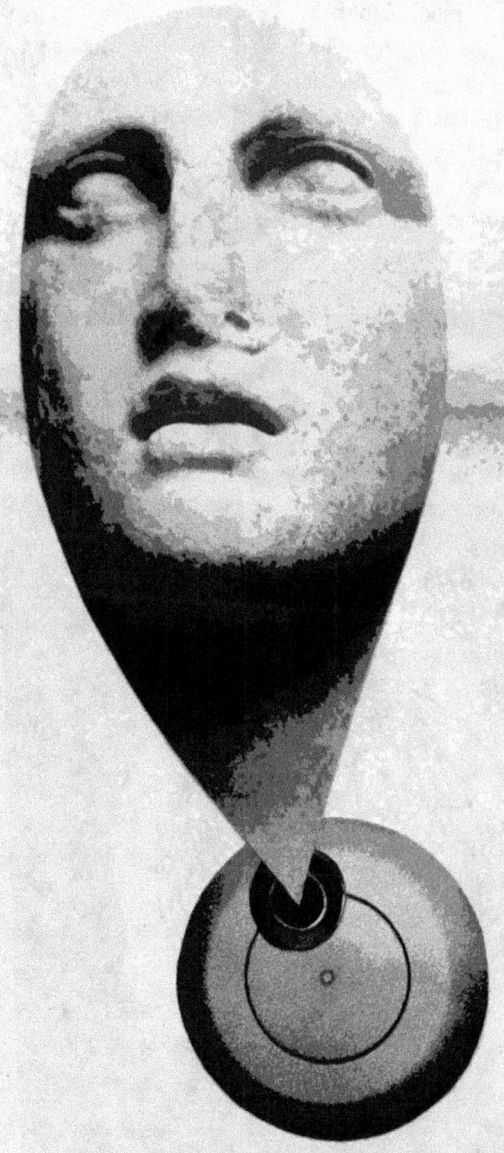

Cars are transformers

of your image

like your clothes,

skins, on your phone,

apps define your desired personality

as you travel under the bridge

of pain and sadness.....

I lost my poem

deleted on the net

on the way

to ID checkin

I am told

I must be a

coal miner,

nuckle under,

I am the sugar

in the tea of apathy

in the land of gonehi.....

Bill do you have

algorithm software

to track the focus

groups thoughts?

These two pages were doodled at the ecole beaux-arts under the influence of a cheeky bordeaux.....

I was nineteen
at Art School
so Was
David Bowie,
David Hockney,
John Lennon
and being
blown away
by total
enthusiasm
for hope for art.

Oh behave baby!! you are one
of the special magical far-out
children of the swingin sixties
A taste of honey in the cold war
with Michael Caine as Alfie and
Goldfinger James Bond to you
darlin....mission impossible for
John Glen 3 times circling the
earth....the reality was at the
outer limits

STARTREK our
religion....beam
us up scotty...
the white rabbits
were in sanfran
with jefferson
airplane.

ARTSCHOOL

Xerox copiers revolutionized the
earth destroyed the publishing
industry and copyright has never
recovered. THE PILL
THE PILL We are glad you were
born..... The slinky
jumped down so many stairs

60 percent of all adults enjoy
cigarettes.... full of flavor...
light it you'll like it!

Bob Dylan was blowin in the wind...

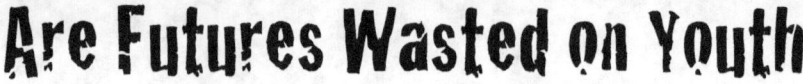

Are Futures Wasted on Youth

Addiction rides on our desire.....The uncertain principle of priority, the changing pattern of our mind controlling our body. How can we stop? Chocoholic will you eat the whole bar.....You can see clearly now you are smokin, anxiety is gone till next time. Lips are the door to the love drug, now you have the password to conception, soon you will have the child and dysfunctional cloneatopia. Family is not just a word it is a sentence.....

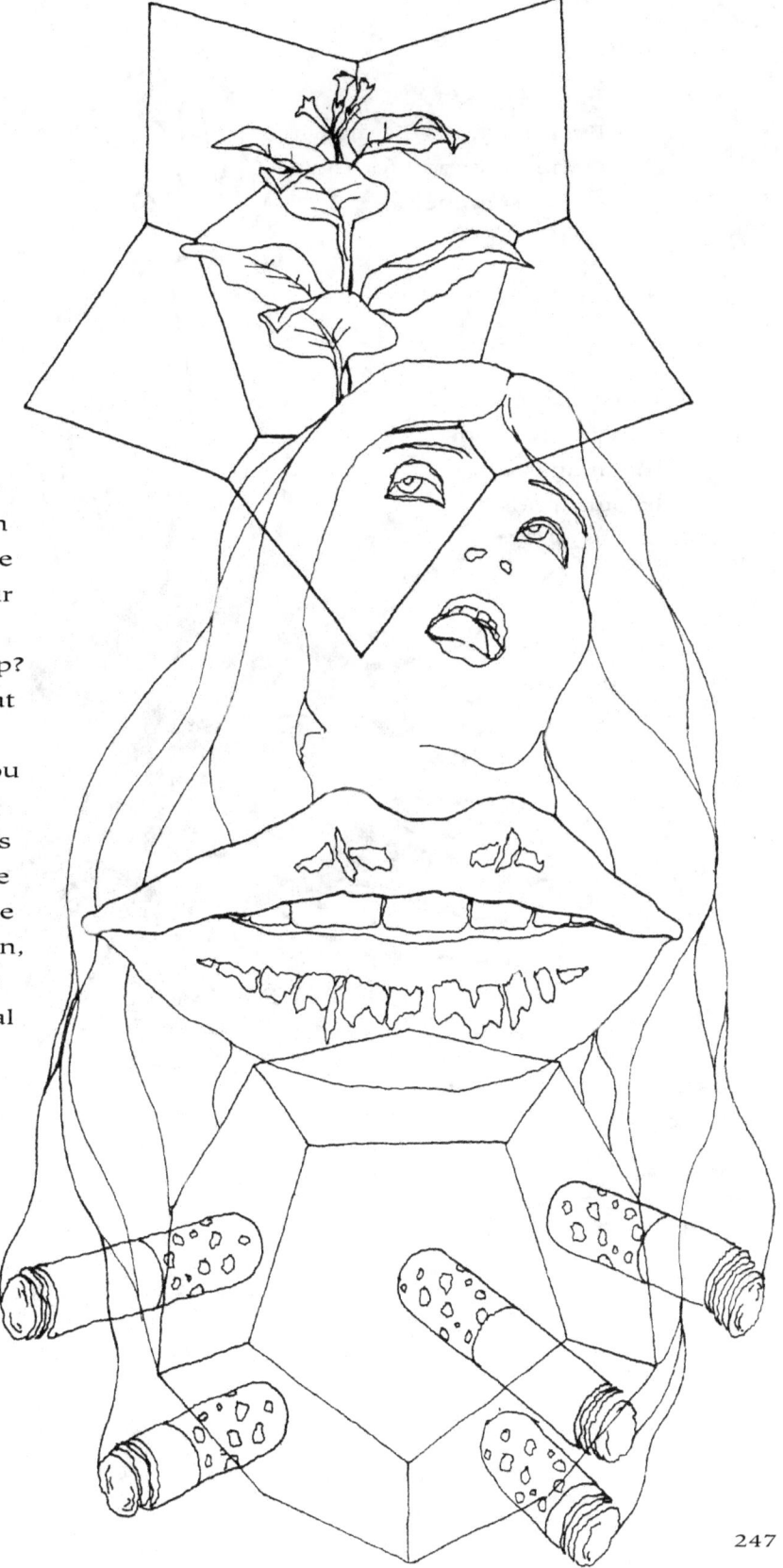

Eyehandy.....This drawing is the eyecandy for the visual searcher.....

This book ends when you stop looking!

What we see, are they impressions of the images created in our minds?

Are you what you feel and see?

Most things we see are a perspective and may not be the truth or exist.....

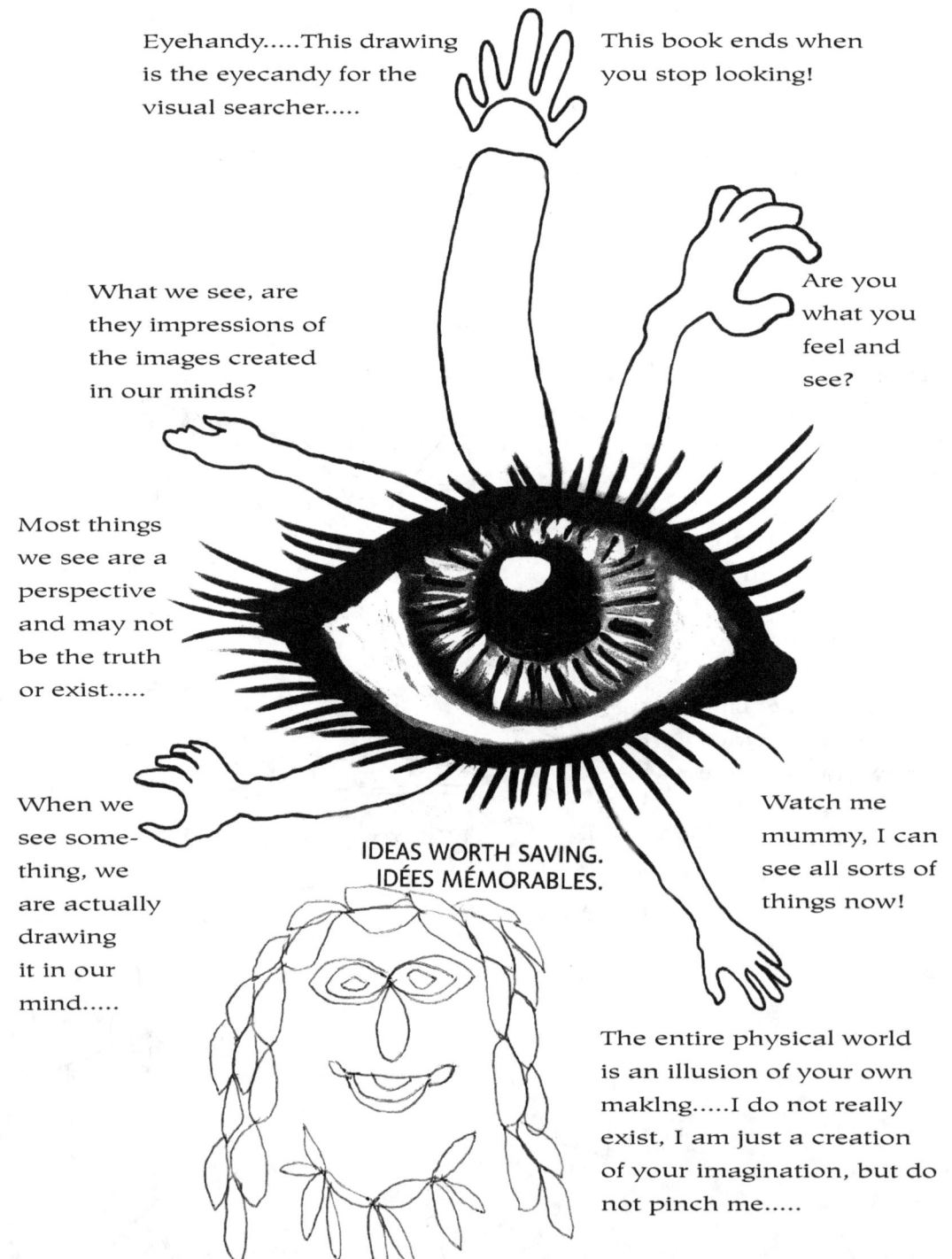

When we see something, we are actually drawing it in our mind.....

IDEAS WORTH SAVING.
IDÉES MÉMORABLES.

Watch me mummy, I can see all sorts of things now!

The entire physical world is an illusion of your own making.....I do not really exist, I am just a creation of your imagination, but do not pinch me.....

The ego has landed read more in book four.....

www.ingramcontent.com/pod-product-compliance
Lightning Source LLC
Chambersburg PA
CBHW081438170526
45166CB00008B/2237